LINCOLN'S HUNDRED DAYS

Lincoln's Hundred Days

The Emancipation Proclamation
and the War for the Union

Louis P. Masur

THE BELKNAP PRESS OF
HARVARD UNIVERSITY PRESS
Cambridge, Massachusetts
and London, England

First Harvard University Press paperback edition, 2014

Library of Congress Cataloging-in-Publication Data

Masur, Louis P.

Lincoln's hundred days : the Emancipation Proclamation
and the war for the union / Louis P. Masur.

p.   cm.

Includes bibliographical references and index.

ISBN 978-0-674-06690-8 (cloth : alk. paper)

ISBN 978-0-674-28409-8 (pbk.)

1. United States. President (1861–1865 : Lincoln). Emancipation
Proclamation.   2. Lincoln, Abraham, 1809–1865—Views on slavery.

3. United States—Politics and government—1861–1865.

4. Slaves—Emancipation—United States.   I. Title.

E453.M266   2012

973.7092—dc23   2012009044

For Dave

Contents

Contents

We care not how the Emancipation Proclamation of President Lincoln may be in the present times considered. . . . It may not be popular now; it may fail in its designs; it may receive contumely without stint; but history will accord to it the proud distinction of immortality. It is "not for the day, but for all time," and happy he who shall remember the trials and tribulation of the time which caused its utterance.

—*Chicago Evening Journal*, January 20, 1863

Liberty is a slow fruit.

—Ralph Waldo Emerson, *Atlantic Monthly*, November 1862

Lincoln Tells a Story

Lincoln began the meeting with a story. He loved stories, jokes, puns, and tall tales, to such an extent that Richard Henry Dana—U.S. Attorney for Massachusetts, abolitionist, and author of the memoir *Two Years before the Mast* (1840)—had lamented that Lincoln "does not act or talk or feel like the ruler of a great empire in a great crisis." What bothered Dana most was that the president focused more on petty details than on grand schemes, and resorted to parables where principles were needed: "He likes rather to talk and tell stories with all sorts of persons who come to him for all sorts of purposes than to give his mind to the noble and manly duties of his great post. It is not difficult to detect that this is the feeling of his cabinet."[1]

If so, several members of Lincoln's cabinet must have murmured when they gathered at noon for that meeting on Monday, September 22, 1862, and the president, after some small talk among the group, began by reading a piece from a book by the humorist Artemus Ward. The selection was called "High-Handed Outrage in Utica," and it tells the first-person story of a showman who arrives in the "trooly grate sitty" of "Uticky" and begins to present his various "Beests and Snaiks." The showman also has a set of wax figures of the Last Supper. Suddenly, a "big burly feller" grabs the figure of Judas and starts to pound and pulverize it. The showman screams, "You egrejus ass, that air's a wax figure!" but the incensed man responds that Judas can't show himself in the town "with impunerty." He destroys the figure but the showman sues, and the "Joory brawt in a verdict of Arson in the 3rd degree."[2]

A visitor had once remarked that Lincoln's stories seemed dull in print: "Unless you could give also the dry chuckle with which they are accompanied, and the gleam in the speaker's eye, as, with the action habitual to him, he rubs his hand down the side of his long leg, you must fail in conveying a true impression of their quaint humour." And yet, the correspondent had noted, "you cannot look upon his worn, bilious, anxious countenance, and believe it is to be that of a happy man." David Davis, an Illinois judge and the floor manager for Lincoln's successful nomination at the Republican National Convention in 1860, had written to the president's good friend Leonard Swett, "It is a good thing he is fond of anecdotes and telling them for it relieves his spirits very much." Lincoln's assistant secretary, William O. Stoddard, had reported: "Mr. Lincoln says that he must laugh sometimes, or he would surely die."[3]

As Davis and Stoddard suggested, Lincoln's storytelling and joke-making served multiple purposes. No doubt his verbal skills, honed while he was riding circuit as a lawyer in Illinois, had helped to make him popular with judges and juries. His ability to tell a funny story and laugh heartily must have made him feel good, countering the other extreme of his temperament, a melancholy that often left him saddened and depressed. If his physical appearance was gawky, even off-putting, his joke-telling drew people to him and made him likable. Lincoln shrewdly used stories and parables in more complex ways as well. They would disarm opponents, or offer an easily digestible truism in support of whatever position he was taking.

Through years of cruel, terrible war, Lincoln never lost his love of humor. "The habit of story-telling," recalled Hugh McCulloch, who was appointed secretary of the treasury on March 9, 1865, "became part of his nature and he gave free rein to it, even when the fate of the nation seemed to be trembling in the balance. . . . Story-telling was to him a safety-valve, and that he indulged in it, not only for the pleasure it afforded him, but for a temporary relief from oppressing cares; that the habit had been so cultivated that he could make a story illustrate a sentiment and give point to an argument." And thus, since Lincoln had a momentous announcement to make at that September meeting, it is no surprise that he chose to read a vignette.[4]

Given Lincoln's penchant for using anecdotes and jokes to instruct as well as amuse, one must wonder whether he had a larger point to make by choosing the Artemus Ward story. One possibility is that, like the showman in the tale, he would be presenting the public with a fearsome figure: emancipation. He knew the Proclamation would evoke a torrent of criticism from some quarters, though unlike the showman, he would have to bear the abuse without recourse to a court of law.

When Lincoln had finished reading the story to his cabinet, the mirth, whether free or forced, subsided and he "took a graver tone." The men no doubt straightened up a bit in their chairs as they looked at the president. He was dressed in his familiar black frock-coat, which he wore so often that, as Nathaniel Hawthorne once observed, "the suit had adapted itself to the curves and angularities of his figure." Lincoln's complexion was "dark and sallow . . . he has thick black eyebrows and an impending brow; his nose is large, and the lines about his mouth are very strongly defined." However coarse his appearance, it was all softened by his kindly eyes which "redeemed, illuminated, softened, and brightened . . . an expression of homely sagacity." Toward war's end, a colonel named Theodore Lyman stood by Lincoln as he reviewed the Army of the Potomac: "The President is, I think, the ugliest man I ever put my eyes on; there is also an expression of plebeian vulgarity in his face that is offensive (you recognize the recounter of coarse stories). On the other hand, he has the look of sense and wonderful shrewdness, while the heavy eyelids give him a mark almost of genius. He strikes me, too, as a very honest and kindly man; and, with all his vulgarity, I see no trace of low passions in his face. On the whole, he is such a mixture of all sorts, as only America brings forth."[5]

Present at the cabinet meeting was William Henry Seward, the secretary of state, a former governor of New York and U.S. senator who had been the favorite for the nomination going into the Republican convention in 1860. Described by one reporter as silver-haired and slight, a "subtle quick man rejoicing in power," Seward had declared in the 1850s that there was a "higher law" than the Constitution and that the conflict between North and South was "irrepressible."[6]

Other cabinet members bristled at Seward's ambitions, perhaps none more so than Salmon P. Chase, former senator from Ohio and now secretary of the treasury. One diplomat described him as a "tall, well-made, robust man, with handsome features, fine blue eyes, and a ready and agreeable smile." (An observer once wondered how "so kind-looking a man can find it in his heart to tax anybody.") Chase himself lusted after the presidency, and in a scheme that backfired, he fed information to a group of radical Republican senators, who called for Seward's dismissal. Both Seward and Chase would offer their resignations by year's end, but Lincoln would refuse to accept them.[7]

Gideon Welles, the secretary of the navy, a former Democrat from Connecticut, was far more conservative than Chase, but he too distrusted Seward, who seemed always to be meeting privately with Lincoln and meddling in affairs. Welles, whose flowing white beard and high naval position had earned him the nickname "Father Neptune," gossiped freely in his diary—he claimed that Edward Bates, the U.S. attorney general, also felt "disgust" with Seward. Bates, from Missouri, was one of the more conservative members of the cabinet; other conservatives included Maryland's Montgomery Blair, the postmaster general, who feuded with Edwin Stanton and called Seward "an unprincipled liar," and Caleb Smith, the secretary of the interior, yet another cabinet member dissatisfied with the secretary of state. Stanton, who had been born in Ohio but had moved to Pennsylvania in 1847 and Washington in 1856, was a prominent lawyer before serving as attorney general under James Buchanan. He opposed Lincoln politically, but had entered the cabinet as secretary of war in January, after Lincoln arranged for the resignation of the inept Simon Cameron. Stanton would remain by Lincoln's side to the end.[8]

Lincoln said to the members of his cabinet: "I have, as you are aware, thought a great deal about the relation of this war to Slavery." He had been waiting for the right time to act and had decided "the time has come now." He knew it wasn't an ideal moment, but such a moment might never arrive. The Confederate army had been driven out of Maryland, and with that the president was determined to "issue a Proclamation of Emancipation such as I thought most likely to be useful." He had made a promise to himself. Lincoln then paused and added that he had also made the promise "to my Maker."[9]

Chase, one of two cabinet diarists to write about the meeting, indicated that Lincoln said nothing more about God, but Welles, in his diary, chose to elaborate: Lincoln "remarked that he had made a vow, a covenant, that if God gave us the victory in the approaching battle, he would consider it an indication of Divine will, and that it was his duty to move forward in the cause of emancipation. . . . God had decided the question in favor of the slaves."[10]

The president did not want his cabinet's advice, not now. He already knew their separate views, and, after months of deliberation and calculation, his own mind was at last fixed. Whatever else might be said about Lincoln, once he arrived at a decision he did not retreat from it. But he sought the cabinet's input on minor matters of wording. He then read the document which he had spent the previous day composing in a clear hand.

Seward spoke first. He suggested that the Proclamation should not state that the incumbent president would sustain the actions; rather, it was the government that would not only recognize but also "maintain the freedom it proclaims." Chase declared that while he himself might have taken a different approach, he was ready "to stand by it with all my heart."

The group agreed to the modification suggested by Seward. The secretary of state then said that with regard to a passage concerning colonization, language should be added providing for the consent of the colonists. Edward Bates brought up the issue of linking deportation to emancipation, a subject of great interest to Montgomery Blair and Caleb Smith as well; but at this meeting, at least, the topic would not be pursued.

Blair announced that he would not oppose issuing the Proclamation, but he intended to file a paper giving his reasons against the expediency of the measure. He feared the influence of the document on the border states—the slave states of Missouri, Kentucky, Delaware, and Maryland—which might join the rebellion; on the army, which might oppose the policy; and on the opposition party, which would now have "a club put into their hands" to beat the administration. Blair claimed that he was in favor of emancipation but concerned about how best to accomplish the objective, and in the end he decided not to submit his objections in writing.[11]

The meeting soon adjourned, and after minor changes had been made in the document, Lincoln sent the preliminary Emancipation Proclamation off to the printers. "It is my last trump card, Judge," he told his supporter Edwards Pierrepont. "If that don't do, we must give up."[12]

The document declared that the war would continue to be waged for the "object of practically restoring the constitutional relation" of the United States with the people of the seceded states, and that Lincoln would use all his authority and power as president and commander-in-chief to do so. It announced that the president would encourage Congress again to offer financial aid to any slave states willing to consider adopting gradual or immediate plans of emancipation, and to "colonize persons of African descent with their consent."

It then stated Lincoln's intentions: "That on the first day of January in the year of our Lord, one thousand eight hundred and sixty-three, all persons held as slaves within any State, or designated part of a State, the people whereof shall then be in rebellion against the United States shall be then, thenceforward, and forever free." Such freedom would be recognized and maintained by the government, including the army and navy, "which will do no act or acts to repress such persons . . . in any efforts they may make for their actual freedom."

The Proclamation proceeded to call attention to two acts of Congress. The first, approved on March 13, 1862, prohibited the military from returning fugitive slaves. The second, approved on July 17, authorized the seizure and confiscation of the slaves of anyone "engaged in rebellion" against the United States and declared that they "shall be forever free of their servitude." It also restated that no escaped slave "shall be delivered up," unless the lawful owner had taken an oath that he himself had not borne arms against the government or supported the rebellion.

The document concluded with the promise to recommend "in due time" that those loyal citizens who lost slaves would be compensated. Lincoln and Seward signed, and on the next day, September 23, the Proclamation was reprinted in newspapers.

January 1 was one hundred days away. Over that time, the Proclamation would be welcomed and feared, praised and damned, analyzed and debated. It would have an impact on military affairs, international relations, domestic elections, and the lives of the enslaved. Anticipation would build. Maybe Lincoln would change his mind. And should he not, what would happen on January 1, 1863? Partially in response to the three months of reaction, the preliminary Emancipation Proclamation would itself undergo transformation. The document Lincoln issued on January 1 differed in significant ways from the one released on September 22.

As the New Year approached, people tried to get word to the president. A politician asked one of Lincoln's electors to "tell him the world will pardon his crimes, and his stories even, if he only makes the proclamation a success, and that if he fails he will be gibbeted in history as a great, long-legged, awkward, country pettifogger, without brains or backbone."[13]

From the start, the Emancipation Proclamation faced withering criticism. Both those opposed to any action against slavery and those craving more than the decree delivered denounced it, and the Proclamation never fully escaped from multifarious allegations—that it was unconstitutional, that it could not be enforced, that it would lead to the horrors of slave rebellions, and that it liberated hardly anyone. The need for additional measures to ensure freedom—most notably the Thirteenth Amendment abolishing slavery, ratified in 1865—further eroded the Proclamation's reputation. And in recent decades, indignation over the meaning and quality of freedom for blacks has led to disparagement of President Lincoln's course of action as too little, too late. At the same time, historians began to look beyond the role of leaders in interpretations of the past and focused instead on the efforts made by those outside traditional channels of power—in this case, the enslaved. And so the decree, deeply contested in its time, has become devalued in ours.[14]

It is lamentable that we have distanced ourselves from the Proclamation, allowed it to be diminished because the prose is legalistic and the document supposedly did not free anyone. In 1863 Frederick Douglass responded to those who said it was nothing but a paper decree: "Our own Declaration of Independence was at one time but ink and paper. The freedom of the American colonies dates from no particular battle during the war. No man can tell upon what particular day we won our national independence. But the birth of our freedom is fixed on the day of the going forth of the Declaration of Independence. In like manner, aftercoming generations will celebrate the first of January as the day which brought liberty and manhood to the American slaves." Indeed, Douglass thought: "The fourth of July was great, but the first of January, when we consider it in all its relations and bearings, even greater."[15]

The Declaration of Independence envisioned a new country; the Proclamation remade one. The Declaration enunciated principles; the Proclamation provided a plan. The Declaration read beautifully, but its effect was delayed; the Proclamation read poorly, but it changed lives instantly. Viewed together, the two documents are the pole stars of American liberty. On July 4, 1865, after the war was over, the men of the 22nd Iowa Infantry, stationed in Savannah, Georgia, held a regimental parade, at the end of which two documents were read aloud: the Declaration of Independence and the Emancipation Proclamation.[16]

Emancipation was a process, not a moment. The movement to emancipate the slaves began long before September 22, 1862, when Lincoln issued the preliminary Emancipation Proclamation, and it continued well after January 1, 1863, when, following a period of one hundred days, he delivered on his promise and promulgated the decree. The idea of one hundred days as the benchmark for presidential success dates to Franklin Delano Roosevelt's first three months in office; and ever since, executive achievement has usually been gauged by what has been accomplished during that interval. Though Lincoln didn't realize the precise timing until later, he had made a decision that would take effect in exactly one hundred days. His hundred days, commencing nineteen months into his term of office, were unlike any other—not the first measure of his presidency, as they were for Franklin Delano Roosevelt and his successors, but a countdown to a momentous event. They allow us to track the unfolding drama of history as Lincoln led a nation at war toward emancipation and, in doing so, traversed the anxieties and expectations of voters, soldiers, scholars, politicians, reformers, foreign leaders, and even the enslaved. Arriving as it did when it did, the Emancipation Proclamation shifted the momentum of the war and, combined with Lincoln's reelection in 1864 and the Confederate surrender the following spring, ensured the eventual destruction of slavery in America.

The Emancipation Proclamation also was the document that first elevated Lincoln to the pantheon of America's transcendent figures—individuals who appear now and again and reshape the nation before they are gone. That he seemed to take forever to act, that he hedged and hesitated, that he irritated not only his political opponents but also his friends, that he appeared at times to shrink from the unprecedented challenges before him, make the story all the more compelling. By revisiting the hundred days between the preliminary version and the final version of the Emancipation Proclamation, we can observe Lincoln as he watched, worried, listened, read, debated, cajoled, prayed, and even joked—then made up his mind and marched the nation toward freedom and the light of the unknown.

The Path to the Preliminary Proclamation

He has not sought to control events, but he has known how to turn events, among the most important of which are to be reckoned the moods of a great people in time of trial, to the benefit of the cause of the nation and of mankind.

—Charles Eliot Norton, *North American Review*, January 1865

1

Toward Emancipation

Lincoln always moved cautiously. He once told the story of a man with a hillside mill whose water supply came from a nearby lake. The man "opened the sluice a trifle & the water rushed out, widening the passage until its volume swept off mill & miller." If not handled with care, emancipation could turn out to be a torrent that would drown one and all. And so Lincoln took his time acting directly against slavery; and even when he took his boldest step, on September 22, 1862, he announced that he did not intend to act until one hundred days later.[1]

Others—members of Congress, military officers, the slaves themselves—were less willing to wait. Indeed, from the very start of the crisis, the call sounded to seize upon the war to abolish slavery, to make emancipation a cause and not merely a possible consequence. In late April 1861, Joshua Giddings, an Ohio congressman from 1838 to 1859 and an antislavery activist, wrote to Charles Sumner, the radical Republican senator from Massachusetts, "The first gun fired at Fort Sumter rang out the death-knell of slavery." He followed that up with a call for some kind of emancipation proclamation, arguing that "such a proclamation would compel every [Confederate] fighting man to remain at home and look to their negroes instead of going into the army to kill our friends." Orville Browning, Lincoln's friend and political supporter, who in June would fill the Illinois Senate seat opened as a result of

Stephen Douglas's death, wrote the president at the end of April: "The time is not yet, but it will come when it will be necessary for you to march an army into the South, and proclaim freedom to the slaves. When it does come, do it. Dont hesitate. You are fighting for national life—for your own individual life. God has raised you up for a great work."[2]

The belief spread that whatever the reasons for the war, and whatever assurances had been given the South that the government would not interfere with the domestic institutions of states, if the union was to survive, slavery could not. "The conviction is permeating the mind of the North," noted one writer, "that in some way or other Slavery is to go down in this struggle to its final death." John Hay, Lincoln's private secretary, observed: "What we could not have done in many lifetimes the madness and folly of the South has accomplished for us. Slavery offers itself more vulnerable to our attack than at any point in any century and the wild malignity of the south is excusing us before God & the world." William Slocum, author of *The War and How To End It*, a pamphlet that went through several editions in 1861, insisted that "slavery is the sole cause of our national troubles, and emancipation the only remedy."[3]

The problem was how to accomplish the abolition of slavery—how to justify emancipation legally and constitutionally, not morally. After all, before the war, the president had time and again assured Southerners that they should have no fear that a "Republican administration would, *directly*, or *indirectly*, interfere with their slaves, or with them, about their slaves." It seemed clear that although the Constitution never used the word "slave" or "slavery," it offered protection to the institution. Article I, Section 8, enumerated the powers of Congress, and legislating on slavery, which was the creation of state or local laws, was not one of them. Indeed, Article I, Section 9, explicitly prohibited Congress from interfering with the slave trade until 1808. And the Constitution also contained a "three-fifths clause," counting each slave as three-fifths of a person for the purposes of taxation and representation, as well as a "fugitive-slave clause," saying that runaway slaves must be returned to their owners in the states from which they had fled. Lincoln would later explain that although he was "naturally anti-slavery," his oath of office, in "ordinary civil administration," forbade him "to practically indulge my primary abstract judgment on the moral question of slavery."[4]

But surely the rebellion made a difference, and in 1861 some wondered in what ways war would change attitudes. The question even troubled men of impeccable antislavery credentials, such as Henry Ward Beecher. The preeminent Congregationalist minister of his day, Beecher was the son of Lyman Beecher, who had helped to fuel the Second Great Awakening in the 1830s and 1840s; he was also the brother of Harriet Beecher Stowe, whose novel *Uncle Tom's Cabin* (1852) helped to revolutionize northern attitudes toward slavery. In a Thanksgiving sermon titled "War and Emancipation," delivered on November 21, 1861, Beecher commented on the popular impulse to "make a declaration of emancipation." The advice, he lamented, cannot be followed: "If we are fighting for our constitution, we must not violate it ourselves. A pretty thing to make war against them for violating the Constitution, when we are willing to violate it ourselves! We may not congressionally declare emancipation. I wish we could!" Beecher later put it this way: The "conflict must be carried on *through* our institutions, not over them. Revolution is not the remedy for rebellion."[5]

Responding not to constitutional scruples but to practical realities, an unlikely figure named Benjamin Butler helped open a path toward emancipation. Butler, a Massachusetts lawyer and politician, was a lifelong Democrat. Indeed, in the election year of 1860 he first supported the nomination of Jefferson Davis and then, in the general election, voted for John C. Breckinridge, nominee of the Southern Democrats. Described by one newspaper correspondent as a "stout middle-aged man, strongly built, with coarse limbs . . . and high forehead," Butler had earned the rank of brigadier general in the Massachusetts militia. In April 1861, the state's governor, John Andrew, sent Butler south to reopen railroad lines destroyed after rioting in Baltimore, but the general astonished the antislavery governor when he offered the militia to the governor of Maryland to help put down any slave insurrections. Andrew rebuked Butler: "Servile insurrection against a community in arms against the federal Union is no longer to be regarded by our troops in a political but solely from a military point of view; and is to be contemplated as one of the inherent weaknesses of the enemy from the disastrous operation of which we are under no obligation of a military character to guard them." In other words, if the slaves rebelled against the secessionists, so much the better for the Union cause.[6]

Butler was not happy with Andrew's admonishment, and he responded tartly. How, he wondered, should he deal with property that consisted of slaves? Should he do this, he asked sarcastically, "by allowing, and of course arming, that population to rise upon the defenseless women and children of that country, carrying rapine, arson and murder—all the horrors of San Domingo a million times magnified—among those whom we hope to reunite with as brethren?" (Butler was alluding to a bloody slave revolt in the 1790s on Santo Domingo, or Hispaniola, the island that today consists of Haiti and the Dominican Republic.) He said that as long as the enemy met him in "honorable warfare," and then called on him for help against slave insurrection, he would provide it.[7]

The dispute seemed likely to fade, but Andrew's letter was leaked to the *New York Tribune,* which denounced Butler's behavior as an example of "that devotion to old fashioned and foolish notions of comity and Constitutional obligation which is bad enough in times of peace, but absolutely intolerable in times of rebellion." The *Tribune* reported inaccurately that "the rebels are arming the negroes," and wondered: "If generals continue the policy of volunteering to put down slave insurrections, and returning runaway slaves, how long will it be before the slaves will come to the conclusion that the Northern people are their worst enemies?"[8]

Leaving Baltimore in mid-May 1861, and accepting a commission as a major general with the U.S. Volunteers, Butler took command of Fort Monroe in Hampton, Virginia. On May 25, he reported to General Winfield Scott an incident that had taken place two days earlier. Three slaves, Frank Baker, Shepard Mallory, and James Townsend, field hands who belonged to Colonel Charles Mallory, the commander of secession forces in the district, had "delivered themselves up" to the picket guards. Butler had investigated and found that the slaves were being transported to aid secession forces. Butler decided to avail himself of their services, as he had a great need for labor. "I am credibly informed," Butler continued in his report to Scott, "that the negroes in this neighborhood are employed in the erection of batteries and other works by the rebels, which it would be nearly or quite impossible to construct without their labor." Why should this property be used against the United States, rather than in support of the cause of the nation?[9]

Two days later Butler wrote again, saying that "the question in regard to Slave property is becoming one of very serious magnitude." The number of slaves coming into his lines was growing, and he confessed "the utmost doubt what to do with this species of property." Recognizing the vital aid these slaves were providing to the enemy (twelve runaways who entered that morning had been forced to help erect the batteries that fired upon Butler's men), he concluded that "as a military question, it would seem to be a measure of necessity to deprive their masters of their services."

Butler decided to declare these runaway slaves contraband of war, and confiscated them as a function of military power. "Contraband" stuck as the term applied to all the slaves who ran off and entered Union lines. As for the Fugitive Slave Act of 1850, which required the return of runaway slaves to their masters, Butler argued that it did not apply to foreign countries and, as far as he was concerned, this was precisely what Virginia had become. Some would privately call it "Butler's fugitive-slave law." On May 30 the secretary of war, Simon Cameron, wrote to Butler approving his action, but leaving uncertain what this meant, exactly, in terms of the status of the contrabands. Were they free? Would they be returned to their masters (or sold back to them) once peace came? Did the policy apply to the slave states still in the Union? All Cameron could say was that "their final disposition will be reserved for future determination." (The secretary of the navy, Gideon Welles, announced in September 1861 that contrabands would be enlisted under the lowest ship's-crew status, known as "boy"; the following December he revised the policy to allow for the advancement of black sailors through the ranks.)[10]

The phrase "contraband of war" as applied to slaves captured the public's imagination. The discussion of what constituted contraband was ubiquitous at the time of Butler's edict, and that may indeed account for his clever application of the doctrine, which had been understood to apply to goods and services being sent into the Confederacy. For example, on May 17, less than a week before Butler's encounter, a headline in the *New York Times* read "What Are Contraband Goods?" The list included such items as food, clothing, timber, munitions, gold and silver coin, and much more. In the weeks leading up to Butler's action, papers in Maryland and elsewhere had been reporting regularly on the seizure of contraband being smuggled into the Confederacy.[11]

Butler was celebrated for his legal and military ingenuity; newspapers reported that the doctrine received "universal approbation" and furnished "unmingled satisfaction to the public." One editor proclaimed the decision "impregnable" because slaves were as "clearly contraband of war as cannon, bombshells, gunpowder, beef and pork, horses and cattle." Later in the year, Charles C. Nott, a lawyer and writer, pointed out that the greatest success of "contraband" was as a word:

> Those who love to ponder over the changes of language and watch its new uses and unconscious growth, must find in it a rare phenomenon of philological vegetation. Never was a word so speedily adopted by so many people in so short a time. In conversation and correspondence, in newspapers and books, in the official dispatches of generals, it leaped instantaneously to its new place, jostling aside the circumlocution "colored people," the extrajudicial "person of African descent," the scientific "negro," the slang "nigger," and the debasing "slave."[12]

Consensus on the meaning of the word, however, broke down on the question of the ultimate status of the contrabands. In a congratulatory letter, postmaster general Montgomery Blair told Butler, "You were right when you declared *secession* niggers contraband of war," but reminded him that "the business you are sent upon . . . is war not emancipation." By contrast, the secretary of the treasury, Salmon Chase, declared he never doubted "that the United States Government under the war power might destroy slavery."[13]

One Democratic newspaper insisted that the contraband policy not be transformed into an "abolition programme," and argued that "a sound policy of economy and humanity cannot be reached by any such processes of a military emancipation." By contrast, an abolitionist paper declared that this was the start of a "practical plan" that would result in "universal emancipation," because the American people would never allow these contrabands, who refused to fight against the federal soldiers and indeed helped the Union cause, to be returned to slavery. "What Shall Be Done with the Slaves Emancipated by War?" asked one headline. "The contrabands are curious as to what shall be their fate," reported a correspondent from Fort Monroe. One writer advised, in effect, not to worry about it: "Use them so far as they can be made useful, pay them fairly for their services, and then dismiss them to shift for themselves." But others saw beyond practicality: the answer was to treat the contrabands like men, because once they crossed over, "the government can know them in no other capacity. . . . It can only know them as men, with all the rights of men." Anything less than that would be so "base and treacherous" that the government would "deserve to be a thousand times overthrown, and be forever accursed among the nations." Henry Ward Beecher fully grasped the political significance of the thousands of runaway slaves: "You may call them 'contraband,'—you may with dexterity call them ingenious or evasive names, but the Southern law that said 'Slave' is broken! Slaves in the possession of the government of these United States can be nothing else than men. They are emancipated."[14]

But where would they live? How would they care for themselves? Perhaps they should be encouraged to settle in open territory or in other countries. And what about the legal and constitutional questions? It was one thing to take the property of rebels fighting against the government; it was another to invade the property rights of loyal citizens. And there was the problem of scale. A few hundred or a few thousand contrabands were one matter; hundreds of thousands, or even millions, another. The war, one writer noted, is putting "ideas into the heads of the slaves." As the three fugitives who appeared at Fort Monroe demonstrated, the Union might wait to make the war one of freedom, but the enslaved would not.[15]

Frederick Law Olmsted was one of the first to suggest a need to organize the contrabands. The superintendent of New York's Central Park, charged with implementing the plan that he and Calvert Vaux had submitted in 1857, Olmsted sought to discover what his mission in the war would be. He thought he would make an able superintendent of contrabands. After all, he had experience supervising some 15,000 workers in the park, and he was quite familiar with the South, having taken three journeys there in 1853 and 1854, and having published three books on the region, including *A Journey in the Back Country*, which had just appeared the previous year. "I have given more thought," he declared in June, "to the special question of the proper management of negroes in a state of limbo between slavery & freedom than anyone else in the country." In December, he published an article in the *New York Times* that called for the government to take possession of certain southern districts located near agricultural regions and use them to establish "a safe harbor for all negroes." These "sanctuaries of freedom" would further destabilize the Confederate cause. By then, Olmsted had accepted a position as general secretary of the U.S. Sanitary Commission, which sought to aid soldiers in the field by furnishing medical care and supplies and by organizing volunteer efforts. Oversight of the contrabands would remain a haphazard affair.[16]

As the slaves came into Union lines, many officers independently advanced the emancipation cause, even though the freedom these contrabands received could hardly have been characterized as benevolent. The actions of Lieutenant Charles Harvey Brewster of the 10th Massachusetts Volunteer Infantry Regiment are illustrative. Writing from Camp Brightwood in Washington, D.C., on November 17, 1861, Brewster noted that nine contrabands had arrived in camp, and he said the regiment's colonel had no intention of sending them back. "This war is playing the Dickens with slavery," he reported, "and if it lasts much longer will clear our Country's name of the vile stain and enable us to live in peace hereafter." A week later he told of a slave in camp who was trying to raise money to buy his freedom. Brewster suggested he take "'leg bail' and save his money" (meaning that the man should simply flee). In the new year, Brewster rejoiced: "I have got a 'Contraband' . . . he is a bright looking mulatto, 17 years old and says his master paid $400 for him six years ago, he was the only slave his master had and his master never will have him again if I can help it."[17]

Brewster "was on the lookout for a servant." In addition to having someone clean and cook for him, he would still have extra money: he was allowed $13 a month for subsistence and $2.50 for clothing, but he figured it would cost only half that to keep a contraband. In February, Brewster reported that the owner of the servant he'd found came looking for his property. The lieutenant sent the runaway off to hide in the woods. The owner said the slave's name was David, and Brewster took it upon himself to "rechristian" him Henry Hastings. Brewster referred to the contrabands as "darkies" and "niggers," and he took pleasure in using them for sport—the company would have them butt heads against each other, like wild rams. At the same time, he vowed: "I never will be instrumental in returning a slave to his master in any way shape or manner." In March, Brewster gave up his contraband, who took off with several others for the Pennsylvania border. But he returned after being confronted by a white man. Brewster scolded him, told him not to be a coward and not to be taken alive, and sent him off again toward uncertain freedom.[18]

Scenes such as these were replayed thousands of times. The war disrupted slavery. It gave slaves a place to which to run, and it introduced soldiers to slavery as a reality, not an abstraction. Encounters between slaves and soldiers, however uncertain, uneven, and unkind, helped to keep the issue of emancipation at the forefront.[19]

Emancipation as a military measure gained added momentum with the defeat of Union forces at Bull Run on July 21, 1861. Lincoln had hoped for a decisive victory that would bring the four-month-old rebellion to a rapid close. He ordered an assault against the Confederate army near Manassas, Virginia. General Pierre T. Beauregard, who had been given command of Confederate forces after his success at Fort Sumter, had an army of 20,000 men that threatened Washington, some twenty-five miles away. Union general Irvin McDowell had 35,000 men under his command, and although he was nervous about proceeding with men so lacking in experience, the advance began on July 16. The march proved chaotic, made worse by the lack of reliable maps of Virginia. With the help of good intelligence and by shifting units around, the Confederate army was able to prepare itself for the assault.

On Sunday, July 21, McDowell reached his destination and prepared to attack. Curious spectators from Washington, thinking it would make a pleasant day's entertainment to watch the Federals fight, rode out in carriages. The initial assault looked promising, but it was repelled when Confederate reinforcements arrived. Late in the afternoon, the rebels launched a counterattack. Their determined rush forward and piercing yell, like the howl of "a thousand dogs," forced a frantic, disorganized retreat by Union military and civilians alike. It didn't help that uniforms this early in the war had not been standardized and Union troops mistook Confederates in blue as Union men. In the end, on each side, several hundred were killed and well over a thousand wounded. Far worse was yet to come.

Reading reports of the battle in London, Henry Adams, serving as secretary to his father, Charles Francis Adams, ambassador to England, wrote that

"Bull's Run will be a by-word of ridicule for all time . . . the disgrace is fright-ful. . . . If this happens again, farewell to our country for many a day." But where Adams saw ignominy, Charles Sumner saw opportunity. "The bat-tle & defeat have done much for the slave," he informed abolitionist Wen-dell Phillips. "I told the Predt that our defeat was the worst event & the best event in our history; the worst, as it was the greatest present calamity & shame,—the best, as it made the extinction of Slavery inevitable." The con-flict could reach no rapid close that would have left slavery intact.[20]

In that same letter, Sumner said: "I have spoken to the Presdt & *a major-ity of the Cabinet* on the new power to be invoked. I assure you there are men who do not hesitate." The new power to be invoked was military power—military necessity. And while the executive branch (except to uphold Butler's contraband policy) may not have been ready to push forward, the legisla-tive was.

On July 22, the day after the defeat at Bull Run, the Senate took up a bill that would give legislative sanction to the military's contraband policy. Ac-cording to Section 4 of this Confiscation Act, if "any person claimed to be held to labor or service under the law of any State" and was required "to take up arms against the United States . . . or work or to be employed in or upon any fort, navy yard, dock, armory, ship, entrenchment, or in any military or naval service whatsoever, against the Government and lawful authority of the United States," then the person who alleged such service or labor "shall for-feit his claim."

In supporting the bill, Lyman Trumbull, Republican senator from Illinois, noted that on the Confederate side "negroes were in the fight which has re-cently occurred." Henry Wilson, Republican senator from Massachusetts, declared: "I think the time has come when this Government should cease to return to traitors the fugitive slaves, whom they are using to erect batteries to murder brave men who are fighting under the flag of their country." In the House of Representatives, where the debate turned acrimonious, Republi-can John Bingham of Ohio proclaimed that "a traitor should not only forfeit his slave, but he should forfeit his life as well." And Pennsylvania's Thaddeus Stevens, perhaps the most radical of the House Republicans, said that he believed "the time had come when the laws of war were to govern our ac-tion." *Inter arma silent leges,* he declared (quoting Cicero): In time of war, the laws are silent. He had no patience for members of the Democratic opposition who said the act under consideration was unconstitutional: "When a country is at open war, with an enemy, every publicist agrees that you have a right to use every means which will weaken him."

The Republicans avoided the question asked by the Democrats: "What was to become of these poor wretches if they were discharged?" Democratic senator James Pearce of Maryland had no qualms about calling the measure what he thought it was: "an act of emancipation, however limited and qualified." Showing that he, too, could use Latin phrases, he labeled it a mere *brutum fulmen*—literally, "inert thunder"—meaning that it could never be enforced. Pearce wondered what court would declare the property confiscated, what procedures would operate, and how any court would see it as constitutional, since, as another member put it, "Congress has no power, and the power exists nowhere in this Government, to set at liberty the slaves now held in bondage in the slave States." Longtime Whig/Unionist senator John J. Crittenden of Kentucky, now in the House, said that the law "undertakes to deprive the owner of slaves of his entire property, and give complete freedom to the slave." Henry Burnett, Democrat from Kentucky, claimed that the act "amounts to a wholesale emancipation of the slaves in the seceding or rebellious states."[21]

Burnett was mistaken. The Confiscation Act, which passed the Senate by a vote of 24 to 11 and the House by a vote of 60 to 46, and which was signed by Lincoln on August 6, 1861, freed few slaves. It merely gave legislative sanction to a military policy already in place. Furthermore, the administration did little to enforce the act. More was needed. Abolitionist and railroad magnate John Murray Forbes, for one, thought it "was a great mistake in Congress to limit the confiscation of property to that of rebels found in arms against us," and insisted "we can no longer afford to 'make war with rosewater.'" Something more acidic was needed, and the doctrine of military necessity, based on the war power, might be used to corrode slavery completely wherever it existed.[22]

On August 30, several weeks after passage of the Confiscation Act, General John Charles Frémont, in his capacity as commander of the Western Department—which had been created on July 3, 1861, and which encompassed all the states and territories west of the Mississippi and east of the

Rocky Mountains—issued a proclamation that imposed martial law in Missouri and announced: "The property, real and personal, of all persons in the State of Missouri who shall take up arms against the United States, or who shall be directly proven to have taken an active part with their enemies in the field, is declared to be confiscated to the public use, and their slaves, if any they have, are hereby declared freemen." It was a bold but perhaps logical step beyond the Confiscation Act. Bold because Missouri, though a slave state, remained in the Union. Logical because, as some Democratic congressmen feared, it was not much of a leap from confiscating the property of rebels who used slaves to fight the war to confiscating the property of rebels who simply owned slaves. And Frémont explicitly went beyond confiscation: he declared the slaves to be free.

"It comes upon us like a thunder clap in a clear sky, and clearly indicates that a new chapter has been opened in the conduct of this war," exulted the *Chicago Tribune,* which also warned that "if we do not emancipate them [the slaves] peacefully they will one day emancipate themselves in fire and blood." The abolitionist Gerrit Smith called the step "the first unqualifiedly and purely right one, in regard to our colored population, which has taken place during the war." One writer reported that soldiers were generally satisfied with Frémont's proclamation, as "it seemed to betoken a more earnest appreciation of the crisis and its dangers than any official document which had previously been issued."[23]

Lincoln could not have been happy to learn of Frémont's proclamation from the morning papers. On September 2, he wrote to the general about his "anxiety" over the proclamation. He feared that the provision "liberating slaves of traitorous owners, will alarm our Southern Union friends, and turn them against us—perhaps ruin our rather fair prospect for Kentucky." He asked Frémont to modify the order. While he waited, he heard from his dear friend Joshua Speed, with whom he had roomed in Springfield after arriving there in 1837 until Speed left Illinois in 1840 to take over his father's plantation in Kentucky. Speed warned the president that Frémont's proclamation "will hurt us in Ky—The war should be waged upon high points and no state law be interfered with—Our Constitution & laws both prohibit the emancipation of slaves among us. . . . All of us who live in slave states whether Union or loyal have great fear of insurrection—Will not such a proclamation read by slaves incline them to assert their freedom?" The proclamation so sickened Speed, he reported, that "I have been unable to eat or sleep."[24]

Frémont refused to amend his proclamation without being explicitly ordered to do so, and the president was more than happy to oblige. On September 11, Lincoln informed the general that the offending clause must be "modified, held, and construed, so as to conform to, and not to transcend" the Confiscation Act of August 6. Lincoln quickly heard from Illinois senator Orville Browning, who expressed his regret over the president's actions. Frémont's proclamation, Browning averred, "had the unqualified approval of every true friend of Government within my knowledge. . . . Its influence was most salutary, and it was accomplishing much good." He concluded that "there has been too much tenderness towards traitors and rebels."[25]

Lincoln responded to his friend, thinking it "odd" that Browning would object. The president argued that "Genl. Fremont's proclamation, as to confiscation of property, and the liberation of slaves, is *purely political,* and not within the range of *military* law, or necessity." Lincoln observed that a military commander could seize a farm, for example, and hold it as long as there was military necessity, but that once the emergency was over the property still belonged to the owner and his heirs. Frémont's proclamation was nothing more than "dictatorship." Only a "thoughtless" person would agree with the action. Furthermore, he had heard that upon issuance of the decree a Kentucky company of volunteers "threw down their arms and disbanded." "I think to lose Kentucky," Lincoln insisted, "is nearly the same as to lose the whole game." Allowing the proclamation to stand would not save the government of the country, but would destroy it: "Can it be pretended that it is any longer the government of the U.S.—any government of constitution and laws,—wherein a General, or a President, may make permanent rules of property by proclamation?"[26]

Lincoln's letter is dated September 22, 1861. A year from that date he would issue the very proclamation which, at the time of addressing Browning, he vigorously opposed. Lincoln had much intellectual work ahead of him; events would help to take him there.

He continued to receive letters from citizens. For everyone who wrote praising Lincoln for his "consistent, prudent, & just course," or for his "conservative policy," many more wrote to express opposition to his order, "which came on the people like a snowstorm in June." People wondered about "propitiating Kentucky" and shaping a policy "so as to make it satisfactory to the loyal slaveholders of Kentucky and wholly repugnant to the twenty millions of loyal people on whom the burthen after war rests." A woman told the president that "when it becomes necessary for a female, a *weak insignificant* female in view of the times to lift up her voice in defence of right," there must be something dreadfully wrong. She added, "Were I a soldier I would lay my arms down in disgust if after the present contest was ended, *Slavery* was to exist." The Union's policy, asserted one writer, should be "that Emancipation not Confiscation should be the rule of our Government," and that such a rule was justified by the "Laws of War." Another correspondent proclaimed: "Now this is a war between Slavery and a Monarcical Government and Freedom[,] and a Military necessity does now Compell us to wipe Out Slavery so far as the Rebells are Concerned or we must loose Our Government forever."[27]

Through the summer and fall of 1861, discussions of emancipation saturated newspaper columns, lecture halls, and Congress. Theophilus Parsons, Dane Professor of Law at Harvard University, identified four ways for the army to address the issue of slaves. It could seize them as contrabands; it could receive all runaway slaves; it could liberate them by a proclamation which "as a matter of law," Parsons affirmed, "I have not the least doubt of the right of an invading army to do.... It would be a right to be exercised only as a *military necessity*"; or it could "put weapons into their hands, and incite them to armed insurrection," a right that could exist only from "extreme necessity." Parsons's idea of an emancipation proclamation may have gotten lost in the more inflammatory final suggestion, but it was clear that intellectuals and activists had now seized on the issue of war power and military necessity to try to persuade Lincoln's administration that it could legally take action against slavery.[28]

Stressing military factors, Charles Loring Brace, a thirty-five-year-old reformer who had graduated from Union Theological Seminary and then founded the Children's Aid Society in New York, declared in August that "the only key to victory is a *Proclamation of Emancipation!*" He explained that the lessons of history demonstrated that smaller, weaker opponents than the Southerners had outlasted more powerful adversaries, and that one need only think back to the Revolutionary War as an example. He predicted why the South might triumph: "They will be in a country they know well; we in a strange. They can retreat to the mountains or the swamps. They can fortify and defend the cities. They can fight in guerrilla-warfare through every mountain-pass and pine-barren and cypress-swamp from the Potomac to the Rio Grande." But a declaration of emancipation would shift the odds in the Union's favor. When such a proclamation "has been widely scattered and proclaimed, and the slaves understand it—as they would marvelously soon—we have a nation of allies in the enemy's ranks. There is a foe in every Southerner's household. . . . A specter of panic is amid the Southern states."[29]

Brace did not articulate any antislavery principles or constitutional concerns. He wished that emancipation might come in some other manner, "but Providence has forced it upon us" in this way. It was left to others to make the case not only for why emancipation should become Union policy, but also for the way to justify it legally. One writer hinted at the case to be made when he declared that "no one has attempted to deny the right of the government, now in a state of war for its very existence, to abolish slavery as a means of preserving that existence." A letter to the editor of the *New York Times* asserted that "a decree of emancipation by the war power would make short work of the rebellion." "It is by no means improbable that his advice will be followed," recorded a reader in his diary.[30]

One of the fullest arguments for emancipation came from an unlikely source. Orestes Brownson was a leading Catholic polemicist who used his *Quarterly Review* to challenge Protestant pieties and address social issues. In the 1840s, after losing faith in Transcendentalism and utopianism, he converted to Catholicism. Politically, before the war, he was a Democrat who opposed slavery but also denounced the abolitionist movement. In late August 1861, he penned a lengthy essay titled "Slavery and the War." He began by acknowledging what his readers knew well: that no man opposed the abolition movement more strenuously than he, "not because we loved slavery . . . but because we loved the Constitution of the Union." He stated that the liberation of the slaves was not the war's purpose; at the same time, the conflict "is no mimic war, is no child's play, and is not to be conducted to a successful issue on the principle of treating the rebels as friends, giving them every advantage, and doing them no harm."[31]

It was time, Brownson thought, to get serious about war. He had endured enough policy aimed at appeasing the border states for fear they would join the rebellion: "This fear . . . has been from the first the bugbear of the administration, and its chief embarrassment." Brownson issued a call for firm, hard war, "real war, downright earnest war, and a war to be conducted not on the principle of respecting the feelings of the enemy, and of doing him no harm, but on the principle of striking him where he is weakest and sorest, and availing ourselves of every advantage against him allowed by the laws of civilized warfare." Toward this end, he argued that traitors could not hide behind supposed constitutional guarantees that the government would not interfere with slavery; the Constitution did not protect those who sought to destroy the document. Whatever it might be that the Constitution did or did not authorize, it was time to make use of all the means authorized by the recognized laws of war, because "in a state of war every thing has to give way to military necessity: private property, liberty, and even life itself." Military necessity, he believed, required going further than the provisions of the Confiscation Act. It required the president, as commander-in-chief, "to liberate all the slaves of the Union and to treat the whole present slave population as freemen." Abolition, Brownson concluded, would "be striking the enemy at his most vulnerable point, precisely where we can best sunder the sinews of his strength, and deal him the most fatal blow." And from a humanitarian point of view, it "would secure us what we now lack, the sympathy and the moral aid of the whole civilized world."[32]

One of Brownson's readers and correspondents was Charles Sumner. Throughout the winter, the two men exchanged letters about the possible appointment of Brownson's son as an officer on Frémont's staff, and the senator shared the belief that emancipation was a necessary and appropriate war measure. Indeed, almost immediately after the war broke out, Sumner went to Lincoln "and told him I was with him now, heart and soul; that under the war power the right had come to him to emancipate the slaves." It was not, however, until October 1, in a speech titled "Emancipation Our Best Weapon," delivered in Worcester, Massachusetts, before the Republican State Convention, that Sumner had a chance to develop the argument.

With his brown hair streaked with gray, and his deep-blue eyes, Sumner attracted attention. An English visitor called him a "man whom you would notice among other men, and whom, not knowing, you would turn around to look at as he passed by you." He had become a living symbol of the violent intransigence of slaveholders when he was caned by South Carolina representative Preston Brooks on the floor of the Senate on May 22, 1856. Recovering from his wounds, Sumner returned to the Senate on only a few occasions during the next three years. For most of that time, his seat remained vacant.[33]

"It is often said," Sumner observed, "that war will make an end of Slavery. This is probable. But it is surer still that the overthrow of Slavery will make an end of the war." The crowd erupted in tumultuous applause and cheers. The war power, he believed, was "positively recognized by the Constitution . . . [and] this law might be employed against Slavery, without impediment from States Rights." No less a figure than John Quincy Adams, first in 1836 and again in 1842, had made the argument. A quarter-century before war erupted, Adams had declared: "From the instant that your slaveholding States become the theatre of war, civil, servile, or foreign, from that instant the war powers of Congress extend to interference with the institution of Slavery in every way by which it can be interfered with." He later said that once the laws of war went into effect, "the commanders of both armies have power to emancipate all the slaves in the invaded territory," and that "not only the President of the United States but the commander of the army has power to order the Universal Emancipation of the slaves." In conclusion, Sumner called for a decree of emancipation and averred that "two objects are before us, Union and Peace, each for the sake of the other, and both for the sake of the country; but without Emancipation how can we expect either?" In a letter to John Jay following the speech, Sumner predicted the future of an emancipation decree: "It is to be presented strictly as a measure of military necessity and the argument is thus to be supported rather than on grounds of philanthropy. At the same time, I do not hesitate in declaring also that thus you will do an act of justice."[34]

It was easy for abolitionists to support Sumner's views, but radicals did not dominate public opinion. In Boston, conservative newspapers denounced the speech as "unfortunate," "impracticable," and "opposed to the spirit of the times." What about "servile insurrection"? What about the economic problem of "supporting four millions of human beings who have never been self-dependent"? The *Caucasian,* a vitriolic anti-abolitionist newspaper in New York, wondered, "Can any patriot read the rodomontade of this classic fanatic . . . without a sense of pain, nausea, and disgust?" Charles Francis Adams, Jr., writing to his brother Henry, clearly wasn't impressed by the references to his grandfather in the speech: "What can Sumner mean by perpetrating historical frauds so sure of detection. . . . Sumner is a humbug! There's no doubt about it. He's been a useful man in his day, but he's as much out of place now as knights in armor would be at the head of our regiments."

Henry Adams responded by saying that while he was against slavery, he agreed with more cautious people such as Seward, who "says the time has not yet come; that we must wait till the whole country has time to make the same advance that we have made within the last six months, till we can all move together with but one mind and one idea."[35]

Lincoln certainly needed no encouragement to move deliberately. His slow pace infuriated those who were more radical than he, but they had nowhere to turn and he knew it. Encouraged by Governor Richard Yates of Illinois to act promptly on emancipation, Lincoln, paraphrasing Exodus 14:13, telegraphed: "Hold fast, Dick, and see the salvation of the Lord." But conservatives such as General George McClellan, appointed general-in-chief of Union forces in November, never wanted that day to come. "Help me to dodge the nigger," he wrote Samuel L. M. Barlow, a New York lawyer and prominent Democrat; "we want nothing to do with him." The general praised Lincoln for focusing only on the preservation of the Union and not on the slavery question. "The Presdt is perfectly honest & is really sound on the nigger question," McClellan reported in November. McClellan would never come to accept the war's transformation into a struggle against slavery, but General Ulysses S. Grant, writing several weeks later, did. Grant told his father that he regretted seeing newspaper coverage that "can look at nothing favorably that does not look to a war upon slavery. My inclination is to whip the rebellion into submission, preserving all constitutional rights. If it cannot be whipped in any other way than through a war against slavery, let it come to that legitimately. If it is necessary that slavery should fall that the Republic may continue its existence, let slavery go."[36]

All sides must have been curious about what Lincoln would say in his An-

nual Message, presented on December 3, 1861. For the most part, it was a so-
ber, stolid document in both content and tone (how different his message
would be a year later!). The president reviewed the affairs of the war. To any
foreign nations that might be considering recognition of the Confederacy, he
warned that such actions often proved "unfortunate and injurious by those
adopting them." He continued to review matters of state, and then he offered
to take action on a measure that appealed to Republicans: he sought recognition of the independence and sovereignty of Haiti and Liberia, both black
republics, one formed through revolution and the other through colonization. Charles Sumner would report the bill in February, and it was debated
in April. It passed the Senate by a vote of 32 to 7, but not before eliciting racial comments about the deleterious effect that black diplomats supposedly
would have on Washington's social life. The House passed the bill 86 to 37,
over the objection of Democrats who opposed "receiving a black man on an
equality with the white men of this country." On June 5, 1862, Lincoln signed
the bill.[37]

Lincoln also mentioned the administration's successful efforts to suppress
the slave trade, and reported on the seizure of five vessels engaged in "this
inhuman traffic," and the sentencing to death of one captain, Nathaniel Gordon, who, after a stay of execution, would be hanged on February 21, 1862.
Seward's finest accomplishment—given the tensions with England over possible intervention, and a crisis at year's end over the removal of two Confederate emissaries from a British packet boat by a Union navy captain—was the
completion of a treaty with Lord Richard Lyons, the British ambassador, to
end the slave trade by permitting Royal Navy vessels to search and seize
American ships carrying Africans, as well as vessels outfitted as slavers even
if no slaves were on board. This was no small concession, given the long-
standing antipathy on the part of Americans to surrendering their rights at
sea, especially to the British. But Seward cleverly manipulated public opinion. He insisted that the draft treaty prepared by the British government be
put forward as a proposal of the Lincoln administration. Moreover, by prear-
rangement with Lyons, he amended the draft so the treaty could be abro-
gated after ten years, with the understanding that the British envoy would
oppose the amendment but then back down when pressed by the secretary
of state. This carefully choreographed diplomatic maneuver averted the risk

that the measure would fall victim to American Anglophobia, and it also gave border-state senators, who worried about any step taken which might contribute to emancipation, jingoistic reasons to vote in favor of the treaty. The Senate, in executive session, ratified the Lyons-Seward Treaty without dissent on April 25, 1862, and after an exchange in London in May, Lincoln proclaimed it on July 7, 1862. The treaty immediately put a stop to New York City's role in helping to organize and finance the illegal trade, and slowed to a trickle slave imports to Cuba, the trade's destination.[38]

Finally, in his Annual Message, Lincoln turned his attention to the Confiscation Act and deemed it possible that, in addition to this legislation, some states would pass their own measures liberating and providing for that class of persons over whom certain other persons made legal claims to the rights of labor and service. Lincoln did not use the word "slave," but he did suggest that, should these states enact plans of emancipation, the government would offer financial compensation and accept "such persons from such States, according to some mode of valuation." When this occurred, the government should require that such persons be "at once deemed free; and that, in any event, steps be taken for colonizing" such persons "at some place, or places, in a climate congenial to them." He added that perhaps free blacks might also be included in such schemes. Lincoln, in the coming months, would have more to say about encouraging individual states to adopt emancipation plans and about colonizing former slaves and free blacks.

Lincoln drew to a close with a tacit explanation for why he was not yet ready to contemplate emancipation as a strategy for ending the rebellion:

> In considering the policy to be adopted for suppressing the insurrection, I have been anxious and careful that the inevitable conflict for this purpose shall not degenerate into a violent and remorseless revolutionary struggle. I have, therefore, in every case, thought it proper to keep the integrity of the Union prominent as the primary object of the contest on our part, leaving all questions which are not of vital military importance to the more deliberate action of the legislature. . . . We should not be in haste to determine that radical and extreme measures, which may reach the loyal as well as the disloyal, are indispensable.

The war was to preserve the Union, not to abolish slavery, and Lincoln had a long way to go before being persuaded that the latter constituted the means necessary to accomplish the former.[39]

After reading the message, abolitionists fulminated. Gerrit Smith excoriated Lincoln: "I have never seen a phrenological chart of his head; but I have no doubt that his veneration is large and his destructiveness small. He would keep all things precisely as they are. He would have the fugitive slave sent back to the very spot he came from, and into exactly his former relations. He would not allow one line or letter of the Constitution to be disturbed by the necessities of war." William Lloyd Garrison, editor of the *Liberator,* had said of Lincoln after he revoked Frémont's order, "If he is 6 feet 4 inches high, he is only a dwarf in mind"; now he derided the "wishy-washy message from the President! It is more and more evident that he is a man of very small caliber, and had better be at his old business of splitting rails than at the head of a government like ours, especially in such a crisis. He has evidently not a drop of anti-slavery blood in his veins; and he seems incapable of uttering a humane or generous sentiment respecting the enslaved millions in our land." Charles Eliot Norton, writer, editor, and devotee of high culture, found the message "very poor in style, manner and thought,—very wanting in pith, and exhibiting a mournful deficiency of wise feeling and strong forecast from the President."[40]

But Lincoln did not need to pander to abolitionists or New England intellectuals, and with Congress now back in session after nearly four months, conservative voices had opportunities galore to encourage the president to stay the course. Aaron Harding, representative from Kentucky, did just that in a speech on the "Emancipation of Slaves in Rebel States." He rose to oppose a resolution introduced by Thomas Eliot of Massachusetts that authorized the president, as commander-in-chief, to make use of the war power "to emancipate all persons held as slaves by rebels in any military district in a state of insurrection." Harding reminded his colleagues that on February 11, 1861, the members of the House had voted unanimously for an amendment proposed by John Sherman of Ohio that stated that Congress did not have the right to "legislate upon, or interfere with, slavery in any of the slaveholding states in the Union." He reminded them that on July 22 they had approved a resolution introduced by John Crittenden stating that the war was not being waged for the purpose "of overthrowing or interfering with the rights of established institutions" of the slave states. Harding insisted on staying true to a "conservative policy," and he argued that "this war should have nothing to do with the institution of slavery any more than with any other state institution." "Let slavery alone," he insisted; "it will take care of itself." Besides, "we have no more right to interfere with slavery in a southern state than with the common school system, or any other local institution of a northern State."

Well aware that Congress had passed a confiscation act, Harding explained that "the right to confiscate property or slaves does not involve the right to emancipate slaves, because emancipation and confiscation are two very distinct things." Emancipation meant destroying the title to property. "I deny," Harding thundered, "that you can emancipate slaves under the idea of confiscation, or that you can turn loose four or five millions of slaves upon the southern people to annoy them, any more than you can kill and destroy other property, burn up and consume houses, and spread desolation over the whole land."

Harding then spoke as if directly to Lincoln. The war, he said, was not to destroy and conquer, but to subdue and reclaim. How could the president imagine "making war upon slavery in the South, by inciting the slaves to insurrection and rebellion, and by a species of warfare so cruel and savage as that of arming or encouraging the slaves to make war upon their masters and upon innocent women and children?" Speaking for the state of Kentucky, he declared that should the war turn into an abolitionist crusade, Kentucky would then have no choice but make war against the Union armies.[41]

Not only would the border states revolt, thought William Gaston Steele, a Democrat from New York, but so would the soldiers generally. A policy of emancipation would demoralize and paralyze the Union army, for whom the slavery question was not at issue. To be sure, many soldiers, in their diaries and letters, expressed opposition to emancipation. A private in the 19th Indiana Volunteers declared that "if emancipation is to be the policy of this war . . . I do not care how quick the country goes to pot." Another soldier, from the 29th Massachusetts, wrote: "If *anyone* thinks that this army is fighting to free the Negro . . . they are terribly mistaken." No doubt a high percentage of soldiers from the border states—and those who, regardless of state, espoused Democratic politics—felt this way, at least in the first year and a half of the war.[42]

Oliver Willcox Norton, however, believed that the war had to be fought against slavery. A private in the 83rd Pennsylvania Volunteers, Norton wrote in October 1861: "Many seem to think that this war is soon to close. I am fully satisfied, however, that it cannot be ended without the emancipation proclamation, and I think that will be made next winter." Told that "we must preserve the union but not touch slavery," Norton wrote his sister: "Away with such nonsense, I say, and the soldiers all say so. Give us a haul-in-sweep of their niggers, their houses, towns, and everything, only conquer them quickly." Norton was prescient, and saw before many others that the war would have to be fought against slavery if the cause of union was to triumph.[43]

For many soldiers, the experience of war turned them against slavery. A soldier in the 3rd Wisconsin Volunteers offered that "the rebellion is abolitionizing the whole army." A soldier from Iowa encountered a slave child who was being sold by her master (who had also fathered her), and wrote: "By G-d I'll *fight* till hell *freezes* over and then I'll cut the ice and fight on." And the flood of contrabands into Union lines certainly helped to humanize slaves for the soldiers, even if it did little to overturn their racial assumptions about black inferiority or their use of racial epithets. James K. Newton, of the 14th Wisconsin, exclaimed, "If the niggers come into camp for a week as fast as they have been coming for two days past we will soon have a waiter for every man in the regiment." He told of two slaves who had arrived and who had been put to work by an officer. Two days later, the owner came looking for his property. "He was told that we didn't keep such men as him in camp and that we would give him just five minutes to leave. He did not leave in that time," Newton wrote his parents, "so we had the pleasure of booting him out of camp." William Thompson Lusk, of the 2nd New York Volunteers, wrote in November 1861, "Negroes crowd in swarms to our lines, happy in the thought of freedom, dancing, singing, void of care, and vainly dreaming that all toil is in future to be spared, and henceforth they are to lead that life of idleness which forms the Nigger's Paradise. I fear that before long they have passed only from the hands of one taskmaster into the hands of another."[44]

At this point, few soldiers, if any, saw the issue of emancipation in terms of military necessity. They either opposed fighting to free the slaves or saw emancipation as an inevitable result of the war, but they did not feel that the Confederate use of slaves was what explained Union defeats or that the contrabands were in any way the key to victory. Indeed, from different political perspectives, the doctrine of military necessity, which held promise as the weapon that would extirpate slavery, came under criticism.

"Giving freedom to five millions of slaves on the principle of a military necessity to suppress insurrection," commented Martin Conway, a Republican representative from Kansas, "is an idle dream." He observed that military exigencies might exist in one place but not another. Officers in command would have to make the decision on a situation-by-situation basis whenever it arose. Under such circumstances, Conway believed, slavery would never be seriously undermined. The "probability for emancipation on the ground of a military necessity based under the Constitution" was remote at best.[45]

In a speech delivered on December 16, George Boutwell, former governor of Massachusetts, seemed to answer Conway. Military necessity, he insisted, "does not depend upon the exigencies of the army in the field; but the great military necessity is to save the government, and whatever is necessary for the salvation of the government is clearly within the right and duty of those who administer it." He asked the audience, "If by the emancipation of slaves we can hasten by one day the return of the power of the Union and our lost prosperity, does not a military exigency exist?" In response they shouted, "Yes! Yes! It does!"

Emancipation, Boutwell, concluded, is inevitable. He said that, as a matter of justice, he hoped it would be implemented by the United States government. Or it might "take place by the efforts of the slaves." And then he raised a third possibility: "It may take place by the action of the slaveholders themselves." The idea of Confederate emancipation was in the air. Wendell Phillips, in his lecture "The War for the Union," had warned that as soon as the Union seemed poised for victory, "the moment our armies do anything that evinces final success, the wily statesmanship and unconquerable hate of the South will write 'Emancipation' on her banner, and welcome the protectorate of a European power." "It is to-day a race between Abe Lincoln and Jeff. Davis [as to] which will arrive at *emancipation* first," warned Phillips, "and which does will succeed in the end."[46]

Boutwell fully developed the scenario. Having staked everything on slavery, Confederates would do anything not to destroy it. And if pushed into a corner, they might gradually emancipate them, and by doing so win the recognition of European governments and triumph in the war. Do not wait, warned Boutwell, for the Confederates to do out of military necessity what the Union should do out of both necessity and humanity. Emancipation was coming—get ahead of it and control the process. Rumors of Confederate action were so rampant that Charles Sumner had to reassure one correspondent that "Jefferson Davis will not proclaim Emancipation."[47]

Sumner believed the president was leaning in his direction. He tried to keep steady pressure on Lincoln, telling other Republicans to visit Washington "to press upon the Presdt. the duty of Emancipation, *in order to save the country.*" No doubt perturbed by the conservative tone of Lincoln's message to Congress, Sumner rushed to the White House, where "the President assured me that in a month or six weeks we should all be together." At year's end he wrote to John Andrew that Lincoln "tells me I am ahead of him only a month or six weeks."[48]

Others were not so certain. Adam Gurowski, a Polish exile who had lived in Berlin, St. Petersburg, and Paris before coming to the United States in 1849, was one of the most volatile and acerbic diarists of the day. Early in the war he held a minor position in the State Department, assigned to read continental newspapers and translate them. But politics was his passion, and the Old World aristocrat stormed about the city in a broad-brimmed hat, flowing overcoat, and colored spectacles, spewing criticism at the administration. Sumner compared him to one of P. T. Barnum's whales in a tank. Welles said, "He is by nature a grumbler, ardent, earnest, rash, violent, unreasonable, impracticable." John Hay called him "venomous." It is possible, if we believe Ward Hill Lamon, the marshal of the District of Columbia, that Lincoln feared for his safety around Gurowski.[49]

Count Gurowski's diary for 1861–1862, published at the end of that year, is scathing, idiosyncratic, and original. It was a tell-all in an age that valued propriety and decorum. The *New York Herald* snorted that "one seems to be overhearing the gossip of a gang of Washington scandal mongers, standing in a dirty barroom and drinking bad whiskey as they chatter. Gurowski has noted down the gossip, but the odor of the bad whiskey clings round it still and makes the reader qualmish." Others feared that the tone, particularly his hostility to Seward and McClellan, might prevent readers from taking his view seriously. "But neither Count Gurowski's overweening conceit of himself, nor his savage criticism," thought one reviewer, "should lead us to overlook the fact that he is a man of great culture, intelligence, and, above all, independence."[50]

"Mr. Lincoln is pulled in all directions," Gurowski wrote in September. "His intentions are excellent and he would have made an excellent President for quiet times. But this civil war imperative demands a man of foresight, of prompt decision, of Jacksonian will and energy." "It may turn out that he is honest," he wrote at another point, "but of not transcendent powers."

Gurowski denounced the doctrine of military necessity as a justification for emancipation. He lamented the fact that emancipation "is spoken of as an expedient, but not as a sacred duty, even for the maintenance of the Union. To emancipate through the war power is an offense of reason, logic, and humanity." He was as critical of other radical Republicans as he was of the conservative policies of the administration: "The question of emancipation is not clear even in the heads of the leading emancipationists; not one thinks to give freeholds to the emancipated. It is the only way to make them useful to themselves and to the community. Freedom without land is humbug, and the fools speak of exportation of the four million of slaves, depriving thus the country of laborers, which a century of emigration cannot fill again. All these fools ought to be sent to the lunatic asylum."

Clearly, Gurowski was far ahead of the nation in his thinking, just as "in decision, in clear-sightedness and soundness of judgment, the people are far ahead of Mr. Lincoln and of his spiritual and constitutional consciencekeepers." With the new year, Gurowski despaired that "Lincoln belittles himself more and more. Whatever he does is under the pressure of events, under the pressure of public opinion. These agencies push Lincoln and slowly move him, notwithstanding his reluctant heaviness and his resistance." In contrast, Jefferson Davis was taking action, leading, trying to establish "a new and great slaveholding empire." Davis was making history. And what was Lincoln doing? "Lincoln is telling stories."[51]

2

Messages and Measures

Like Count Gurowski, George Templeton Strong was also an inveterate diarist. Indeed, when Gurowski's diary was published in late 1862, Strong admitted that it "makes some impression on me," and he called the count "the Thersites of our camps and councils, denouncing and decrying every chief and every measure, but I fear his denunciations are justified."[1]

A prosperous New York lawyer and devoted Episcopalian, Strong supported many philanthropic causes. He also cast a wary eye on the Republicans, and had reluctantly voted for Lincoln. In January, he visited the president. Strong described him as "lank and hard-featured, among the ugliest white men I have seen." After a return visit, Strong confessed "he told us a lot of stories." When Lincoln was asked about the way antislavery congressmen and newspaper editors were pressuring him to take action on the status of the slaves, he had said:

> Wa-al that reminds me of a party of Methodist parsons that was travelling in Illinois when I was a boy, and had a branch to cross that was pretty bad—ugly to cross, ye know, because the waters was up. And they got considerin' and discussin' how they should git across it, and they talked about it for two hours, and one on 'em thought they had ought to cross one way when they got there, and another another way,

and they got quarrellin' about it, till at last an old brother put in, and he says, says he, "Brethren, this here talk ain't no use. I never cross a river until I come to it."[2]

But talk he did, finally, on March 6, 1862, when he sent a message to Congress that contained a recommendation on the subject of slavery, the first emancipation proposal ever submitted to Congress by a president. (One writer noted that it marked "the first time [anyone had heard] lisping from the seat of government the word *Emancipation*"). Charles Sumner knew it was coming. In December, he leaked it to a liberal statesman in England: "The *Presdt now meditates an early Message to Congress* proposing to buy the slaves in the still loyal states of Mo.-Ky.-Md.-&Del. & then proclaim Emancipation with our advancing armies."[3]

The distance between what the radical senator had hoped for and what he got was vast, and would have been wider had not Lincoln deleted a sentence that had appalled Sumner when he'd read it in draft: "Should the people of the insurgent districts now reject the councils of treason, revive loyal state governments, and again send Senators and Representatives to Congress, they would, at once find themselves at peace, with no institution changed."[4]

It was what every antislavery advocate dreaded: the war would end and the Union would be restored to what it had been, with slavery intact. Lincoln bracketed the line for deletion, but the sentiment indicates that even as he now proposed support for the voluntary adoption of a gradual emancipation plan, he was willing still to accept slavery in some states in order to end the war and preserve the Union.

In the end, Lincoln asked Congress to provide "pecuniary aid" to any state that would "adopt gradual abolishment of slavery." The individual states could use the money as they wished. He argued that if the border states abolished slavery, this would end the hope of the rebels that they would one day create a Confederacy of united slave states. Lincoln talked in terms of "initiation of emancipation," because "in my judgment, gradual, and not sudden emancipation, is better for all." He assured the states that accepting money from the federal government "sets up no claim of a right, by federal authority, to interfere with slavery within state limits." He did warn that as the war progressed "it is impossible to foresee all the incidents, which may attend, and all the ruin which may follow." But declaring emancipation had no place, as yet, in any part of his strategy.[5]

Reactions to the announcement were mixed. Of course, Lincoln would not have expected most abolitionists or radical Republicans to be happy with the proposal. The former had been fighting the idea of gradual, compensated emancipation for more than thirty years, at least since William Lloyd Garrison had started the *Liberator* in 1831. Garrison feared that the message would serve as a decoy to restrain Congress from taking more aggressive action. George Barrell Cheever, pastor of the Church of the Puritans in New York City, wrote to Sumner lamenting: "How pitiable the attitude of President Lincoln, beseeching rebel States to do what God, justice, humanity, and our Constitution *requires* him to do." Count Gurowski called the proposal a "crumb," thrown to relieve the pressure of public opinion. Charles Eliot Norton criticized Lincoln's prose: "Could anything be more feebly put, or more inefficiently written?" he asked. "His style is worse than ever, and though a bad style is not always a mark of bad thought,—it is at least proof that thought is not as clear as it ought to be."[6]

But Frederick Douglass saw it differently: "That I should live to see the President of the United States deliberately advocating Emancipation was more than I ever ventured to hope." Douglass went on to argue that the various qualifications included in the proposal should not dishearten opponents of slavery. "There are spots on the Sun," Douglass observed, but "a blind man can see where the President's heart is. I read the spaces as well as the lines of that message. I see in them a brave man trying against great odds, to do right."[7]

Others besides Douglass felt relief. Samuel Gridley Howe, who lamented Lincoln's "habit of procrastinating: he puts off and puts off the evil day of effort, and stands shivering with his hand on the string of the shower-bath," called the message a "bomb-shell." The president had "at last had a change of heart, and has set his face steadily Zionward, though he is as yet rather ashamed of his Lord." And Henry Ward Beecher was ecstatic. In a sermon titled "The Beginning of Freedom," preached on March 9, he exulted: a "Message, we call it, and yet it is inevitably a Proclamation. . . . Never before has [there] been in the history of this government such a message. . . . Dates will begin from it. In the year of this Message of President Lincoln will begin a new cycle of our national career." Beecher went through the message, nearly line by line, rejoicing at every turn, and he invited parishioners to imagine a call for "the abolishment of slavery, as Lincoln peculiarly styles it," issued by any previous administration. This was unthinkable, and it was a measure of how far the nation had come: "There never was such a revolution since the world began, upon such a scale, involving such interests, and taking place within so short a time." Less than four months before, Beecher himself had said that "revolution is no remedy for rebellion." His new stance showed how attitudes were changing under the war's impact.[8]

William Aikman—pastor of the Hanover Street Presbyterian Church in Wilmington, Delaware—agreed. Aikman observed that "we are as likely to undervalue as to overestimate events which occur just beneath our eye." Lincoln's message was "clothed in very plain and homely garb, but of meaning not to be misunderstood. . . . It is that *the government of these United States deems slavery an evil, wishes it to cease,* and will do what it can to help it to an end. . . . That simple message marked an era in the history of the world, and will be looked back upon in all future time as one of the grand events of this century."[9]

Newspaper responses were equally favorable, and Lincoln followed them avidly. The antislavery *Independent* declared: "Considered simply as a stroke of home and foreign policy, this is masterly but that is its least merit. It is a noble moral act. To inaugurate the policy of emancipation in the United States of America, is of itself a claim and a title to an undying fame. Henceforth, President's Lincoln name will be associated with those of the Founders and Fathers of the Country and Constitution." The *New York Tribune,* often critical of the administration, proclaimed that "this Message constitutes of itself an epoch in the history of our country." As far as the opposition *New York Herald* was concerned, the best thing about the message was that it would "demolish the abolitionists," who had to endorse a proposal that offered compensation and depended on the choice of voters in the states—a proposal which, in the *Herald's* view, "sinks them forever." The moderate *New York Times* declared that "the president has placed the Government on the side of freedom. He has pronounced it to be better than Slavery. His words will echo round the globe." The *Times* also suggested that the plan might not be practical, on account of the expense. This elicited a private letter from Lincoln to the editor, Henry J. Raymond, in which the president explained that "less than one half-day's cost of this war would pay for all the slaves in Delaware, at four hundred dollars per head" and that "eighty-seven days' cost of this war" would pay for all the slaves in all the border states and Washington, D.C., combined. Lincoln asked whether adopted plans of gradual emancipation would not shorten the war by at least this many days, in which case the expense was neutral.[10]

As pleased as he must have been with the editorial response to his message, he was disturbed by the torpid reaction of the border-state congressional representatives, to whom he had pitched the plan. "Not one of them has yet said a word to me about it," he told Missouri representative Francis (Frank) Blair, Montgomery's brother. Even before he delivered the address, he knew the outcome of his November meeting with Delaware representative George Fisher and the state's leading slaveholder, Benjamin Burton, in which he had enlisted them to present a bill for gradual, compensated emancipation of the state's 1,800 slaves (with total abolition by 1893, and a payment of $500 to each slaveholder). The measure met a predominantly hostile response in Delaware and was not enacted into law despite the efforts of Fisher and pro-emancipation members of the legislature. Indeed, Fisher may have arranged for the bill to be withdrawn from consideration.[11]

Lincoln asked the postmaster general, Montgomery Blair—who continually reinforced the president's belief that there was strong emancipation sentiment in the border states—why there was so little action. Blair said he thought that the congressmen were waiting for a military victory. But that was precisely the problem, Lincoln answered: "If we should have successes, they may feel and say, the rebellion is crushed and it matters not whether we do anything about this matter. . . . If they will take hold and do this, the war will cease. . . . If they do not the armies must stay in their midst."[12]

On March 10, 1862, Lincoln spoke with a delegation of border-state representatives. He reviewed his litany of reasons for desiring gradual emancipation, especially to resolve the problem of "conflicting and antagonistic complaints" by armies coming into contact with slaves, and to stifle Confederate hopes that the border states would join the rebellion. He restated the commonly held belief that "emancipation was a subject exclusively under the control of the states," and expressed hope that they would give his proposal serious consideration.[13]

From the start of his administration, the disposition of the border states had preoccupied Lincoln. Following the assault on Fort Sumter, and Lincoln's call to the states for troops to put down the rebellion, Virginia, Arkansas, Tennessee, and North Carolina had seceded. But through a variety of means, both military and political, the slaveholding states of Delaware, Maryland, Missouri, and Kentucky remained in the Union, though residents in those areas were divided in their loyalties. (There was never any real danger that Delaware would secede.) The border states were crucial to the Union cause in a number of ways. Their geographic position was of strategic importance; their manufacturing and agricultural capacities provided essential support; and tens of thousands of their citizens would fight under the Union banner. No wonder Lincoln moved gingerly on the issue of slavery.[14]

In the conversation that followed at the March 10 meeting, John Noell of Missouri said that slavery in his state was waning due to natural causes, which made Lincoln's proposition unnecessary. The president responded that so far the operation of natural causes had neither prevented "irritating conduct" nor brought an end to Confederates' hopes that Missouri would join them. John Crisfield of Maryland asked what the consequences of refusal would be and what else the President had in mind, to which Lincoln answered that he would lament their failure to act and had no further designs in mind. John Menzies of Kentucky then asked if there was any power except in the states themselves to carry out emancipation. According to Crisfield, who took notes on the conversation, "The President replied, he thought there could not be. He then went off into a course of remarks not qualifying the foregoing declaration, nor material to be repeated to a just understanding of his meaning." Perhaps Lincoln had here spoken about war power and military necessity, which he did not necessarily see as contradicting the assertion that the states, not Congress, controlled slavery.

Toward the meeting's end, a congressman asked Lincoln about his personal feelings toward slavery. According to Crisfield, who wrote his summary immediately after the meeting ended, Lincoln "said that he did not pretend to disguise his Anti-Slavery feeling; that he thought it was wrong and should continue to think so; but that was not the question we had to deal with now. . . . He recognized the rights of Property which had grown out of it, and would respect these rights as fully as similar rights in any other property."[15]

Despite Lincoln's entreaties, the congressional debate over the resolution containing the president's message became rancorous. Opponents, mainly Democrats and border-state representatives, denounced it as unconstitutional; rejected the idea that nonslaveholding states should in effect be taxed to pay slaveholders; believed that its effect, if not intent, was to stimulate antislavery agitation in the border states; declared it was not legislation, but a policy statement that failed to specify any details of compensation; derided it for not addressing what would become of the slaves if freed; and suspected it was the forerunner of "a series of measures of confiscation and emancipation by which the institution of slavery is suddenly and violently to be uprooted in all the border, and, indeed, in all the seceding states."

Supporters of the measure lamented that the issue of emancipation could not be brought up, in even the most benign way, without eliciting indignation and excitement. Rather than the proposal being some sort of "entering wedge" for a string of radical proposals, it seemed more to be "a *counter project* to any such series of measures." Shocked by the anxiety the measure had triggered, Thaddeus Stevens brought one day's debate to a close by calling the president's suggestion "the most diluted, milk and water gruel proposition that was ever given to the American nation," and asserting that the only reason to postpone a vote was "for the purpose of having a chemical analysis to see whether there is any poison in it." Eventually, both chambers passed a resolution to aid states in abolishing slavery, the House by a vote of 89 to 31 and the Senate by a vote of 32 to 10. A little over a month after proposing it, the president signed the measure.[16]

Lincoln could not have been happy. If this benign proposal generated such vocal opposition, then what would come of anything more forceful? He had always believed that abolishing slavery first in the border states would be the key to victory—that with the border states secured from any chance of joining the Confederacy, the rebellion would falter and fold. But maybe it was the other way around: attack slavery first in the Confederacy, and the border states would have to follow.

For the moment, Lincoln would bide his time. The war seemed to be going well, with the Union capturing Fort Henry and Fort Donelson in February and winning some lesser battles in March. The debate over the president's message may have given Lincoln pause, but it did not slow down the Republican majority in Congress, which had just addressed the issue of fugitive slaves being returned by the military and which had begun debate on the existence of slavery in Washington and on a more stringent confiscation act.

When Congress discussed a bill creating a new article of war prohibiting all commissioned officers from using their forces to return fugitives "from service or labor who may have escaped from any persons to whom such service or labor is claimed to be due," the debate took less time than the debate over the president's message. Discussion centered on whether the proposal constituted a tacit repeal of the Fugitive Slave Act of 1850. John Bingham, Republican of Ohio, argued that, if anything, it served to uphold the integrity of the act, which provided for civil magistrates, not military authorities, to adjudicate claims. Robert Mallory of Kentucky brought laughter to the House when he said that, while he greatly admired Bingham's legal accomplishments, "I am very suspicious of the accuracy of the working of his mind upon questions of this character." Undeterred, Bingham went on to denounce as "military despotism" any "attempt by the military power to assume and exercise civil authority in contempt of the civil power of the land." On the Senate side, Henry Wilson of Massachusetts made the same point: "The return of fugitive slaves is a civil question, a judicial one, not a military one." The bill passed the House 83 to 42 and the Senate 29 to 9, and Lincoln signed it on March 13. True to Bingham's claim, the Fugitive Slave Act remained in effect until June 28, 1864, when it was repealed by Congress.[17]

It may have been widely acknowledged that Congress had no authority over slavery in the states, but it was also widely acknowledged that Congress alone had authority over slavery in the District of Columbia. As a congressman in 1848, Lincoln had offered a plan for emancipation in the District of Columbia, and the issue had come up again in his debates with Stephen Douglas in 1858. The presence of slavery in the capital rankled, and a resolution was first introduced in the Senate on December 16, 1861, calling for the immediate emancipation of the slaves in the District, with compensation to be paid to the owners. Spirited and extensive discussion occupied several weeks, from mid-March until early April 1862.[18]

From the start, debate raged less over emancipation than over freedom, less over the slavery question than over the *"negro question."* James Doolittle, a Wisconsin Republican, put the issue this way: "What is to be done in relation to this race of people when they are emancipated?" Freedom, he said, must be something more than just in name; it must be "a thing in substance, freedom in fact." But equality in America, he believed, could never be achieved. Men might theorize all they wanted about "social and political equality between the white and colored race," but "it is simply an impossibility."

Doolittle did not specify why he believed equality impossible; other Senators were less reticent. Senator Garrett Davis of Kentucky declared that "a negro's idea of freedom is freedom from work," and he labeled the entire population "thriftless, worthless, indolent [and] inefficient." He had no doubt that liberation would lead to "a war of extermination between the two races." Senator Waitman Willey of Virginia added that abolition would make the war that was then raging into a "war of total extermination," because it would drive southern Unionists into the ranks of rebels. Willey asked his colleagues to consider the effects of the eventual emancipation of four million ignorant, helpless, and degraded slaves. Did northern senators want them in their communities? Where would the slave be entitled to vote or to serve as a juror? "You may emancipate the slave, and call him free, but he is still a slave," observed Willey.

It was telling that Willey made the leap from a bill that would free some three thousand slaves in the District of Columbia to the idea of the emancipation of all the slaves in the United States. Opponents saw the bill, if it passed, as a first step toward total abolition. "It is an entering wedge," warned Garrett Davis. "You want to get the head in, and then you intend to push the monster through." Even as he spoke, other bills were pending, including one that would permit the confiscation of slaves.[19]

Believing that, once emancipated, slaves could never achieve equality, and fearing a war of extermination, Davis proposed an amendment stipulating that all persons freed as a result of this act "be colonized out of the limits of the United States," and that "Congress authorize $100,000 for those purposes." Some supporters of colonization, however, opposed compulsory emigration, and Doolittle proposed an amendment to the amendment that offered support for whoever "may desire" to emigrate to Haiti, Liberia, or some other country. On March 24, Doolittle's amendment passed by a vote of 23 to 16. But on a subsequent vote to incorporate the amended measure into the bill, the Senate deadlocked 19 to 19. Vice President Hannibal Hamlin broke the tie by voting against the amendment. For now, colonization, as well as the appropriation of money to assist those who wanted to resettle, would not be part of the bill.

Radical Republicans spoke eloquently in favor of emancipation in the District of Columbia. Henry Wilson was outraged to learn that some sixty free blacks were currently imprisoned in Washington's jail under suspicion of being fugitive slaves. "That color is presumptive evidence of slavery" was a doctrine that had to be repudiated. Wilson concluded that "this bill proposes to strike the chains from the limbs of three thousand bondmen in the District of Columbia, to erase the word 'slave' from their foreheads, to convert them from personal chattels to free men, to lift them from the degradation of personal servitude to the dignity and responsibilities of manhood, to place them in the ranks of free colored men, to perform with them the duties and bear with them the responsibilities of life."

James Harlan of Iowa denounced those senators who sought to raise fears of emancipation by warning that amalgamation between the races would result. Such expressions of prejudice as describing a black woman as a "greasy old wench" had no place in the chamber. He went on to suggest that slaveholders might not desire too close an investigation of the issue, because one former senator "lived notoriously and publicly with a negro wench, and raised children by her."

Harlan denounced the idea of compulsory removal. Why should blacks be forced to go "homeless and penniless and friendless into a land of strangers"? All that was needed was to make the transition from slave labor to wage labor: "Let them work on for their masters; if their masters choose to pay them for their labor, all well; and if they decide to work on without pay, be it so."[20]

Democratic senator Willard Saulsbury of Delaware responded. He inquired how many free blacks lived in Iowa. Answer: very few. No wonder Harlan could speak so hopefully. Saulsbury did not want to discuss the bill, which he opposed, and which he felt tampered indirectly with slavery in neighboring Maryland. Irritated, he proposed an amendment that required all persons freed by the act to be removed to northern states within thirty days. The amendment fell, 31 to 2. When it was raised again a few days later by another senator, Saulsbury's fit of pique had subsided and even he voted against it.[21]

Opponents continued to press for a conservative policy, and reminded senators of Lincoln's pledges not to tamper with slavery but only to restore the Union. William Pitt Fessenden of Maine answered for most Republicans when he asked, "Do you suppose we came into power to sit still and be silent on this subject; that we came into power to do nothing; to think nothing; to say nothing lest by some possibility a portion of the people of the country might be offended?"

Frustrated, Garrett Davis took to attacking the "abolition" party. He blamed Massachusetts for originating secession and nullification in its opposition to Jefferson's embargo and the War of 1812. He identified Horace Greeley, Wendell Phillips, and George Cheever as men willing to overthrow the Constitution. "They remind me of the fable," Davis said. "When the whole host of apples went swimming down the current, some of them exclaimed 'how we apples swim.'" The gallery erupted in laughter.

Hoping still to salvage something for the more conservative Republicans, Orville Browning brought colonization back into the discussion. Browning no doubt shared the president's belief in colonization. Lincoln had said in 1848 that he envisioned emancipation in the District of Columbia as being gradual, requiring approval by District residents in a referendum, and including compensation. The current bill contained only the last feature. Adding colonization would fit with the president's earlier messages and would make the measure more palatable to Browning and other conservative Republicans. "We may confer upon them all the legal and political rights we ourselves enjoy," said Browning, but "they will still be in our midst a debased and degraded race, incapable of making progress. . . . We owe something to these people more than simply to strike from them the fetters of bondage that now hold them, and turn them loose among us, with scarcely the means or the ability of providing the most ordinary necessities of life, much less with the means of any advance in the exaltation of character and of the attainment of a position in society. They can never do that." He conceded that the time might come when compulsory emigration would be needed, but that in this case voluntary emigration would do just fine.[22]

A House Select Committee on Emancipation and Colonization, dominated by conservatives, concluded that "the highest interests of the white race, whether Anglo-Saxon, Celt, or Scandinavian, require that the whole country should be held and occupied by those races alone. . . . There are irreconcilable differences between the two races which separate them, as with a wall of fire. . . . The home of the African must not be within the limits of the present territory of the Union. The Anglo-American looks upon every acre of our present domain as intended for him, and not for the negro."[23]

With little debate and little controversy, a Senate amendment that included colonization passed by a vote of 27 to 10. Even Henry Wilson voted in favor of it, but not Charles Sumner, who despised colonization. He saw it as a dodge to avoid the question of equal rights. Why remove freedmen from the country when what was needed most was labor? In a speech delivered in Massachusetts he proclaimed, "It is vain to say that this is the country of the 'white man.' It is the country of man. Whoever disowns any member of the human family as brother disowns God as father, and thus becomes impious as well as inhuman. It is the glory of republican institutions that they give practical form to this irresistible principle. If anybody is to be sent away, let it be the guilty and not the innocent."[24]

Sumner also took issue with compensation, but he rationalized the problem by considering it ransom rather than compensation, "so that freedom shall be yielded rather than purchased." After all, during the Barbary Wars the government had paid ransom to free American sailors who were Algerine captives. He had once declared, "Never should any question of money be allowed to interfere with human freedom. Better an empty treasury than a single slave." He stood fast by that belief now, and his rhetoric soared as he concluded his speech on the Senate floor: "At the national capital, slavery will give way to freedom; but the good work will not stop here. It must proceed. What God and nature decree, rebellion cannot arrest." On April 3, 1862, the bill passed the Senate by a vote of 29 to 14: all twenty-nine of the aye votes were cast by Republicans. Discussion in the House occupied only two days, and it was passed on April 11 by a vote of 92 to 38. It had been only a year since the crisis at Fort Sumter plunged the nation into war.[25]

April 11 was a Friday. Orville Browning took on the responsibility of presenting the bill to Lincoln, but he delayed until Monday. Lincoln told the senator that he would sign it, but that he had concerns about infants and the aged, and would recommend supplemental bills. Still, Lincoln held on to the bill—an action that infuriated Sumner who told Lincoln that while the bill rested on his desk he was "the largest slave-holder in the country." During the delay, slaves, fearing they would be sold out of the District of Columbia, "were in concealment, waiting for the day of Freedom to come out of their hiding places."[26]

In his diary, Browning explained Lincoln's delay: "He told me that he would not sign the bill before Wednesday—that old Gov Wickliffe had two family servants with him who were sickly, and who would not have benefitted by freedom, and [he] wanted time to remove them." Lincoln's action illuminates the personal, emotional, and philosophical dilemmas he faced as he wrestled with the question of emancipation. Charles Wickliffe was a Kentuckian, and Lincoln felt sympathy for the plight of slaveholders as well as slaves. His action was, in one sense, admirable, for he used his discretion to permit what he saw as an act of kindness to slaves whose best course seemed to be to remain with a kindly master. At the same time, it was reprehensible for Lincoln to skirt the act he was about to sign. He might have advised Wickliffe to free his slaves and then allow them to remain with him if they wished, or pay them wages for their service, or offer, should they stay in Washington, to find a suitable place for them.[27]

Upon signing the bill, Lincoln sent a message to Congress expressing gratification that the principles of compensation and colonization were recognized. He would have preferred gradual emancipation and a vote by the D.C. electorate, but this did not stop him from approving the measure. To Frederick Douglass, for one, "the events taking place seem like a dream," and he wrote to Sumner to thank him for his Senate speech and to rejoice that "you have lived to strike down in Washington, the power which lifted the bludgeon against your own free voice."[28]

Douglass had already anticipated the issue of "What shall be done with the slaves if emancipated?" He had asked this question in an essay with this title, published in his monthly magazine in January 1862. His answer: "Do nothing with them; mind your business, and let them mind theirs. Your *doing* with them is their greatest misfortune. They have been undone by your doings, and all they now ask, and really have need of at your hands, is to just let

them alone." (From the opposite side, in a debate in March, John J. Crittenden, speaking for Kentucky about the president's plan for gradual border-
state emancipation, declared that "the way to conciliate Kentucky is not by
pressing these questions upon her. The way to conciliate her is to leave her
alone.") Douglass believed that the best course to take after emancipating the
slave was to "deal justly with him. He is a human being, capable of judging
between good and evil, right and wrong, liberty and slavery." He also addressed the issue of colonization: "Would you let them all stay here?—Why
not? What better is there than here? Will they occupy more room as freemen
than as slaves? Is the presence of the black freeman less agreeable than that
of a black slave? . . . Would it be safe? No good reason can be given why it
would not be. There is much more reason for apprehension from slavery
than from freedom."[29]

Many people thought slavery wrong, but wondered what would happen
after abolition. Henry Ward Beecher put the matter this way: "Loyal citizens
differ exceedingly as to the character of the African; as to the benefit of slavery or liberty to him; as to his rights; as to the best way of letting him go free;
as to the disposal of him afterward; but I think it may be said that, while these
discrepancies exist there is a united and settled popular conviction that slavery is bad all around."[30]

Slavery was bad but insurrection was worse, and opponents of abolition
kept alive stories of "the horrors of Santo Domingo," by which they meant
"fire, rape, and slaughter; dwellings burned, children butchered, wives and
daughters ravished upon the dead bodies of their husbands and fathers."
These were the words of Senator James Doolittle, who was speaking out
against the abolition of slavery in the District of Columbia unless it was coupled with colonization. His point was not that such atrocities had occurred,
but that after John Brown's raid Southerners feared them—and their fears
led them to secede and to take up arms. Months later, Lincoln would receive
a letter from a supporter of emancipation who advised: "It is the custom of
those at the North who claim to be the particular friends of the southern people, to assert that any effort at freeing the slaves would cause a repetition of
the 'Horrors of San Domingo.'"[31]

Abolitionists recognized that historical comparisons would be made. Even before the war, they had offered summaries of how emancipation had been achieved elsewhere, and they had defended against comparisons to Santo Domingo. In *The Right Way the Safe Way*, Lydia Maria Child proclaimed that "whenever immediate emancipation is urged, the 'horrors of St. Domingo' are always brought forward to prove it dangerous." But the statement, she insisted, showed little understanding of the actual history. The problem on Santo Domingo had occurred only when Napoleon sought to "*restore slavery*, after it had been for some years abolished." Everywhere else, across the West Indies and elsewhere, "history proves that emancipation has *always* been safe."[32]

Elizur Wright provided a less simplistic history. One of the founders of the American Anti-Slavery Society in 1833, in May 1861 Wright had published a pamphlet titled *The Lesson of St. Domingo: How To Make the War Short and the Peace Righteous.* He narrated the violent struggles that eventually led to a declaration of emancipation in 1793, and then described the years of Anglo-French war when the British sought unsuccessfully to take over the island. If the French commissioners had only remained true to the promise of abolition, "they would have saved some ten thousand white and some thirty thousand colored lives." Looking at the American scene, he asked: "If we have not justice or philanthropy enough to do spontaneously what France was *obliged* to do, ought we not to have *wit* enough?" A mere six weeks after the attack on Fort Sumter, Wright predicted that while both Lincoln and Davis "should agree at first perfectly in ignoring the negro, and even join their forces to suppress 'seditious movements' of slaves, one or the other will at last be obliged to recognize black men as a raw material of military power."[33]

The Catholic polemicist Orestes Brownson also challenged those who equated emancipation with horror:

The horrors of San Domingo did not result from the emancipation of the slaves, but from the obstinate refusal of the slave proprietors to recognize the partial emancipation decreed by the mother country. It was not the liberation of the slaves, but the refusal of that liberation by their owners, and their severe and barbarous punishments inflicted on those who simply asked that the laws in their favor should be practically observed, that led to those terrible scenes of pillage, murder, and incendiarism which slaveholders take a savage delight in holding up as the horrors of San Domingo.

Brownson suggested that slaveholders should take a very different message from what happened on the island of Santo Domingo: "Deny the slave, even the negro, all hope of being one day delivered from his bondage, and of standing up, sable though be his complexion, as a freeman, drive him to utter desperation, and you make him a tiger in ferocity, and he will rend you in pieces." Weary of the phrase "as a kind of algebraic expression for all that is most frightful in cruelty, revenge, and brutal violence," one writer offered a different equation: "The 'horrors' of Santo Domingo were the horrors of *slavery*, not of *emancipation*."[34]

As antislavery activists continued to argue that there was nothing to fear from emancipation, Republican politicians continued to offer new arguments to justify the legality of a proclamation of emancipation. A doctrine of military necessity derived from the war power had already been propounded as a way around the widely held belief that slavery was a local institution under the control of the states, and that Congress had no authority to interfere. On February 11, 1862, Sumner introduced resolutions in the Senate declaring that states in rebellion had abdicated all rights under the Constitution, and that the "termination" of statehood meant, as well, the termination of all the state's "peculiar local institutions." Sumner continued to develop the argument for what was called "state suicide," and to claim that slavery thus "died constitutionally and legally with the state from which it drew its malignant breath." Privately Sumner wrote, "I rejoice to believe that Slavery itself has lost its *slender* legality in this suicide." Reading Sumner's resolutions, Orestes Brownson admitted that "there is something severe in treating the rebellion of a state as state suicide; but we have yet to learn that the way of rebellion ought not to be graded, macadamized, and made easy. We see no wisdom or humanity in leaving a state free to rebel, convulse the nation, create a fearful civil war, with all its sacrifices and men and money, and be free to resume its former *status* the moment it ceases fighting."[35]

Senator Garrett Davis responded immediately to Sumner's resolutions and proposed several of his own, including the stricture that no state could abdicate its rights and obligations under the Constitution, and that no loyal citizen could have his property forfeited or confiscated. During the early spring of 1862, conservative Republicans and northern Democrats as well as border-state representatives must have grown anxious as they watched Congress abolish slavery in the District of Columbia, prevent military forces from returning fugitive slaves, debate a more encompassing confiscation act, and even endorse the president's message for initiating gradual, compensated emancipation.[36]

From London, in early May, Henry Adams wrote to his brother Charles that "the emancipation question has got to be settled somehow, and our accounts say that at Washington, the contest is getting very bitter. The men who lead the extreme Abolitionists are a rancorous set. They have done their worst this winter to over-ride the administration rough-shod, and it has needed all of Seward's skill to head them off."[37]

The issue assumed even greater gravity for both conservatives and radicals when they learned, at the same time the president did, that General David Hunter had taken action against slavery. Hunter was head of the Department of the South, comprising South Carolina, Georgia, and Florida (only small parts of which were actually in Union hands). He was also avidly anti-slavery. Hunter had befriended Lincoln, even accompanying the president-elect on his journey from Springfield to Washington in February 1861. Had Lincoln known of the general's letter to secretary of war Edwin Stanton, in January 1862, pleading to have his own way on the issue of slavery, he might not have been so keen to promote him. On May 9, acting on his own authority, and arguing that slavery was incompatible with the martial law he had imposed two weeks earlier, Hunter issued General Order No. 11, declaring all slaves in his Department "forever free." This went far beyond General John C. Frémont's order of the previous August, which had freed only the slaves of owners who were in rebellion. News of Hunter's action spread quickly, and again, as with Frémont's order, so did a response.

One outraged New Yorker wrote the president that if Hunter's order "is not disowned by the administration and himself disgraced, I shall place my whole property to the value of three millions in the hands of the rebels for the use of the traitor Jeff Davis and his base ends." "For Heaven's sake," exclaimed another, "at once, repudiate it, & recall the officer. . . . I look on the policy thus inaugurated, if to be followed, as fatal to all our hopes." One newspaper editor wondered what possibly could have led the general to issue an order "so wild in its statement of facts, and so impolitic in its probable effects, and so violently opposed to the officially declared policy" of the administration. Another denounced Hunter's action as "by far the most arbitrary exercise of power yet attempted in this country by any public officer," adding sarcastically that "the only wonder is that he did not go on and free the whole of the four millions of slaves in the south."[38]

Of course, those who had been pushing all along for a more aggressive policy against slavery rejoiced. George Templeton Strong, no radical, marveled at the news: "Very strange and startling. John Brown *IS* a-marching on, and with seven league boots." And Salmon P. Chase urged the president not to revoke the order: "It has been made as a military measure to meet a military exigency" and should stand. Newspapers picked up on tensions in the cabinet over the issue, and claimed that at least four members were in favor. "It will probably produce a split in the Cabinet," predicted one editor.[39]

Lincoln also heard from Carl Schurz, who had left Germany after the revolutions of 1848 and settled in Wisconsin, where he became an early, influential member of the Republican Party. In return for his support, Lincoln had appointed him ambassador to Spain. He had resigned that position in April 1862, and would eventually receive a commission as a brigadier general. On May 16, Schurz wrote Lincoln that "I am convinced it must and will come to this all over the Cotton states," and that in a month or so Hunter's proclamation would be seen "as the most rational thing in the world." He acknowledged that it might, at the moment, seem a bit premature, and that he would have preferred allowing emancipation to happen through the incidents of war rather than by military proclamation. Still, if Lincoln endorsed it the people would follow, because "your personal influence upon public opinion is immense; you are perhaps not aware of the whole extent of your moral power."

Schurz also warned the president that if he chose to modify Hunter's proclamation, he should not declare any policies that later, out of necessity, he might have to abrogate. "You can hardly tell at the present moment," Schurz noted, "how far you will have to go in six weeks hence. The best policy would be to avoid public declarations altogether. The arming of negroes and the liberation of those slaves who offer us aid and assistance are things which must and will inevitably be done; in fact they are being done, and it would perhaps be best boldly to tell the whole truth and to acknowledge the necessity."[40]

On May 19, Lincoln revoked Hunter's order. He declared that he had had no knowledge of Hunter's intentions, and that neither Hunter nor any other commander or person "has been authorized by the Government of the United States to make proclamations declaring the slaves of any State free." He added, "I further make known that whether it be competent for me, as Commander-in-Chief of the Army and Navy, to declare the Slaves of any state or states, free, and whether at any time, in any case, it shall have become a necessity indispensable to the maintenance of the government, to exercise such supposed power, are questions which, under my responsibility, I reserve to myself, and which I can not feel justified in leaving to the decision of commanders in the field." Not content to stop there, Lincoln went on to make reference to his March 6 message to Congress. He again appealed to the people of the border states to initiate plans of gradual abolition. "I beseech you," he pleaded, "to make the arguments for yourselves. You can not if you would, be blind to the signs of the times."[41]

Lincoln's statement that he reserved solely to himself the decision as to whether he had the authority to issue a declaration of emancipation and, if so, when to do this, did not go unnoticed. Salmon Chase excitedly wrote to General Benjamin Butler that Lincoln's language "clearly shows that his mind is not fully decided. It points to a contingency in which he may recognize the same necessity." Indiana representative George Julian rejoiced that "while the President saw fit to revoke the recent sweeping order of General Hunter, he took pains to couple that revocation with words of earnest warning, which have neither meaning nor application, if they do not recognize the authority of the Executive, in his military discretion, to give freedom to the slaves." William Lloyd Garrison, who personally despaired over the "wet blanket . . . thrown upon the flame of popular enthusiasm" by Lincoln's veto and lamented that "the President is still disposed to treat the dragon of slavery as though it was only a wayward colt," nevertheless reprinted an editorial from another paper that stated: "We do not overlook that feature of the Proclamation which apparently anticipates the possibility of future action by the

President in the same direction with the Order of General Hunter, on a wider scale, should the rebel states fail to respond to the President's beseeching appeal." "The tone of the President's proclamation," observed the *New Bedford Republican,* "shows that he is almost at the turning point."[42]

It was not only Lincoln's reference to the ultimate holder of authority that alerted attentive readers, but also his comment about the "signs of the times." *Harper's Weekly* read the president's message as "a threat and a warning. . . . 'The signs of the times,' he warns them, point to the abolition of an institution which is not in harmony with the spirit of the age or reconcilable with the peace of the country." The conservative *Weekly Patriot and Union,* however, challenged the president, declaring that "the 'signs of the times,' we assure Mr. Lincoln, are understood to be in his keeping. He could stop this clamor for a *new* Union in an hour" if he simply reiterated his earlier commitment not to touch slavery in the states. The president's most inflammatory radical critic, Adam Gurowski, fulminated in his diary: "Of course Mr. Lincoln overrules General Hunter's Proclamation. It is too human, too noble, too great, for the tall Kentuckian. . . . Mr. Lincoln again publishes a disquisition, and points to the signs of the times. But does Mr. Lincoln perceive other, more awful, signs of the times? Does he see the bloody handwriting on the wall, condemning his unnatural, vacillating, dodging policy?"[43]

When General George Gordon Meade met Lincoln prior to a review of the troops, he told the president that the army supported his decision with respect to Hunter. Lincoln, according to Meade, responded: "I am trying to do my duty, but no one can imagine what influences are brought to bear on me." Lincoln was suffering. Personally, he was still mourning the loss of his eleven-year-old son, Willie, who had died in February 1862 of typhoid. Militarily, the war news—which would ebb and flow, a Union victory here, a Confederate one there—turned horrific with reports of the carnage at Shiloh on April 6 and April 7, which resulted in the worst death toll in a single battle to that point. Shiloh put an end to any northern hopes for a quick resolution to the war. And politically, Lincoln felt pressure. At that very moment, Congress was engaged in debate over a bill "to confiscate the property and free the slaves of rebels."[44]

The debate over confiscation, which began in the Senate toward the end of February, pulsated for months. Amendments came forward in waves, and no sooner had one been dealt with than others rolled in to take its place. Senators offered substitute bills and engaged in all manner of parliamentary maneuvers. Speeches went on for hours, and every misunderstanding led to a rejoinder that led to another misunderstanding. Typical of the comments was the remark of one peevish senator who complained, "I thought it very unjust in him in the assault he made upon my State." "There is a spirit of denunciation and browbeating on this subject," lamented Garrett Davis of Kentucky, "which I have never seen equaled."

On April 11, Illinois senator Lyman Trumbull, the bill's sponsor, chided his colleagues that no public measure would ever be passed if it was debated only an hour here and an hour there, and then put aside for other business, as had become commonplace with this bill. To pass or fail on its merits, a bill must be pressed forward and not "killed by inches." Trumbull's appeal did little good. In May the Senate voted 24 to 14 to refer the bill and its myriad alternatives (at least a dozen had been printed) to a select committee that grew from five to seven and finally to nine members. Trumbull viewed this as dooming his bill, and he asked to be excused from service on the committee, saying he did not have "much confidence from anything growing out of it."

The House, too, stuttered and stammered. On March 20, the House Judiciary Committee reported five bills, six joint resolutions, and four House resolutions—and recommended that none of them pass. In April, the initial bills were referred back to a select committee, but not before Republican Schuyler Colfax of Indiana thundered, "Standing here before the living and the dead, we cannot avoid the grave and fearful responsibility devolving on us. The people will ask us when we return to their midst, when our brave soldiers went forth to the battle-field to suffer, to bleed, and to die for their country, what did you civilians in the Halls of Congress do to cripple the power of the rebels whom they confronted at the cannon's mouth. . . . Why do we hesitate. . . . I plead only for action."[45]

For months, members of both chambers of Congress posed an array of questions: Was any confiscation bill constitutional? Was it a bill of attainder (a legislative act declaring a person guilty of a crime, without trial), which is expressly forbidden by the Constitution? Under the war power, who held the authority to confiscate—Congress or the president? What were the differences between confiscation and emancipation? Would freeing the slaves weaken or strengthen the rebellion? What would be done with the emancipated slaves?

In response to the conservative claim that the Constitution protected citizens against loss of property without due process of law, radical Republicans and abolitionists argued that the rebels, in waging war, had forfeited their rights as citizens; that the "ultimate power over the sword" was vested in Congress and that "Congress has full authority under the war-making power to free the slaves of rebel enemies"; that the act was not a bill of attainder because it operated only against those who could not be reached judicially, it was not directed against a particular person, and it did not exact a "corruption of blood"; and that "if there is anything that will tend to make the constitution a less sacred thing in the minds of the people, it is the use that is made of it to shield those who are in open rebellion against it." Sumner put the matter in typical axiomatic form: "The Rebels have gone outside the Constitution to make war upon their country. It is for us to pursue them as enemies outside of the Constitution, where they wickedly place themselves, and where the Constitution concurs in placing them also." Years later, revising the speech for publication, Charles Sumner added, "So doing, we simply obey the Constitution, and act in all respects constitutionally."[46]

But opponents of the measure could see no reason to pass a constitutionally dubious bill that would have no effect because the property to be confiscated was beyond the government's reach. Orville Browning said the bill was "little more than a bravado, for however much we may declare by proclamation or resolution or statute that their property shall be confiscated, no confiscation will ensue until we can actually seize the property and enforce the penalty; and when we are in a condition to do that, neither proclamation nor law of Congress nor resolution will be necessary." Republican Edgar Cowan of Pennsylvania agreed: to pass this law "is a mere *brutum fulmen;* it is the mere idle blowing of a trumpet, and of no more efficacy than that, just because it achieves nothing."[47]

Opponents saw the bill as "an invidious attempt to do indirectly what its advocates will not attempt to do directly—it is an attempt to destroy the institution of slavery in the southern States." And at times they gave vent to their racial hatred, proclaiming "the supremacy of the white man," denouncing free blacks as "worthless, thriftless, lazy," insisting that "the black man, the negro, cannot live and prosper in the presence of the white man," and warning against a freedom that would exist in name only and lead to "extermination or reenslavement."[48]

One of the more humorous exchanges in the debate occurred on May 1, when the Unionist senator from Kentucky, Garrett Davis, said he favored confiscation of slaves but not emancipation. Republican senator Daniel Clark of New Hampshire wondered if he'd heard the senator correctly—if the objection was "not that the slave is taken from the rebel, but that he is not sold, and the proceeds put into the treasury of the United States." Davis said yes. Clark then wondered, "Suppose we take a mule from a rebel, and cannot sell him, and have nothing to do with him; cannot we turn him loose?" Davis replied, "Yes, but anybody can pick him up afterwards if he chooses." To which Clark responded, "So anybody can pick the negro up if he can find him." The Senate erupted in laughter.[49]

The inclusion of a provision for voluntary colonization did little to win anyone over. Most radical Republicans disdained the measure and thought it "unworthy of Christian men anywhere to talk about the laborer not being permitted to live in a country on account of his color." Representative Luther Hanchett of Wisconsin insisted, "We have no right to expatriate them without their consent . . . and we cannot afford to send away from the country such a vast capital of labor." Senator Samuel Pomeroy of Kansas suggested that instead of colonizing freed slaves, the Senate should consider colonizing the rebel leaders, a class of men who were "more dangerous to the Government of this country than are the slaves; who produce less, and who can be spared, provided we can find any government of any country under heaven" that would take them.

Some conservatives of both parties also saw little in the colonization proposal. Those from western states averred that "our people want nothing to do with the negro," but did not believe in colonization as anything other than "a wild, impracticable scheme." Garrett Davis called voluntary colonization "moonshine": "It never did take place, and it never will." Republican representative Francis Blair of Missouri, however, staunchly supported colonization as a remedy that would make the "boasted freedom conferred by this bill" something more than a "bill of exile" as state after state passed laws prohibiting free blacks from entering. Without colonization, he saw the bill only as a measure "to make them homeless, houseless, to make them destitute and despairing wanderers upon the face of the earth."[50]

The most virulent opponent not only of colonization but also of emancipation was congressman Samuel Sullivan Cox, Democrat of Ohio. In a speech titled "Emancipation and Its Results: Is Ohio To Be Africanized?" Cox declared he wanted to hear "no more poetry about striking off chains and bidding the oppressed go." Emancipation would result "in the flight and movement of the black race by millions northward," a population hurled "in hordes upon the North." The "plain people" of his state would not tolerate the influx, Ohio soldiers would lay down their arms, and a "conflict of races" would ensue that would destroy the weaker side. "The white and black races thrive best apart," insisted Cox, and "the mixture of the races tends to deteriorate both." Cox concluded that if "the negro cannot be colonized without burdens intolerable, and plans too delusive; if he cannot be freed and left South without destroying its labor, and without his extermination; if he cannot come North without becoming an outcast and without ruin to Northern industry and society, what shall be done? Where shall he go? He answers for himself. The pater familias of a drove of negroes, the other day in the valley of Virginia, was asked, 'where are you going?' 'Dun' no, massa, dun' no; gwine somewhere I recken.'" Cox's supporters laughed heartily.[51]

Republicans largely ignored Cox's race-baiting and pressed on with their legislative goals. Colonization was an add-on and had nothing to do with the raison d'être of the bill. It fit with what the president had already called for, and if it eased the reservations of some Republicans, so much the better. It was clear that Congress intended the act to strike at the heart of the rebellion, its cause and its sustenance. Practical emancipation was already occurring: the number of slaves who "as our armies advance further and still further into rebel territory . . . will become separated from their masters, and thus practically set to liberty, will be constantly increasing."

The moment had arrived, many thought, for declaratory emancipation as well. No one expressed more forcefully the rationale for attacking slavery directly, as a military necessity, than Republican representative Elijah Babbitt of Pennsylvania. Confiscation and emancipation, he proclaimed, "would utterly exterminate the rebellion at incomparably less cost and in fewer months than it might take of years if we should not adopt it." He explained:

The slave system, unassailed, is the great element of rebel power. In it, as in the locks of Samson, lies the secret of their great strength. Slave labor feeds and clothes their armies, supplies them with all the munitions and means of war. Slave labor sustains the aged and the infirm, the women and children, leaving every able-bodied adult white male with nothing to do but fight for the overthrow of the Union. Shorn of this institution, rebeldom would be as powerless as was Samson shorn of his locks in the lap of Delilah. These slaves, composing nearly half the population of the cotton States, are, I believe, about the only true Union men to be found there. . . . I think the time has arrived, and we have reached a point in this great war, when we should employ them on our side, and grant them freedom as a boon for faithful assistance, if they are willing to render it.

In response to the argument that the slaves would be prevented from leaving, Babbitt insisted that the slaves "being informed, as they soon would be—for no surveillance could keep it from them—that under the stars and stripes they would certainly find freedom—the great absorbing desire of their souls—it would require the attention of all the armies of all rebeldom to prevent the exodus of its slaves, and thus leave to them no time to fight against the Union. Or, if they would still attempt to fight, each soldier would have to hold a negro by the throat with one hand while fighting against the Union with the other."[52]

The time for hard war had come, and the confiscation of property and slaves signaled the turn. After all, the rebels had already passed confiscation laws, and under those laws "there is but little property of loyal men left in their States." No longer should the rebels be treated kindly as wayward sons to be coaxed back into union; they were fierce enemies. "This rebellion cannot be put down by soft words and lenient measures," declared Samuel Steel Blair of Pennsylvania. "Since slavery made the war, let slavery feel the war," thundered New York's Rodolphus Duell. Senator Edgar Cowan, his conservative inclinations notwithstanding, feared that the "contagion of our supineness and inertness" had carried over to the armies in the field, who seemed only "to set and set and set." Even the conservative Orville Browning thundered, "If it is *war*, let it be war in earnest. Let it be quick, fierce, terrible."

"We must destroy our enemies, or they will destroy us," concluded Ohio's John Sherman.[53]

Opponents of the bill warned that its passage would "array . . . every white being in all the slave States, the border States as well as those that have seceded, against your law." But the argument that taking action against slavery would unite the South and alienate loyal slaveholders had lost much of its potency. Henry Wilson of Massachusetts reviewed each of the actions that had been taken previously by Congress and noted that before each one had passed—whether it was the First Confiscation Act, or the ban on the military returning fugitive slaves, or the abolition of slavery in the District of Columbia—advocates had been warned that "you will unite the hearts of the people of the slave States against you" and lose the border states to the rebellion. Yet none of those fears had come to pass. Attacking slavery would not threaten the republic; rather, as Wilson noted, "every hour of thought and reflection brings me to the conclusion that death to slavery is life to the Republic."[54]

The Republicans had done their duty—but would the president sign a sweeping confiscation act? Lincoln preferred moderation to severity, restraint to upheaval. Always thinking about the political implications of any act, he would warn Congress that "the severest justice may not always be the best policy."[55]

3

A New Departure

"Thought and reflection," Henry Wilson had advised. Indeed, it was impossible not to think deeply about the issues surrounding slavery, and, over time, men changed their minds about what was to be done. Benjamin Wade, Republican senator from Ohio, was most articulate in explaining how his position had evolved. Wade conceded that, in the past, he had been willing to tolerate the practices of otherwise law-abiding slaveowners:

> Abhorrent as slavery is to man and God, I had agreed that in their States they might have it, provided they would keep it there, and let us alone; but when they repudiated the Constitution of the United States, when they waged violent war against it, when they made use of those very slaves as the fulcrum by which to overturn the Constitution of the country, I lost all my veneration—no, not veneration, for I never had any veneration for slavery; I repudiate the idea; but it absolved me from all my sense of duty in that regard, and allowed me to give full scope to my sense of justice in dealing with slaves and their masters.

Wade would no longer feel any obligation toward slaveholders, and would sooner see the rebels hang on the gallows and the enslaved "remitted to his rights."[1]

As the confiscation bill moved toward a vote, discussion of what it would require of Lincoln began to surface. Congressmen believed that it necessitated the "assent and cordial cooperation of the President." Indeed, one version explicitly required the president "thirty days hence to issue a proclamation" supporting emancipation. The president and Congress, declared one legislator, were "running in the same channel," and another averred that "it is the duty of the President to declare universal emancipation to the slaves." Of course, even many of those who believed the authority to emancipate under the war power rested solely with the Executive, and not with Congress, contended that any proclamation by the president would in practice be "utterly without force."[2]

By the end of June 1862, Lincoln knew that a confiscation bill would find its way to his desk. The House had passed such a bill on May 26. (It is worth noting that the House also took up a *separate* though closely related bill for the emancipation of the slaves of rebels and their voluntary colonization. This emancipation bill was defeated 74 to 78, with sixteen Republicans voting in the negative; but when it was brought up again on June 18, it carried 82 to 54, with eighty-one Republicans plus George Fisher of Delaware voting for it; only six Republicans opposed it this time around. The bill, however, never made it to the floor of the Senate for consideration.) The Senate agreed to an amended version on June 28. On July 3, the House voted nonconcurrence with the Senate bill, and it went to conference committee for resolution. The final bill was reported and approved by the House on July 11, and by the Senate on July 12—only two House and two Senate Republicans voted against it (Bradley Granger of Michigan and Benjamin Franklin Thomas of Massachusetts, and Orville Browning and Edgar Cowan). It remained to be seen whether or not the president would sign.[3]

On June 2, the abolitionist John Murray Forbes had written to congressman Charles Sedgwick, "I would trust to old Abe's being pushed up to the use of the military powers of emancipation." Forbes himself confessed to a change of mind. He wrote to Charles Sumner, "I used to think emancipation only another name for murder, fire, and rape, but mature reflection and considerable personal observation have since convinced me that emancipation may, at any time, be declared without disorder."[4]

Pressing ahead, Lincoln seemed to be in motion. It is little more than a telling detail, but on June 16 he borrowed from the Library of Congress Harriet Beecher Stowe's *Key to Uncle Tom's Cabin.* In that volume, Stowe provided documentary evidence for the fictional stories she told in her novel. That fictional characters had become true to life was evident in the Confiscation Act debate, when Representative William Lansing of New York declared, "No matter to me whether every slaveholder was either a Legree or a St. Clair, my detestation of the system would be the same in either case."[5]

A few days later, a delegation from a group called Progressive Friends met with the president to urge him to issue a proclamation of emancipation. After wryly observing that slavery was the most troublesome issue he faced after the problem of office seekers, Lincoln remarked: "If a decree of emancipation could abolish Slavery, John Brown would have done the work effectually. Such a decree surely would not be more binding upon the South than the Constitution, and that cannot be enforced in that part of the country now. Would a proclamation of freedom be any more effective?" The conversation turned to the need for divine guidance, and newspapers reported that Lincoln said "he had sometime thought that perhaps he might be an instrument in God's hands."[6]

Lincoln's mention of John Brown in this context did not go unnoticed. One abolitionist wondered just what the president might have meant: What possibly could be the relationship between the "supposition and the conclusion"? "How," the writer wondered, "could any sensible man compare, even by implication, an edict issuing from John Brown at Harper's Ferry and the same from Abraham Lincoln at Washington? The one, a private citizen, without commission or authority, and, above all, assuming a position hostile to laws State and National; the other, the Chief Magistrate of the whole people, the Commander-in-Chief of the whole army, and invested by the Constitution with the absolute, undisputed control of the War Power, together with ample means for the execution of any order or policy in his judgment necessary." Another declared that the reply "is an insult to an intelligent people. In it he has not given the reason—while pretending to give it—for not decreeing *emancipation.*" Lincoln's logic continued to confound those pressing for action.[7]

In early July, Lincoln still had deep reservations about issuing an emancipation proclamation. His friend Orville Browning kept hammering away both publicly in Congress and privately with the president about its inadvisability, and he had the president's ear. After Browning visited Lincoln at the White House on July 1, he recorded in his diary that he had "had a talk with him in regard to the Confiscation bills before us." Lincoln had shared with Browning

> a paper embodying his views of the objects of the war, and the proper mode of conducting it in its relations to slavery. This, he told me, he had sketched hastily with the intention of laying it before the Cabinet. His views coincided entirely with my own. No negroes necessarily taken and escaping during the war are ever to be returned to slavery— No inducements are to be held out to them to come into our lines for they come now faster than we can provide for them and are becoming an embarrassment to the government. At present none are to be armed. It would produce dangerous & fatal dissatisfaction in our army, and do more injury than good.[8]

But Browning was not the only politician calling on the president. On July 4, Sumner went to the White House not once but twice to implore the president "to make the day more sacred & historic than ever" by issuing a decree of emancipation. He came away from the first visit thinking Lincoln might at least declare the slaves in Virginia free; but by the second visit, later in the day, the president had again shifted course, fearing that if he issued such a decree "half the officers would fling down their arms & three more States would rise." Sumner believed the president "plainly mistaken." For the moment, Sumner's optimism flagged. It had reached a high point on May 28, when he'd breathlessly reported to Massachusetts governor John Andrew: *"Stanton told me this morning that a decree of Emancipation would be issued in two months. . . .* The cause of Emancipation cannot be stopped."[9]

Perhaps emancipation could not be stopped, but General George McClellan's army could, and the prospects for freedom to the enslaved gained with the army's military setbacks. In March, McClellan had finally launched his Peninsula Campaign, aimed at taking Richmond. In late March, tens of thousands of troops sailed from Alexandria to Fort Monroe. McClellan had superior forces to the Confederate army (the Army of the Potomac had 105,000 men; Richmond was defended by 60,000)—but he balked at attacking, under the mistaken impression that the southern army was at least equally strong. On April 9, Lincoln wrote to McClellan: "It is indispensable to *you* that you strike a blow. *I* am powerless to help this. . . . *you must act.*"[10]

Although Union forces gained access to the James River, McClellan made only halting progress toward Richmond and in efforts to subdue the Confederates. Two days of fighting, on May 31 and June 1, yielded heavy casualties (a total of more than 11,000) but little change in position. The Peninsula Campaign concluded with a series of savage engagements known collectively as the Seven Days Battles, fought from June 25 to July 1. The sixth and final battle took place at Malvern Hill, where Robert E. Lee attacked an entrenched Union position and paid for it with heavy casualties. "It was not war—it was murder," agonized one Confederate general. McClellan was eager to get away; the Army of the Potomac pulled back, and Richmond was no longer threatened.[11]

"Affairs at Richmond are in a very critical condition, and the President is deeply anxious—So am I," wrote Orville Browning on July 2. Unable to sleep, losing weight, Lincoln tried to maintain a positive outlook, but the only unadulterated good news all spring had been the capture of New Orleans by Admiral David Farragut in late April. On July 7, Lincoln traveled to Harrison's Landing, a stretch of five miles or so on the north side of the James River, to see McClellan and visit the troops. He reviewed the army in the moonlight. "It was a magnificent scene," wrote one lieutenant. And an artillery officer declared: "If our good and noble President loves his army as well as it loves him, he must have a good big heart."[12]

McClellan presented Lincoln with a letter explaining that he thought the war "should be conducted upon the highest principles known to Christian Civilization. It should not be a War looking to the subjugation of the people of any state, in any event. It should not be, at all, a War upon population; but against armed forces and political organizations. Neither confiscation of property, political executions of persons, territorial organization of states or forcible abolition of slavery should be contemplated for a moment."[13]

Lincoln already knew McClellan's attitude toward the war. The general consistently overestimated the enemy's troop strength and was reluctant to commit his men to battle. He had become a master of inactivity. And he seemed unwilling to take any actions that Southerners might view as unchivalrous. In June, for example, McClellan would not allow an estate owned by Mrs. Robert E. Lee to be used as a hospital for wounded soldiers. McClellan said he had made a promise—but Lincoln apparently told a noted physician, *"I will break it for him."*[14]

On July 11, Lincoln named Henry Halleck general-in-chief of all land forces, filling a post McClellan had once held but that had been vacant since March 11, when the president had reassigned him to focus exclusively on the Peninsula Campaign. Halleck's elevation marked the beginning of a change in strategy. The war would be prosecuted more energetically and aggressively. The property of civilians would become a legitimate military target, and the struggle began to be transformed from a war against an enemy army to a war against a people in rebellion. As naval secretary Gideon Welles explained in his diary, "The reverses before Richmond, and the formidable power and dimensions of the insurrection . . . impelled the Administration to adopt extraordinary measures to preserve the national existence."[15]

The mood of the people also suffered. George Templeton Strong expressed the feelings of many when he wrote, on the day Lincoln made the military change, "We have been and are in a depressed, dismal, asthenic state of anxiety and irritability. The cause of the country does not happen to be thriving just now." Salmon Chase lamented that "the defeat of McClellan before Richmond was shameful, and attributable only to gross neglect & incompetency for which he should at once have been dismissed the service in disgrace."[16]

Count Gurowski could not have agreed more. In his diary, starting as early as October 1861, he maintained a steady screed against McClellan. After meeting the general, he called him "altogether unmilitary and inexperienced. It made me sick at heart to hear him, and to think that he is to decide over the destinies and the blood of the people." His animadversions grew even harsher thereafter. In January, he thought "McClellan is either feeble as a reed, or a bad man." Observing the Peninsula Campaign, Gurowski concluded that if French, Prussian, or Russian military leaders were to show such incompetence, "they would be condemned as unfit to have any military command whatever." It drove Gurowski mad that all McClellan did was ask for more troops and dig entrenchments: "If McClellan could know anything, then he would know this—that nothing is so destructive to an army as sieges, as diggings, and camps, and nothing more disciplines and re-invigorates men, makes them true soldiers, than does marching and fighting." Denouncing the general as a "mud-mole" intent only on executing a "bloodless strategy," Gurowski wondered why Lincoln kept him on for so long; he concluded that it was because of an "unnatural, vacillating, dodging policy" that failed to "perceive other, more awful, signs of the times."[17]

George Templeton Strong, in his diary, likewise expressed growing dismay with Lincoln: "We begin to lose faith in Uncle Abe"; "I fear Lincoln is what Wendell Phillips calls him, 'a first-rate second-rate man'"; "Lincoln himself has gone down at last, like all our popular idols of the last eighteen months."[18]

The day after appointing Halleck, Lincoln met with representatives and senators from the border states, who numbered twenty-eight, including several loyalists from Virginia and Tennessee. Knowing that adjournment of Congress was imminent, he read an address in which he again appealed to them to enact plans for compensated, gradual emancipation. He chided them, saying that if they'd voted for the message Lincoln had delivered in March, "the war would now be substantially ended." Again he warned that as long as their states continued to allow slavery, the Confederacy would hold out in hopes of their eventually joining in the rebellion. He pleaded with the delegation to recognize that "the incidents of the war can not be avoided. If the war continue long, as it must, if the object be not sooner attained, the institution in your states will be extinguished by mere friction and abrasion—by the mere incidents of the war. It will be gone, and you will have nothing valuable in lieu of it." Why not, he asked, take a step that would undoubtedly shorten the war, restore the Union, and provide compensation for what otherwise would certainly be lost? Lincoln assured his listeners, "I do not speak of emancipation *at once,* but of a *decision* at once to emancipate *gradually.*" He added that there was room for colonization in South America, and thought with "company and encouragement for one another, the freed people will not be so reluctant to go." He reminded these mostly conservative politicians that he had repudiated General Hunter's proclamation, but that, in doing so, he had angered many whose support the country needed. "The pressure in this direction, is still upon me, and is increasing," Lincoln admitted. He begged them to relieve him and the country by merely stating that they would begin a process that would gradually lead to emancipation.[19]

Lincoln must have known by their reaction, before the men filed out, that he had not persuaded them. Two days later, he received a formal response signed by Kentucky governor Charles Wickliffe as chairman and nineteen of the other twenty-seven border-state congressmen to whom Lincoln had appealed. They characterized his message of March 6 as unconstitutional and an undue interference with the rights of states to have slavery; said that it was too expensive and that they could not, in good conscience, add to the national debt; expressed admiration for the president, but feared doctrines and measures propounded and passed in Congress; acknowledged being troubled by his reference to Hunter's proclamation and the pressure upon him; and wondered whether there was a tacit threat in his admonition. Disagreeing about denying the "necessity of emancipating the Slaves of our States, as a means of putting down the rebellion," they emphasized that the people in their states could not consider the president's proposition "in its present impalpable form." A minority response offering "to ask our people to consider the question of Emancipation *to save the Union*," which arrived the following day, did little to ease Lincoln's mind.[20]

On Sunday, July 13, the day after addressing the border-states representatives, Lincoln attended the funeral of Edwin Stanton's infant son. He invited Gideon Welles to accompany him. William Henry Seward was also in the carriage. On the trip, which took the party a few miles away toward Georgetown, Lincoln brought up the subject of issuing an emancipation proclamation, "in case the Rebels did not cease to persist in their war on the Government and the Union, of which he saw no evidence." According to Welles, he "dwelt earnestly on the gravity, importance and delicacy of the movement, said he had given it much thought and had about come to the conclusion that we must free the slaves or be ourselves subdued, etc., etc."[21]

As the journey continued, the president asked his two cabinet members for their opinion. According to Welles, Seward said "the subject involved consequences so vast and momentous" that he needed to reflect further before giving a final opinion; but his initial thought was that the measure was "justifiable, and perhaps he might say expedient and necessary." Welles concurred. During the ride, they kept returning to the subject. Lincoln "was earnest in the conviction that something must be done. It was a new departure for the President, for until this time in all our previous interviews, whenever the question of emancipation or the mitigation of slavery had been in any way alluded to, he had been prompt and emphatic in denouncing any interference by the General Government with the subject." It was time, in the face of McClellan's failures in the field, to shift policy. The rebels were making use of the slaves; that weapon had to be removed from the Confederates and placed at the disposal of the Union army. Welles also mentioned, in an article published ten years later, the "last hopeless interview" with the border-states representatives, from whom the president "received little encouragement." The interview had made Lincoln realize that "emancipation of the slaves in the rebel States must precede that in the border States." "War had removed constitutional obligations and restrictions," and, believing that the rebels "could not at the same time throw off the constitution and invoke its aid," Lincoln was ready to proceed.[22]

While Lincoln's position since the firing on Fort Sumter had not been static, this was a decisive move—albeit from the perspective of the more radical Republicans, one that had been too long delayed. The "new departure," as Welles called it, came for a variety of reasons: the failure of the Peninsula Campaign, which gave additional legitimacy to an argument based on military necessity; the ongoing debate over confiscation and emancipation in Congress, which allowed for a full and prolonged airing of all the issues on both sides of the question; and the negative response of the border states to Lincoln's repeated entreaties to move against slavery. Lincoln had long believed that the abolition of slavery in Kentucky, Missouri, Delaware, and Maryland would help to end the rebellion and lead to emancipation in the Confederacy. He now realized that, if anything, it would have to be the other way around. Attack slavery in the rebellious states first, which he now was convinced his war power as commander-in-chief of the armed forces gave him constitutional warrant to do, and let emancipation filter up to the border states. Lincoln still clung to the idea of gradual, compensated emancipation, and he still favored colonization, but he was now preparing to issue some sort of proclamation of emancipation.

Just what would emerge, and when, remained to be seen; but something was coming. The *New York Times* reported, "It is generally understood that the President's consultation with the Border State men is only preliminary to some new stroke of policy which the Executive contemplates—and speculation as to its general character and purpose is very active and diverse. . . . Nothing that Mr. Lincoln ever said or did commits him against the proposition that Slavery must die if necessary, in order that Freedom may live."[23]

The day after Lincoln's revelation to Seward and Welles, Orville Browning brought him a copy of the Confiscation Act as passed by Congress and implored the president not to sign it. He contended that it was unconstitutional, that Lincoln needed to show he controlled the radicals, not the other way around, and that a veto would unleash "a storm of enthusiasm in support of the Administration in the border states which would be worth to us 100,000 muskets, whereas if he approved it I feared our friends could no longer sustain themselves there."[24]

Lincoln told Browning "he would give it his profound consideration." On July 15, he wrote to Solomon Foot, the president pro tempore of the Senate, and to Galusha Grow, Speaker of the House, to ask that they postpone adjournment of their respective bodies for one day, because he might return the Confiscation Bill with objections and he wanted Congress to have a chance to respond. Lincoln's objections, it turns out, were not Browning's. The president's major concern was that, under the terms of the bill, not only would title to the landed property of persons guilty of treason or disloyalty be forfeited for the remainder of their lives, but the title would not revert to their heirs upon their death. Lincoln regarded the latter provision as unconstitutional.

Lincoln spent Tuesday morning writing in his library, having left instructions not to be disturbed. Apparently this was when he drafted a veto message to Congress explaining in detail why he was returning the bill. Browning observed that the president "looked weary, care-worn and troubled. . . . He looked very sad, and there was a cadence of deep sadness in his voice. We parted I believe both of us with tears in our eyes."[25]

That same day, Representative Horace Maynard introduced a joint resolution that said none of the punishments or proceedings under the acts would be "construed as to work a forfeiture of the real estate of the offender beyond his natural life." Lincoln's response was completed before he learned of the adoption of the joint resolution. Once he had heard about it, he signed the Confiscation Act. But perhaps feeling that he shouldn't let a thoughtful response go to waste, he went ahead and sent the message anyhow, attaching it to a note informing Congress that, in light of the Maynard resolution, he had approved the bill. It was unprecedented for a president to submit a veto message in conjunction with a bill he had signed into law, and it caused much irritation among members of Lincoln's own party. Angry Republican senators even employed a filibuster to prevent approval of a motion to print the document.[26]

Three different sections of the Confiscation Act dealt with emancipation, mandating freedom for, respectively, slaves who belonged to persons convicted of treason, those whose owners were convicted of aiding and abetting the rebellion, and those who belonged to disloyal owners and managed to flee to Union lines, or were captured by Union forces, abandoned by their owners, or found by invading Union forces in areas previously held by Confederate troops. In his draft veto message, Lincoln said he had no objection to the substance of these three sections of the bill. But he admitted to finding it "startling" that Congress claimed the right to emancipate slaves within a state. He thought the bill should have provided, instead, that ownership of such slaves would first be transferred to the federal government, with Congress specifying in advance that they were to be liberated, not sold (as other confiscated rebel property often was). This rather technical consideration was not sufficient, however, to cause Lincoln to reject the bill.[27]

One peculiarity of the Confiscation Act was that it simultaneously—indeed, in adjoining sections—authorized the president to make provision for colonization and to "employ as many persons of African descent as he may deem necessary and proper for the suppression of this rebellion." The latter meant enlisting blacks as soldiers; and, along with the Confiscation Act, Congress passed a revision of the Militia Act to "receive into the service of the United States . . . persons of African descent." What was intended initially was enlisting blacks to work as military laborers, thereby freeing white troops for combat.

But the issue of arming the slaves erupted sporadically in the debate over the Confiscation Act. In an exchange with Senator Willard Saulsbury of Delaware, Lyman Trumbull of Illinois declared: "If the Senator asks me whether I will arm negroes in insurrection to murder their masters, I say, I will disturb no slave masters at home; but if the master of the slave comes to destroy this Government, to murder Union soldiers, I will put a gun in the hands of his negro to shoot him. That is my feeling about it. I would resort to all the means God has given us to put down this rebellion." By comparison, Representative William Allen, Democrat from Ohio, called the arming of the slaves "the most odious and inhuman of all propositions," according to which, if carried into effect, "our soldiers would be as apt to become victims of these ignorant and treacherous creatures as those of the confederates, and which would at most accomplish the inhuman massacre of innocent children and helpless females."[28]

The debate over revisions of the Militia Act turned rancorous, especially once Senator Preston King of New York introduced an amendment stating that whenever "any man or boy of African descent, who by the laws of any State shall owe service or labor to any person who, during the present rebellion, has levied war or has borne arms against the United States, or adhered to their enemies by giving them aid and comfort, shall render any such service as is provided for in this act, he, his mother and his wife and children, shall forever thereafter be free." In other words, rebellious slaveowners forfeited their human property. Saulsbury denounced the measure as "a wholesale scheme of emancipation," and derided the attempt on the part of his colleague "on every occasion to change the character of this war, and to elevate the miserable nigger, not only to political rights, but to put him in your Army, and to put him in your Navy, and while this policy is pursued, the Union never will be restored, because you can have no Union without preservation of the Constitution." Senator Garrett Davis of Kentucky did not want blacks in the military in any capacity, certainly not as soldiers or even as laborers. "I know the negro well," he claimed, "I know his nature. He is, until excited, mild and gentle; he is affectionate and faithful too; but when his passions have been inflamed and thoroughly aroused, you find him a fiend, a latent tiger fierceness in his heart, and when he becomes excited by the taste of blood he is a demon." "Has it come to this," the Kentuckian asked, "that we cannot command white soldiers enough to fight our battles to put down this rebellion. . . . If the Union cannot be preserved by the white man, making him the soldier and the hero of the battle for the Union, there are no conditions upon which it can be saved."

With less demagoguery than his colleagues, Orville Browning likewise raised objections to the bill, though he would end up voting in favor of an amended version of it. Recognizing that in all likelihood a slave's mother, wife, and children might be held by another owner, he wondered what would happen if that owner was loyal to the Union, because Congress had no power to emancipate the slaves of loyal citizens. Senator James Henry Lane of Kansas interrupted and asked, "What would freedom be worth to you if your mother, your wife, and your children were slaves?" Browning admitted that such a situation "would detract very greatly from the value of life," but, nevertheless, loyal slaveholders had to be protected. In any event, words codified by laws do not free slaves: "It is not your paper declaration that is either to confiscate the property or emancipate the slaves of rebels. It is marching with your Army, and by the strong hand of war seizing hold of the property, taking it from their possession." John Sherman, now a senator, having been elected to fill the vacancy created by the resignation of Salmon P. Chase, proposed an amendment to restrict the emancipation clause to the slaves of rebels; and after a heated debate during which radical Republicans fervently opposed it, the amendment was adopted by a vote of 18 to 17.

Though modified, the emancipation clause remained, most Republican senators agreeing with Edgar Cowan's plea: "Shall we bring these people, in this condition of things in the country, into the public service, and not guarantee to them their liberty? Why, sir, we should hardly deserve their services, if after they have preserved our rights, and our liberties, we would return them into slavery." The bill passed the Senate by a vote of 28 to 9, and in the House an attempt to lay it on the table failed, yeas 30, nays 77. On July 17, Lincoln signed the measure. He approved of using blacks as laborers. It would still be some time before blacks became fighting soldiers, but a discussion had been initiated that linked service in the military to freedom.[29]

The measure won the support of many, including the octogenarian Horace Binney, a conservative nationalist who had served as a Whig for one term in Congress in the 1830s. In August 1862, Binney declared: "I am not going myself to become an abolitionist, which I have never been; but if within the ACT of Congress the government shall use slaves for military labour, and freedom is the result, I shall not complain of it. The negroes are a part of the force of our enemy. I would dare, as freely as the act of Congress permits, to use that force against the enemy."[30]

4

Movement

Treasury secretary Salmon Chase sensed movement on the part of the president. On July 20, 1862, he wrote to a correspondent: "The Slavery question perplexes the President almost as much as ever and yet I think he is about to emerge from the obscurities where he has been groping into somewhat clearer light." On the same day, John Hay, Lincoln's private secretary, wrote that the president "will not conserve slavery much longer. When next he speaks in relation to this defiant and ungrateful villainy it will be with no uncertain sound. Even now he speaks more boldly and sternly to slaveholders than to the world." At this time, the writer and editor Charles Eliot Norton wondered: "Will Lincoln be master of the opportunities, or will they escape him? Is he great enough for the time?"[1]

On Monday, July 21, Lincoln assembled his cabinet to discuss "some definitive steps in respect to Military action and slavery." Only Montgomery Blair, the postmaster general, was absent. The president had prepared orders that included giving generals authority "to subsist their troops in hostile territory" (that is, allow their soldiers to seize provisions from local residents), to employ blacks as laborers, to require officials to keep careful records of property taken (including slaves), and to make arrangements for compensation and colonization. The next day the cabinet met again and adopted the first three orders, while agreeing to drop the colonization order. The question of arming the slaves then came up. Chase advocated the measure "warmly," but Lincoln was opposed.[2]

The three War Department orders (as they were known) may have seemed unobjectionable to most, but at least one abolitionist was livid over the implications of the specific language used, which referred at one place to "property and persons of African descent." Did these Africans, the writer wondered, "descend with *property* other than dusky hides to this country?" The phrasing, he said, must have been another example of the president's "fatal repute of being a joker; and however much it is to be deprecated in the private citizen, it is most deplorable when it crops out on the most serious occasions in the outgoings of the chief magistrate of a great nation. . . . Mr. Lincoln's jokes are now becoming chronic with him. . . . It may be esteemed 'cool' [impudent or audacious] for the Chief Magistrate to indulge in whimsicalities in regard to serious matters, but we submit that his 'quips and jibes' are, to say the least, UNTIMELY."[3]

At the next cabinet meeting, on Tuesday, July 22, Lincoln, according to Chase, "proposed to issue a Proclamation, on the basis of the Confiscation Bill, calling upon the States to return to their allegiance—warning the rebels the provisions of the Act would have full force at the expiration of sixty days—adding, on his own part, a declaration of his intention to renew, at the next session of Congress, his recommendation of compensation to States adopting the gradual abolishment of slavery—and proclaiming the emancipation of all slaves within States remaining in insurrection on the first of January, 1863."[4]

Two years later, Lincoln apparently told the artist Francis B. Carpenter, who was living in the White House while painting a portrait of the first reading of the Emancipation Proclamation: "I felt that we had reached the end of our rope on the plan of operations we had been pursuing; that we had about played our last card, and must change our tactics, or lose the game."[5]

Welles later recalled that the president said there were "differences in the Cabinet on the slavery question, and on emancipation, but he invited free discussion on the important step he was about to take; and to relieve each one from embarrassment, he wished it understood that the question was settled in his own mind." He had personally "dwelt much and long on the subject" and had reached his conclusion, but he wanted to hear what the members of the cabinet thought.[6]

Lincoln then read the first draft of what became the Emancipation Proclamation. It began by citing Section 6 of the Confiscation Act, which gave those in rebellion sixty days to resume their allegiance after a public warning and proclamation made by the president, or else face seizure and confiscation of their property. In the draft, Lincoln also noted that he intended to urge the next Congress to provide pecuniary support for schemes of gradual, compensated "abolishment of slavery" and to restore constitutional relations among the states. Finally, "as a fit and necessary military measure for effecting this object, I, as Commander-in-Chief of the Army and Navy of the United States, do order and declare that on the first of January in the year of Our Lord one thousand, eight hundred and sixty-three, all persons held as slaves within any state or states, wherein the constitutional authority of the United States shall not then be practically recognized, submitted to, and maintained, shall then, thenceforward, and forever, be free."[7]

In the ensuing discussion, Chase said he would give the measure his "cordial support," but he preferred that there be no new initiatives on compensated emancipation, and that instead of a presidential proclamation of emancipation, the objective be "quietly accomplished by allowing Generals to organize and arm the slaves (thus avoiding depredation and massacre on the one hand, and support to the insurrection on the other) and by directing the Commanders of Departments to proclaim emancipation." Montgomery Blair opposed the policy of emancipation on the grounds that it would "cost the Administration the fall elections." Edward Bates, the attorney general, offered his approval but "wished deportation to be coupled with emancipation." According to naval secretary Gideon Welles, Bates argued "it was impossible . . . for the two races to assimilate but by amalgamation and they could not amalgamate without degradation and demoralization to the white race." As a result, Bates favored deportation. "These were also the President's views," added Welles.[8]

The secretary of state, William Seward, then spoke. According to Welles, he said nothing about the merits of the issue—but then Welles and Seward did not get along. According to Francis Carpenter, Seward approved of the policy but opposed the timing. Welles also said that Seward thought issuing a proclamation should be postponed to a "more auspicious period" when it would not be "received and considered as a despairing cry—a shriek from and for the Administration, rather than for freedom." In Welles's account, the president said Seward's idea "'was that it would be construed our last shriek on the retreat.' (This was his precise expression)." Seward was particularly concerned about European reaction, and feared that rather than dissuade England and France from intervening on behalf of the Confederacy, it might induce them to do so for fear of losing their supply of cotton and out of concern for the safety of slaveholders. And so Lincoln decided to put aside the proclamation for the moment, awaiting a reversal of military fortunes. He did, however, issue the proclamation required of him by the sixth section of the Confiscation Act, a proclamation identical to the first paragraph of the draft discussed at the cabinet meeting on July 22.[9]

The delay came as a surprise to Francis B. Cutting, a New York lawyer and former Democratic congressman. Nearly seven years later, Cutting sent Edwin Stanton a lengthy account of a meeting he recalled having with the president on the morning of July 22. Cutting was visiting with Stanton, and when he told the secretary of war he "fully & heartily concurred" that slavery was the root of the war and that something needed to be done, Stanton brought him to meet with Lincoln. Stanton must have felt that the president would be encouraged to hear from a New York Democrat who supported "the necessity & expedience, as a war measure, of issuing without delay a Proclamation of Emancipation."

Cutting recounted to Stanton that in his meeting with the president, "I argued that the emancipation of the slaves would produce a very important & beneficial effect on our relations with foreign powers . . . that in the face of a Proclamation striking off the shackles of the bondsmen, and making their freedom . . . an issue of the struggle, their Governments would not dare to take sides in favor of the masters or to recognize the Confederacy based as it was on human slavery, not merely as its cornerstone but as the main and entire foundation." The president, according to Cutting, "from time to time made various suggestions & inquiries. Finally he remarked he had no doubt that the proposed measure would result most advantageously to our Foreign Relations, which had given him much uneasiness."[10]

But Lincoln told Cutting that "his difficulty was in foreseeing its effects upon the people of the border States, and he requested me to consider what would be its practical operation on them." Cutting answered that "we had already sacrificed too much in the vain attempt to conciliate these people, a majority of whom were at heart disloyal, or not better than neutral." Cutting left the president believing that an emancipation proclamation would be issued.[11]

Lincoln's ongoing concern with the fate of Kentucky led him to read the Proclamation to James Speed, a lawyer and antislavery Unionist state senator in Kentucky, as well as older brother of Joshua Speed, Lincoln's closest friend since he had arrived in Springfield in 1837. James, Lincoln's future attorney general, wrote from Louisville on July 28 that he had pondered the document and concluded "it will do no good; most probably much harm. The negro can not be emancipated by proclamation." Speed went on to articulate a position that looked beyond the wartime abolition of slavery. He believed that giving freedom to slaves meant nothing unless they desired it, because once military force had been removed, the freedmen "would sink into slavery again." "If the negro is to be free," declared Speed, "he must strike for it himself."[12]

At this point, Lincoln was not ready to give thought to how to make freedom endure. There was a war to be won, and, with the decision made, he began the work of preparing the public for his shift in policy. As was his wont, he did it piecemeal—a private letter here, a public statement there, sometimes a hint hidden in a feint in the opposite direction. In response to a letter from Reverdy Johnson of Maryland, who was sent to New Orleans by the State Department as a special agent to investigate complaints from foreign consuls about the conduct of the military in the occupied city, and who reported to Lincoln that Union support had weakened as a result of the belief that "it is the *purpose* of the Govt. to force the Emancipation of the slaves," the president asked: If the people of Louisiana did not simply take their place in the Union as before, "should they not receive harder blows rather than lighter ones?" As for heeding the advice of supposed friends of the Union, he confessed that "this appeal of professed friends has paralyzed me more in this struggle than any other thing." He was not about to "surrender this game leaving any available card unplayed."

Lincoln was equally direct with Cuthbert Bullitt, acting collector of customs in New Orleans: "The paralysis—the dead palsy—of the government in this whole struggle is, that this class of men will do nothing for the government, nothing for themselves, except demanding that the government shall not strike its open enemies, lest they be struck by accident. . . . It is a military necessity to have men and money; and we can get neither, in sufficient numbers, or amounts, if we keep from, or drive from, our lines, slaves coming to them." "What would you do in my position," he asked rhetorically: "Would you drop the war where it is? Or would you prosecute it in future with elder-stalk squirts, charged with rose water?" To the New York financier August Belmont he explained that "broken eggs cannot be mended. . . . This government cannot much longer play a game in which it stakes all, and its enemies stake nothing." (Two days before Lincoln's letter to Belmont, the Harvard botanist Asa Gray had written to Charles Darwin: "There is no use trying any longer to pick up our eggs gently, very careful not to break any. The South forces us at length . . . to act with vigor, not to say rigor.")[13]

At the same time, Lincoln was clearly so good at weighing the pros and cons of any action that he confused his good friend Leonard Swett, an attorney with whom he had practiced law in Illinois. After discussing the issue of emancipation with the president, Swett informed his wife, "He will issue no proclamation emancipating negroes."[14]

To some correspondents Lincoln, as far as we know, did not respond. A letter from the Pennsylvania journalist Benjamin Bannan, dated July 24, urged the president "to emancipate the Slaves as a military necessity."

> You may overrun the South with an Army of 7 or 800,000 men, but after that is done, it will require at least a half million stationed in the South to keep the slaveholders in subjection. . . . Let me tell you that *you can never conquer and hold the South, so long as slavery exists— except at an expense that no nation can sustain.* . . . A decree of general Emancipation by you now would be hailed as the greatest stroke of policy that any Government ever practiced, not only by the people of this Nation, but throughout the whole Christian world, and would immortalize the man who dared to do it.[15]

By August, word was circulating in Washington that Lincoln had decided to issue an emancipation proclamation. *"Vulgatior fama est"* ("Rumor is rather widespread"), proclaimed Gurowski. The count then went on, in his inimitable style, to offer his understanding of what had transpired in July:

> Mr. Lincoln was already raising his hand to sign a stirring proclamation on the question of emancipation; that Stanton was upholding the President's arm that it might not grow weak in the performance of a sacred duty; that Chase, Bates, and Welles joined Stanton; but that Messrs. Seward and Blair so firmly objected that the President's outstretched hand slowly began to fall back; that to precipitate the mortification, Thurlow Weed was telegraphed; that Thurlow Weed presented to Mr. Lincoln the medusa-head of Irish riots in the North against the emancipation of slaves in the South; that Mr. Lincoln's mind faltered ... before such a Chinese shadow, and that thus once more slavery was saved.[16]

Thurlow Weed, an influential New York editor and political operator who in 1860 thought he had sewn up the Republican presidential nomination for his friend Seward, was always antislavery, but he favored an approach that, earlier in his career, he had called "rational emancipation." Sensitive to public opinion, Weed's beliefs, according to one rival, "were convictions so long as they harmonized with the majority, and on that majority depended his earnestness in their utterance. He realized at an early day that nothing so offends as unpopular views, and he made it a point never to offend in that way. As he had no views of his own, this was easy." Less kindly, Sumner called him "one of the marplots [meddlers] of our history."[17]

It so happened that early on the morning of July 23, Francis Cutting ran into Weed at Willard's Hotel in D.C. The two exchanged greetings, and then Weed—as Cutting reported in a letter to Stanton—"stated in substance that he had undone in the evening what I had nearly accomplished in the morning; that after further reflection the President had decided to postpone the Proclamation." Weed had told the president that the Proclamation could not be enforced in rebel states; it would merely add to their hatred, and it would "occasion serious disaffection" in the border states. Sumner, who wanted the Proclamation issued without delay, would later offer this assessment of Weed: "He did not understand the crisis. His diagnosis was utterly wrong, & his nostrums ever since have been injurious. He & Seward set themselves against Emancipation."[18]

Weed was overjoyed when, several weeks later, Lincoln issued a public statement that the New Yorker took as evidence that the president opposed a policy of emancipation. Lincoln had responded to a lengthy public letter by Horace Greeley, the eccentric and impetuous editor of the *New York Tribune,* printed on August 19 and titled "The Prayer of Twenty Millions."

Lincoln's relationship with Greeley had seesawed over the years. In 1858, the editor had encouraged Illinois voters to support the Democratic nominee, Stephen Douglas, during the senatorial debates. But after hearing Lincoln's Cooper Union address on February 27, 1860, Greeley had called him "one of Nature's orators," and his opposition to Lincoln's New York rivals Seward and Weed had led him to play a role in Lincoln's nomination later that year. But then, after Bull Run, Greeley's bold headline "Forward to Richmond" had brought derision to the editor and embarrassment to the administration. On January 3, 1862, Lincoln had attended a lecture by Greeley at the Smithsonian. He'd sat on the platform, along with Salmon Chase and other dignitaries. He'd listened as Greeley, with his pince-nez glasses and flowing white hair, proclaimed that in the war "slavery is the aggressor, and has earned a rebel's doom." In March, Lincoln had written to Greeley to thank him for supporting his emancipation policy, but cautioned the influential editor that "we should urge it *persuasively,* and not *menacingly,* upon the South." Relations between the men would cool as Greeley turned defeatist—he would take the initiative on peace negotiations held at Niagara Falls in 1864, which would cause Lincoln consternation—and he would fail to support Lincoln's reelection. By August 1864, Lincoln would reportedly tell Welles that Greeley "is an old shoe—good for nothing now, whatever he has been."[19]

But in August 1862, Greeley still was treading heavily. In his public letter, he stated that those who had supported Lincoln's election were "sorely disappointed and deeply pained by the policy you seem to be pursuing with regard to the slaves of the Rebels." Greeley went on to issue a series of indictments: that Lincoln had failed to discharge his duties with respect to the emancipation provisions of the Second Confiscation Act; that Lincoln was too subservient to the opinions of border-state politicians; that Lincoln was too deferential to "Rebel slavery." Greeley closed by insisting that the president enforce the Second Confiscation Act and give freedom to the slaves coming into Union lines.

Lincoln took the unusual step of responding to Greeley with a letter of his own, published in the *Daily National Intelligencer* and reprinted in numerous newspapers, including the *Tribune*. Dated August 22, Lincoln's pithy letter included a statement expressed with syllogistic precision: "My paramount object in this struggle *is* to save the Union, and it is *not* either to save or destroy slavery. If I could save the Union without freeing *any* slave I would do it, and if I could save it by freeing *all* the slaves I would do it; and if I could save it by freeing some and leaving others alone I would do that." He concluded by distinguishing his *"official"* duty from his "oft-expressed *personal* wish that all men every where could be free."[20]

Readers gathered from the letter whatever message they most wanted to believe. No wonder, then, that Thurlow Weed wrote that it "warmed the hearts, inspired the hopes, and stirred the patriotism of the People. Upon *that* Platform all can stand and work." Weed was content to let slavery "by its madness . . . inevitably destroy itself"; he felt he now had assurance, however, that the president would not be the agent of its destruction. But just as Weed saw Lincoln's response as making the case for restoring the Union regardless of slavery, Sydney Gay, the *Tribune*'s managing editor, wrote that the letter to Greeley "has infused new hope among us at the North who are anxiously awaiting that movement on your part which they believe will end the rebellion by removing its cause. I think the general impression is that as you are determined to save the Union tho' Slavery perish, you mean presently to announce that the destruction of Slavery is the price of our salvation." The *Daily Morning Chronicle* called the letter a "concise, expressive, and intelligent exposition," and the *Daily National Republican* thought it "decidedly Lincolnic."

By comparison, Adam Gurowski, never a fan, labeled Lincoln's response "the eternal dodging of a vital question." One writer called Lincoln's bluff: "The President says, in his letter to Mr. Greeley, that if he could save the Union by freeing *all* the slaves, he would do it. Why does he not set himself about it? He seems to talk as if he was able to free the slaves, if he would only undertake it."[21]

Lincoln could continue to maintain the distinction between the official and the personal when it came to the abolition of slavery; it was far more difficult, however, to separate the two when it came to the issue of the place of blacks in American society and what role they might play in military affairs. Lincoln was a longtime supporter of colonization—the resettlement of blacks in Africa or in other countries. The doctrine won support for any of a number of reasons: racial hatred, the belief that whites and freed blacks could not live peaceably together, opposition to social and political equality, anxiety over competition for labor. The American Colonization Society dated from 1816, and Henry Clay, Lincoln's political hero, had proposed various colonization schemes. Lincoln had espoused the doctrine throughout the 1850s, and would even remind Congress: "I cannot make it better known than it already is, that I strongly favor colonization."[22]

On August 14, Lincoln met with a group of five black leaders residing in Washington and spoke to them about the imperative of colonization. He argued that blacks should leave the country because "you and we are different races. We have between us a broader difference than exists between almost any other two races.... I think your race suffer very greatly, many of them by living among us, while ours suffer from your presence." "Even when you cease to be slaves," he said to these freemen, "you are yet far removed from being placed on an equality with the white race." Lincoln lamented the evil effects of slavery on the white race, effects which could be seen in the amount of blood poured out on the battlefields. "It is better for us both," he concluded, "to be separated." He had in mind a location in Central America for a colony, a central spot with good harbors, natural resources, and coal mines. He admitted that the political situation in Central America was not stable, but "to your colored race they have no objection." He asked for volunteers. One hundred? Fifty? "If I can find twenty-five able-bodied men, with a mixture of women and children," he thought, "I could make a successful commencement."[23]

Assorted colonization schemes had emerged since the start of the war, but none had succeeded. In 1861–1862, some 2,000 free blacks emigrated to

Haiti, but they became disillusioned with life there and many returned to the United States. At various times, Lincoln entertained colonization projects for Honduras, Costa Rica, Ecuador, Guadeloupe, Martinique, Santo Domingo, the British West Indies, and Dutch Surinam. There was even a proposal, made by a Republican congressman at an early point in the war, to confiscate slaves and colonize them in Florida. At the moment of his speech to the delegation of black leaders, Lincoln had in mind a plan to acquire from the Chiriqui Improvement Company two million acres in what is today western Panama. Lincoln appointed Senator Samuel Pomeroy of Kansas as colonization agent, and authorized him to begin recruiting blacks for a new colony. Some thought the new colony should be called "Lincolnia."

Blacks had long opposed colonization, and they continued to do so. The men Lincoln spoke with replied that they believed it "inexpedient, inauspicious and impolitic to agitate the subject of emigration of the colored people of this country anywhere." One abolitionist, writing in the *Liberator,* noted that at the end of the August 14 meeting the president had said to the men, "Take your full time—no hurry at all" in responding. "That has been the character of the war from the beginning," he chided, "and will be to the close of his authority. . . . I am soul-sick of all this cant about the President, to prove that he is an honest man. Away with it all! And judge him by his acts, not his intentions." Another writer could not comprehend how the president, "in the midst of a war that is threatening the very life of the nation, is turning aside the work of crushing the rebellion, to see if he can find 'twenty-five able bodied men, with women and children,' with whom to commence a settlement somewhere in the Central American region, and, by his own account, not under very inviting prospects." Gurowski thought the whole address "clap-trap," and pointed out that Lincoln could not deliver what he promised because it is "utterly impossible and beyond his power" to form an independent community in an already sovereign country. Lincoln's views were a "display of ignorance or of humbug, or perhaps of both." Reading an account of the interview in the newspaper, an exasperated Salmon Chase wrote in his diary, "How much better would be a manly protest against prejudice of color!—and a wise effort to give freemen homes in America!"[24]

Lincoln's address became fodder for the humorist Robert Henry Newall, who published satirical pieces under the name Orpheus C. Kerr (as in "Office Seeker"). Newall was one of Lincoln's favorite writers, and the president read him avidly, though whether he found humor in the send-up of his colonization address is unknown:

> Perhaps you have not been here all your lives. Your race is suffering the greatest wrong that ever was; but when you cease to suffer, your sufferings are still far from an equality with our sufferings. Our white men are now changing their base of operations daily, and often taking Malvern Hills. This is on your account. You are the cause of it. How you have caused it I will not attempt to explain, for I do not know; but it is better for us both to be separated, and it is vilely selfish in you (I do not speak unkindly) to wish to remain here in preference to going to Nova Zembla. The fact that we have always oppressed you renders you still more blamable.[25]

Frederick Douglass could find nothing to laugh about. The president, he thought, was "making himself appear silly and ridiculous. . . . He has been unusually garrulous, characteristically foggy, remarkably illogical and untimely in his utterances, often saying that which nobody wanted to hear." Douglass went on at length, puncturing the fallacies in Lincoln's argument. To say that blacks caused the war was like a horse thief's pleading that the existence of the horse is the reason for his theft; and Lincoln was wrong in denying that in other countries distinct races lived peaceably together, that racial prejudice was the result of slavery, and that if blacks had come as free immigrants "they never would have become the objects of aversion and bitter persecution, nor would there ever have been divulged and propagated the arrogant and malignant nonsense about natural repellency and the incompatibility of races." Douglass also criticized the tone of Lincoln's speech, constructed "as to think any but the simplest phrases and constructions would be above the power of [his black listeners'] comprehension." In his endless delaying, his constant concern for the border states, his refusal to take any bold, decisive action, and his seeming antipathy to principles of justice and humanity, the president had turned his back on those who had elected him.[26]

Not everyone denounced Lincoln for the message he had delivered to the black leaders. One writer believed, "The negro may well say that under President Lincoln he has had his first hearing in the White House. Other President's have bought and sold him, and driven them from the territories, and closed their eyes to the nefarious system under which he was captured in Africa and dragged over the ocean in chains. But President Lincoln has listened to his story and given him counsel and advice. It may not be what his most ostentatious friends would like to hear," but the reality, concluded the writer, was that "there must forever be an antagonism of race" and that "the star of the black man is in the east."[27]

Lincoln's most recent colonization scheme came at the very moment that, with the passage of the Militia Act, blacks were being accepted for service into the military, though not yet as armed soldiers. Earlier in the year, Frederick Douglass had called for enlistment of blacks, warning: "We are fighting the rebels with only one hand, when we ought to be fighting them with both. We are recruiting our troops in the towns and villages of the North, when we ought to be recruiting them on the plantations of the South. We are striking the rebels with our soft, white hand, when we should be striking with the iron hand of the black man, which we keep chained behind us."[28]

As early as December 1861, Simon Cameron, Edwin Stanton's predecessor as secretary of war, had stated in his annual report: "It is as clearly the right of the Government to arm slaves when it may become necessary as it is to use gunpowder taken from the enemy." Lincoln rejected the report and ordered it recalled. Some generals managed on the quiet to raise regiments—David Hunter in South Carolina, for example. But after writing a sarcastic response to a congressional inquiry, Hunter was ordered to disband the unit. On August 25, 1862, Stanton, as secretary of war, authorized General Rufus Saxton, military governor of contrabands on the Sea Islands of South Carolina, to "arm, uniform, equip, and receive into the service of the United States such number of volunteers of African descent as you may deem expedient, not exceeding 5,000." But this was an experiment, not a policy.[29]

Lincoln remained firmly opposed to arming the slaves. At a cabinet meeting on July 22, Chase reported that "the question of arming the slaves was then brought up and I advocated it warmly. The President was unwilling to adopt this measure. . . . The impression left upon my mind by the whole discussion was, that while the President thought that the organization, equipment and arming of negroes . . . would be productive of more evil than good, he was not unwilling that Commanders should, at their discretion, arm, for purely defensive purposes, slaves coming within their lines." On August 4, Lincoln told a delegation from Indiana which had come to offer two black regiments that "he was not prepared to go the length of enlisting negroes as soldiers"; he feared that "to arm the negroes would turn 50,000 bayonets from the loyal Border States against us that were for us." According to one account, the "discussion gradually became warm," and ended with Lincoln declaring: "Gentlemen, you have my decision. I have made my mind up deliberately and mean to adhere to it. It embodies my best judgment, and if the people are dissatisfied, I will resign and let Mr. Hamlin try it."[30]

One soldier, in the 8th Illinois Infantry, wrote: "We are all 'rejoicing' that Abe refuses to accept the negroes as soldiers. Aside from the immense dissatisfaction it would create in our army, the South would arm and put in the field three negroes to our one." On August 11, Senator Sumner informed the Duchess of Argyll: "The President's great difficulty now is to arming the blacks. He invites them as laborers, but he still holds back from the last step to which everything irresistibly tends. He says, 'Wait; time is essential.' That is, after an interval of time we shall be able to do what he thinks we cannot do now."[31]

What was he waiting for? A military victory might allow him to issue an emancipation proclamation and make it appear that it was not an act of desperation, but military defeat might force him to act without worrying about public opinion, because to lose the war would be to lose all—union for the nation and freedom for the slaves. At the end of August, Union forces were again defeated at Bull Run. This second battle began with Stonewall Jackson cutting off the federal supply base at Manassas. In a battle that raged from August 28 to August 30, Union general John Pope was outsmarted and outmaneuvered by generals Robert E. Lee, Stonewall Jackson, and James Longstreet, whose forces arrived in time to reinforce the Confederate line. Longstreet's force of 28,000 counterattacked and drove the Union forces more than a mile. Sixteen thousand of Pope's 60,000 men were killed, wounded, or missing; the Confederates suffered some 9,000 casualties out of 50,000 men. It was a humiliating, demoralizing defeat for the Union. "For the first time I believe it possible that Washington may be taken," wrote the correspondent for the *New York Tribune.* An officer confessed that "our men are sick of war. They fight without an aim and without enthusiasm." Lincoln fell into depression. Edward Bates described him as "wrung by the bitterest anguish—said he felt almost ready to hang himself." Gideon Welles said the president was "sadly perplexed and distressed by events."[32]

If so, it's no wonder he thought more than ever about divine providence. In a fragment on divine will he wondered which side God truly favored, because "God can not be *for,* and *against* the same thing at the same time." "He could have either saved or destroyed the Union without a human contest," thought Lincoln, "yet the contest began. And having begun he could give the final victory to either side any day. Yet the contest proceeds."[33]

On September 13, a delegation of Christian clergymen from Chicago presented Lincoln with a memorial (petition) in favor of a national proclamation of emancipation. Lincoln explained that he had been dwelling on the subject "for weeks past, and I may even say for months." Noting that he had been given "the most opposite opinions and advice" about emancipation "by religious men, who are equally certain that they represent the Divine will," Lincoln went on to remark that he hoped it wouldn't be "irreverent" for him to say that if God "would reveal his will to others, on a point so connected with my duty, it might be supposed he would reveal it to me . . . for . . . it is my earnest desire to know the will of Providence in this matter. *And if I can learn what it is I will do it!* These are not, however, the days of miracles, and I suppose it will be granted that I am not to expect a direct revelation." What he needed to do was "study the plain physical facts of the case."

The lawyer in Lincoln had mulled over "the merits of the case," but this was a particularly difficult subject, one on which "good men do not agree." On the one hand, he questioned whether under current circumstances an emancipation proclamation would do any good—perhaps it would be seen as "inoperative, like the Pope's bull [edict] against the comet!" How could the president's word alone free any slaves? Even the Confiscation Act had so far freed no one. And even if a proclamation of freedom liberated the enslaved, there was the problem of *"what should we do with them?* How can we feed and care for such a multitude?" He expressed dismay that when the rebels took black prisoners and sold them off at auction, *"I am very ungenerously attacked for it!* . . . What *could* I do?" Lincoln just didn't know what good a proclamation would accomplish. On the other hand, he told the Chicago delegation he had no objections to a proclamation on legal or constitutional grounds, for he believed he had the right as commander-in-chief to take any measures necessary. Nor was he concerned about the risk of insurrection or possible "massacre at the South" on account of emancipation. It was simply a matter of whether or not it was a "practical war measure."

The delegation of clergymen presented the other side: they argued that while good men disagreed, *"the truth was somewhere"* and the president's job was to locate it. Lincoln wondered how he could enforce an emancipation proclamation when he couldn't even enforce the Constitution, and the delegation responded that the former was a means to accomplishing the latter. A sea change in opinion on emancipation had been taking place, "especially since late reverses have awakened thought as to the extreme peril of the nation." Emancipation, they argued, would provide "a glorious principle for which to suffer and fight," would win over European support, and would bring *"both laborers and soldiers"* into the army.

Lincoln conceded a few of these points, emphasizing that emancipation "unquestionably . . . would weaken the rebels by drawing off their laborers, which is of great importance." But the president again wondered what to do with the blacks: "If we were to arm them, I fear that in a few weeks the arms would be in the hands of the rebels." And though he anticipated that the delegation would respond with "scorn and contempt," he expressed his long-standing fear that an emancipation proclamation would cause "fifty thousand bayonets in the Union armies from the Border States" to go over to the rebels.

The delegation responded one more time, arguing forcefully that the unifying idea of constitutional government had been threatened by slavery alone and that "the people demand emancipation to preserve and perpetuate" it. Lincoln agreed: "That is the true ground of our difficulties." As for the fear of the border states' reaction—even if there was a certain amount of loss it would be more than made up for by the "increased spirit" nourished by emancipation. In drawing the discussion to a close, Lincoln assured the delegation: "I have not decided against a proclamation of liberty to the slaves, but hold the matter under advisement. And I can assure you that the subject is on my mind, by day and night, more than any other."[34]

It was a vintage performance by Lincoln. John Hay recalled that, with respect to an emancipation proclamation, "if any one tried to dissuade him from it, he gave the argument in its favor. If others urged it upon him, he exhausted the reasoning against it. Even when it was resolved upon, written, copied, and lying in his desk only waiting promulgation, a delegation of clergymen waited on him to insist upon such a measure, and he confounded them all by his close and logical argument against it."[35]

On the same day that Lincoln discussed matters with the Chicago clergymen, three soldiers, camping in a field of clover near Frederick, Maryland, came upon a document wrapped around three cigars in an envelope. It turned out to be Robert E. Lee's Special Order No. 191, detailing plans for a Confederate invasion of the state. General McClellan, now back in command, exulted over the discovery, and expected, as a result, nothing less than "decisive results" over Lee and the Army of Northern Virginia. Providence had chosen sides.

Yet McClellan again failed to act, waiting nearly eighteen hours to put his army into motion. By then, Lee's army had shifted position. Finally, on September 17, McClellan's forces attacked Lee's army, situated on high ground east of Sharpsburg, near Antietam Creek. The armies fought through a day that saw repeated attacks, counterattacks, and missed opportunities to exploit temporary advantages. The battle ended with combined casualties of over 23,000. Each side suffered more than 2,000 battlefield dead, and thousands more would perish from their wounds. It remains the single bloodiest day in American military history. A private with the 14th Indiana called it "one of the hardest fought battles as ever was known on the American Continent." Afterward a New Hampshire surgeon wrote to his wife, "When I think of the battle of Antietam it seems so strange. Who permits it? To see or feel that a power is in existence that can and will hurl masses of men against each other in deadly conflict—slaying each other by the thousands—mangling and deforming their fellow men is almost impossible. But it is so and why we cannot know."[36]

Though the battle was a draw tactically, strategically it was a victory for the Union. Lee's invasion had been stopped, and newspapers throughout the North played up the triumph, celebrating a restoration of the "hopes of the nation" and proclaiming that Antietam would be "seen and felt in the destinies of the Nation for centuries to come." Lincoln had the victory he had been waiting for; God had decided. It came at a horrific price, but Lincoln had met adversity with equanimity time and again. As Gurowski put it with typical pungency, "In the midst of the most stirring and exciting—nay, death-giving—news, Mr. Lincoln has always a story to tell."[37]

On September 19, Lincoln received a letter from Robert Dale Owen, a socialist who had helped to found the utopian community of New Harmony in Indiana, and who was elected to two terms in the House of Representatives as a Democrat in the 1840s. Imploring Lincoln to act on emancipation, he declared: "It is within your power at this very moment not only to consummate an act of enlightened statesmanship, but, as the instrument of the Almighty, to restore to freedom a race of men." He insisted that the rebels expected it; indeed, "they read EMANCIPATION in all the signs of the times." He reminded the president that the sixty-day warning period for those in rebellion to resume their allegiance—a period which, pursuant to Section 6 of the Second Confiscation Act, Lincoln had proclaimed on July 25—was nearly up, and that therefore the government would soon be able to act on the seizure of property. "The twenty-third of September approaches," Owen pointed out, "the date when the sixty-day notice you have given to the rebels will expire—expire without other reply to your warning than the invasion of Maryland and a menace to Pennsylvania. Is it to rest there? Patiently we have waited the time. Is nothing to follow? Are our enemies to boast that we speak brave words—and there an end to it? What a day, if you will it, may that twenty-third of September become! The very turning point in the nation's fate!"[38]

Secretary Chase, to whom Owen had sent the letter for transmission to Lincoln, made certain the president saw it. "I lost no time," he informed Owen on September 20, "in placing it in the hands of the President." "It cannot fail to impress him powerfully," thought Chase. "God grant that it may impel him to action."[39]

John Hay knew what was coming. The handsome, boyish, twenty-three-year-old secretary lived in the White House and was devoted to the president. In addition to his executive duties, he kept his hand in journalism and wrote anonymous pieces for a number of newspapers, including the *Missouri Republican*. In those reports, he commented on events, explained the actions of the administration, and, most of all, defended Lincoln who "has so long and successfully maintained an attitude of dignified reticence." The phrase aptly described the man who disappointed fanatical abolitionists and slave-mongers alike, and Hay tried to explain the president's stance:

[He] had the best possible reasons for his reticence. He was not unde-cided, apathetic or stubborn in the matter. He knew that, in the first place, the contest in which we are engaged is the one unique of its kind, without precedents or analogies in history. Its character shifts with the shifting seasons; its complexion changes with the staining leaves. He knew that any declaration of opinion which he might publicly make would be rendered obsolete by the progress of events before it had reached the newer States. Secondly, his utterances would instantly form an issue upon which would divide and fiercely fight those who were now most strongly united in defense of the Union. While the contest could be better carried on without an executive pronunciamento, the President thought best to keep silent.[40]

But no more. Lincoln had been consistent in his approach. He had tried to conduct the war in such a way as to make the rebellious states return to their allegiance; he had neither returned to slavery those slaves who came into Union hands nor encouraged them to run away or rebel; he had advo-cated a voluntary system of colonization; he had sought repeatedly to per-suade the border states to embrace a policy of gradual emancipation; he had supported a judicious confiscation act and retained wide discretion in matters of amnesty and exemption; he had never vacillated from opposition to the extension of slavery in the territories; and, finally, "his highest hope has been the restoration of the Old Union." Hay, in his desire to reassure Missouri readers, exaggerated when he insisted that the president had time and again "stood between slavery and those who would destroy it, as a strong and steadfast bulwark, waiting, hoping, praying to God that the Bor-der States would read the signs of the times that the National arms would prevail, that the maniacy of treason would give way to the truth and the light of returning loyalty." Yet if not a bulwark, Lincoln had certainly drawn a boundary that allowed slavery to continue where it already existed. All of that had now passed; eighteen months of war had stripped away his reticence.[41]

On September 22, five days after Antietam, Lincoln called a special cabinet meeting. As the men gathered, they sensed that the president wanted to make an important announcement. But first, he read a story.

THE (FORT) MONROE DOCTRINE.

1. Once the war began, slaves fleeing to Union lines were labeled "contrabands." This print recognizes the new situation: a slaveholder calls for the runaway to return, while the slave thumbs his nose at him and declares he is now a contraband. *The (Fort) Monroe Doctrine* (1861; Library of Congress).

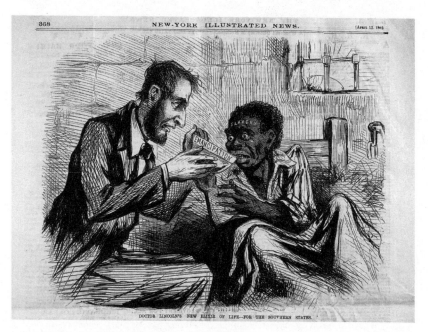

2. Issued after the abolition of slavery in Washington, D.C., this cartoon shows a bedridden slave being nourished back to health by Lincoln, who offers the cup of emancipation. "Doctor Lincoln's New Elixir of Life—for the Southern States," *New-York Illustrated News*, April 12, 1862 (courtesy of the American Antiquarian Society).

"A HUMANE BUT OFFICIOUS HUNTER."

Mr. Lincoln—"NOW THEN, YOU BOY, THAT BURD AIN'T YOURS—WHAT DO YOU LET HER LOOSE FOR? I'LL HAVE YOU UNDERSTAND THAT, WHEN I WANT ANY BURDS LET LOOSE, I'LL LET THEM LOOSE MYSELF."

3. In May 1861, Lincoln revoked General David Hunter's order that freed slaves in the Department of the South, comprising South Carolina, Georgia, and Florida. A cartoon in *Frank Leslie's Budget of Fun* depicts the president slapping Hunter, who is mesmerized by the black crow of slavery, and declaring that "when I want any birds let loose, I'll let them loose myself." "A Humane But Officious Hunter," *Frank Leslie's Budget of Fun*, June 1, 1862.

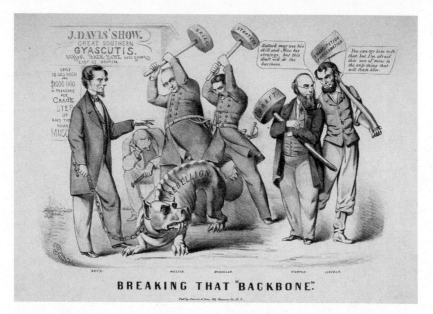

4. This popular Currier & Ives print reads left to right: Jefferson Davis displays the monster of rebellion; General Henry Halleck's skill and General George B. McClellan's strategy have failed to overcome it; Horace Greeley is confident a military draft will do the job. But Lincoln brandishes the axe of the preliminary Emancipation Proclamation as the sure way to break the monster's back. *Breaking That "Backbone"* (1862; Library of Congress).

5. *Punch,* an English weekly of satire and humor, depicts Lincoln's Emancipation Proclamation as the last card being played by a crazed gambler atop a keg of gunpowder. Unknown to the cartoonist, Lincoln had privately told one supporter that the Proclamation "is my last trump card." "Abe Lincoln's Last Card," *Punch,* October 18, 1862.

6. Adalbert Johann Volck, a Baltimore dentist, created a series of anti-Union etchings. Here he portrays Lincoln as using a devil's inkstand to draft the Emancipation Proclamation. On the wall are a portrait of John Brown and a painting of the insurrection against the French on Santo Domingo, representing two of the slave South's worst nightmares. Beneath Lincoln's foot is the trampled Constitution. Adalbert Johann Volck, *The Emancipation Proclamation* (1864; Library of Congress).

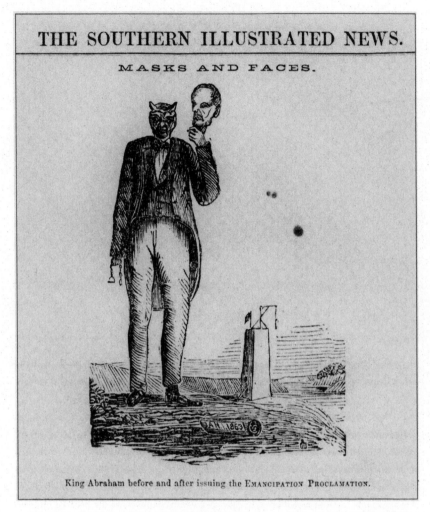

7. The *Southern Illustrated News* depicts "King Abraham" as a dictatorial devil hiding behind a human face. In the background, a gallows for Lincoln's enemies stands atop the partially completed Washington Monument. "Masks and Faces," *Southern Illustrated News,* November 8, 1862.

GRAND SWEEPSTAKES FOR 1862.
Won by the Celebrated Horse "EMANCIPATION"

Emancipation. Old Abe 1.1.1. Contraband. C. S. 2.3.2. John Brown. J. A. 3.2.3. Philosopher. H. G. 4.4.4

8. This rare print suggests that Lincoln is using emancipation opportunistically to win the elections of 1862 and outflank the more radical members of his party. He rides "Emancipation," and finishes ahead of Senator Charles Sumner on "Contraband," Massachusetts Governor John Andrew on "John Brown," and antislavery editor Horace Greeley on "Philosopher." A black family in racist caricature celebrates as a white couple views the proceedings with distaste. *Grand Sweepstakes for 1862* (1862; courtesy of the American Antiquarian Society).

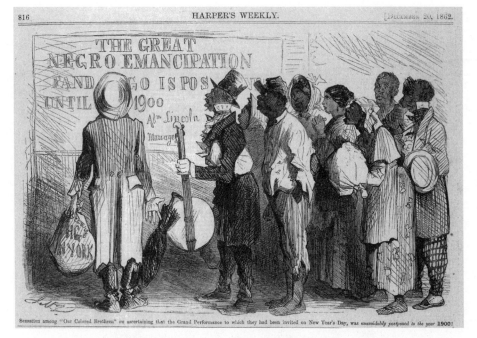

Sensation among "Our Colored Brethren" on ascertaining that the Grand Performance to which they had been invited on New Year's Day, was *unavoidably postponed to the year* **1900!**

9. Lincoln's Annual Message to Congress in December 1862 perplexed supporters of emancipation, who did not know what to make of his recommendation for a constitutional amendment that would abolish slavery gradually no later than January 1, 1900. In this cartoon, a group of blacks stand in shock as they read that emancipation has been postponed until 1900. "The Great Negro Emancipation," *Harper's Weekly,* December 20, 1862 (courtesy of the American Antiquarian Society).

10. During the Civil War, Thomas Nast's work for *Harper's Weekly* redefined the art of the cartoon. He emerged as the premier political cartoonist of the day, and he remained with the magazine until 1886. "Emancipation" is typical of his panoramic, narrative style: on the left is slavery's past, while in the center and on the right are scenes of freedom's future. In prints issued after the war, the pendant of Father Time was replaced with a portrait of Lincoln. Thomas Nast, "Emancipation," *Harper's Weekly,* January 24, 1863 (courtesy of the American Antiquarian Society).

One Hundred Days

It was a somewhat remarkable fact . . . that there were just one hundred days between the dates of the two proclamations, issued upon the 22nd of September and the 1st of January. I had not made the calculation at the time.

—Abraham Lincoln, quoted in Francis B. Carpenter,
Six Months at the White House with Abraham Lincoln (1866)

5

Judgments

Handbills appeared all over town: citizens in Washington had organized a serenade for 9 P.M., on September 24, 1862, to honor the president at the Executive Mansion. Gideon Welles reported that the Emancipation Proclamation "has been in the main well received, but there is some violent opposition, and the friends of the measure have made this demonstration to show their approval." When the music came to an end, Lincoln came out to speak. He pretended not to know what had occasioned the spontaneous celebration, and then he admitted, "I suppose I understand it." The crowd laughed, yelling back, "That you do!" and "You thoroughly understand it!"

"What I did," Lincoln said, "I did after very full deliberation, and under a very heavy and solemn sense of responsibility. . . . I can only trust in God I have made no mistake."

"No mistake," responded the serenaders. "Go ahead, you're right."

"I shall make no attempt on this occasion to sustain what I have done or said by any comment."

"That's unnecessary; we understand it."

"It is now for the country and the world to pass judgment on it."[1]

Whitelaw Reid, a young writer and editor from Ohio who contributed dispatches to the Cincinnati *Gazette* under the pen name "Agate," was among "the surging crowd." He thought,

It is a scene well worth remembering—one that History will treasure up forever: the President of a great Republic—great even in its misery and shame—standing at his window, amid the clouds and gloom with which his decree of Universal Emancipation is ushered in, receiving the congratulations of his People for his bold word for Freedom and the Right, as against all constituted guarantees of Wrong, hesitating as he thanks them, doubting even amid the ringing cheers of the populace, trusting in God he has made no mistake, tremulously (so tremulously this utterance seems choked by his agitation) awaiting the judgment of the Country and the World.[2]

Reid captured something essential about Lincoln's character: his humility. Other politicians might have trumpeted how momentous their actions were, but not Lincoln. He worked methodically, carefully, deliberately; but still, when he made a decision, he understood that it might prove to be ineffectual or even wrong. He realized that intentions did not guarantee outcomes. There was no guidebook for him to follow. And so he stated his determination to act in one hundred days, and then paid close attention to the myriad responses.

From the White House, the serenade moved on to treasury secretary Salmon Chase's residence, where a number of Republican politicians and generals had gathered. They all chirped with joy. John Hay, Lincoln's secretary, noted: "They gleefully and merrily called each other and themselves abolitionists, and seemed to enjoy the novel sensation of appropriating that horrible name. . . . They all seemed to feel a sort of new and exhilarated life; they breathed freer; the Prest. Procn. had freed them as well as the slaves."

It was an astute observation. For a long time, many who detested slavery felt they could not act on their convictions, because the slaveholder had a legal right to his property and the nonslaveholder was obligated to respect that right. This was the point of Lincoln's remarkable letter to Joshua Speed, written in August 1855: "I bite my lip and keep quiet. The great body of the Northern people do crucify their feelings, in order to maintain their loyalty to the Constitution and the Union." The preliminary Emancipation Proclamation freed from the cross those who, like Lincoln, were "naturally antislavery," and at last allowed their feelings to unite with their thoughts.

When, after the serenade, Hay spoke to Lincoln about the newspaper editorials on the Proclamation, the president said "he had studied the matter so long that he knew more about it than they did."[3]

Those judgments came quickly, and from all quarters: radicals, moderates, and conservatives, Confederates and Europeans, soldiers and slaves. An anonymous correspondent to *Forney's War Press* in Philadelphia stated at September's close: "As I write millions are discussing it in every section that is traversed by the telegraphic wires. It will be greeted by many differences of opinion. It will startle the weak, confirm the conscientious, and for a brief period supply a new weapon to the sympathizers with the common enemy."[4]

Newspapers seemed to compete with one another for the boldest claims. "The country is electrified this morning," wrote a correspondent to San Francisco's *Daily Evening Bulletin*. The *New York Tribune* declared: "It is the beginning of the end of the rebellion; the beginning of the new life of the nation. God bless Abraham Lincoln." The *Lowell Daily Citizen* deemed the Proclamation "a paper which marks an epoch in the history of this nation and the world. . . . [Lincoln] has written his name in history in letters of light." The *Albany Evening Journal* called it "the most solemn and momentous declaration the world ever witnessed," and the *New York Times* stated, "There has been no more far reaching document ever issued since the foundation of this government." Said the *New York Evening Post:* "The 22d of September in this year will hereafter be a day to be commemorated with peculiar honor. . . . On that day, it will be recorded, the chains of bondage were struck from the limbs of three millions of human beings." And according to the *Philadelphia Press,* it was a "second Declaration of Independence from slavery, which is certain to awaken more excitement than the first, and, if possible, to lead to results more novel and wide reaching."[5]

"The axe is laid to the root of the tree": this was a popular metaphor. A cartoon in *Harper's Weekly* showed Lincoln swinging an axe at a withered tree labeled "Slavery," and warning a rebel cowering in the top branch: "Now, if you don't come down, I'll cut the Tree from under you." And a popular print showed Jefferson Davis displaying the "Great Southern Gyascutis," a monstrous-looking dog with fangs and talons. The print depicted various Union officials trying to break the backbone of the beast; a dejected man sitting with head in hand, holding a tiny hammer labeled "Compromise";

Generals Halleck and McClellan wielding hammers representing "Skill" and "Strategy"; Secretary of War Stanton preparing to strike with the "Draft"; and Lincoln, with an axe labeled "Emancipation Proclamation," telling Stanton: "You can try him with that, but I'm afraid this axe of mine is the only thing that will fetch him."[6]

Lincoln's mail bag filled with expressions of gratitude. "May God bless & prosper Abraham Lincoln for his great & sublime act of justice & humanity," wrote the editor of the *Christian Inquirer*. An abolitionist declared that "the People are jubilant over your emancipation message as a measure alike Military & Philanthropic." "It is the noblest act of the age on this continent," averred one correspondent. Others claimed that "the cloud is lifted from our country's future—our cause receives an inspiration unknown before; and having now won God to our side, and established our policy upon Eternal Justice, the Nation *cannot die.*" One writer, unable to find the right words, sent the President a barrel containing half a dozen hams.[7]

The vice president, Hannibal Hamlin, who had been kept pretty much out of the decision-making process, predicted that the Emancipation Proclamation "will stand as the great act of the age." Lincoln wrote back to Hamlin: "While I hope something from the proclamation, my expectations are not as sanguine as are those of some friends. . . . It is six days old, and while commendation in newspapers and by distinguished individuals is all that a vain man could wish, the stocks have declined, and troops come forward more slowly than ever. This, looked soberly in the face, is not very satisfactory. . . . The North responds to the proclamation sufficiently in breath, but breath alone kills no rebels."[8]

For some, the Proclamation restored faith and cleared the air. Jane Stuart Woolsey, a nurse in New York and Virginia, wrote:

There *was* a time,—I confess it because it is past, when your correspondent turned rather cold and sick and said "It is enough!" and when my sister Abby . . . went about declaiming out of Isaiah "To what purpose is the multitude of yours: your country is desolate, strangers devour it in your presence." We came out of that phase, however, at any rate I did, and concluded that despondency was but a weak sort of treason: and then with the first cool weather came the Proclamation, like a "Loud wind, strong wind, blowing from the mountain," and we felt a little invigorated and thanked God and took courage.[9]

Charles Eliot Norton also spoke of God's glory. He wrote to his dear friend George W. Curtis:

> I can hardly see to write,—for when I think of this great act of Freedom, and all it implies, my heart and my eyes overflow with the deepest, most serious gladness. I rejoice with you. Let us rejoice together, and with all the lovers of liberty, and with all the enslaved and oppressed everywhere. I think to-day this world is glorified by the spirit of Christ. How beautiful it is to be able to read the sacred words under this new light. "He hath sent me to heal the broken-hearted, to preach deliverance to the captives, and recovery of sight to the blind, to set at liberty them that are bruised, to preach the acceptable year of the Lord." The war is paid for.[10]

In a sermon delivered on September 28 at the First Congregational Unitarian Church in Philadelphia, the Reverend William Furness declared that the Proclamation gave meaning to the "dear and honorable lives . . . sacrificed" at Antietam, and that it moved citizens from a state of private sorrow to public blessing. "The Proclamation of the President," stated Furness, "is a Proclamation of Emancipation to *us. We,* the white race of the North, who have been under the galling chain of obligation that bound us to connive at oppression and to hurl back into the hell of bondage the fugitive grasping for his sacred and God-given freedom,—it is we, whose emancipation this great act of the President announces."[11]

It was a measure too sweeping to be the act of any individual; rather, it was an act of destiny. "This proclamation of the President is the decree of fate rather than the utterance of any man," declared an editorial in the *North American.* "The storm is not over, but it is no longer gathering. We can now see that there is to be an end, and we know the end is to be favorable to the future unity and prosperity of this great nation."[12]

Other commentators, however, played down the Proclamation's significance. The *New York World,* the country's leading Democratic paper, asserted: "This new proclamation really amounts to little. The President proclaims in substance that on the first of next January he will issue still another proclamation, putting in force the main provisions of the confiscation act." The *Boston Post* agreed: "There is nothing strikingly new in the measures advocated in the proclamation. . . . The declaration that slaves are free where our armies cannot penetrate, of course, is a nullity, and will excite the ridicule that follows impotency." "It is on the whole a curious document," concluded the *Journal of Commerce.*[13]

One writer, who opposed Lincoln's action, suggested to readers that "emancipation is not abolition," and that even if by virtue of the Proclamation all the existing slaves in South Carolina are emancipated, *the right to hold slaves still remains,* and may be exercised by the people of South Carolina whenever the State is again in the Union. The Proclamation merely takes from them the slaves they now own."[14]

Not all conservatives were so temperate in their reaction. Democratic opponents denounced the Emancipation Proclamation as the triumph of "Greeley, Sumner & Co." in an administration "fully adrift on the current of radical fanaticism." The *New York Herald,* while not a strict Democratic Party paper, warned that the Proclamation would inaugurate a "social revolution." Another editor railed that it was "an outrage upon the humanity and good sense of the country, to say nothing of its gross unconstitutionality"; it would lead blacks to "massacre white men, women and children till their hands are smeared and their appetites glutted with blood." The *Louisville Journal* opposed the measure as "wholly unauthorized and wholly pernicious. . . . Kentucky cannot and will not acquiesce in this measure. Never!" The *Springfield Register,* in Lincoln's hometown, warned of "the setting aside of our national Constitution, and, in all human probability, the permanent disruption of the republic, a permanent standing army, endless civil war, the Africanization of the Southern States, anarchy in the North, to end in despotism."[15]

Opponents of the Proclamation predicted so many diverse consequences that the *Liberator* mocked the divergent claims made by the Democratic press:

It will destroy the Union.

It is harmless and impotent.

It will excite slave insurrections.

The slaves will never hear of it.

It will excite the South to desperation.

The rebels will laugh it to scorn.[16]

Whether supportive or opposed, newspaper writers speculated wildly about "the mystery of how and why the Emancipation Proclamation was issued." Indeed, one correspondent reported that conjectures "are so multitudinous and various, and, I may add, so irreconcilable, that people know just less than nothing at all about the why and wherefore and the circumstances of the issue." Some said that Edward Bates, Montgomery Blair, Caleb Smith, and William Seward had opposed the measure, that Lincoln decided to issue it anyhow, and that Seward was going to resign, to be replaced by Massachusetts politician Edward Everett. Some said that Bates, Blair, and Smith had given in, but that "Mr. Blair continued to make very wry faces up to the last minute." A few even suggested that it had been agreed to and "received with great applause" by a unanimous cabinet. Another report speculated that Chase had led the movement to issue the Proclamation. Gideon Welles was following the press reports, and remarked in his diary that "the speculations as to the sentiments and opinions of the Cabinet in regard to this measure are ridiculously wild and strange."[17]

One writer offered a cogent analysis of the timing of the Proclamation. C. C. Hazewell, editor of the *Boston Traveller* and a frequent contributor to the *Atlantic,* thought Lincoln had chosen September 22 for three reasons:

(1), that the American mind had been brought up to the point of emancipation under certain well-defined conditions, and that, if he should not avail himself of the state of opinion, the opportunity afforded him might pass away, never to return with equal force; (2), that foreign nations might base acknowledgment of the Confederacy on the defeats experienced by our armies in the last days of August, on the danger of Washington, and on the advance of Rebel armies to the Ohio, and he was determined that they should, if admitting the Confederacy to national rank, place themselves in the position of supporters of slavery; and (3), that the successes won by our army in Maryland, considering the disgraceful business of Harper's Ferry, were not of that pronounced character which entitles us to assert any supremacy over the enemy as soldiers.[18]

Other explanations of the timing were more far-fetched. Some thought Lincoln had issued the Proclamation so as to act before the Confederacy did. One writer predicted in the *New York Times* that "the rebels intended, when pressed to the wall, as they will be, to issue a proclamation freeing all the negroes themselves, as a last desperate means of inducing England to acknowledge their independence. This done, they would have placed the United States government in the false attitude of fighting to perpetuate Slavery. And all there is of the matter is simply this: Mr. Lincoln has taken the start of Jeff. Davis." A correspondent for the *Boston Journal* claimed: "Lincoln was induced to issue the proclamation through assurances that unless he did so, Jeff Davis would forestall him and issue a proclamation first, and that the sympathies of Europe would be with the section which first adopted the measure." This explanation, thought one of the *Journal*'s editors, "manifestly absurd as it is, is no more silly than that of a hundred others I have seen within the last few days." As for the assertion that the preliminary Emancipation Proclamation had turned Confederates' thoughts toward emancipation, the *New York Times* reported: "They have thus far only breathed out threatenings and slaughter, not only against us but also against the slaves. Their thoughts have turned to extermination instead of counter emancipation."[19]

Another theory, circulated by the Democratic press, suggested that Lincoln was hoping to influence the upcoming October and November elections. "The proclamation was probably issued to operate upon the fall elections," declared the *Boston Herald*, "and to save the abolitionists from defeat." Confederates thought similarly. The *Richmond Enquirer* stated: "We are of the opinion that his main idea was to carry the elections which are about to take place in the Northern States."[20]

If so, Confederates believed it would do no good: the preliminary Emancipation Proclamation would serve to unite secessionists and aid their war effort, because it would divide and distract the North. The *Charleston Cou-*

rier declared that Lincoln had harmed his own cause: "The South rejoices in the publication of his emancipation proclamation. It cannot do us any harm; it will do us great good. It breeds divisions in his own borders; it will compose differences and produce a greater unanimity throughout these Confederate States." One diarist in North Carolina noted that "evidences of division at home appear in the Northern journals—the Emancipation Proclamation meets with some bitter opponents & M[c]Clellan is like to have a fire in his rear." Josiah Gorgas, the Confederacy's chief of ordnance, observed that the Proclamation had triggered "marked opposition at the north, & is denounced by the democrats generally."[21]

Politically, Lincoln immediately gained the support of the majority of loyal-state governors who had been meeting in Altoona, Pennsylvania, on September 24 when word of the Proclamation arrived. Twelve governors (counting Austin Blair of Michigan, who arrived late) had gathered in Altoona at the invitation of Pennsylvania's governor, Andrew Gregg Curtin. Governor John A. Andrew of Massachusetts served as cohost. That conference, scheduled well before September 22, could have led the radical governors to pressure the moderates to join them in urging the president toward more decisive action with respect to the war—but the Proclamation effectively undercut anything that might have emerged. The governors, except for Augustus Bradford of Maryland, hurried to Washington and presented an address in which they congratulated "the President upon his proclamation to emancipate the slaves, believing it will be productive of good as a measure of justice, humanity, and sound policy."[22]

Whatever the Proclamation's origins and political implications, its genius, thought abolitionist James Miller McKim, lay not in "its extent and depth to be judged of by out ward appearance," but in the fact that virtuous, reflective, intelligent, patriotic people would understand its import. The historian Richard Hildreth—writing from Trieste, where he served as United States consul—rejoiced that the act solved the riddle of Lincoln's public letter to Greeley: "How preserve the Union? The utterances of the President on this point have been mystical, obscure, oracular. He has shown himself a very sphinx. If, he says, to preserve the Union, slavery must be abolished, I go for abolishing; but if, to preserve the Union, slaveholding must be tolerated, I go for tolerating it. The Proclamation cuts the Gordian knot. It abandons the idea of tolerating." John A. Dahlgren, commander of Washington's Navy Yard, also thought about the public letter of a month earlier: "The President says in his letter to Greeley, that 'he will not interfere with slavery if not required to this end, but will interfere if it is necessary.' This, then, is equivalent to saying that slavery and the union cannot exist together." Republican governor John Andrew distinguished between text and meaning: "It is a poor *document,* but a mighty *act;* slow, somewhat halting, wrong in its delay till January, but grand and sublime after all." The *Independent,* an antislavery paper published in New York, wished that the decree had been immediate and unconditional and that it had been based on the grounds of justice—but no matter: "The Decree of Emancipation is the dividing line between a dark past and a hopeful future."[23]

Harriet Beecher Stowe decided to travel to Washington to satisfy herself that "I may refer to the Emancipation Proclamation as a reality and a substance, not a fizzle out at the little end of a horn." She met with Lincoln, who, according to Stowe family tradition, asked the author of *Uncle Tom's Cabin,* "Is this the little woman who made this great war?" Inspired by the preliminary Emancipation Proclamation, Stowe then wrote a letter to England that was nearly ten years overdue. In 1853, she had received a document titled "An Affectionate and Christian Address" from a group of prominent British women, who were calling for the abolition of slavery. Organizers had asked women throughout British society to sign the document; they had sent Stowe twenty-six leather-bound volumes containing more than half a million signatures.[24]

All too aware of the threats of British intervention in the war, Stowe explained to the women abolitionists that the Emancipation Proclamation "has been much misunderstood and misrepresented in England. It has been said to mean virtually this: 'Be loyal, and you shall keep your slaves; rebel, and they shall be free.' But that is not what the decree meant. Rather, building upon all the anti-slavery measures of the thirty-seventh Congress, it sent a message to the states in secession, 'Come in, and emancipate peaceably with compensation; stay out, and I emancipate, nor will I protect you from the consequences.'" Stowe informed her sisters overseas that, with the Emancipation Proclamation, "universal emancipation will have become a fixed fact in the American union."[25]

Other abolitionists were less sanguine. William Lloyd Garrison, who had fought his entire adult life for this moment, thought the Proclamation was "certainly matter for great rejoicing, as far as it goes," but lamented that "it leaves slavery, as a system or practice, still to exist in all the so-called loyal Slave States. . . . What was wanted, what is still needed, is a proclamation, distinctly announcing the total abolition of slavery. . . . The President can do nothing for *freedom* in a direct manner, but only by circumlocution and delay. How prompt was his action against Fremont and Hunter!"[26]

Orestes Brownson wondered, "What sort of military necessity is that, it may be asked, which admits to a delay of a hundred days?" He still believed that "the instant and complete emancipation of all the slaves in the whole United States, as a war measure, immediately after the first battle of Bull Run, with the assurance of a reasonable compensation to loyal owners, would have been effectual, and speedily ended the war." N. H. Eggleston, writing in the *New Englander and Yale Review,* admitted: "It would have pleased us better had the president proclaimed emancipation on the instant rather than after a lapse of an hundred days. It would have been more just, more dignified, more manly, and more Christian."[27]

But Horace Greeley saw the hesitation as strength: "The very hesitation of the President to take the decisive step gives weight to his ultimate decision." After all, conservatives and compromisers repeatedly praised the president for his firm, patient, independent course, refusing to buckle to radical pressures. No one could question the policy as being anything other than his own, and he was responding solely to the "emphatic conviction of the great mass of our loyal citizens." "The Proclamation," Greeley declared, "is an immense fact. If it were no more than a recognition from the highest quarter of the deadly antagonism between slavery and the Union, it would have inexhaustible significance."[28]

Frederick Douglass turned Lincoln's "peculiar, cautious, forbearing and hesitating way" into a virtue. He predicted that the Proclamation, "this righteous decree," would face virulent opposition and that the president would be urged to retract it. But Douglass felt certain that although Lincoln "may be slow," he would not reverse the policy. "Abraham Lincoln may desire peace even at the price of leaving our terrible national sore untouched, to fester for generations, but Abraham Lincoln is not the man to reconsider, retract, and contradict words and purposes solemnly proclaimed over his official signature. The careful, and we think, the slothful deliberation which he has observed in reaching this obvious policy, is a guarantee against retraction."[29]

Whether it was retracted or not, Richard Henry Dana thought little of the document:

It is good for platforms and rhetoricians, but I fear it is not *statesmanship*. I can not give this course a hearty, intelligent support. But I can support the President. I fear it is to be a *dead failure*. Unless we meet with decisive success before that Proclamation takes effect, the war is over, the slaves are not free, and the managers of the war, from the President down (I mean the civilians), are doomed to the wall. The Proclamation is not what your friends suppose it to be. It does not interfere with slavery in the loyal states. It only threatens to abolish it in the States that continue disloyal,—that is to say, in the States which we cannot conquer, and in which we cannot emancipate one slave. It is Slavery where we can emancipate, and freedom where we cannot.[30]

Lydia Maria Child—at age sixty-one one of the oldest abolitionists, and one of the most progressive (she had proclaimed, "I identify myself so completely with the slaves" and "I have no prejudice against color")—was the most disappointed. Writing in October 1862, Child feared what would happen by the New Year. She dreaded the kind of cooperation with slaveholders that would emerge—aided, she was sure, by Seward and McClellan. "Everywhere I see signs that the subtle poison is working." Child would not change her mind over the hundred days:

As for the President's Proclamation, I was thankful for it, but it excited no enthusiasm in my mind. With my gratitude toward God was mixed an under-tone of sadness that the moral sense of the people was so low, that the thing could not be done nobly. However we may inflate the emancipation balloon, it will never ascend among the constellations. The ugly fact cannot be concealed from history that it was done reluctantly and stintedly, and that even the degree accomplished was done selfishly; was merely a war-measure, to which we were forced by our own perils and necessities; and that no recognition of principles of justice or humanity surrounded the politic act with a halo of moral glory.[31]

Among radicals, Count Gurowski was the most merciless in his denunciation. On September 23, 1862, he wrote in his diary:

Proclamation *conditionally* abolishing slavery from 1863. The *conditional* is the last desperate effort made by Mr. Lincoln and by Mr. Seward to save slavery. Poor Mr. Lincoln was obliged to strike such a blow at his *mammy!* The two statesmen found out that it was dangerous longer to resist the decided, authoritative will of the masses. The words "resign," "depose," "impeach," were more and more distinct in the popular murmur, and the proclamation was issued. Very little, if any, credit is due to Mr. Lincoln or to Mr. Seward for having thus late and reluctantly *legalized* the stern will of the immense majority of the American people.

Gurowski persisted, seemingly unable to control the flow of words: "The absurdity of colonization is preserved in the proclamation. How would it have been otherwise?" He wondered what would happen if the rebellion ended before January 1? Happily, "for humanity and for national honor . . . the rebels will spurn the tenderly proffered leniency."

Gurowski reread the document and exploded anew: "The proclamation is written in the meanest and the most dry routine style; not a word to evoke a generous thrill, not a word reflecting the warm and lofty comprehension and feelings of the immense majority of the people on the question of emancipation. Nothing for humanity; nothing to humanity. Whoever drew it, be he Mr. Lincoln or Mr. Seward, it is clear that the writer was not in it either with his heart or with his soul; it is clear that it was done under moral duress, under the throttling pressure of events."[32]

Another European revolutionary, who knew something about manifestos, saw the document differently: Karl Marx expressed his appreciation for the mechanical language of the Proclamation. He told Friedrich Engels, "Lincoln's acts all have the appearance of inflexible, clause-ridden conditions communicated by a lawyer to his opposite number. This does not, however, impair their historical import and does, in actual fact, amuse me when, on the other hand, I consider the drapery in which your Frenchman enwraps the merest trifle." In an article for the Viennese daily *Die Presse* published on October 12, 1862, Marx reiterated those views:

> Lincoln is a *sui generis* figure in the annals of history. . . . He gives his most important actions always the most commonplace form. . . . He sings the bravura aria of his part hesitatively, reluctantly and unwillingly, as though apologizing for being compelled by circumstances "to act the lion." The most redoubtable decrees—which will always remain remarkable historical documents—flung by him at the enemy all look like, and are intended to look like, routine summonses sent by a lawyer to the lawyer of the opposing party. . . . His latest proclamation, which is drafted in the same style, the manifesto abolishing slavery, is the most important document in American history since the establishment of the Union, tantamount to the tearing up of the old American Constitution.[33]

What Marx saw, others such as Gurowski clearly did not; for them, the document failed because it didn't do enough, say enough, or go far enough. To conservative Republicans and most Democrats, however, its mere existence was too much because they believed the Proclamation was patently unconstitutional. "The proclamation is *an outrage upon the humanity and good sense of the country,* to say nothing of its gross unconstitutionality," thundered the *Weekly Patriot and Union* of Harrisburg, Pennsylvania. "Whatever there was of absurdity, of folly, of impotency, of unconstitutionality in the proclamations of Fremont, of Phelps, and of Hunter, may be found in this Proclamation," concluded one editorial. "A complete overthrow of the Constitution," shrieked the *Chicago Times.*[34]

Many opponents labeled the decree a *brutum fulmen*—an empty threat. For example, according to the *New York Express,* "The President has no more Constitutional Power to issue such a Proclamation than any other man. If he has any Constitutional authority to free negroes, he has a corresponding Constitutional authority to enslave them. The power exercised is an assumption, therefore, throughout and hence is mere *brutum fulmen,* the more, therefore, to be deplored, as mere paper thunder, because it but re-excites, re-arouses and demonizes the South. . . . It changes the character of our civil, Constitutional Government, into a mere Abolition Military Despotism."[35]

One pro-administration paper, tiring of the sudden enthusiasm for Latin phrases, quipped in response:

> We see so much Latin now-a-days in the Northern Confederate news-papers that we are becoming quite familiar with it. They quote it just now with reference to the President's emancipation proclamation and declare it to be a *"brutum fulmen."* Whether this meant *brutally foolish,* or that it would make fools of brutes, or implied something like *et tu brute* we didn't know until we found out. But we have found out and it means "a loud but harmless menace." And this phrase is applied to a proclamation which, while they profess to care little about, stirs up all their gall and wormwood and would lash them into paroxysm of trea-sonable fury.[36]

Rather than posing an empty threat, the preliminary Emancipation Proc-lamation, argued the *Springfield Republican* in Massachusetts, breathed revolution:

> The President's action is timely—neither too soon nor too late. It is thorough—neither defeating itself by halfway measures nor by passion-ate excess. It is just and magnanimous—doing no wrong to any loyal man, and offering no exasperation to the disloyal. It is practical and ef-fective—attempting neither too little nor too much. And it will be sus-tained by the great mass of the loyal people, North and South; and thus, by the courage and prudence of the President, the greatest social and political revolution of the age will be triumphantly carried through in the midst of civil war.[37]

Most commentators understood that, in one way or another, there was nothing inert about the preliminary Emancipation Proclamation. But no one could predict precisely in what ways it might operate, what its consequences would be, or, with one hundred days of anticipation and debate lying ahead, how the situation might change. Americans imagined various scenarios: the Proclamation would rapidly bring the war to a close; it would lead, at last, to the abolition of slavery and the liberation of some four million slaves; it would induce the Confederacy to sue for peace or, alternatively, reinforce its citizens' determination to win their independence; it would compel European nations to enter the conflict or else foreclose the possibility of their aiding the Confederacy; it would lead to mass desertions among Union soldiers; it would ignite violent insurrection among the enslaved; it would be political suicide for the Republicans. And some observers continued to cling to the hope that it would have no effect whatsoever.

Given the way Lincoln had introduced the document to his cabinet—with a humorous story by Artemus Ward—the comment by Henry Knowlton, writing to a friend from Joliet, Illinois, on the letterhead of the Michigan Central Rail Road Company, may have been the most fitting: "What do you think of Lincoln's 'emancipation proclamation'? To use Artemas Ward's elegant phraseology I think that it is 'hunky' every way."[38]

6

The Reactions of Scholars and Soldiers

Isaac Morris, a former Democratic congressman from Illinois, was agitated. In a lengthy letter to Lincoln dated November 20, 1862, he objected to the emancipation decree. "The war," he asserted, "must be fought through with arms and not with proclamations. I am firmly convinced that if no proclamations had been issued by yourself or by your Generals since it commenced we would be in a much better condition today than we are. If every one has not done an injury no one has certainly done any good." He went on to denounce as heretical and dangerous the doctrine of military necessity. "This should be a war to restore the Constitution and not destroy it."[1]

For more than a year, politicians had debated the constitutionality of such a proclamation, and now, with the decree issued, jurists and scholars took up the discussion. What further animated the argument was Lincoln's decision, two days after the preliminary Emancipation Proclamation, to issue another proclamation, this one suspending the writ of habeas corpus (which prevented people from being detained without sufficient cause or evidence) for anyone arrested or imprisoned by any military authority. Navy secretary Gideon Welles, for one, had not known of the suspension until he'd read about it in the papers, and he questioned "the utility of a multiplicity of proclamations striking deep on great questions."[2]

Democratic opponents quickly connected the two documents. In a speech before the Democratic Union Association in New York on September 29, James Brooks, a conservative Democrat who had served previously in Congress, derided the Emancipation Proclamation as unconstitutional and mocked the colonization proposal as "utterly impossible": "never did a dreamier idea enter the head, it seems to me, of any wild, Utopian scheming philosopher." Brooks predicted that if the president's Proclamation were carried through, there would inevitably follow "the arming of the slaves, their adoption into the army of the United States, not only as fellow soldiers but as fellow citizens." The crowd erupted in laughter.

Brooks went on to argue that Lincoln's second proclamation was linked directly to the first—"a corollary" which "substantially says to the free white people of the North, if you discuss and agitate this subject of emancipation, if you make war against the Administration on this subject, you shall be incarcerated." One Democratic newspaper in New York alleged that "the freeing of negroes involved, of necessity, the enslaving of the white race, and hence it does not surprise us that this attempted change in the *status* of the negro is accompanied by a corresponding change in the *status* of the white man." The only remedy, Brooks advised, was the ballot box. Looking ahead to the November elections, he implored the voters not to allow unconstitutional paper proclamations to rob them of their freedom.[3]

Later in the fall, one Democratic writer mocked what he viewed as Lincoln's proclamation frenzy:

> Having thus disposed of Secession, the President could turn his attention to slavery in Brazil and Cuba, and finish it there, by the stroke of the pen! Canada could, in the same way, be separated from England, and the European dynasties overturned. Cannibalism in the Fejee Islands, small feet in China, polytheism in the rest of Asia might share the same fate. . . . Wives could be divorced from husbands, instantly; and children released from obedience to parents. . . . We know of nothing else for the President to do, for himself or for humanity, except to declare, by proclamation, that the Northwest Passage is henceforth free and open for navigation to all the nations of the world.[4]

The two proclamations generated less derisive responses as well, begun when former Supreme Court justice Benjamin Curtis published a pamphlet titled *Executive Power.* Curtis had dissented in the *Dred Scott* case, and he soon thereafter resigned from the court, though not because of the decision. A practicing attorney in Boston, Curtis believed that only "public discussion" could resolve the thorny constitutional issues involved, and that one of the reasons the Emancipation Proclamation was to take effect in three months was "for the very purpose of allowing such discussion." Curtis wrote clearly, with authority and force. He argued that the Emancipation Proclamation and the proclamation suspending habeas corpus were "assertions of executive power" that had no grounding in the Constitution. Curtis argued that the two proclamations "do not relate to exceptional cases—they establish a system. They do not relate to some instant emergency—they cover an indefinite future. They do not seek for excuses—they assert powers and rights. They are general rules of action applicable to the entire country, and to every person in it." Curtis refused to accept that Lincoln possessed a military power that could "overcome us and the civil liberties of the country." The Emancipation Proclamation was an executive decree that repealed and annulled valid state laws regulating domestic relations. The military power, he argued, was a power to act immediately, not to "prescribe rules for *future* action."[5]

Curtis wondered: by virtue of what power could the president act? He quoted Lincoln's response to the Chicago clergymen—namely, that as commander-in-chief he believed he could take any measures necessary to end the rebellion. But if the president could claim an "*implied* constitutional right" based on his role as commander-in-chief, could he not then "disregard each and every provision of the Constitution" in order to do what he thought best to subdue the rebels? Could he not also appropriate any other powers that were reserved to the states or the people? The powers that were being asserted by the Executive, Curtis insisted, were "not found in any express grant of power made by the Constitution to the President." The result "of this interpretation of the Constitution is, that, in time of war, the President has any and all power, which he may deem necessary to exercise, to subdue the enemy; and that every private and personal right of individual security against mere executive control, and every right reserved to the States and the people, rests merely upon executive discretion."[6]

From the start of the war, the powers of the president and Congress had been topics of great controversy and the subject of numerous books, articles, and speeches. But Curtis's pamphlet alone, serving as a direct commentary on the constitutionality of the Emancipation Proclamation and the suspension of habeas corpus, generated a series of direct responses. With a final emancipation decree in sight, the legitimacy of such a proclamation mattered more than ever to those who had been pressing upon the president the use of the doctrine of military necessity as the instrument needed to free the slaves. There were reasonable people, perhaps apolitical people, whose support would be needed, and writers set out to persuade them of the constitutionality of Lincoln's acts.

In a letter to the *Boston Daily Advertiser,* Harvard professor Theophilus Parsons claimed that Curtis was conflating several distinct questions: civil power, military power, and expediency. Parsons argued that while the president did not have power to emancipate as a civil act, he held the power to act as commander-in-chief, and was best positioned to decide whether or not to proceed. "Judge Curtis' argument," Parsons concluded, "would give the Constitution and the law to the rebels, as their sword to smite with, and their shield to save them, and leave it to us only as a fetter." It was a matter of common sense, wrote one editor of the *New York Times.* He wondered how it was that "we might wage war against them—that we could bombard their towns, kill their troops, confiscate their goods, occupy their lands, forfeit their cattle, their crops, and everything else that they possessed—but that we could not strip them of their slaves. What gave such supreme sanctity to this specific form of property or labor? Not the Constitution, which does not even, in explicit terms, mention its existence."[7]

"If your argument can avail," the lawyer Charles Mayo Ellis wrote to Curtis, "you will have done more for the traitor cause than all the rebel armies." Ellis put no faith in Curtis's claim that the jurist did not belong to any political party. Noting that the judge had once ruled in favor of the Fugitive Slave Act as well as against the *Dred Scott* decision, Ellis insisted that "really, there are few persons more biased than you are on this topic." He found incredible the implication of Curtis's argument that popular, democratic government must be impotent in times of war. The commander-in-chief possessed implied power—"not implied in the sense of being only constructive or incidental. It is implied in the sense of being necessarily involved in the command with which he is invested." Not only could the president act; he *must* act, or else "sit with folded hands and see a band of conspirators in garb of civilians vote another State into open Rebellion." It did not matter whether the army could act directly on a decree—"martial law can be declared over a city without a soldier in every house"—or whether the decree applied only at a future date—"it is but fair, as well as expedient, to give notice beforehand." Sadly, Ellis concluded, Curtis's course "is not the cause of the Constitution and the law. It would lead to anarchy."[8]

Grosvenor Lowrey, a prominent New York attorney, assailed Curtis for the polemical use of the term "Executive Power." Lincoln was not acting as executive, but as commander-in-chief, and the Emancipation Proclamation was "a lawful and necessary measure of war." Curtis "utterly confounds" the two classes of powers exercised by the president as commander-in-chief. The first consisted of routine duties, matters of organization and appointment; and the second arose out of enemy acts which allowed the president to use all means necessary to defeat the enemy. The rebels, Lowrey argued, had abandoned any constitutional protection: *"Rebels in arms against the Constitution, must not be spoken of, as men having Constitutional rights."*

Lowrey gave an example of what he thought the Emancipation Proclamation meant and how it worked. What it "proposes to do is to suspend the relation between Robert Toombs, a voluntary white resident of Georgia, who is, by that fact, presumptively a rebel, and Tom, his slave, who is presumptive loyal, as far as he is free to be anything. The civil *status* of Tom was slavery, because certain civil interests demanded it. His military *status* is to be freedom, because the general military interests demand it. This does not abolish slavery; it only abolishes the slave." Lowrey's distinction was an important one and it helps explain why, after January 1, 1863, opponents of slavery pressed for a constitutional amendment to abolish the institution. Yet Lowrey did make clear that, once freed, a person could never be reenslaved: "The slave, whom we have heretofore considered merely as a chattel, now stands up and asserts his manhood."[9]

Another New York attorney, Charles Kirkland, not only wrote and published a letter to Curtis; he also sent a copy to Lincoln. Kirkland began by objecting to Curtis's inability to distinguish the two presidential proclamations, "which differ radically and essentially in subject and in intent." One was limited, the other broad; one led to permanent results, the other to temporary results. What, Kirkland wondered, did the former justice believe was "the distinguishing fatal error of each"? Whatever the case, the problem, Kirkland thought, was that Curtis argued as if there were "no rebellion and *no war.*" But "the intent and design of the proclamation, its actual effect, if it has its *intended* operation, is to forever deprive the 'enemy' of this vital, absolutely essential, and . . . *indispensable,* means of carrying on *the war.*" The president's action of divesting the rebels of their ability to sustain the rebellion by depriving them of their slaves, who constituted one of their most effective and available means for continuing the war, was "sanctioned by the laws of war, and, consequently, this act of the President is, within your own doctrine, perfectly legal and constitutional."[10]

Kirkland's tone shifted as his anger deepened. To Curtis's argument that the Emancipation Proclamation would annul state laws, he countered that "never was more error, gross, palpable, grievous, found." The states were in rebellion; they repudiated the Constitution; they denied its authority and sought to overthrow it, and yet "you claim the inviolability of their *State* laws under *that constitution.* . . . It is difficult to imagine what hallucination you were laboring [under] when you gave utterance to those sentiments." In response to Curtis's question, "What is to come out of this great and desperate struggle?" Kirkland answered: not an autocratic government, not an executive dictatorship, but rather "a great, a united, a powerful, a free people, purified by the fires of adversity, and taught by their tremendous calamities the lessons of moderation and humility." Lincoln read the pamphlet and sent Kirkland a note: "Under the circumstance I may not be the most competent judge, but it appears to me to be a paper of great ability."[11]

One conservative Boston lawyer expressed an opinion different from most of the others. A childhood spinal injury had kept John Codman Ropes from volunteering for military service, but not from writing lengthy letters to his future law partner, John Chipman Gray. Ropes disdained radicals such as Sumner, who thought only in terms of the abolition of slavery. He did not belong to that class of men. But there was an even larger class "who look upon the destruction of slavery as necessary to the restoration of the authority of the government. . . . To this class I have always belonged since the war began. I have not gone in for waging the war for the emancipation of the slaves, but I have made up my mind that the slaves must be emancipated in order that we may again be a united nation. I have been willing to let the President take his time for it, but I have been pretty certain that it must come sooner or later." As to whether the measure was constitutional, Ropes could not say, but he added that it didn't matter: "I can conceive of men *wisely* insisting upon the destruction of slavery at any rate, even at the expense of the infraction of the Constitution, under the present circumstances. The life is more than meat, the body is more than raiment, and the Country is more than the Constitution." A contributor to the *New Englander and Yale Review* agreed: "Union is nothing, constitutions are nothing, compared with the nation itself.[12]

Embedded in the pamphlet war over the constitutionality of the Emancipation Proclamation was another issue that appeared repeatedly whenever abolition was discussed, and that exploded with new intensity upon issuance of the preliminary Emancipation Proclamation: slave insurrection. Benjamin Curtis wondered how the enslaved might "overturn these valid laws of States," and he imagined that they could only be *"violated by physical force."* Although he said he did not believe this was the intent of the president, the result of the Proclamation would be to "incite a part of the inhabitants of the United States to rise in insurrection against valid laws."[13]

At other places in his analysis, Curtis talked of "scenes of bloodshed" and "servile war." Charles Kirkland pounced on this, wondering how the former Supreme Court justice could make such allegations. "I am not an abolitionist," Kirkland confessed, "nor a believer in the social and political equality of the white and black races. . . . I am even called by some a pro-slavery man. Yet I see no 'scenes of bloodshed,' no 'servile war,' in the event of the practical carrying out of this proclamation." Grosvenor Lowrey went further. He said that no one could predict whether a "servile insurrection will ensue"; but if it did, the rebels had only themselves to blame. He wondered, "What is there about a black insurrection so much more obnoxious to the law of nations than a white insurrection, except for the bare possibility that the debased black—for whose continued debasement, in the midst of Christian civilization, the enemy alone is responsible—may be more cruel in his proceedings; and which result the enemy, but for misguided persistence in treason, might surely prevent?"[14]

Lincoln himself inadvertently invited the controversy by including in the preliminary Emancipation Proclamation an assurance that the government "will do no act or acts to repress such persons, or any of them, in any efforts they may make for their actual freedom." Charles A. Dana, for one, immediately recognized the problem with this sentence. On September 23, he wrote to secretary of state William Seward: "The 'Proclamation' wd. Please me better if it had omitted *one short paragraph* 'and will do no act or acts to repress such persons or any of them in any efforts they may make for their actual freedom'—this *jars* on me like a *wrong tone in music*—nor do I believe either of the two names signed to it would hesitate one moment to shoulder a musket and 'go in' to crush out an effort to repress what is intimated *they will not.*—This is the only 'bad egg' I see in 'that pudding'—& I fear may go far to make it less palatable than it deserves to be."[15]

The editor of the *Patriot and Union* in Harrisburg said that now the slaves "may rise, if they will, and massacre white men, women and children till their hands are smeared and their appetites glutted with blood. They may do it with impunity—for they have the assurance of the President of the United States that the government" would not repress them. The *Richmond Whig* proclaimed: "It ordains servile insurrection in the Confederate States. . . . It is . . . a bid for the slaves to rise in insurrection, with the assurance of aid from the whole military and naval power of the United States." The *Charleston Daily Courier* rejoiced that Lincoln "has been forced to throw off the mask. The world now beholds the rottenness of his heart. Disastrous and humiliating defeats, unexpected and ruinous reverses have compelled him to make known the base design he formed at the beginning of the war. The measure announced in the proclamation . . . is an invitation to murder, rape, and spoliation." The mask motif appeared as well in the *Southern Illustrated News,* which printed an image of the devil removing his Lincoln mask and holding it in his hand. The caption read: "King Abraham before and after issuing the Emancipation Proclamation."[16]

On September 29, 1862, the Confederate Congress considered a joint resolution that called the Proclamation "a gross violation of the usages of civilized warfare, an outrage on the rights of private property, and an invitation to an atrocious servile war, and *therefore should be held up to the execration of mankind,* and counteracted by such severe retaliatory measures as in the judgment of the President may be best calculated to secure its withdrawal or arrest its execution." One Confederate legislator said that the resolution did not go far enough; he thought that "upon any attempt being made to execute the proclamation of Abraham Lincoln, we immediately hoist the 'black flag' and proclaim a war of extermination against all invaders of our soil."[17]

Southerners, always fearful of slave plots, began to suspect various conspiracies were under way, designed to trigger a general insurrection. For example, in Culpepper County, Virginia, seventeen blacks, most of them free, were arrested on suspicion of fomenting an uprising. According to one report, "copies of late newspapers, which published Lincoln's Emancipation Proclamation, were found in their possession. The fact that such a proclamation has been made is well-known among all the negroes, and it produces the most startling effect. The terror of the whites is beyond description. Apprehensions of a re-enactment of the Nat Turner horrors are felt to an alarming extent." (Turner was a Virginia slave who had led an insurrection in 1831.) Charles Sumner, for one, had little sympathy for the Southerners: "I know of no principle of war or reason by which our rebels should be saved from the natural consequences of their own action. When they rose against a paternal government, they set the example of insurrection, which has carried death to so many firesides. They cannot complain if their slaves, with better reason, follow it. It is according to an old law, that bloody inventions return to plague the inventor."[18]

Richard Busteed, a brigadier general of volunteers, was delighted that *"the emancipation arrow has pierced the heart of treason."* If indeed the Proclamation led to insurrection, the secessionists had the power in their own hands to prevent catastrophe. The rebels had three months to decide to "lay down their arms; let them return to their allegiance; let them disperse and go to their homes; let them cease to be usurpers and murderers, and there will be no confiscation of their property, no emancipation of their slaves, no servile insurrection."[19]

Count Gurowski made an important distinction. "In St. Domingo," he explained, "the slaves were obliged to tear their liberty from the slaveholding planter, and from a government siding with the oppressor. Here the lawful government gives liberty to the peaceful laborer, and the planter is an outlawed traitor."[20]

Insurrection was a fear; flight was a reality. Sumner predicted that the "slave telegraph" would do its work: "The glad tidings of freedom will travel with the wind, with the air, with the light, and will gradually quicken and inspire the whole mass." But slaves on the move created nearly as much anxiety as slaves in rebellion. One northern writer, in an article titled "Workings of the Emancipation Proclamation," reported on the situation in Union-occupied La Grange, Tennessee:

> As many as four or five hundred negro families have arrived here, and are now taking up quarters in the church buildings, vacant houses, stores, &c. To-day I saw some who had been here a week, and they said that they had eaten nothing since they had left their masters. . . . What they can do here, or what is going to be done with them, I don't know. Our army is already overstocked with negro cooks, teamsters, &c. They cannot be sent north because the free States will not receive them. They cannot live here, for they have nothing to live upon. . . . They may well sing, "Then what shall a poor nigger do?" And, think, if Abraham Lincoln carries his proclamation into effect, as he threatens to do, on the 1st of January next, he will be called upon many times to answer to the poor negro's song.[21]

The preliminary Emancipation Proclamation stated that "the effort to colonize persons of African descent" would continue; and in the context of the increased movement of the black population, slave and free, the subject continued to receive Lincoln's attention. Indeed, on September 24 he called a special meeting of the cabinet to discuss making treaties with foreign governments for the voluntary colonization of blacks. At that meeting, treasury secretary Salmon Chase opposed treaties, preferring instead simple legislative arrangements. According to Chase's account of the meeting, Seward favored treaties but spoke against the wisdom of sending needed laborers out of the country. Gideon Welles favored only voluntary emigration—"the emigrant who chose to leave our shores could, and would go where there were the best inducements." Postmaster general Montgomery Blair and attorney general Edward Bates, however, argued strenuously in favor of compulsory deportation, saying that blacks were unlikely to go voluntarily. On this point, the president was resolute. According to Welles, he "objected unequivocally to compulsion. Their emigration must be voluntary and without expense to themselves." Ardent opponents of colonization, such as William Lloyd Garrison, argued that "voluntary" was an illusion: "No one will leave on their own accord; but only to flee from cruel prejudice and hateful proscription, which they despair at seeing removed, and which are upheld as natural and permanent, on account of their complexion." But Lincoln held on to it as a panacea.[22]

Two days later, Lincoln raised the issue again. Secretary of war Edwin Stanton was not present. Welles and Chase opposed such treaties. Everyone else agreed. Lincoln realized he needed such treaties because foreign governments understandably opposed the creation of autonomous communities within their borders. On September 30, Seward sent a circular to Britain, France, the Netherlands, and Denmark offering to enter into agreements for the colonization of blacks in their New World territories. Little came of Seward's initiative, which had begun because of foreign opposition to a project Lincoln had been promoting on and off since 1861. At that time, he had met with an individual who claimed to have several hundred thousand acres of coal-rich land in Chiriqui, on the Isthmus of Panama. The plan had unraveled, and Lincoln should have known better: Welles had refused to have anything to do with the idea that the area might make a good naval station, and believed that "there was fraud and cheat in the affair"; a congressional committee had found that the land was "uninhabitable" and that the Chiriqui Improvement Company did not have title to it; the coal itself had turned out to be not only without value but potentially hazardous—it was prone to spontaneous combustion. A first expedition to Chiriqui had been planned to depart in fall 1862, but the administration had been forced to cancel it.[23]

In New York, free blacks gathered at the Bridge Street Methodist Church to discuss the Proclamation and colonization. Those assembled stated "they had been pained to hear from his [Lincoln's] lips that they had been the cause of all this bloodshed, and that his race and theirs could never dwell together in this land on terms of equality. And what was it proposed to do with us? Why send us to Chiriqui—a place than which, if Satan himself had been sent to search, he could not have selected worse."[24]

Massachusetts senator Charles Sumner did not allow the colonization schemes to undermine his joy over the preliminary Emancipation Proclamation. On October 6, at an overflowing Faneuil Hall in Boston, he delivered a speech titled "Emancipation! Its Policy and Necessity as a War Measure for the Suppression of the Rebellion." "Thank God that I live to enjoy this day," he exclaimed. "Thank God, that my eyes have not closed without seeing this great salvation. The skies are brighter and the air is purer, now that slavery has been handed over to judgment." On this day he would offer no criticisms or qualifications of the preliminary decree: "For myself, I accept the Proclamation without note or comment." It did not matter where slavery was struck, so long as it was attacked directly and with seriousness of purpose. He quoted from Alexander Pope's *Essay on Man:* "Whatever link you strike, tenth or ten thousandth, breaks the chain alike."

Sumner celebrated the fact that the "war in which we are now engaged has not changed in *object,* but it has changed in *character.*" He used the opportunity to respond to objections to the Proclamation. One of them was that the army would refuse to fight to liberate the slaves and that officers "will fling down their arms." Let those who want to leave go, said Sumner; but he was convinced that "as officers, they must know their duty too well, and, as intelligent men, they must know that the slaves are calculated to be their best and surest allies."[25]

However much Sumner tried to allay anxieties that the army would refuse to fight for freedom, rumors spread that mass mutiny was imminent. Thomas T. Ellis, a surgeon with the Army of the Potomac, claimed that the Proclamation "has caused considerable discontent among the regiments of Maryland, Virginia, Pennsylvania, New York, and the West." Just as some generals were in favor of emancipation, others were resolutely opposed. General Fitz-John Porter, a close comrade of George McClellan, called the Proclamation the act "of a political coward" and said it was "ridiculed in the army." McClellan, who had already expressed his opposition to such a policy, considered resigning over it and declared that it would "inaugurate servile war."[26]

Lincoln was disturbed by whispers that the Army of the Potomac had intentionally failed to follow up after Antietam. (Major John Key, an aide to General Henry Halleck, said defeating the Confederate army was not the objective, and Lincoln immediately cashiered him.) The president was also concerned that a week had passed and still McClellan had not issued a General Order with respect to emancipation. Intent on sending the message that McClellan must pick up the pace of action, and eager to visit the soldiers who had fought so valiantly, Lincoln left Washington on October 1 to visit the headquarters of the Army of the Potomac and review the troops. "It was neither holiday recreation nor idle curiosity that took the President on this excursion, but the all-absorbing business of this war," reported one newspaper.[27]

Lincoln's visit received much play in Southern newspapers. The *Charleston Mercury* and the *Richmond Examiner* reported that, as a result of the Proclamation, "McClellan's army was thrown into a terrible ferment, which threatened to break into an open and general riot. The Republicans and Democrats were instantly arrayed in deadly hostility, the latter declaring that if the proclamation was not withdrawn they would throw down their arms, or if forced to use them, would turn them against the Abolitionists. All the efforts of their commanders having failed to pacify the troops, Lincoln was telegraphed for and set out at once for the army." The Confederate press had an interest, of course, in exaggerating military opposition to the Emancipation Proclamation. Whatever the common soldier felt, McClellan's antipathy set a tone that the president could not abide.[28]

Finally, on October 7, after being advised by a close friend that "it is my duty to submit to the Presdt's proclamation & quietly continue doing my duty as a soldier," McClellan issued a General Order. It included a civics lesson, explaining that armed forces exist only to "sustain the Civil Authorities," who make all policy. He added, however, the dictum that "the remedy for political Errors if any are Committed is to be found only in the action of the people at the polls." Adam Gurowski noted, "McClellan's order to the army concerning the President's proclamation shows up the man. Not a word about the object of the proclamation, but rather unveiled insinuations that the army is dissatisfied with emancipation, and that it may mutiny."[29]

Lincoln's visit may not have moved McClellan, but it buoyed the troops. Lincoln's smile "was like an electric shock. It flew from elbow to elbow and with one loud cheer which made the air ring, the suppressed feeling gave vent, conveying to the good president that his smile had gone home and found a ready response." Charles Fessenden Morse, an officer with the 2nd Massachusetts, guided the presidential party to the summit of Maryland Heights. Lincoln on horseback sometimes provided a comical sight; a soldier once described him as looking like "a pair of tongs on a chair back."

Morse "showed the way until we got to a path where it was straight up, when Abraham backed out. I think it must have reminded him of a little story about a very steep place; at any rate, around they turned and went down the mountain." At the end of the visit, Morse recalled in a letter to his family, "I gave 'Uncle Abe' a few parting words of advice with regard to the general management of things, bade them farewell, and rode back to camp."[30]

In that same letter home, Morse wrote:

Have you made up your mind about the Emancipation Proclamation? At first, I was disposed to think that no changes would be produced by it, but now, I believe its effect will be good. It is going to set us straight with foreign nations. It gives us a decided policy, and though the President carefully calls it nothing but a war measure, yet it is the beginning of a great reform and the first blow struck at the real, original cause of the war. . . . It may have the effect to cause disturbances among the troops from the extreme Southern States, who will think, perhaps, that their presence is needed more at home than up in Virginia. There is no mistake about it, if the fact becomes generally known among the slaves of the South that they are free as soon as within our lines, there will be a much more general movement among them than there has been before. It is evident that Jeff Davis is frightened by it, to judge by the fearful threats of retaliation he is making.[31]

Morse's response is a fragmentary piece of evidence that begins to answer the question posed by a *New York Tribune* headline: "How Will the Army Like the Proclamation?" The question, responded the *Boston Journal,* "may be difficult to answer because military subordinates will restrain the expression of opinion upon acts of the commander in chief. Obedience is a soldier's first duty, and criticism of the acts of a superior officer is a direct violation of the articles of war." The writer wondered, however, what beliefs lay beneath the silence: "Will the hearts of the men go with their work? Will they be willing to strike at the cause of the rebellion?"

The answer seemed to be a resounding yes: "The evidence is abundant, and we think conclusive, that the soldiers belonging to the old regiments who have been longest in the field, and who, from observation and experience, have learned to estimate the strength which Slavery has given to the Rebels, are in favor of emancipating the slaves upon military grounds." As proof, the article included a letter from someone described as a former pro-slavery Democrat. He wrote: "With very few exceptions the *whole* army is in favor of the most stringent prosecution of the war, using every means in our power to stifle the rebellion, and regards emancipation as one of our most potent weapons. Even among the officers of the old army, many of whom talked loudly of resigning, &c. if they were to be used as 'nigger stealers' there has been a great and most marked change of sentiment."[32]

In a "Letter from Baltimore," a correspondent to the *New York Times* reported that "the Emancipation proclamation is discussed *pro* and *con,* in the army, opinion seeming to incline toward its endorsement." But some, the writer continued, "are very bitter against it," saying they refuse to engage in "political warfare." "Most of our troops," however, "seem to concern themselves only with the question 'Qui Bono?' Harsh experiences have destroyed in them all feeling of sentiment in regard to the negro, and they only wish to know how he can be put to service in the suppression of the rebellion." Sergeant Henry Tisdale of the 35th Massachusetts reported in November that the Proclamation "has caused many debates among us soldiers. Somehow feel the measure to be unwise and tending only to exasperate the rebels. Yet feel that our President has an honest disinterested desire for the welfare of the country and would not act rashly in anything pertaining to its interests. Therefore have reason to wait quietly for the results, and in good hope that they will be such as to show the wisdom of the President in this action."[33]

Perhaps the most joyous reaction came from Lieutenant John Quincy Adams Campbell of the 5th Iowa, who predicted that January 1 would be "the day of our nation's second birth. God bless and help Abraham Lincoln— help him to 'break every yoke and let the oppressed go free.' The President has placed the Union pry under the corner stone of the Confederacy and the structure *will* fall." Writing from Jackson, Tennessee, to his wife on the one-year anniversary of his enlistment, John P. Jones, of the 45th Illinois, also waxed eloquent: "The 'year of Jubilee' has indeed come to the poor slave. The proclamation is a deathblow to slavery. . . . The name of Abraham Lincoln will be handed down to posterity, as one of the greatest benefactors of his Country, not surpassed by the immortal Washington himself. . . . We now know what we are fighting for, we have an object, and that object is avowed." Frederick Wilkinson, a second lieutenant with the 2nd Michigan, agreed: "The men look more like doing something since the President's Proclamation. That is better than 100,000 men or fifty victorys. I hope the people of the North will now find that they have now something to fight for." Private Levi Hines of the 11th Vermont wrote his parents, "The late proclamation of the President makes it a war on Slavery and I am ready to die fighting . . . for the purpose of ending that *hellish curse* of our country." One Illinois volunteer proclaimed, "The sentiment of the army is 'God bless Abraham.' Hitherto the great trouble has been just here: the president has been governed by the sentiments of the people at home, in a great measure disregarding the sentiments, feelings, and suggestions of the army. On this question [emancipation] the army has been far in advance of the people."[34]

The timing of the Proclamation, which came after an extended gestation period, seemed to be critical to the document's acceptance by some soldiers. The army correspondent to the *Cincinnati Gazette* reported, "I have conversed with a number of intelligent and, I believe, truly loyal men, who declare that, if this had been done 'ten months since' they would not have remained in the service 'ten minutes.' But now they say, (and this is the universal expression,) there is a military necessity which fully justifies the President in this course." At the same time, another soldier believed that "if the President's proclamation had been proclaimed one year sooner than it was I think the war would have been just so much nearer the end." John Quincy Adams Campbell agreed: the "proclamation would have been in better time . . . if it had been made a year ago. But better late than never." One private in the 15th Massachusetts supported the Proclamation but told his brother: "I fear it won't do any good because we cant enforce it. Time will tell." But a colonel with the 9th Indiana declared, "This army will sustain the emancipation proclamation and enforce it with the bayonet."[35]

Some soldiers started out opposed, but over the hundred days changed their minds. A sergeant in the 8th Illinois Infantry reported that when the Proclamation was issued "a number of our officers became very much excited. Several of them talked strongly of tendering their resignations in consequence thereof, and one of them really did. But we are too strong for the d—d compromising lickspittles, and to-day you can't hear a whimper against it." A soldier in the 16th Illinois confessed to his brother-in-law in the 99th Illinois: "I think old Abe's proclamation is all right and there is very few soldiers that is against it[;] it is my opinion that yourself and the greater part of your Regiment will be in favor of it before you are in the service six months. I was of the same opinion of your self when I first came in service but I have learned better." And a second lieutenant in the 28th Illinois, stationed in Mississippi, admitted: "I did not like it at first myself, but I have now come to the conclusion that it is the best thing that can possibly be done. It just brings these proud southerners down to a level with other people in their own imagination as well as in other peoples. Here lately they cant hold up their heads & put on 'airs' & talk independently like they did before the Proclamation came out."[36]

To be sure, many soldiers vehemently opposed the Proclamation; and some commissioned officers resigned, and enlisted men deserted, as a result of it. After all, two-fifths of Union men had a Democratic background and at least one-tenth hailed from the border states. Henry Hubbell of the 3rd New York Volunteers reported in October, "I have heard but one expression of opinion by Officers, Regular or Volunteer, in regard to the Pres' Emancipation Proclamation—viz, that of disapproval, and fear of its bad effect at the north by causing division." A captain in the 91st New York said, "The emancipation act is alarmingly unpopular. . . . There has been a great many resignations." Another New Yorker, a lieutenant in the 1st New York Light Artillery, said in November: "I am really getting tired of the way [the war] is carried on and some of our rabid abolitionists are making it nothing but a nigger war, and that is not what I came for." Another soldier, from the 19th Indiana, asserted that "no one who has ever seen the nigger in all his glory on the southern plantations . . . will ever vote for emancipation." And Corporal William Ross of the 40th Illinois wrote: "The soldiers are swaring that they will stack their arms, desert, or go to the confederate army or anything before they will fight to free the negroes and I suppose they are all to bee free by the first of January." But he added that whether the troops favored the Proclamation did not matter, because "they are sworn to stand by Abryhham and what he says must be law and gospel."[37]

Overcoming racial hatred and fear would not be easy, and some soldiers made it plain that they despised slavery and blacks equally. Charles Chase, a private with the 23rd Massachusetts, informed his brother, "Ere this you probably have read Pres. Lincoln's proclamation declaring all slaves free after Jan. 1st 1863, the people I think say 'amen.' What would they have said had he issued it a year ago? I think it is fast being proven that slavery is wrong, a curse to all that have any thing to do with it. But we cannot have the Negro in this country unless we give him one or two states and let them go it, they and the whites never can get along together. I can't bare them."[38]

In the end, most soldiers kept their personal feelings subordinate to their military duty. William Ross, a corporal in the 40th Illinois, claimed that "a majority of the Volunteers is against the Presidents Proclimation but they have about come to the conclusion that they will have to submit to what ever Old Abe says." Lieutenant Robert Stoddart Robertson of the 93rd New York proclaimed, "I did not and I presume two thirds of the officers did not come out to fight for slave emancipation, but if it becomes a military necessity we will do it. In the Army, we attach little, if any, importance to the proclamation. It is no doubt intended to bring the South to their senses, & end the war sooner, & in that light it is a good idea." John W. Chase, a private with the 1st Massachusetts Light Artillery, thought it odd to talk about freeing slaves before conquering some of the slave states, and decided the Proclamation was issued to placate the abolitionists and radicals: "He must do something to keep the nigger worshippers quiet and this seems to prove a very good sugar tit for them." Oliver Willcox Norton, a private with the 83rd Regiment Pennsylvania Volunteers, offered a dose of realism: "I approve of the proclamation, but I don't think it is going to scare the South into submission."[39]

For Norton, as for many soldiers, the experience of going south and encountering slavery firsthand had altered his perceptions of the institution, though sometimes the experience hardened racial antipathies. In January 1862, Norton wrote: "I thought I hated slavery as much as possible before I came here, but here, where I can see some of its workings, I am more than ever convinced of the cruelty and inhumanity of the system." As for the idea that "this is not a war against slavery, . . . away with such nonsense, I say, and all the soldiers all say so. Give us a haul-in-sweep of their niggers, their houses, towns, and everything, only conquer them quickly." In June, Norton reported that "a man named George Taylor who had inhumanely whipped a slave, came into our camp after him and he came near losing his life by the operation. He escaped by taking the oath of allegiance, but he lost his nigger." At the same time, Norton thought some radicals were hoping that the army would go down in defeat, which would prove the need "to make the abolition of slavery a military necessity." Horace Greeley, he assured his siblings, would not survive twenty-four hours were he to arrive in camp. "I used to be something of an abolitionist," he confessed, "but I've got so lately that I don't believe it is policy to sacrifice everything to the nigger."[40]

Soldiers were especially shocked to see slaves who appeared as light-skinned as they themselves were. Captain Charles Haydon of the 2nd Michigan wrote in his journal on November 17: "I saw to day a white slave, a girl about 18 with blue eyes, yellow hair nearly straight and a complexion lighter than a majority of northern women. I should never have suspected her African blood if I had not seen her with other slaves." Wilder Dwight, a lieutenant colonel with the 2nd Massachusetts Infantry Volunteers, was shocked by the response when he asked a contraband what he was doing in camp:

"I ran away last night," the curly-haired man said.

"Ran away! From whom?" asked Dwight.

"From my mistress."

"Are you a slave?"

"Yes."

"Nothing could have been more unexpected than this reply," confessed Dwight. "The fellow says he has brothers and sisters as white as himself, and all slaves. His father is a white man, his mother a yellow woman. The man's features and accent were European. O, this is a beautiful system, in its practical details—a firm basis for a Christian commonwealth! It is an order of things worth fighting for! Bah!" "Masters deal in their own blood!" reported one soldier. "We only heard of this, before. Now we see it, and *know* it! If that won't change politics, what will?"[41]

Such encounters became more common. "Contrabands are pouring in on us every day," wrote Oliver Willcox Norton in May from the encampment at Cold Harbor, Virginia. One soldier reported "a sight that I would gladly photograph for you. A large wagon full of negro men, women, and children, overrunning like the old woman's shoe. It had come from the farm, near town, of some disloyal Rebel. There stood the load of helpless and deserted contrabands; an embarrassment and a question typifying the status of the slave everywhere, as the army marches on." This, said Wilder Dwight, was "the practical effect of invasion. Where the army goes, slavery topples and falls."[42]

The exodus stood only to increase as word of the Emancipation Proclamation spread among the enslaved. "Intelligence of 'Massa' Lincum's emancipation proclamation has doubtless reached every negro household from Mason and Dixon's line to the Gulf of Mexico," reported Corporal Stephen Fleharty from Tennessee. Private Joseph Richardson Ward, Jr., of the 39th Illinois, stationed in Suffolk, Virginia, wrote his parents in October: "If the Presidants Proclemation works all over as it does here the south will soon begin to feal the effects of it. Already hundreds have come from North Carolina within our lines and say they heard of the Proclemation a way in the south where they never saw a Yankee soldier." Moncure Conway, Unitarian minister and abolitionist, believed that "the blacks know all that is said and done with reference to them in the North; that their longing for freedom is unutterable; that once assured of it under Northern protection, the institution would be doomed. . . . If he were on the upper Mississippi and proclaimed emancipation, it would be told in New Orleans before the telegraph could carry the news there." Louis Hughes recalled in his narrative *Thirty Years a Slave* that "as the war continued we would, now and then, hear of some slave in our neighborhood running away to the Yankees. It was common when the message of a Union victory came to see the slaves whispering to each other: 'We will be free.'" "The Proclamation is not barren of results," announced Frederick Douglass in November; "the negroes have heard of it, and are flocking in thousands to the lines of our army."[43]

But the slaveholders did not tolerate attempted acts of self-emancipation. Hughes told of two slaves who had tried to escape to Union lines but "were caught, brought back and hung." All the slaves were "called up, told every detail of the runaway and capture of the poor creatures and their shocking murder, and then compelled to go and see them where they hung. I never shall forget the horror of the scene—it was sickening. The bodies hung at the roadside, where the execution took place, until the blue flies literally swarmed around them, and the stench was fearful. This barbarous spectacle was for the purpose of showing passing slaves what would be the fate of those caught in an attempt to escape."[44]

The Proclamation enraged Confederates. "Now, any man who pretends to believe that this is not a war for the emancipation of the blacks, and that the whole course of the Yankee government has not only been directed to the abolition of slavery, but even to a stirring up of servile insurrections, is either a fool or a liar," reported a Confederate soldiers' newspaper. A Kentucky cavalry sergeant, believing that now men from the border states would pour into the rebel army, declared: "The Proclamation is worth three thousand soldiers to our Government at least. It shows exactly what this war was brought about for and the intention of its damnable authors." "After Lincoln's Proclamation," threatened a captain in the 27th Virginia, "any man that would not fight to the last should be hung as high as Haman."[45]

Some Union soldiers feared that the Proclamation might make the rebels fight more fiercely. On September 24, Corporal George Tillotson, of the 89th New York Infantry, informed his wife: "We have just got news that the president has issued a proclamation freeing all the slaves on the first of January. It may be for the best but stil my hopes (if I had any) of a speedy termination of the war is thereby nocked in head for I know enough of the southern spirit so that I think they will fight for the institution of slavery even to extermination." Lieutenant Robert Gould Shaw, still with the 2nd Massachusetts but soon to become an officer of the 54th Massachusetts, also had reservations. Shaw, a member of a prominent family, had impeccable abolitionist credentials, but he thought that the preliminary Emancipation Proclamation would yield no "*practical* good" because "wherever our army has been, there remain no slaves, and the Proclamation will not free them where we don't go." He worried that "Jeff Davis will soon issue a proclamation threatening to hang every prisoner they take, and will make this a war of extermination." After hearing back from his mother, who upbraided him for his apostasy, Shaw softened his tone and praised the Proclamation as "an act of justice"; indeed, he said he thought it should have been issued long before.[46]

In the end, the decree lifted the spirits of those soldiers who had come to despise slavery, as well as of those who, whatever their feelings about the institution, were more than ready for any policy that would speed the end of the war. Private Edward Edes of the 33rd Massachusetts told his mother, "I hope that the President's Proclamation will hurry the close of rebellion somewhat." A private in the 48th Illinois informed his sister that "the army as far as I know likes his (lincolns) proclamation very well and think that the plan will work so well that wee that are a live yet will be Home against June next." One writer, from conservative La Salle County in southern Illinois, took ideology out of the equation and probably summarized the feelings of many soldiers when he declared: "You have no idea of the change salt pork, hard crackers, burnt coffee and long marches have made in the political opinions of your La Salle county soldiers. They would make an abolitionist of the most inveterate Democrat that ever lived."[47]

7

Intervention and Election Fever

While Northerners and Southerners considered the effect of the Emancipation Proclamation at home, they obsessed over its influence abroad. From the start of the war, what Count Gurowski aptly called the "paroxysm of the foreign intervention fever" waxed and waned. It had begun as soon as Lincoln declared a naval blockade of the Confederate States. Such a measure, typically used against sovereign nations, threatened to invite European powers into the conflict by inducing them to recognize the Confederacy. England, in particular, had much to gain. Some 80 percent of Britain's cotton came from the United States; without it, England's burgeoning textile and manufacturing industry would come to a halt. Furthermore, many Englishmen, especially among the aristocracy, disdained the democratic politics of a nation that had repudiated its mother country, and they felt some sympathy for the southern effort at nation making. When, on May 14, 1861, the British government had issued a proclamation of neutrality, Lincoln and Seward, after initial concern that it signaled a prelude to recognition, had expressed relief. The British, who had preferred a blockade to Lincoln's other option—closing the ports—awarded the Confederacy belligerent status, but did not extend official recognition.[1]

William Seward's diplomacy with England early in the war seemed to fluctuate between aggression and appeasement. The secretary of state instructed Charles Francis Adams, minister to the Court of St. James's, to insist on certain conditions and to refuse to deal with the government unless it stopped meeting with Confederate emissaries; at the same time, he notified Adams and William Dayton, the minister to France, that the position of the United States was that the war was being fought not over slavery, but over disunion. When these dispatches became public, Massachusetts senator Charles Sumner howled that this was the "policy which has turned Europe against us." But Seward thought differently. He was reacting to a belief among some Europeans that the North was out to build an empire, and that attacking slavery would serve as an excuse for conquest, not a cry for freedom. Seward argued that so long as the issue was self-preservation rather than aggrandizement, foreign nations would not be tempted to come to the aid of the Confederacy.[2]

The delicate maneuvering almost came to an abrupt halt when an event toward the end of 1861 nearly brought Great Britain into the war on the Confederate side. On November 8, Captain Charles Wilkes, of the U.S. warship *San Jacinto,* boarded a British vessel, the *Trent,* and removed two Confederate commissioners, James Mason of Virginia and John Slidell of Louisiana, headed to Europe on a diplomatic mission. The Confederate commissioners, who had instructions to argue that the blockade was illegal whereas secession was legal, and that Great Britain would benefit from a Confederate victory, were brought to a prison in Boston.

The British government reacted with indignation. The prime minister, Lord Palmerston, considered it "a deliberate and premeditated insult" intended to provoke England. One correspondent writing from England informed Seward, "The people are frantic with rage, and were the country polled I fear 999 men out of one thousand would declare for immediate war." In his annual message to Congress, on December 3, Lincoln observed that "a nation which endures factious domestic division, is exposed to disrespect abroad; and one party, if not both, is sure, sooner or later, to invoke foreign intervention." He also warned European powers against becoming involved.[3]

The *Trent* affair terrified John Lothrop Motley, newly appointed minister to the Austrian Empire. Educated at Harvard and at the University of Göttingen, Motley was a distinguished historian whose book *The Rise of the*

Dutch Republic was a bestseller. But now, he said, he could no longer immerse himself in the sixteenth century: "I can think of nothing but American affairs." "I wish I could get back to the sixteenth and seventeenth centuries," he confessed, "but, alas! the events of the nineteenth century are too engrossing." Motley was well-connected in diplomatic circles, and knew personally most members of the British ministry. Sumner called him "a true American who knows well how . . . to inspire the confidence of foreign statesmen." In June 1861, from Boston, Motley had written sorrowfully to his wife: "We are treated to the cold shoulder of the mother-country, quite as decidedly as if she had never had an opinion or a sentiment on the subject of slavery, and as if the greatest *war of principle* which has been waged, in this generation at least, was of no more interest to her, except as it bore on the cotton question."[4]

Later that month, Motley went to Washington to meet with Lincoln. "I found the President better and younger-looking than his pictures. He is very dark and swarthy, and gives me the idea of a very honest, confiding, unsophisticated man, whose sincerity of purpose cannot be doubted." After another meeting, he wrote: "I believe him to be as true as steel, and as courageous as true. At the same time, there is doubtless an ignorance about State matters, and particularly about foreign affairs, which he does not affect to conceal, but which of necessity we must regret in a man placed in such a position at such a crisis."

Motley also met with treasury secretary Salmon Chase, whom he called a "frank, sincere, warm-hearted man." Writing to his family on June 23, Motley quoted Chase:

If the insurrection is unreasonably protracted, and we find it much more difficult and expensive in blood and treasure to put it down than we anticipated, we shall then draw that sword which we prefer at present to leave in the sheath, and *we shall proclaim the total abolition of slavery on the American continent.* We do not wish this, we deplore it, because of the vast confiscation of property, and of the servile insurrections, too horrible to contemplate, which would follow. We wish the Constitution and Union as it is, with slavery, as a municipal institution, existing until such time as each state in its wisdom thinks fit to mitigate or abolish it, but with freedom the law of the Territories and the land; but if the issue be distinctly presented, death to the American republic or death to slavery, slavery *must die.*"

As Motley looked ahead to October, he worried that when the new cotton crop was harvested, England might be tempted to violate the blockade. "I refuse to contemplate such a possibility," he wrote—while, of course, doing little else but contemplating it. "It would be madness on the part of England, for at the very moment when it would ally itself with the South against the United States, for the sake of supplying their English manufacturers with their cotton, *there would be a cry of twenty millions as from one mouth for the instant emancipation of all the slaves.*"[5]

With the *Trent* affair, Motley passed from sanguine (in September, he had written that "there will be no foreign interference" and that European cotton manufacturers were trying to supply themselves from India) to despondent ("If the South has now secured the alliance of England, a restoration of the Union becomes hopeless"). Tensions and threats mounted, until Lincoln's administration informed the Palmerston ministry that Captain Wilkes had acted without authorization, which Palmerston chose to interpret as a disclaimer of any intention on the part of the U.S. government to violate international law. The two prisoners were released on New Year's Day and made their way to England. For the time being, the war remained an internal affair between the United States and the Confederate States.

Throughout 1862, anxiety grew. Motley became convinced the only way to prevent European intervention was to declare that the war was specifically against slavery. "If we continue to dally with the subject of emancipation much longer," he wrote from Vienna on January 13, "and continue on efforts to suppress the rebellion without daring to lay a finger on its cause, we shall have the slave Confederacy recognized by all the governments of Europe before midsummer." The reason, he argued, was simple: the pro-Confederacy party in England could not publicly avow itself in favor of slavery, "for that institution is so odious to the great mass of the English nation as to consign any party *openly* supporting it to destruction; but it contents itself with persuading the public that slavery has nothing to do with secession, that the North is no more anti-slavery than the South, and that therefore all the sympathies of liberal Englishmen ought to be given to the weaker of the two sections, which is striving by a war of self-defense to relieve itself from tyrannical oppression." Motley repeated in February:

> Our great danger comes from foreign interference. What will prevent that? Our utterly defeating the Confederates in some *great* and *conclusive* battle, or our possession of the cotton ports and opening them up to European trade, or a most *unequivocal policy* of slave-emancipation. Any one of these three conditions would stave off recognition by foreign powers. . . . The last measure is to my mind the most important. . . . We are threatened with national annihilation, and defied to use the only means of national preservation. The question is distinctly posed to us, Shall slavery die, or the great Republic?[6]

The situation seemed even more urgent in late February, when rumors circulated that Confederate agents in London and Paris were quietly offering to abolish slavery in return for diplomatic recognition. But then Union victories in the spring, especially the capture of New Orleans in April, seemed once and for all to forestall talk of mediation, recognition, or intervention. An exhausted Charles Francis Adams wrote from London in May, "I have been here now more than a year, during which time I have gone through nearly every variety of emotion in connection with this war. The time is approaching, I trust, when this anxiety will disappear."[7]

Motley praised each successive step taken by the administration and Congress: the message on compensated emancipation, the abolition of slavery in Washington, the movement toward confiscation. Whatever his feelings about Lincoln's overturning of Hunter's proclamation, he did not confide them to his correspondents. Instead, on June 22, he commended the president for "his wisdom, courage, devotion to duty, and simplicity of character." Indeed, he grasped something essential about Lincoln's way of proceeding: "I think Mr. Lincoln embodies singularly well the healthy American mind. He revolts at extreme measures, and moves in a steady way to the necessary end. He reads the signs of the times, and will never go faster than the people at his back. So his slowness seems like hesitation; but I have not a doubt, that when the people will it, he will declare that will, and with the disappearance of the only dissolvent [slavery] the dissolution of the union will be made impossible."[8]

By late August, however, he was worried anew about the threat of European intervention. The cotton supply in England was dwindling, mills were closing, and the failure of General McClellan's campaign to take Richmond, followed less than two months later by Robert E. Lee's smashing victory at Second Bull Run, had again made ultimate Union military success seem doubtful in the eyes of Europeans. Luckily, Charles Francis Adams pointed out, the reports of Union setbacks came during "the most dead season of the year," when Parliament was not in session.[9]

England was not the only foreign nation with an interest in American affairs. Louis-Napoleon of France was urging the English government to participate in a joint Anglo-French mediation effort, and Napoleon was himself scheming in Mexico. Motley claimed, "The only thing that saves us yet from a war with the slaveholders allied with both France and England is the antislavery feeling of a very considerable portion of the British public. . . . I am entirely convinced, not as a matter of theory, but as a fact, that nothing but a proclamation of emancipation to every negro in the country will save us from war with England and France combined."

At his post in Vienna, Motley hung on every scrap of news from home and from other European capitals. He subscribed to American newspapers and relived events weeks after they occurred. His letters went on for pages, and he begged his correspondents for observations and information. And there, in Austria, four thousand miles from home, the historian and diplomat became radicalized. "The very reason which always prevented me from being an abolitionist before the war," he confessed, "in spite of my antislavery sentiments and opinions, now forces me to be an emancipationist. I did not wish to see the government destroyed, which was the avowed purpose of the abolitionists. When this became the avowed purpose of the slaveholders, when they made war upon us, the whole case was turned upside down. The antislavery men became the Unionists, the slaveholders the destructionists. This is so plain that no mathematical axiom is plainer. There is no way of contending with the enemy at our gates but by emancipation."[10]

Motley expressed those thoughts to his daughter on September 21. The next day the president, having arrived at the same conclusion, but by a different route, followed the advice that so many had been urging for so long. To what extent concern over possible English and French intervention entered into his calculations is difficult to say. Neither Welles nor Chase, in their diary entries, make mention of it as a factor. Indeed, it is striking how little concern over European affairs enters into their accounts. Seward, of course, had been navigating relations with European powers all along, and by the summer of 1862 he had heard regularly from his ministers—not only Motley, but also Carl Schurz (Spain), Cassius M. Clay (Russia), and James S. Pike (Netherlands)—that a policy attacking slavery would win overseas support. But Seward did not initially endorse Lincoln's decision to issue an emancipation proclamation, so it is unlikely that he offered any pro-emancipation arguments based on diplomatic considerations. Indeed, the case could be made that while attacking slavery would win the support of more liberal, antislavery constituencies in Europe, it would antagonize the textile makers, who feared that an end to slavery would also end southern cotton production, and alarm all manner of conservatives, who feared that abolition would lead to "servile warfare"—uprisings by the enslaved against the slaveholders. Seward himself had shrewdly made the economic argument in messages to Charles Francis Adams during the summer. "Intervention will end the exportation of cotton," he predicted, "by extinguishing the slavery which produces it." He warned that should England and France intervene, "the civil war will, without our fault, become a war of continents—a war of the world; and whatever else may revive, the cotton trade built upon the slave labour in this country will be irredeemably wrecked in the abrupt cessation of human bondage within the territories of the United States."[11]

Previous to the preliminary Emancipation Proclamation, the issue of European attitudes had come up in Lincoln's meeting with Francis Cutting on July 22, and in his reply on September 13 to a delegation of Chicago Christians, who had told him that "to proclaim emancipation would secure the sympathy of Europe and the whole civilized world, which now saw no other reason for the strife than national pride and ambition, an unwillingness to abridge our domain and power. No other step would be so potent as to prevent foreign intervention." Lincoln had responded, "I will also concede that emancipation would help us in Europe, and convince them that we are incited by something more than ambition."[12]

At most, fear of European intervention was a subsidiary reason for Lincoln's decision to issue the Emancipation Proclamation. He was more directly concerned with taking measures out of military necessity that would subdue the rebellion. He acted because he had finally lost patience with the border states, and because he believed public opinion now supported such action. Still, at the same time that Lincoln decided to issue the preliminary Emancipation Proclamation, Seward gave notice in a letter circulated to American diplomats. The time had come, the letter read, to make it clear to the rebel states that if "they persist in imposing upon the country the choice between . . . this Government, at once necessary and beneficial, and the abolition of Slavery, it is the Union and not Slavery that must be maintained and saved."[13]

Regardless of the degree to which Europe entered into Lincoln's decision to issue the Emancipation Proclamation, the question of intervention figured prominently in how some Americans received the document. Charles Fessenden Morse declared that "no foreign nation can now support the South without openly countenancing slavery." A private in the 72nd Pennsylvania noted that "foreign nations will now have to come out flat-footed and take sides; they dare not go with the South, for slavery, and consequently they will all be ranged on our side." One editor noted, "we infer from its adoption at this particular time that the President anticipates trouble from abroad, and that he is determined that foreign interventionists, if there shall be, shall assume the parts of champions of slavery." And Frederick Douglass asserted:

> The effect of this paper upon the disposition of Europe will be great and increasing. It changes the character of the war in European eyes and gives it an important principle as an object, instead of national pride and interest. It recognizes and declares the real nature of the contest, and places the North on the side of justice and civilization, and the rebels on the side of robbery and barbarism. It will disarm all purpose on the part of European Governments to intervene in favor of the rebels and thus cast off at a blow one source of rebel power.[14]

Yet reaction to the preliminary Emancipation Proclamation, particularly from the British, must have come as a surprise to those who argued that making the war an explicit assault on slavery would win over Europe and put an end to talk of intervention; instead, it nearly caused it. To be sure, many workingmen in England and elsewhere praised the document. They saw the war as a struggle over labor—free versus slave—and whatever hardship the blockade caused them, they could not root for a southern slaveholding aristocracy. One observer said that mill operatives in England look "upon slavery as the author and source of their present miseries." Liberal papers such as the *London Star* asked, "Is this not a gigantic stride in the paths of Christian and civilized progress? Is not here a reason, abundant and unquestionable, why every man to whom personal or political freedom is dear should pray for the success of the Union Arms?"[15]

But even the most radical papers, such as the *Guardian,* found the Proclamation to be "nothing more than a compound of 'bunkum' on a grand scale with the swaggering bravado" present throughout the war. It had been "too hastily regarded as announcing an approaching abolition of slavery throughout the United States"; instead, "it still leaves the door open for a reconstruction of the Union without the slightest practical effort to reduce the power of slavery." And "the fact that [Lincoln's] proclamation once more brings forward the scheme of negro colonization . . . will not make it more palatable in Europe."[16]

For different reasons, foreign diplomats were deeply troubled by the Proclamation. Lord Palmerston, the British prime minister, called it a "singular manifesto that could scarcely be treated seriously." Lord Russell, the British foreign secretary, thought that it would provide a premium for "acts of plunder, of incendiarism, and of revenge." The British chargé d'affaires in Washington, William Stuart, wrote Lord Russell: "There is no pretext of humanity about the Proclamation. It is cold, vindictive, and entirely political." Diplomats from other nations agreed. Henri Mercier of France labeled the Proclamation "an act of desperation, atrocious in the intent it reveals and the consequences it might entail." Edouard de Stoeckl of Russia lamented that "emancipation is used by President Lincoln as a military weapon to subdue his enemies and is not at all a proclamation of human liberty." And the Spanish minister, Gabriel García y Tassara, called it "an act of vengeance and cowardliness." Writing from Paris, William Dayton warned Seward in October of "another spasmodic effort for intervention . . . based upon the assumed ground of humanity but based upon the real ground that emancipation may seriously injure the cause of the South, and will interfere for years to come, at least, with the production of cotton."[17]

To make matters worse from an administration perspective, on October 7 in Newcastle, William E. Gladstone, chancellor of the exchequer, declared: "There is no doubt that Jefferson Davis and other leaders of the South have made an army; they are making, it appears, a navy; and they have made what is more than either—they have made a nation. . . . We may anticipate with certainty the success of the Southern States so far as regards their separation from the North." Gladstone said he was speaking only for himself, not the government, but clearly some prominent British figures favored an offer of mediation followed by recognition of the Confederacy, even after learning of the preliminary Emancipation Proclamation.[18]

The influential *London Times,* which from the start of the war had sympathized with the Confederacy and promoted intervention, attacked the Proclamation, calling it a "very sad document," contemptible and wicked. The editor accused Lincoln of "doing his best to excite a servile war. . . . He will appeal to the black blood of the Africans; he will whisper of the pleasures of spoil and the gratification of yet fierce instincts; and when blood begins to flow and shrieks come piercing through the darkness, Mr. Lincoln will wait till the rising flames tell that all is consummated, and then he will rub his hands and think that revenge is sweet."[19]

The *Liverpool Mail* called the Proclamation "a mere waste of paper unless it should have the effect of stimulating the slaves to take up arms against their masters, and thus precipitate a servile war." Slave revolts, predicted the *Newcastle Daily Journal,* would occur "on the remote plantations where every white man would be murdered, every traveler waylaid, every white woman seized, and every pale-faced child tossed into the flames of the burning homestead." Reactions in France mirrored the English response. *La France* said the measure "looks no higher than a general butchery of defenseless women and children," and *Le Constitutionnel* declared that, as a war measure, it "does not do honor to the moral sense of its signer or the government that approved it."[20]

And so the preliminary Emancipation Proclamation did little to dissuade the British and the French from considering formal recognition of the Confederacy; indeed, it very well might have served as an excuse to hasten intervention. Lincoln was seen as acting in desperation, the Proclamation being "the last resource of a desperate trader to burn down his own house." The editors of the *London Times* declared that Lincoln *"has played his last card"* and that they did not believe "it will prove to be a trump." The British humor magazine *Punch* included a cartoon that showed a demoniacal Lincoln holding up the ace of spades and playing it atop a keg of gunpowder. The Proclamation was seen as lacking humanity and nobility. Even the *London Spectator,* which supported the Union cause, declared: "the principle is not that a human being cannot justly own another, but that he cannot own him unless he is loyal to the United States." The *Raleigh Register* believed that "instead of enlisting the sympathy of foreign powers with the so-called 'Union' cause, [the Proclamation] will inspire them with thorough disgust at a cause which requires for its support and success means at which humanity shudders."[21]

Gurowski correctly predicted this reaction to the document: "It may not produce in Europe the effect and the enthusiasm which it might have evoked if issued a year ago, as an act of justice and of self-conscientious force, as an utterance of the lofty, pure, and ardent aspirations and will of a high-minded people. England may see now in the proclamation an action of despair made in the duress of events; (and so it is in reality for Mr. Lincoln, Seward and their squad)."[22]

John Stuart Mill, British philosopher and avid supporter of the Union, whose essay "The Contest in America" helped to shape public opinion in England, wrote to Motley that while he personally exulted over the Proclamation, in England it "has only increased the venom of those who, after taunting you so long with caring nothing for abolition, now reproach you for your abolitionism as the worst of your crimes."

But Motley refused to succumb to such disillusionment. On November 25, he exclaimed: "The President's Proclamation was just in time. Had it been delayed it is possible that England would have accepted the invitation of France, and that invitation was in reality to recognize the slaveholders' Confederacy, and to make with it an alliance offensive and defensive. I am not exaggerating. The object is distinctly to unite all Europe against us, to impose peace, and to forcibly dismember our country." But the antislavery sentiment of the people of England, if not the rulers, combined now with a war against slavery, would make any meddling politically untenable.[23]

As it turns out, the issuance of the Emancipation Proclamation probably mattered less with respect to the question of English and French intervention than did the military victory that gave rise to it. Believing that the Confederacy was on the verge of success, the English cabinet inched toward accepting the proposal for joint mediation that had been put forward by the French emperor earlier in the summer. Such a measure would either lead to an agreement to end the war or—if Lincoln refused the offer, as time and again his administration had said he would—lead directly to Anglo-French recognition of the Confederacy. But after Lee's invasion of Maryland was defeated by Union forces under George McClellan, the mediation movement faltered. Adams reported that McClellan's victory "has done a good deal to restore our drooping credit here." Although Russell and Gladstone continued to press for recognition of the Confederacy, other cabinet members—most notably George C. Lewis, the secretary for war, and the Duke of Argyll, Lord Privy Seal—were strongly opposed. Finally, Palmerston declared in October that he thought it best for the British government to "continue merely to be lookers-on till the war shall have taken a more decided turn."[24]

More than forty years later, Henry Adams was still trying to piece together what had actually taken place and who had actually believed what. He had come to conclude that no politician could be trusted. Russell had lied to Adams's father about the possibility of intervention, though "the 'truth' was not known for thirty years." And, unknown to Charles Francis Adams, even as late as November Gladstone was still pressing for involvement in "the business of America." As Henry Adams looked back, it seemed that his political education was complete: "All the world had been at cross-purposes, had misunderstood themselves and the situation, had followed wrong paths, drawn wrong conclusions, and had known none of the facts."[25]

One of the events Europeans and Americans watched closely was the fall elections. In October 1862, voters in Pennsylvania, Ohio, and Indiana went to the polls; in November, Illinois, Missouri, Massachusetts, New York, and New Jersey held critical contests. New York and New Jersey would elect not only congressmen but governors as well. Coming in the aftermath of the Emancipation Proclamation and the suspension of habeas corpus, as well as the bogging-down of any military progress, the elections worried the Republicans. As early as July, when the cabinet first discussed the Emancipation Proclamation, postmaster general Montgomery Blair had expressed his concern that "it would cost the Administration the fall elections." Writing to Salmon Chase in September, Senator John Sherman informed him that "the election this Fall is feared by all our friends."[26]

When the returns came in, Blair was proven prescient, though the meaning of the final tallies was not entirely clear. In certain ways the outcome—sweeping Democratic victories in many states—mattered less than how they were interpreted, both at home and abroad. Were they a referendum on emancipation, civil liberties, or the war? Were they typical of off-year congressional elections, when the majority party nearly always lost seats? What effect would the elections have on the policies of Lincoln's administration? This debate over the meaning of the fall elections preoccupied politicians, editors, and everyday citizens. Even Lincoln engaged in some testy correspondence over how to read the results.

Historians have pointed out that the elections did not turn out as badly as they may have appeared. The consensus is that Democrats gained thirty-four seats. But according to the Clerk of the House of Representatives, the 37th Congress contained forty-four Democrats and the 38th contained seventy-two, which made for a pickup of twenty-eight seats. An article on the elections in the New York *Saturday Evening Post* arrived at the same number. Part of the complexity of establishing a fixed number is that the 38th Congress, according to the Clerk, contained sixteen Unconditional Unionists and nine Unionists, some of whom leaned heavily to the Democratic side. The difficulty of resolving nomenclature is typified by the Missouri state election, which went very well for Lincoln's party. Official records give the result as six Unconditional Unionists and three Unionists elected. But on November 14, Francis Blair wired Lincoln that Missouri had elected "5 Republicans one Emancipationist Democrat 2 Unconditional Union & 2 proslavery Dem's to Congress." Not only were the labels different, so too was the total. Even Salmon Chase found the nomenclature puzzling. He referred to the triumph of "the Conservative—Union—War & Anti-War—in fact all sorts of party," and suggested that they should "take boldly the name of Democratic Republicans & say above-board that we are Democratic & are Republican. . . . Such a party might be made invincible."[27]

It is certain, however, that the Democratic Party gained: Pennsylvania, Illinois, Indiana, Ohio, and New York all sent majority Democratic delegations to Congress, with Republicans losing five seats in Pennsylvania, eight in Ohio, and nine in New York. In Illinois, Democrats captured nine of fourteen seats, even taking Lincoln's home Eighth District. Democrats gained in Wisconsin as well. State legislatures in Indiana and Illinois came under Democratic control, and New Jersey and New York elected Democratic governors. Following the first wave of results in October, John G. Nicolay wrote, "We are all blue here today on account of the election news."[28]

Still, it could have been more catastrophic from a Republican standpoint: Pennsylvania and Ohio elected their governors in odd-numbered years, and Illinois and Indiana had elected governors to four-year terms in 1860. Republicans still controlled Congress, as well as the vast majority of governorships and state legislatures. And where they lost, the margins of defeat were slim: 4,000 votes in Pennsylvania, 6,000 in Ohio, and 10,000 in New York and Indiana.[29]

But the meaning of the elections rested not in numbers but in perceptions and reactions. John Lothrop Motley admitted to the "spleen and despondency into which I was thrown by the first accounts of the elections in New York, Pennsylvania, and Ohio." And Count Gurowski wrote, "The future looks dark and terrible. I shudder." It would be difficult to find two men with more contrasting temperaments and beliefs than Motley and Gurowski, yet both arrived at similar states of mind.[30]

So far as Gurowski was concerned, the meaning of the elections was simple: they "evidence the deep imprint upon the country of Lincoln-Seward disorganizing, because from the first day vacillating, undecided, both-ways policy. The elections reverberate the moral, the political, and the belligerent condition in which the country is dragged and thrown by these two *master spirits*. No decided principle inspires them and their administration, and no principle leads and has a dreaded majority in the elections; neither the democrats nor the republicans prevail; neither freedom nor submission is the watchword.... All is confusion."[31]

In the lower Midwest, candidates were convinced the preliminary Emancipation Proclamation would secure their defeat. One candidate for Congress from Ohio, Hezekiah Bundy, informed Chase that "the President's proclamation has come just in the nic of time to save the country perhaps, while from present appearance it will defeat me and every other Union Candidate for Congress along the border. But we stand square up to the proclamation let personal consequences be what they may."[32]

Bundy was prophetic: he was defeated, but two years later was elected to the 39th Congress. The elections in the Midwest seemed to turn, however, not so much on the preliminary Emancipation Proclamation per se as on the racial fears of the electorate. Of course, the two were connected, but Democratic politicians had played on racial fears long before Lincoln issued the Proclamation, and the ongoing actions of Congress dating back to the First Confiscation Act irked conservatives more than the actions of the president, who at least, it seemed, had taken measures time and again to keep the war focused on restoring union, not ending slavery. In June 1862, during the debate over the Second Confiscation Act, Samuel Cox had asked, "Is Ohio to be Africanized?" The summer had already brought scenes of racial violence to Cincinnati, Toledo, and Chicago as blacks and whites battled over wages and jobs. Indeed, in his public appeal to Lincoln in August, Horace Greeley had made mention of the "late anti-Negro riots in the North" and the propagandistic uses to which the rebels put them.

Violence against blacks was sporadic, but civil inequality seemed permanent. Illinois, Iowa, Indiana, Ohio, Wisconsin, Minnesota, and Michigan denied free black men the right to vote. Blacks were even forbidden legally to immigrate to Iowa and Indiana. On June 17, voters in Illinois rejected a new state constitution, but passed separate amendments that forbade black immigration and black suffrage. Midwesterners became especially alarmed when Edwin Stanton issued an order on September 18 that a group of contrabands, living in an army camp in Cairo, Illinois, be shipped northward to help alleviate the shortage of labor for the fall harvest resulting from the absence of so many men who had gone off to war. When a few days later Lincoln acted on slavery, the *Chicago Times* called it a "proclamation of negro equality" and predicted that blacks traveling into the state would be "the first fruits of emancipation." One newspaper directly addressed voters: "Democrats, recollect that you want to send men to the legislature who will take the means to prevent the State from being overrun by free niggers." Summarizing the feelings of most Democrats, one politician declared: "The Constitution as it is, the Union as it was, and the niggers where they are."[33]

Republicans did their best to offset this new slogan. In an essay published in October in the *Continental Monthly,* the editor wrote that the phrase "the Constitution as it is—the Union as it was" was being used "to distract and perplex the public mind." The Constitution did not stand in the way of taking necessary measures to win the war and preserve the Constitution. And "the Union 'as it was' is a thing that never can be again." The rebels would never lay down their arms "until they are conquered by overwhelming military force." Those who used the phrase "the Constitution as it is" meant it as a defense of slavery. But "most wise men believe that in the end of the war there is not likely to be much slavery to need constitutional protection." The phrase was the domain not of those who wanted to save the Constitution and the Union, but of those who wanted to destroy it.[34]

As it turned out, the man credited with coining the phrase, Clement Vallandigham of Dayton, Ohio, was not reelected to Congress. His advocacy of an immediate armistice to be followed by negotiations riled Unionists, and many felt that his accusations against Lincoln and the government skated upon the line of treason. Redistricting also cost him some of his most avid supporters. Adelaide Case wrote to her friend Charles Tenney, a private in the 7th Ohio, "You are glad Valandingham [*sic*] was defeated. So was I. What an insult to Ohio's brave soldiers was the nomination of such a man—no not a man—a traitor. He is now—and always has been working against us—working with all the energy of which demons are capable to destroy this noble republic."[35]

Treason was one matter; racial demagoguery another. And it seemed that no degree of Republican counterargument could blunt the effect of a Democratic Party that sought "to galvanize a dead and rotten party into life by yelping 'nigger! Nigger! NIGGER!' around its corpse." But voters were concerned with more than blacks inundating their region. They deplored Lincoln's suspension of habeas corpus, accusing the president of "seeking to inaugurate a reign of terror in the loyal states by military arrests . . . and to destroy all constitutional guaranties of free speech, a free press, and the writ of habeas corpus." The issue of blacks entering Illinois and the suspension of civil liberties probably did more than the Emancipation Proclamation to cause the defeat of Lincoln's friend Leonard Swett in the president's home district of Springfield. Indeed, Republicans initially believed that the Emancipation Proclamation would help their cause in places where voters wanted to see sterner war measures taken. Swett declared on September 27 that "the Proclamation fell upon" his opponent, John T. Stuart, "like an exploding shell and since then he has not known what to say." Instead, Stuart said nothing, refusing to debate Swett on the grounds that he could be arrested for the content of his speech. The ploy worked, and Swett was not elected.[36]

The electorate also bemoaned a war that had bogged down. Lincoln himself became so disgusted with McClellan's inertia that, in October, in response to a dispatch about "sore tongued and fatigued horses," he inquired: "Will you pardon me for asking what the horses of your army have done since the Battle of Antietam that fatigue anything?" In Pennsylvania, military developments played a key role in Republican defeat. On October 9, just five days before that state's elections, Confederate General J. E. B. Stuart launched a sensational reconnaissance mission in which he and some 1,800 cavalry troopers rode completely around McClellan's immobile army. On the 11th, they occupied Chambersburg, Pennsylvania, cutting telegraph lines, seizing horses, and demolishing railroad machine shops, a depot, and several trains before returning safely to Virginia on the 12th. The only Confederate casualty was one wounded trooper. Blame was placed on the Union army, which not only failed to protect citizens against incursions, but also seemed, since Antietam, unwilling to fight at all. Pennsylvania congressman James Moorhead informed the president, "The tardiness of our Army movements had more to do with our political defeat in Penna than the Proclamation." One commentator wryly noted that it was unfortunate that "Republican candidates should lose because Democratic Generals won't fight." A Republican newspaper offered an analysis of the Democratic gains in the state: "The people have availed themselves of the elections to render manifest their dissatisfactions with the lingering course of the war, the events of which have not been commensurate with the enormous expenditures of blood and treasure."[37]

In other states, such as Illinois, it was not the direct threat posed by the

Confederates, but the inertia displayed by Union forces that aggravated voters. Horace White, correspondent for the *Chicago Tribune,* informed the president in late October, "*If* we are beaten in this State two weeks hence, it will be because McClellan & Buell [commanding Union forces in Tennessee and Kentucky] *wont fight.*" Governor Oliver Morton of Indiana informed the president that the Democrats would gain because the voters "believe that the Administration has grossly mismanaged the war. They think that irresolution, imbecility, and dishonesty have characterized its management; and whether the fact be so or not, *they believe it.*"[38]

By November, Lincoln's administration was especially anxious about the elections in New York, in particular the governor's race, which pitted Republican James Wadsworth against Democrat Horatio Seymour. Wadsworth was an affluent New Yorker who had been with the Republican Party from the start. When war erupted, he was commissioned a major general in the New York State Militia, and then became a brigadier general with the U.S. Volunteers and commanded the 2nd Brigade in McDowell's division of the Army of the Potomac. Through much of 1862, he commanded the military district of Washington. Wadsworth was the choice of the Greeley wing of the Republican Party in New York; Thurlow Weed, his antagonist, had preferred John A. Dix, a strongly pro-war Democrat who had a lengthy record of service to the country dating back to the War of 1812. Wadsworth expressed the concerns of the administration when he declared, "Here in this city of New York, more even than the Shenandoah or in the valleys of Kentucky, is the battle field to be fought, which is to preserve our liberties and perpetuate our country."[39]

Horatio Seymour, a conservative Democrat from upstate New York, where he had been mayor of Utica, had already served a term as governor in 1853–1854. During the campaign, Seymour defended himself against the charge that he favored a compromise to bring the war to an end and would not, if elected, send more troops into the field. But a year earlier, at the Democratic State Convention, Seymour had said: "I believe that we are either to be restored to our former position, with the constitution unweakened, and the powers of the States unimpaired, and the fireside rights of our citizens duly protected, or that our whole system of government is to fail." And the Democratic Party platform in New York called for an end to arbitrary arrests and denounced emancipation as "a proposal for the butchery of women and children, for scenes of lust and rapine, and of arson and murder, which would invoke the interference of civilized Europe." Republican David Dudley Field insisted that Seymour "would have half war and half accommodation. He is for peace on any terms." In his diary, Gideon Welles described Seymour as having "smartness, but not firm principles. He is an inveterate place-hunter, fond of office and not always choice of means in obtaining it. More a party man than patriot."[40]

The rhetoric of the campaign played heavily on the questions of emancipation and civil liberties. Wadsworth had publicly approved of the Emancipation Proclamation, and he argued that once freedom came, rather than New York being inundated with blacks looking for work and competing against recent immigrant groups, the free black population in the city would "drift to the South where they will find a congenial climate and vast tracts of land." But Democratic opponents called the Proclamation a "barbarous, disgraceful, hideous violation of the morality of Christendom," and denounced "sudden, secret, lawless arrests" and the infringement of free speech.

The prosecution of the war, however, may have played an even greater part in the election results than the dual proclamations. William Cullen Bryant, editor of the *New York Evening Post,* wrote to Lincoln on October 22 that "we are distressed and alarmed at the inactivity of our armies in putting down the rebellion. . . . These inopportune pauses, this strange sluggishness in military operations seem to us little short of absolute madness. Besides their disastrous influence on the final event of the war they will have a most unhappy effect upon the elections here, as we hear they have had in other states. The election of Mr. Seymour as Governor of New York would be a public calamity. A victory or two would almost annihilate his party and carry General Wadsworth triumphantly into office."

Those victories did not arrive, and Seymour was elected by a majority of some 10,000 votes out of 600,000 cast, a total that was 70,000 fewer than in 1860 because so many New York voters were away in the army and there was no provision for absentee balloting. Hearing that Seymour was elected, a Chicago editor lamented, "It does not seem possible that a majority of the men in . . . the great State of New York has swung round into the dark cesspool of Democracy." (The same editor, commenting on a Democratic clean sweep in New Jersey, exclaimed: "New Yorkers are wont to insist facetiously that New Jersey is not a part of the United States, and the result of her election yesterday certainly indicates that she scarcely deserves to be." Perhaps he should not have been surprised: in the election of 1860, New Jersey was the only northern state from which Stephen Douglas received electoral votes.) After New York's election, the *Tribune* concluded that Wadsworth had lost because of "general dissatisfaction with the slow progress or no progress of our Armies, and a wide-spread feeling that, through the incapacity of our military leaders, the blood and treasure of the loyal Millions are being sacrificed in vain." It also did not help that Weed, in all likelihood, had done little to support the candidate, and that Wadsworth, who disdained campaigning, had not arrived in New York until a week before the election.[41]

On October 31, Chase wrote: "We are looking with much anxiety to the result of the New York elections. Every element of opposition is combined. There are however many Americans and Democrats who strenuously support the Republican Ticket, believing that high patriotic duty demands it. The most recent advices indicate that Wadsworth will carry the state handsomely and that we shall have the Legislature. The Union men are thoroughly aroused. Still it is impossible to predict results in these days. Nothing need astonish us."

A few days later, an astonished Chase tried to rationalize the results: "The elections—on the whole—are well enough. We can still save a majority in the House, &—except the great loss of the moral prestige & influence of Wadsworth as Governor of New York—I think the result not really damaging." Others could not dismiss the results so easily, and an extensive debate about the meaning of the elections ensued—a debate in which widely divergent interpretations of the outcome were voiced. Although the choices of the electorate certainly mattered, so did the controversy over what the returns signified.[42]

For the Confederates, the meaning was clear. "This news produce great rejoicing, for it is hailed as the downfall of Republican despotism," wrote the proslavery journalist and novelist John Beauchamp Jones, who was working as a clerk in Richmond's War Department. "Some think it will be followed by a speedy peace, or else that the European powers will recognize us without further delay." The *Charleston Mercury* exulted that "we do not see how the defeat of the Administration can do otherwise than paralyze the war," and asked whether Lincoln and Seward "would dare carry into effect their Emancipation Proclamation, and thus persist in urging on upon the people the ruin which they have, by their votes, declared shall not prevail."[43]

But there was also a note of caution in the Confederate reaction. The *Charleston Mercury* warned, "It will not do to trust to the success of Democratic elections for our salvation." After all, many northern Democrats were as opposed to the Confederacy as Republicans. Perhaps even more unsettling, "It is quite uncertain what they will do," as "they have even less of a fixed purpose and definite policy than their opponents." Democrats might be just as fixed on war as on peace, and would do what was necessary to maintain political power." To be sure, better that the Democrats had won than the Republicans, but "we by no means expect this result to put an end to the war." The best that could be said was that "it is likely to bring distraction and division in the conduct of the war and among the people of the North," and this would benefit the Confederate cause.[44]

Northern Democrats defined the elections as a repudiation of the administration. Representative Samuel Sullivan Cox of Ohio thundered that "the people have registered their oaths at the ballot-boxes, that no infraction of the Constitution shall be suffered." What baffled him was the response of the administration, which, rather than withdrawing the Emancipation Proclamation and restoring the writ of habeas corpus, had offered "mockery, defiance, and persistency in wrong doing." Cox quoted the *London Times,* which said: "In the results of these elections we think we see hope that the word 'compromise' will soon come into general use." It was not, Cox averred, that the elections indicated "sympathy with the Southern rebellion." It was that "the war must be carried on *under* and not *over* the Constitution." Cox's colleague in Congress, William Richardson of Illinois, insisted that "the people are sick and tired of this eternal talk upon the negro, and they have expressed that disgust unmistakably in the recent elections."[45]

The *New York Herald* keyed on the Emancipation Proclamation: "It is now made plain to the President that the people do not desire to see the proclamation carried out, and that declarations of their will in the recent elections will enable him to postpone action on the proclamation." But proadministration papers such as the *Evening Post* responded, "It is more ingenious than ingenuous in the opposition prints to argue that the results of the late elections are a specific popular rebuke of the principles under the President's Proclamation. They have hitherto represented that document as a mere dead letter, without validity or effect, and they cannot now affect to regard it as an agency so living and real as to have been capable of working a serious revolution in public sentiment." The *Illinois Daily State Journal* speculated that the results might have been taken as a referendum, but only if the opposition party had articulated some sort of policy. Rather, "The opposition was a *mere* opposition. It had no line of policy, and was careful to enunciate none." As a result, the administration was free to interpret the results as they saw fit. William Owner, a southern sympathizer living in Washington, realized that although "the Presdt is grieved at the result of the elections . . . if any believe that he will change his course or policy because of the result they are woefully mistaken."[46]

Following New York's election, Lincoln said he felt "somewhat like that boy in Kentucky, who stubbed his toe while running to see his sweetheart. The boy said he was too big to cry, and far too badly hurt to laugh." He received numerous letters, none longer than the one that arrived from Isaac N. Morris, a Democratic Representative from Illinois in the last two pre-war Congresses. The manuscript letter goes on for twenty-two pages. Morris, who had sought in the election of 1860 to discredit Lincoln by seeking proof that the candidate had attended a meeting of the Know-Nothing Party, a group opposed to foreigners, now wrote to offer his assessment of the failures of the president's policy. He said "the Democratic triumphs . . . as I interpret them, do not mean a condemnation of the war, do not mean that the Government is to be abandoned, as an old wreck or allowed to be boarded by political pirates,—do not mean that secession and rebellion shall be allowed to plant their bloody flag upon the ramparts of the Constitution but do mean that the abuses and blunders of the war shall be corrected,—do mean that it shall be prosecuted to restore the Union and maintain the Constitution as it is and not as a partisan war."[47]

Morris saved his criticism of the Emancipation Proclamation for separate paragraphs. The Proclamation "alarmed the Union men of the South, and led the conservative men of all parties in the North to believe that your object was more to overthrow the Institutions of the South, than to restore the Government. . . . There never was a greater heresy or more dangerous doctrine than that which pleads a 'military necessity' as an excuse for violating a National Organic Law. . . . The war must be fought through with arms and not with proclamations. I am firmly convinced that if no proclamations had been issued by yourself or by your Generals since it commenced we would be in a much better condition today than we are."[48]

Some of Lincoln's friends were just as harsh as his political opponents. Orville Browning was back in Washington, and on November 29 he called on the president. "We had a long familiar talk," Browning wrote, relieved that the president "was apparently very glad to see me." They spoke about the recent elections, and Browning told him "that his proclamations had been disasterous to us. That prior to issuing them all loyal people were united in support of the war and the administration. That the masses of the democratic party were satisfied with him, and warmly supporting him, and that their disloyal leaders could not rally them in opposition—They had no issue without taking ground against the war, and upon that we would annihilate them. But the proclamations had revived old party issues—given them a rallying cry—capitol to operate upon and that we had the results in our defeat. To this the President had no reply."[49]

Many writers furnished other explanations for the defeats, none of which blamed the preliminary Emancipation Proclamation for the results at the polls, and some of which suggested that without the decree the Republicans might have done worse. If the decree was to be blamed for defeats in states such as Illinois and Ohio, it needed to be credited for victories in Massachusetts and Michigan. When Zachariah Chandler asked Lyman Trumbull to campaign for the Republicans in Michigan, Trumbull replied: "I do not believe there is the least danger in Michigan. Lincoln's Proclamation should do the trick to swing the election to Michigan." Chandler and Jacob Howard, both radicals, were elected to the Senate, and Austin Blair was reelected governor.[50]

Francis Springer, an Iowa attorney, reported to a local official that "the canvas on the republican side dragged, not because of the emancipation proclamation of the president, but because of the lamentable want of vigor and energy in the conduct of the war." Schuyler Colfax, representative from Indiana, wrote that the address of March 6 recommending compensated emancipation in the border states "lost us many votes, the charge being 'taxing the people hundreds of millions to pay for negroes to be turned loose to work North at 10 cts a day' but your glorious Proclamation came in the nick of time & gave us victory."[51]

From New York, David Dudley Field claimed that "the elections are very significant; nobody who observes carefully can fail to understand them. The people are dissatisfied. What they are dissatisfied with, is the question you & every Statesman will desire to have answered, for upon that answer depends the future." Field thought the Proclamation was not the central issue: "It lost us some votes, but it gained us more." He provided an example of how local events swung specific contests. In Erie County, the large vote against the Republicans was due "in great part to the taking away by your Marshall of A clergyman whom Judge Hall had ordered to be discharged on Habeas Corpus. In one of the towns of Chenango County, where one of the arrests had been made, it was proposed to give every vote in the town against you on that account, and every vote but six, was so given."[52]

Lincoln also heard from John Cochrane, a Republican activist in New York and an officer with the 65th New York. Cochrane did not think that the vote could be easily interpreted. Some people objected to the Emancipation Proclamation, but most "have been impelled by some uncertain indefinite sense that all was not right; and the greatest number have greedily visited their disappointment that the war is not finished & was not finished in 60 days upon the first responsible party they could discover—They have been aching *for a head* to smash—They thought they saw one, and they smashed Wadsworth's." John Codman Ropes crudely observed, "The New York and other elections are simply a reproof of the inactivity of the Government—and the confused state of the finances. They have nothing to do with the nigger-question." Prior to the election, George Templeton Strong predicted that defeat at the polls, should it come, "will be due not so much to the Emancipation Manifesto as to the irregular arrests the government has been making." But afterward he changed his mind and reasoned simply that the citizens of New York were "impatient, dissatisfied, disgusted, disappointed. We are in a state of dyspepsia and general, indefinite malaise, suffering from the necessary evils of war and from irritation at our slow progress. We take advantage of the first opportunity to change, for its own sake, just as a feverish patient shifts his position in bed, though he knows he'll be none the easier for it."[53]

John Hutchins, a Republican congressman from Ohio, tried to put the results in historical perspective. "There is no cause for discouragement in the recent elections," he argued, because "it has generally happened that the elections of the second Congress after the advent of a new Administration have resulted in the defeat of the party electing a President. That was the case in 1827, 1835, 1839, 1843, 1847, 1851, 1855, and 1859." The *Boston Evening Transcript* concurred: "For nearly twenty years past every Congress chosen with and favorable to the new President has been succeeded by a second Congress decidedly adverse to his policy." If this was the situation in ordinary times, there was no reason to think that the pattern in extraordinary times would be any different.[54]

In a letter to his brother General William T. Sherman, Senator John Sherman of Ohio blamed the defeat on two factors. First, "The people were dissatisfied at the conduct and results of the war. The slow movements on the Potomac and worse still in Kentucky dissatisfied and discouraged people. It was a little singular that the Democrats some of whom opposed the war should reap the benefit of this feeling, but such is the fate of parties." He thought the Emancipation Proclamation and suspension of habeas corpus also contributed. But he was especially peeved with the president, who "voluntarily abandoned" the Republican organization for a "no-party Union . . . to run against an old, well-drilled party organization." Forsaking ward meetings, committees, and conventions was as ridiculous politically as spurning drills and marches militarily, and the result in both cases was defeat.[55]

Carl Schurz, the former U.S. ambassador to Spain, also blamed Lincoln's administration, and his letter to the president received a pointed response. Schurz wrote saying that "the defeat of the administration is owing neither to your proclamations, nor to the financial policy of the Government, nor to a desire of the people to have peace at any price. I can speak openly, for you know that I am your friend. The defeat of the Administration is the Administration's own fault." Schurz went on to criticize Lincoln's decision to place opposition party members in key military roles. Lincoln had strengthened his enemies "by placing them on an equality with your friends." For all the effort and sacrifice, there had been few positive results, and "the people felt the necessity of a change."[56]

Schurz's letter is dated November 8; Lincoln responded on November 10.

"We have lost the elections," Lincoln began, "and it is natural that each of us will believe, and say, it has been because his peculiar views was not made sufficiently prominent." Lincoln attributed the defeat to "three main causes [that] told the whole story. 1. The democrats were left in a majority by our friends going to the war. 2. The democrats observed this & determined to re-instate themselves in power, and 3. Our newspapers, by vilifying and disparaging the administration, furnished them all the weapons to do it with. Certainly, the ill-success of the war had much to do with this."

Lincoln then took a scalpel to Schurz's arguments, pointing out all the opinions and assertions the general presented as if they were indisputable facts. The president had his own reading of "the plain facts, as they appear to me," and those were that the administration came into power with "a minority of the popular vote," that "the war came," and that it "was mere nonsense to suppose a minority could put down a majority in rebellion." Democrats had to be appointed to command, argued the president, merely because of their military knowledge and experience, and "I have scarcely appointed a democrat to a command, who was not urged by many republicans and opposed by none"—including Schurz. He concluded by observing that the success of the Republican generals was no greater than that of the Democrats.[57]

Remarkably, Schurz, who never lacked for gall, responded to the president in another letter, continuing the argument, saying the president was mistaken in his view that the losses were because of Republican soldiers in the field. He repeated, this time in italics, that *the result of the election was a most serious and severe reproach administered to the Administration,*" and that "the result of the election has complicated the crisis."

Displaying infinite patience, Lincoln replied one final time. He told Schurz that he had read his latest missive and "the purport of it that we lost the late election, and the administration is failing, because the war is unsuccessful; and that I must not flatter myself that I am not justly to blame for it. I certainly know that if the war fails, the administration fails, and that I *will* be blamed for it, whether I deserve it or not. And I ought to be blamed, if I could do better."[58]

A number of commentators agreed with Lincoln that a major reason for the Republican losses was that too many of the party's supporters were in the army and thus unable to go to the polls. General Benjamin Butler received a letter informing him that "the administration has been defeated in New York, New Jersey, Pennsylvania, and Ohio, in the first-named as well as in the latter two states by majorities which would probably have been overcome had the Volunteers from there been allowed to vote." Sumner agreed. He informed John Bright, the foremost liberal reformer in the British House of Commons, that the election losses for the administration "may be explained by the larger proportion of Republicans who have gone to war." One analyst asserted that in Pennsylvania, "a hundred thousand men . . . go out in the proportion of about three Republicans to one Democrat, an excess of fifty thousand men from the side which those who stay at home say is beaten in the election which follows."[59]

The most sustained analysis of the elections came from overseas. Karl Marx wrote that "the elections have been a defeat for the Washington government," but then he looked more closely at their meaning. He pointed out that since this Congress would not be seated until December 1863, "for the time being . . . the elections are nothing more than a demonstration." In New York, "a large part of their men entitled to vote is in the field." New York City, he pointed out, had always been Democratic, but the rural districts of the state voted Republican. Combining urban and rural, he claimed that the Democratic majority in the state came to only 8,000–10,000 votes. In Pennsylvania he reported the majority as only 3,500 votes. In Ohio it numbered 8,000, but the "efficient farmers in Indiana and Ohio hate the Negro almost as much as the slaveholder." The point, Marx thought, was how much had changed in two years: "If Lincoln had had *Emancipation of the Slaves* as his motto at that time, there can be no doubt that he would have been defeated." But now, the policy of the administration had received majorities in many states and significant minorities in the states where Republicans were defeated.[60]

The message was not to read the results as a referendum on emancipation, because they weren't, but rather to embrace the new war effort that made the emancipation of the slaves critical to the defeat of the rebellion. Republican leaders immediately seized upon this opportunity. Senator William Pitt Fessenden reflected, "I am not clear that the result of the elections is not fortunate for the country, for it has taught the President that he has nothing to look for in that quarter." "The hesitation of the Administration to adopt the policy of Emancipation," Charles Sumner argued after the October elections, "led democrats to feel that the President was against it & they have gradually rallied. I think a more determined policy months ago would have prevented them shewing their heads." But, as he had with the defeat at First Bull Run, Sumner saw "consolation even in our disasters, that they have brought the Presdt to a true policy. . . . The elections will doubtless encourage the Rebellion; but their *contrecoup* on the Administration has been good. The President is immensely quickened, & the War Department is harder at work than ever."[61]

The senator then referred to a fable that the president doubtless also knew: One winter, a farmer found a stiff and frozen snake. Showing compassion, he took it in, and held it by the fire to warm it. The snake revived and, reverting to its natural instincts, bit the farmer and inflicted a mortal wound. With his last breath the farmer cried, "Oh, I am rightly served for pitying a scoundrel." "The President himself," opined Sumner, "has played the part of the farmer in the fable who warmed the frozen snake at his fire."[62]

It is a measure of the popularity of *Aesop's Fables* that, in a letter to his father, a soldier in the 1st Minnesota, stationed in Louisiana, referred to a slightly different version of the tale: "It really looks as though the People of the North, would forgoe everything rather than be just to themselves, or the Negro. Assuredly slavery has been a greater evil to this country than the snake the foolish Blacksmith in the Fable, took in too his house to warm, but the smith had no compunction to kill the Pesky thing when it commenced Biting at him."[63]

The journalist Noah Brooks, who was also a friend and confidante of Lincoln's, reported "that the slow conduct of the war had more to do with the result of the elections than anything else. This is the view which the President took of it and it must be admitted that adopting, as he did, that hypothesis, he was more deeply chagrined than if he had supposed that his emancipation policy had received a signal rebuke."[64]

Immediately following the November elections, Lincoln acted on his earlier decision to remove McClellan, who had slithered around too slowly for too long. Perhaps he had kept him on in hopes that having a Democratic general at the head of the Army of the Potomac would pay dividends at the polls. It did not, and regardless of whether Republicans or Democrats had emerged victorious, McClellan's handling of the war effort in the weeks after Antietam had doomed him. John Nicolay's diary provides an apt résumé of Lincoln's exasperation. On October 13, after Stuart's dash around McClellan's army, the secretary reported that "the President has well-nigh lost his temper over it." A week later, concerning the Army of the Potomac, "the President is anxious that it should move and fight." On October 26, Nicolay wrote to Hay that "the President keeps poking sharp sticks under Mac's ribs" to get him to move across the Potomac. And finally, on November 9, "the President's patience is at last completely exhausted with McClellan's inaction and never-ending excuses, and has relieved him from command of the Army of the Potomac. . . . He is constitutionally *too slow,* and has fitly been dubbed the great American tortoise. I am sure sensible people everywhere will rejoice that he, and not the army, goes into 'winter quarters.'" Count Gurowski, certainly not thought sensible by the likes of Hay, exulted: "Great and holy day! McClellan's gone overboard! Better late than never."[65]

The administration responded to the elections of 1862 by more vigorously prosecuting the war. "New vigor has been infused into all departments of the military service," reported one editor. "Inactive commanders have been relieved by those who are believed to possess the elements necessary to insure success. Along our whole line, from the Potomac to the western frontier of Missouri, our armies have been advancing. This may not have been just what the leaders of the opposition desired, but in the absence of more explicit instructions (which they carefully avoided to give), the administration had the right to assume" what it wanted. Furthermore, with a majority of the popular vote still in the Administration's favor, with some 800,000 voters absent from their homes serving in the field, and with four-fifths or nine-tenths of these supporting the policy of the administration, one could plausibly claim, after a few months' time, that "the fall elections of 1862 provided unmistakably, that the loyal sentiment of the nation, instead of being against the Administration policy, was overwhelmingly in its favor."[66]

As for the Emancipation Proclamation, David W. Bartlett, the Washington correspondent for the *Independent,* heard two versions of a story. Following the New York election, a prominent gentleman sought out the president to argue in favor of withdrawing the Proclamation. In one version, the president said peremptorily, "I will not go back. Having taken my position I am not the man to retreat." In the second version, Lincoln refused to meet with the gentleman and declared, "I will not talk upon so preposterous a proposition. He knows I will not revoke the proclamation, and we will not waste time over the matter." Either way, Bartlett concluded, "no one can doubt . . . that the President has expressed himself very decidedly in favor of standing by his proclamation."[67]

8

"We Cannot Escape History"

Following news of the election in New York, Charles Sumner wrote to Lincoln. Never one to squander an opportunity afforded by defeat, the Massachusetts senator encouraged the president to press forward with the Proclamation. "The country must be made to feel," he advised, "that there will be no relaxation of any kind, but that all the activities of the country will be yet further aroused." One of those activities he had in mind was the enlistment of black troops, and toward that end he sent Lincoln a copy of George Livermore's book *An Historical Research Respecting the Opinions of the Founders of the Republic on Negroes as Slaves, as Citizens, and as Soldiers.* Sumner directed Lincoln's "especial attention to the last half," which concerned the use of blacks as soldiers. Livermore, a Boston merchant, conservative Republican, and amateur historian, had delivered the text as an address to the Massachusetts Historical Society on August 14, 1862, and it had been published soon thereafter.[1]

Livermore began his commentary with an examination of the Declaration of Independence, which, he averred, "is not an ethnological essay, or a disquisition on the physical or intellectual capacity of the various races of men, but a grave announcement of Human Rights." These rights were re-affirmed by several of the States and adopted as part of their constitutions. Livermore reviewed the opinions of the Founders with regard to slavery, quoting Washington, Jefferson, Adams, and Franklin, whose parody of a proslavery speech, published in 1790, may not have been read as comical in 1862. Franklin, writing in the voice of a Muslim ruler in 1687 defending the enslavement of Christians, declared: "Let us hear no more of this detestable proposition,—the manumission of Christian slaves; the adoption of which would, by depreciating our lands and houses, and thereby depriving so many good citizens of their properties, create universal discontent, and provoke insurrections, to the endangering of government, and producing general confusion."[2]

Part II of Livermore's work was titled "Negroes as Soldiers," and here the author directly addressed the president, "on whom, more than on all others, rests the responsibility of taking the final step in this direction." Livermore wrote with passion about blacks during the American Revolution: Crispus Attucks at the Boston Massacre and Peter Salem at Bunker Hill. Citing speeches and memoirs, Livermore wished to show that "many slaves were manumitted that they might become soldiers. They served faithfully to the close of the war. Their skill and bravery were never called in question, but, on the contrary, were frequently commended." But Livermore could discover no legislation authorizing the enlistment and emancipation of slaves, and noted that, while the issue may have proven controversial in Congress, Lord Dunmore, the royal governor of Virginia, had issued a proclamation that gave freedom to slaves who fought for the British. Livermore walked a fine line. He carefully denounced Dunmore, and praised the slaves who were not taken in by his offer, while at the same time he saw the precedent and idea of enlisting slaves as a course of action relevant to the current conflict. He showed that blacks had served the patriot cause, particularly in Rhode Island, where "not only were the names of colored men entered with those of white citizens on the rolls of the militia, but a distinct regiment of this class of persons was formed." Livermore quoted a letter from Alexander Hamilton: "I have not the least doubt that the Negroes will make very excellent soldiers with proper management." Having demonstrated that "it was general practice among the Founders of the Republic to employ negroes, both slaves and freemen, as soldiers regularly enrolled in the army," the author brought his study to a close.[3]

Despite having used the word "citizen" in the title, Livermore said little about the subject in his commentary. *Dred Scott*, the 1857 Supreme Court decision in which Chief Justice Roger Taney had ruled that blacks were not citizens, seemed to remain in force, and in the racially toxic atmosphere of the Civil War, there seemed little incentive, even for Republicans who had disparaged the decision, to do anything about it. But a few weeks after Lincoln was given Livermore's book, his attorney general, Edward Bates, issued an opinion on "whether or not *colored men* can be citizens of the United States." Bates was asked by treasury secretary Salmon Chase to issue his judgment after a federal revenue steamer stopped a schooner mastered by a black man. Under a late eighteenth-century law, only citizens could be shipmasters and obtain licenses for their vessels. The question of citizenship, Bates explained, was little understood, and he had "been pained by the fruitless search" for a definition. Rights enjoyed and powers exercised—such as holding office or voting—did not bear on the question of citizenship. After all, women, children, paupers, and lunatics could not vote, but certainly were citizens. Bates argued that "the Constitution uses the word citizen only to express the political quality of the individual in his relations to the nation; to declare that he is a member of the body politic, and bound to it by the reciprocal obligation of allegiance on the one side and protection on the other." As for *Dred Scott,* he argued that whatever was said in that case "respecting any supposed legal disability resulting from the mere fact of color ... was 'dehors [outside] the record,' and of no authority as a judicial decision." Bates concluded that "every person born in the country is, at the moment of birth, *prima facie* a citizen ... without any reference to race or color, or any other accidental circumstance."[4]

Bates's decision said nothing about the status of slaves, but it marked a significant step forward in thinking about the place of blacks in the United States. The conservative Bates, a one-time slaveholder from Missouri, who had favored the preliminary Emancipation Proclamation but thought it should be linked to deportation, had moved ahead in his thinking. The attorney general had come to admire the president, though he was troubled by his "easy good nature" and his "never-failing fund of anecdote." Bates explained Lincoln's tendency this way: "His thought habitually takes on this form of illustration, by which the point he wishes to enforce is invariably brought home with a strength and clearness impossible in hours of abstract argument." In its own way, Bates's opinion on citizenship also brought home with clarity an argument that newspapers such as the *New York Tribune* recognized as significant: "It properly precedes and ushers in that other great act which is to come from the president on the 1st of January."[5]

With January 1, 1863, drawing near, and with excitement, anxiety, and uncertainty building, preachers began to devote their Sunday sermons to questions related to emancipation. On November 2, the Reverend Frederick Starr delivered a discourse at the First Presbyterian Church in Penn Yan, New York, titled "What Shall Be Done with the People of Color in the United States?" Starr had been born in Rochester, had graduated from Yale in 1846, and had then attended Auburn Seminary. Praised for his strong convictions, Starr had always advocated the abolition of slavery. Now, he stood before his congregation and condemned those "drunken men, upstart boys, and conceited politicians of shallow brains [who] denounce and threaten to oppose the proclamation." Lincoln had prayed for "guidance and light; his patience, his honesty, his cautious judgment, his long deliberation" served the will of God, who actually "hath given to us this proclamation." Here, in a tiny village in western New York, and no doubt in towns and villages throughout the Union, the apotheosis of Abraham Lincoln took flight.

When Reverend Starr looked back from the heavens, he posed the issue that no one, including the president, could answer: "How much may directly result from the proclamation no one can tell." He believed that slavery would be ended, because behind the paper Proclamation stood the iron military ready to enforce it. As he turned to the question posed in his title, his answer restated widely held racial assumptions: the freedmen would not come north, because blacks gravitate to warm climates; amalgamation would not take place, because intermixture was created by slaveholders' lust and not by blacks, who are "prouder of pure black blood than the whites are of theirs"; voluntary colonization would be a blessing through which the emancipated slaves would become "the instrument of Christianizing that benighted continent [of Africa]." Sadly, Starr's answers were no answers at all, and they spoke to the fears that would do much to make the transition from slavery to freedom an excruciating one for blacks and for the nation.[6]

On Thanksgiving Day, in a sermon preached at the South Presbyterian

Church in Brooklyn, the Reverend Samuel T. Spear wondered, "How far . . . will the Proclamation be likely to go in the direction of freedom? How much will it actually accomplish?" Spear thought that it would accomplish a great deal because "capture forever extinguishes the master's title, and devotes the slave to freedom. By his own act in escaping from the master, and under the Proclamation making himself an ally of the Union, he does that which is equivalent to a capture. He captures himself and forever becomes a freeman." The minister mocked the idea that rebellious states, which had withdrawn from the Union, should presume to plead for states' rights. The single constitutional right they had, he affirmed, was to be "constitutionally hung." The only remaining issue, he thought, was whether slavery would be abolished in all the slave states. The president's effort to cajole the border states into taking the initiative on emancipation was commendable, but something more would soon be needed. It was time, Spear thought, "to march squarely up to the question" of applying the theory of confiscation not just to rebels but to all slaveholders. As Spear looked ahead to victory, he imagined "Southern society will itself be *reconstructed* and enter upon a new style of life." He apologized for devoting his sermon to emancipation, and acknowledged that he could have chosen other themes. But he felt obligated, with emancipation only weeks away, to consider these questions; and he also felt obligated, though he regretted evoking the "unmingled detestation and horror of war," to exhort his congregation to stand firm for war, "persistent, energetic, unrelenting, until this rebellion is entirely subdued."[7]

In Philadelphia, the Reverend Albert Barnes delivered a Thanksgiving discourse at the First Presbyterian Church. Barnes had long opposed the involvement of the church in maintaining slavery. In a provocative lecture entitled "What to the Slave Is the Fourth of July?" delivered in 1852, Frederick Douglass had quoted Barnes as declaring, "There is no power out of the church that could sustain slavery an hour, if it were not sustained in it." On this day of thanks in 1862, Barnes, too, posed questions. When, he asked, would the war end? How would it end? What good would be accomplished by it? The events of the year had already furnished many reasons to give thanks. "It has been such a year as our country has never experienced before," he proclaimed, "and will make more work for the calm and impartial historian of future times, than any one year in all our public history." In 1862, slavery had been abolished in Washington, D.C., "and so quietly and calmly that the nation has scarcely been aware of it." In the same year, the territories had been made "forever free from the tread of the slave." In the same year, the international slave trade had been struck down. In the same year, compensated emancipation in the border states had been proposed—"never before has a suggestion on that subject been made by the President of the United States . . . and yet it was so wise, so calm, so free from any attempt at compulsion." And in the same year, at that very moment, the passing days were bringing the nation closer to realizing the "idea of Emancipation." There was much cause to grieve, Barnes acknowledged; "our minds are indeed pensive and filled with sadness." But "there is light beyond; and those who will live in the future, may see, even in what gives us sorrow now, reasons for adoration and praise in a land made more happy; a land without our conflicts and troubles; a land where man everywhere shall be recognized and treated *as a man;* a land that shall be truly free."[8]

The word "man" was one of the most important in the vocabulary of the era. Frederick Douglass had made it central to his riveting memoir, *Narrative of the Life of Frederick Douglass, an American Slave.* "You have seen how a man was made a slave," he affirmed at a critical juncture in the story; now "you shall see how a slave became a man." The sin of slavery was that it robbed the enslaved of his or her status as a person. This meant more than liberty: it meant the freedom of self-determination, control over one's body, autonomy of mind. If you robbed someone of his manhood, you robbed him of his individuality. And with the loss of individuality, independence vanished. Lincoln's "Order of Emancipation," observed one writer, "recognized the manhood of three millions of Africans."[9]

In the 1830s and 1840s, some northern writers, ministers, and intellectuals pressed hard on the question of what it meant to be an individual, none more so than Ralph Waldo Emerson. "Whoso would be a man must be a nonconformist," proclaimed Emerson in his essay "Self-Reliance." But Emerson's journey was not one of social activism—he called himself "a seeing eye, not a helping hand." Rather than join, he observed; but when he commented, his words carried power. It was Emerson who predicted that the war with Mexico "will be as the man swallows the arsenic which brings him down in turn. Mexico will poison us." And it was Emerson who said of John Brown that his death "would make the gallows as glorious as the cross." Still, Emerson mistrusted political parties (he called them "an elegant incognito designed to save a man from the vexation of thinking") and, although opposed to slavery, thought little of philanthropic efforts to help others.

But the outbreak of the war changed him. He labeled the war "a new glass to see all our old things through." War was a "teacher," "instructor," "searcher," "magnetizer," and "reconciler." Emerson the individualist and idealist may have bristled at the churning power of the machinery of war, but Emerson the patriot and realist welcomed the struggle for the birth of a new social order. "The War," Emerson realized, "is serving many good purposes. . . . War is a realist, shatters everything flimsy & shifty, sets aside all false issues, & breaks through all that is not real as itself."[10]

Earlier in the year, on Sunday, February 2, Emerson had been in Washington, and Sumner had introduced him to Lincoln. "The President impressed me more favorably than I had hoped," Emerson confided in his journal. "A frank, sincere, well-meaning man, with a lawyer's habit of mind, good clear statement of his fact, correct enough, not vulgar, as described; but with a sort of boyish cheerfulness, or that kind of sincerity & jolly good meaning that our class meetings on Commencement Days show, in telling our old stories over. When he has made his remark, he looks up at you with a great satisfaction, & shows all his white teeth, & laughs."

"Great is the virtue of the Proclamation," Emerson observed, because "it works when men are sleeping, when the Army goes into winter quarters, when generals are treacherous or imbecile." So taken was he with the document that he spoke about it publicly in September, and the speech appeared in the *Atlantic Monthly* in November. The Sage of Concord marveled that once in a century "a poetic act and record occur." "Liberty," he observed, "is a slow fruit. It comes, like religion, for short periods, and in rare conditions, as if awaiting a culture of the race which shall make it organic and permanent." Emerson listed the Augsburg Confession, the English Commonwealth of 1648, the Declaration of Independence, and the passage of the British Reform Bill as examples of "acts of great scope, working on the long future, and on permanent interests, and honoring alike those who initiate and those who receive them."

Emerson regarded the Emancipation Proclamation as such an act, delivered by Lincoln in a carefully calibrated manner:

> The extreme moderation with which the President advanced to his design,—his long-avowed expectant policy, as if he chose to be strictly the executive of the best public sentiment of the country, waiting only till it should be unmistakably pronounced,—so fair a mind that none ever listened so patiently to such extreme varieties of opinion,—so reticent that his decision has taken all parties by surprise, whilst yet it is just the sequel of his prior acts,—the firm tone in which he announces it, without inflation or surplusage,—all these have bespoken such favor to the act, that, great as the popularity of the President has been, we are beginning to think that we have underestimated the capacity and virtue which the Divine Providence has made an instrument of benefit so vast. He has been permitted to do more for America than any other American man.

Now, Emerson reasoned, all the bad days of the war mattered less: "The acts of good governors work a geometrical ratio, as one midsummer day seems to repair the damage of a year of war." He reminded his audience that the Proclamation itself mattered, apart from whatever effect it might have: "It is by no means necessary that this measure should be suddenly marked by any signal results on the negroes or on the Rebel masters. The force of the act is that it commits the country to this justice." But of course it could not just be a "paper proclamation"—it must be followed up, must be made irresistible. Emerson's prose soared:

> It is not a measure that admits of being taken back. Done, it cannot be undone by a new Administration. For slavery over-powers the disgust of the moral sentiment only through immemorial usage. It cannot be introduced as an improvement of the nineteenth century. This act makes that the lives of our heroes have not been sacrificed in vain. It makes a

victory of our defeats. Our hurts are healed; the health of the nation is repaired. With a victory like this, we can stand many disasters.... The first condition of success is secured in putting ourselves right. We have recovered ourselves from our false position, and planted ourselves on a law of Nature.

Emerson looked forward to that auspicious January day when the Proclamation would be issued: "A day which most of us dared not hope to see, an event worth the dreadful war, worth its costs and uncertainties, seems now to be close before us. October, November, December will have passed over beating hearts and plotting brains: then the hour will strike, and all men of African descent who have faculty enough to find their way to our lines are assured of the protection of American law." He could hardly contain his anticipation: "Do not let the dying die: hold them back to this world, until you have charged their ear and heart with this message to other spiritual societies, announcing the melioration of our planet."[11]

With December, that fruit of liberty seemed nearly ripe. Thanksgiving had passed, and Lincoln had remained firm. Indeed, in remarks to a visiting group of Kentuckians, he was quoted as saying "he would rather die than take back a word of the Proclamation of Freedom." He was not shaken by the fear of soldiers throwing down their arms; he was not fazed by the threat of European intervention; he did not cower before the results of the fall elections. But as he drafted his annual message to Congress, some abiding fears resurfaced and he addressed them at great length. His Annual Message to Congress on December 1, 1862, was one of the longest documents he composed during his presidency, and it left many readers befuddled and perplexed—left many wondering if he would, indeed, affirm the Proclamation in a month's time.[12]

In that message, Lincoln disposed of formalities quickly. He addressed foreign affairs and financial matters, and advised those seeking additional details to refer to the reports of his cabinet members. He mentioned a Sioux uprising in Minnesota and wondered whether "our Indian system shall not be remodeled." Then he turned his attention to the preliminary Emancipation Proclamation and asked Congress to recall the section on compensated emancipation. For several pages, he turned geographer, making the argument that physically the United States "is well adapted to be the home of one national family; and it is not well adapted for two." He quoted two paragraphs from his First Inaugural Address, which he had delivered before the opening shots of the war and in which he had wondered, "Suppose you go to war, you cannot fight always; and when, after much loss on both sides, and no gain on either, you cease fighting, the identical old questions, as in terms of intercourse, are upon you."

If slavery was the root cause of "our national strife," then only by resolving the issue of its existence could the strife be "hushed forever with the passing of one generation." Toward this end, Lincoln made his proposal: the adoption of three constitutional amendments. The first encouraged every state to abolish slavery before January 1, 1900, and urged that it be compensated for doing so through interest-bearing bonds. The second provided that slaves who had already "enjoyed actual freedom by the chances of war" would remain "forever free" and that their owners, so long as they had not been disloyal to the Union, would be compensated for the loss. And the third authorized Congress to appropriate funds to colonize "free colored persons, with their own consent."

Lincoln tried to address the dissatisfaction of all groups: those who defended slavery, those who advocated immediate emancipation, those who desired gradual emancipation without compensation. He maintained that gradualism "spares both races from the evils of sudden derangement" and protected blacks from "the vagrant destitution which must largely attend immediate emancipation." Since the effects of slavery were national, and since so many had profited from its existence, the cost should be carried "at a common charge." Lincoln then turned demographer and economist, offering population statistics, predicting rates of growth, seeking to show that the per capita cost of compensated emancipation would be quite manageable in a rapidly growing nation, and calculating its total cost in comparison to the cost of continuing the war.

In his message, Lincoln warmly advocated colonization, but he also sought to refute the widespread belief that the labor of free blacks would be injurious to the job prospects of whites. "Emancipation, even without deportation, would probably enhance the wages of white labor." Lincoln meant "colonization," not "deportation"—his typically precise, lawyerly use of language for once had apparently eluded him. He argued that even if the freedmen remained, and even if they fanned out across the country, there would be only "one colored to seven whites." But, he argued, they would not leave the South. Gradually freed, they could work for wages "till new homes can be found for them, in congenial climes, and with a people of their own blood and race." In the meantime, states would be allowed to decide whether to permit former slaves to settle within their borders.

Lincoln made clear that merely *recommending* the plan would stay neither the war nor "proceedings under the proclamation of September 22, 1862." But *adopting* it "would bring restoration and thereby stay both."

Only toward the end of the address did Lincoln achieve any rhetorical power. "Fellow-citizens," he closed, "*we* cannot escape history." In defense of his proposal, he averred that "the dogmas of the quiet past, are inadequate to the stormy present. . . . As our case is new, we must think anew, and act anew. We must disenthrall ourselves, and then we shall save our country." "In *giving* freedom to the slaves," he concluded, "we *assure* freedom to the free—honorable alike in what we give, and what we preserve. We shall nobly save, or meanly lose, the last, best hope of earth. Other means may succeed; this could not fail."[13]

The fear of failure haunted Lincoln, and it helps to account for his end-of-year proposal, which seemed like a retreat. He believed it was a gamble whether the Emancipation Proclamation would actually accomplish anything. And even if it did initially, by what process would freedom become permanent? How would slavery be eradicated? Furthermore, there was the question of whether, in the future, the courts would uphold an Executive Order based on the doctrine of military necessity. Saying that the Proclamation freed the slaves did not mean that it would. Lincoln had once told the story of a lawyer who tried to maintain that a calf had five legs by including the tail in the count. "But," Lincoln said, "the decision of the judge was that calling the tail a leg, did not make it a leg, and the calf had four legs after all." And so, the president concluded, "proclaiming slaves free did not make them free." He was no gambler, and he preferred what he believed was a surer way to end the war and abolish slavery, even if that path included certain features—gradualism, compensation, and colonization—that antagonized so many opponents of the institution.[14]

Lincoln's address received widespread comment. Sumner told the abolitionist Wendell Phillips that "the Message is a curiosity, & its Confection was a curiosity. It is the Presdt's exclusive and unaided work." In fact, Lincoln had shared a draft with Chase, who advised the president not to go forward with the proposal. "Is it expedient to propose the measure if there is not a strong probability of its adoption?" he wondered. "Will not such an act weaken rather than strengthen yourself and your Administration?"[15]

On reading the text of the address, Count Gurowski growled, "Grammarians may criticize the syntax of the President's message, and the style. It reads uneasy, forced, tortuous, and it declares that it is *impossible* to subdue the rebels by force of arms." Another commentator, in the *San Francisco Bulletin,* observed "that it was written by Abraham Lincoln and nobody else is as clear as tangled, crooked sentences and homely, honest, earnest and not quite practicable suggestions could possibly make." "The President is eminently foggy in his style," wrote an editor in the same newspaper. Frederick Douglass thought "the President is not competent to write his own official papers—It is evident that they are all from his pen; for they all bear the same marks of crudeness, incongruity, feebleness, and lack of method." The president, he concluded, is "demented."[16]

Congressman Henry L. Dawes no doubt spoke for many Republicans when he confided to his wife, "How it makes one's heart bleed for his country to have its chief magistrate proposing measures to be accomplished in 1900 as a remedy for evils and perils which have thrust us . . . into the very jaws of death. Whether the Republic shall live six months or not is the question thundering in our ears and the chief magistrate answers I've got a plan which is going to work well in the next century."[17]

It was not only opponents of slavery who despaired. On the opposite side of the political and social spectrum, anti-abolitionists who believed in maintaining slavery, and who thought government existed only for the benefit of the white race, maintained that "a more silly, contemptible, ungrammatical, unstatesmanlike document surely never before appeared from any President of the United States. . . . We could easily forgive bad grammar, rough diction and spavined sentences, if we could detect among the rubbish a single ray of light or a single hope for the future."[18]

Not everyone criticized the address. The *New York Times* called it "a concise, clear and perspicuous document." The *New York Herald* labeled it a "remarkable document." One soldier wrote that the president's Annual Message "meets my views exactly. It is broad and deep, but yet so simple a child can understand it. Nothing he has ever said or done pleased me so much as his reasons for his policy, and his earnest appeal to Congress and the people to support it." And Daniel Dickinson, who served as a Democratic senator from New York from 1844 to 1851, but who supported Republican James Wadsworth in his failed gubernatorial campaign, thought that "while it lacks elegance and compactness, . . . it is frank, sincere, and manly; and anything that is manly excites my admiration."[19]

The *Boston Journal* viewed the president's address as "co-operative" with the Emancipation Proclamation and not a contradiction of it. "To that war measure," the editor observed, "which dealt only with rebel communities, he would add universal emancipation under the flag of the Union, so that the nineteenth century should close on no American slave." "The proclamation was a purely military measure taken by the commander in chief," noted the newspaper, whereas "the emancipation plan of the message is a purely legal measure recommended by the civil head of the government." Emancipation was not the same as abolition: "it is only the *freeing of individual slaves.*" Added to that, Lincoln's proposal, however dilatory and far-fetched, sought the abolition of the entire institution of slavery.[20]

Lincoln's failure to make much mention of the war itself irked readers. *Harper's Weekly* noted that "persons who take up the Message in the hope of finding in it some retrospect of the past operations of the war, and some intimation of what is to happen hereafter, will meet with disappointment." "In his message he hardly alludes to the army," lamented the Catholic polemicist Orestes Brownson, "and says not a word to encourage it and reward it for its deeds and sacrifices." William Richardson, an Illinois Democrat, lambasted the president: "No page, no sentence, no line, no word, is given to laud or even to mention the bravery, the gallantry, the good conduct of our soldiers, in the various bloody battles which have been fought."[21]

Illinois senator Orville Browning was likewise "surprised . . . by its singular reticence in regard to the war." The president, thought Browning, was laboring under a "hallucination . . . that Congress can suppress the rebellion by adopting his plan of compensated emancipation." His propositions, declared the *Liberator,* are "lame and impotent." Congressman John Hutchins of Ohio called the plan "entirely impracticable." The humor magazine *Vanity Fair* provided a parody of the speech:

> The idea I have labored to convey is, that if we buy the slaves of the rebels and set them free, paying in U.S. bonds due January 1, A.D. 2035, that they will immediately lay down their arms, and fall upon our bosoms in a fraternal embrace; for this is all our Southern brethren have been fighting for. It was the hope of "compensated emancipation," even in the dim distance, that nerved them to the enormous expenditures of blood and treasure that they have made in the past two years. . . . In conclusion, fellow-citizens, I beg to state that we cannot hope to escape History, who will be after us with a very sharp stick.[22]

Brownson, however, found nothing funny in Lincoln's proposals, and he alone took them seriously long enough to dismantle them. The editor proposed doing the math. He was willing to stipulate that Congress would pass the proposals, which required a two-thirds vote, even though that was highly unlikely. It would then have to be ratified by twenty-five states, assuming that for these purposes all thirty-four were still in the Union. Even if all the free states voted in favor, and the border states, Lincoln would still need three Confederate states to vote yes. "Does the president expect his amendments to be approved by the rebellious legislatures of a single slave state?" Brownson wondered. To get the needed ratification from the states, eleven states would have to be considered as "having committed suicide or lapsed," which would then leave twenty-four states, counting the soon-to-be-admitted state of West Virginia, and requiring eighteen to ratify. Equally confusing was how this proposed policy, if adopted, "is to give us military success or put an end to the war." Finally, Brownson pointed out that the president's amendments "will not authorize the federal government to free a single slave, nor will they render certain emancipation in a single state." There was nothing to stop states from passing a gradual emancipation act, taking the money, and then, on New Year's Eve 1900, passing a law making slavery perpetual. The federal government would ask for its money back—but what if the state refused to pay it? You would have "but the present rebellion over again."[23]

The critical question was not the feasibility of Lincoln's proposals, but what they augured for the Emancipation Proclamation. "What becomes of the president's proclamation of the 22d of last September?" asked Brownson. "Is it to be recalled, and no slave to be freed under it?" "If the President means to carry his edict of freedom on the New Year," wondered one writer, "what is all this stuff about gradual emancipation?" Observing that the document would be read around the world, the *Independent* informed readers that "men speaking in twenty diverse languages will study the Message with a common eagerness to see whether the Proclamation of the 22nd of September will be adhered to." The proslavery *Plain Dealer* of Cleveland rejoiced: "Their hope of immediate and unconditional emancipation and setting loose of four million negroes has received a terrible blow from which we doubt they will ever have strength to recover. Think of it, *thirty seven years* in which to accomplish the gradual emancipation of slaves contrasting with a Proclamation which was to have set them immediately, nay, instantaneously free! Wont the Abolitionists howl?"[24]

A Boston writer recalled the story of a man who believed that if he took a two-mile head start, then he could jump over a mountain: "We are reminded of this individual by the President's Message. Taking a hundred days' start, he nears the base of his mountain; but, it seems, he is very tired, and sits down to rest. He nods. Never did wide-awakes usher in a more heavy-eyed President. Here, evidently fallen asleep, he takes to dreaming of the year 1900! Is he that despairing of the present, he is turning his attention to future salvation?"[25]

But the *Chicago Tribune* found a different moral: "If any reader is disappointed in finding no reference to the Emancipation Proclamation promised as a New Year's present to Human civilization, it is enough to borrow a phrase from the President himself. He 'will not cross Fox River before he gets to Fox River.'"[26]

The *Charleston Mercury* thought the message had to be a ruse and that Lincoln was a "rogue." "Why, then, propose to Congress to do that in 1900 which he does next January, so far as the power of the United States can accomplish it?" The Confederate paper thought the message was designed to "disguise the scope and atrocity of his unconstitutional and fiendish policy," to mask what would actually occur on January 1. The editor of the *Girard Union,* in Pennsylvania, had the same thought: "We judge this proposition to be merely a pad or cover, so to speak, for the dagger which he intends soon to send home to the vitals of slavery and secession. Any other interpretation, it seems to us, would evince a lack of that practical common sense which has hitherto been accorded to Mr. Lincoln."[27]

Wendell Phillips could only hope that was true. In fact, he saw the Annual Message as a retreat, and he contrasted its meaning with that of the Proclamation: "The message belonged to the past, the proclamation to the present and future; the message was a word, the proclamation a blow; the message was a bugle to summon the camp to surrender, the proclamation a mine whose explosion would scatter the camp into the air, and carry death and confusion to our enemies; the message was like the address of our fathers to the tyrants of Great Britain in 1774, the proclamation was the Declaration of Independence on the Fourth of July." Sumner tried to ease Phillips's fears. "The last paragraph of the message is every thing," he wrote. "All the rest is surplusage."[28]

One editor had had enough of Lincoln's penchant for designing and proposing plans: "He is not the *Thinker* but the Doer. Congress is to think. The President is the man of action. There is the enemy. Defeat him. There is Slavery, the magazine and base of this rebellion. The President threw a bomb into it with a three-months fuse. It is his next business to stand by for the explosion and prepare to make the most of the enemy's disasters."[29]

Charles K. Whipple, printer of the *Liberator,* predicted that "the vacillations of President Lincoln will greatly perplex the future historian. Why, having the war power in his hands, he did not proclaim emancipation at the beginning—why, having proclaimed a restricted measure of it, he did not push that with vigor—and why, when the time for the beneficent action of the Proclamation approached, he impaired that action by a Message, running counter to it—all these are difficult of explanation."[30]

9

Standing Firm

With Congress now in session, many members seized the opportunity to comment on the Emancipation Proclamation, which Lincoln had issued during the recess. With the president's Annual Message in mind, some hoped to forestall the Proclamation, whereas others embraced it. Representative George Yeaman of Kentucky moved "that the policy of emancipation, as indicated in that proclamation, is not calculated to hasten the restoration of peace, was not well chosen as a war measure, and is an assumption of power dangerous to the rights of citizens and to the perpetuity of a free people." Yeaman's motion was tabled. Afterward, he denounced the Proclamation as unconstitutional and as an exercise in unfettered executive power. He derided the idea of military necessity as a justification for the act. He was baffled by the administration's repudiation of earlier assurances not to interfere with slavery in the states. He insisted the war was not caused by slavery—one could just as easily say that the abolitionists had precipitated it. He mocked the idea of colonization and the scheme suggested in the message to Congress as impracticable and absurd. And he raised the specter of servile insurrection, leading "to bloodshed of the most revolting character to the history of the world!" "The proclamation of emancipation," he concluded, "was an impolitic, an unwise, and a frightfully unfortunate measure. . . . I protest against it as being malicious, revengeful, and blood-thirsty."[1]

Representative John Crisfield of Maryland also spoke against the Proclamation. It came, he said, "as the thunder-bolt from the cloudless sky. . . . Men stood in amazement. Its suddenness, its utter contempt for the Constitution, its imperial pretension, the thorough upheaving of the whole social organization which it decreed, and the perspective of crime, and blood, and ruin, which it opened to the vision, filled every patriotic heart with astonishment, terror, and indignation." Crisfield then wondered about the army. "Do you think they will be willing to fight for the abolition of slavery and to break the Constitution?" he asked. "Have no murmurs reached you? Do you not hear the inquiry what are we fighting for? Are there no desertions or resignations?" He predicted that with the Proclamation the army would melt away, and that the South would never make peace.[2]

Republicans did not much bother to respond to "the invective and denunciation" cast at the Proclamation. John Hutchins of Ohio suggested an argument against the likelihood of servile insurrection that reversed the logic of emancipation's opponents: "It will tend to prevent rather than encourage such an insurrection. Slaves will only risk an insurrection—which, if it fail, must result in a terrible death—when they despair of all hope of freedom from other means. This proclamation, if a knowledge of it reach them, will hold out to them the prospect of freedom; and, if a knowledge of it does not reach them, it cannot effect them at all." And William Darrah Kelley of Pennsylvania simply asked rhetorically, "Has not the question as to whether four millions of stalwart people shall labor for us or for those with whom we are at war, some importance, and a direct bearing on the issue?" Responding to Crisfield's metaphor, Kelley testified that "the only thing about the President's proclamation that struck me as amiss was, that it was not, like the lightning, to take instant effect." The Republicans showed their support by backing the resolution proposed by Samuel Clement Fessenden of Maine "that the policy of emancipation, as indicated in that proclamation, is well adapted to hasten the restoration of peace, was well chosen as a war measure, and is an exercise of power with proper regard for the rights of the States, and the perpetuity of free government." On December 15, 1862, the resolution passed by a vote of 78 to 51. The black community was particularly relieved by the action of Congress. According to *Pacific Appeal*, an African American paper, "The ordeal in the House may be considered as passed. Its members are direct from among the people, and this vote may be considered as expressing the voice of the people, and 'the voice of the people is the voice of God.'"³

That same day, General Ambrose Burnside retreated across the Rappahannock River following a devastating series of assaults on a dug-in Confederate position on Prospect Hill and Marye's Heights, near Fredericksburg. Burnside's men time and again tried to take the Heights, but a 400-yard-long, four-foot-high wall shielded Robert E. Lee's troops. By nightfall, dead and dying Union soldiers littered the terrain. The Union absorbed more than 12,000 casualties; the Confederates, fewer than 5,000. Lee is supposed to have said during the fight, "It is well that war is so terrible, or we should grow too fond of it." Lincoln's popularity sank. "A year ago," remarked George Templeton Strong, "we laughed at the Honest Old Abe's grotesque genial Western jocosities, but they nauseate us now. If these things go on, we shall have pressure on him to resign." The president groaned, "If there is a worse place than hell, I am in it."⁴

Joel Parker, Royall Professor of Law at Harvard and a critic of the constitutionality of Lincoln's emancipation policy, intimated that the assault had been made to justify the doctrine of military necessity. "Is this the mode by which your Constitutional emancipation is to be worked out?" he asked. Parker's allegations disgusted Boston attorney John C. Ropes. If anything, he thought, it would be in the interest of supporters of the emancipation policy "not to go ahead till after January 1, 1863." The attack near Fredericksburg, no matter how misguided, was purely a military decision, not a civil one.⁵

With the defeat, Lincoln faced a serious threat to his cabinet, and to his own power. Many Republicans, both radical and moderate, had long been unhappy with William Seward. They saw him as the power behind the president, and schemed to force him out. Salmon Chase worked furtively with the radicals to compel the resignation of the secretary of state, telling tales not only about Seward's supposedly baleful influence on Lincoln, but also about disharmony in the cabinet and the president's failure to consult its members. David W. Bartlett of the *Independent* thought that the threshold issue was support for the Proclamation: "The Old Cabinet will be preserved," he reported, "but upon the distinct understanding that the Emancipation policy of the President shall be cordially supported by every member of the Administration."[6]

On December 18, Lincoln met with a delegation of nine senators who claimed that Seward was "the real cause of our failures." The next day, he gathered with the entire cabinet, except for Seward, who had given the president a letter of resignation in order to save him from the ordeal. Chase would not speak openly against Seward, and he, too, offered his resignation to the president. Lincoln refused to accept either resignation. He had made his point to the radicals: he was the one who held power, and he alone would decide who filled his cabinet. Navy secretary Gideon Welles aptly noted in his diary, "A Senatorial combination to dictate to the President in regard to his political family in the height of a civil war which threatens the existence of the Republic cannot be permitted." Despite resolving the imbroglio, Lincoln confessed to Orville Browning, "We are now on the brink of destruction. It appears to me the Almighty is against us, and I can hardly see a ray of hope."[7]

Lincoln was suffering. Noah Brooks saw him at church in November and described the president: "His hair is grizzled, his gait more stooping, his countenance sallow, and there is a sunken, deathly look about the large, cavernous eyes, which is saddening to those who see there the marks of care and anxiety such as no President of the United States has ever before known." And yet, notwithstanding the misery and gloom he felt so deeply, Lincoln managed on December 23 to write one of the most hopeful condolence letters ever composed, a letter that in many ways reveals more about his temperament than almost anything else. Lieutenant Colonel William McCullough of the 4th Illinois Cavalry had been killed in battle, and Lincoln wrote to McCullough's daughter Fanny: "In this sad world of ours, sorrow comes to all; and, to the young, it comes with bitterest agony, because it takes them unawares. The older have learned to ever expect it. I am anxious to afford some alleviation of your present distress. Perfect relief is not possible, except with time. You can not now realize that you will ever feel better. Is not this so? And yet it is a mistake. You are sure to be happy again. To know this, which is certainly true, will make you some less miserable now."[8]

On that same day, Lincoln asked the members of his cabinet for their opinions on the constitutionality and expediency of a bill establishing the statehood of West Virginia. The western, mountainous part of Virginia, where slavery was far less widespread than in the eastern, Tidewater region or in the Piedmont, had opposed secession from the start of the war. In October 1861, residents in numerous western counties approved creation of a new Unionist state, and in May 1862 received permission, as required by the Constitution, from the restored Virginia government (created in June 1861) to form the state of West Virginia. The Senate passed a statehood bill on July 14, but not before defeating an amendment that called for the immediate emancipation of all slaves to take place on July 4, 1863. The Senate bill did include, however, a measure proposed by Waitman Willey of Virginia: "The children of slaves born within the limits of this State after the fourth day of July, eighteen hundred and sixty-three, shall be free; and all slaves within the said State who shall, at the time aforesaid, be under the age of ten years, shall be free when they arrive at the age of twenty-one years; and all slaves over ten and under twenty-one years, shall be free when they arrive at the age of twenty-five years; and no slave shall be permitted to come into the State for permanent residence therein." As much as most Republicans wanted to see a new Union state created, the gradual emancipation provision was anathema to some. The bill passed 23 to 17, but Republicans Charles Sumner (Massachusetts), Lyman Trumbull (Illinois), Preston King (New York), and Zachariah Chandler (Michigan) were among those who voted against it.[9]

In the House, consideration was postponed until December. Believing it was unconstitutional to create the new state in this way, conservatives opposed the bill; radicals opposed it over the gradual emancipation measure. But the bill passed by a vote of 96 to 55 (eleven Republicans voted against it), and was placed on the president's desk. The members of the cabinet responded quickly to the president's request for their views. Attorney general Edward Bates argued that the bill was unconstitutional because Congress could only "admit" states, not "form" them, and that it was inexpedient because it "may disjoint the fabric of our national government, and destroy the balance of power in Congress, by a flood of senators representing a new brood of fragmentary States." Welles likewise opposed it, much to the surprise of Edwin Stanton, the secretary of war, who "thought it politic and wise to plant a Free State south of the Ohio." But Welles believed expediency should not trump constitutional obligation, and that so far as freedom went, all of the slaves would be free when the president issued the Emancipation Proclamation. Montgomery Blair, the postmaster general, also recommended against West Virginia's admission. Seward, however, believed the measure was constitutional, the only possible objection being that the "political body which gave the consent is not in fact and in law really the State of Virginia." But it was up to the United States to decide, out of necessity and expediency, which of the two political bodies, the seceded one or the restored one, would be recognized. Chase agreed that there was "no valid constitutional objection." As for expediency, he thought the act of "vital importance." Privately, he wrote the president to say he would be "better satisfied . . . by a provision for immediate compensated emancipation."[10]

On December 31, Lincoln gave his opinion in support of the measure. "Can this government stand," he asked, "if it indulges constitutional constructions by which men in open rebellion against it, are to be accounted, man for man, the equals of those who maintain their loyalty to it?" He thought it constitutional, and he also thought it expedient: "We can scarcely dispense with the aid of West-Virginia in this struggle." Always attuned to the meaning of words, Lincoln responded to those who said the creation of West Virginia was merely secession against Virginia and was "tolerated only because it is our secession." "Well," Lincoln thought, "if we call it by that name, there is still difference enough between secession against the constitution, and secession in favor of the constitution."[11]

Lincoln said nothing about the provision for gradual emancipation, which voters in West Virginia would approve on March 23, 1863; the state would officially enter the Union on June 20. He would have been content had any of the border states adopted such a policy, so West Virginia's action must have pleased him. As his address to Congress earlier in the month indicated, when emancipation occurred mattered less than the simple fact that it *did* occur. Perhaps, as well, the issue of emancipation in West Virginia did not register as a significant one because there were only some 18,000 slaves in the state. They would have to wait for freedom until February 1865, when the governor would sign an act immediately abolishing slavery in the state.

As 1862 came to a close, with military and political turmoil raging, the question remained whether Lincoln would follow through and issue the Proclamation. On December 12, Harriet Beecher Stowe reported to Charles Sumner: "Everybody I meet in New England says to me with anxious earnestness —*Will* the President stand firm to his Proclamation?" George Templeton Strong wondered, "Will Uncle Abe Lincoln stand firm and issue his promised proclamation on the first of January, 1863? Nobody knows, but I think he will." A few days later, on December 30, Strong was less sure. "I am not sanguine on the subject," he admitted. "If he postpone or dilute his action, his name will be a byword and a hissing till the annals of the nineteenth century are forgotten." William Lloyd Garrison also had his doubts: "A man so manifestly without moral vision, so unsettled in his policy, so incompetent to lead, so destitute of hearty abhorrence of slavery, cannot be safely relied upon."[12]

Admiral Samuel Du Pont also had his concerns. In November he informed his friend William Whetten, a Philadelphia businessman, "With you, I thank my God we have that proclamation—will the President reaffirm it on 1st January?" Over the course of the war, Du Pont had been transformed from a conservative Whig to an advocate of abolition. In a Christmas Eve letter to his wife, he expressed his concerns: "I see the border-state men are pressing him [Lincoln] to at least postpone the emancipation proclamation—headed by Mr. Crittenden, etc. If he does this, he will be abandoned by the Republicans." The *Independent* reported on Christmas Day that "the Border-State men sent a deputation up to him a few days ago, and they came away dissatisfied. The President refused to comfort them."[13]

Lincoln not only refused to comfort the border-states representatives in general; he refused to comfort a particular Kentucky slaveholder as well. In November, a jury in Lexington, Kentucky, indicted Colonel William L. Utley of the 22nd Wisconsin Regiment for his refusal to return five slaves to their owners. One of those owners turned out to be the former chief justice of the Kentucky Court of Appeals, George Robertson, who came to camp and demanded his property—a boy named Adam, who, according to Utley in a letter to the president, entered camp "cold, bare-foot and hungry in the midst of a dreary snow storm." Utley emphasized that it was the slave himself who had refused to go with his master and had instead claimed protection from an owner whose treatment "had already made him a dwarf instead of a man." Just as the slave asked protection from Utley, so Utley sought Lincoln's protection for having obeyed and honored the laws of Congress and the preliminary Emancipation Proclamation.[14]

Utley wasn't the only one to appeal to Lincoln. Robertson also wrote the president and asked him to declare that "military force will not be permitted" for the detention of slave property. Robertson's relationship with Lincoln traced back nearly two decades. As a Kentucky lawyer, he had once served as legal counsel for the heirs of Lincoln's father-in-law. Visiting Springfield in 1855, Robertson had left a copy of his speeches on slavery and other topics for Lincoln to read. In his letter acknowledging the gift, Lincoln, who understood that Robertson was not "a friend of slavery in the abstract," wrote: "I think, that there is no peaceful extinction of slavery in prospect for us. . . . So far as peaceful, voluntary emancipation is concerned, the condition of the negro slave in America, scarcely less terrible to the contemplation of a free mind, is now as fixed, and hopeless of change for the better, as that of the lost souls of the finally impenitent. . . . Our political problem now is 'Can we, as a nation, continue together *permanently—forever*—half slave, and half free?' "[15]

Now, with his prophecy having come to pass, and in the midst of a great Civil War, Lincoln drafted a distinctly more intemperate letter to Robertson: "Do you not know that I may as well surrender this contest, directly, as to make any order, the obvious purpose of which would be to return fugitive slaves?" Lincoln did not send the letter. Six days later, he wrote Robertson and offered to pay him $500 to convey his slave to Colonel Utley, who would free him. Robertson rejected the offer and pursued Utley in civil court, where he won a judgment in 1871 that was paid by Congress with passage of an act in 1873 to relieve Utley's financial burden.[16]

Though few know of the incident, Lincoln had demonstrated that even when it came to the property of a loyal slaveowner in the border states, the day was passing when the Union army would return anyone to slavery. At the same time, he displayed his abiding belief in compensatory emancipation as the most just way to eradicate the institution in the border states—even, as in this case, if the money had to come out of his own pocket.

Utley was far from alone among soldiers upholding the preliminary Emancipation Proclamation and anticipating the final decree. On December 28, Taylor Pierce of the 22nd Iowa wrote to his wife, "We are all looking anxiously for the 1st of January and the workings of Old Abe's proclamation. We all feel that it will end the war and that it is the only thing that will give us a chance of seeing our homes very soon since Burnsides defeat on the rappahanock." Surgeon Thomas Hawley of the 111th Illinois wrote to his parents: "I cincerely hope President Lincoln will stand by his proclamation and see that it is carried out to the letter. I have no fears of the result every negro will assert his freedom and if necessary maintain it by force. If pleased with his master will remain so long as he is remunerated for his labors. I do not anticipate a great uprising on the 1st of January but the dawning of a new era in this nation's history and the history of the world."[17]

No one was more nervous than the abolitionist John Murray Forbes. On Christmas Eve, he forwarded a petition signed by the electors who had certified Lincoln's selection as president (only one, abroad in Europe, did not sign). The electors "beg leave to congratulate you upon your having begun the greatest act in American history; the emancipation of three millions of blacks and of five millions of whites from the power of an aristocratic class." They prayed that Lincoln might "complete now your great work" by carrying into effect the proclamation of September 22.

Forbes heard from New York congressman Charles Sedgwick that "every conceivable influence has been brought to bear upon him [Lincoln] to induce him to withhold or modify—threats, entreaties, all sorts of humbugs, but he is as firm as a mule." Typical of the efforts being made against the Proclamation, Orville Browning, working behind the scenes, suggested to Benjamin Franklin Thomas, a former judge on the Massachusetts Supreme Court, that he visit the president and "have a full, frank conversation with him in regard to the threatened proclamation of emancipation—that in my opinion it was fraught with evil, and evil only and would do much injury." Thomas told Browning that he had taken his advice and met with Lincoln, but that "the President was fatally bent upon his course, saying that if he should refuse to issue his proclamation there would be a rebellion in the north, and that a dictator would be placed over his head. . . . The proclamation will come." Forbes also heard from Charles Sumner, who, on Christmas Day, wrote to say that he had met with the president about "how to proclaim on 1st January. It will be done. He says of himself that he is hard to be moved from any position which he has taken."[18]

One newspaper, the *Commercial Advertiser* in New York, provided its readers with an astute analysis of why, despite the clamoring of Democratic journals to the contrary, Lincoln would proceed with the Emancipation Proclamation. "We imagine these writers little understand the President's character," observed the editor. "He is in the first place a man not given to hasty judgments or conclusions, and in this matter he certainly formed no sudden resolution or purpose." As for his oft-quoted remark to the Chicago clergymen that a proclamation would be as effective as a Pope's bull against a comet, it was the president's habit to "draw from his visitors their most powerful arguments in support of what he had already resolved to do." In preparation for litigation, this lawyerly habit had served Lincoln well over the years, and it served him equally well as president. Another paper, the *North American* in Philadelphia, reminded readers that "Mr. Lincoln is a man of deliberate mind, slow to form a judgment, patient in hearing all sides and investigating facts; but once having arrived at a conclusion, and convinced himself of its rectitude, no power can swerve him from it."[19]

With the Proclamation but a few days away, the *Chicago Tribune* could not resist observing that Democratic newspapers "say nothing now of the Pope's bull against the comet. Their danger is too imminent for ridicule. In three days time . . . the Emancipation Proclamation blesses the world and civilization, that has waited for it. . . . It will establish through *all coming time,* New Year's day as the birthday of a new people, 'a nation born in a day.'"[20]

On December 27, Forbes wrote to tell Sumner about the electors' petition, adding that the abolitionist poet John Greenleaf Whittier was going to write separately, and including other letters for Sumner to give to Lincoln. "I sincerely hope that you & others will have sufficient influence with the President," implored Forbes, "to ensure his giving us on the 1st of January such a Proclamation as will only need the 'General Orders' of his subordinates to carry into effect not only Emancipation but all the fruits thereof in the perfect right to use the Negro in every respect *as a man*—& consequently, as a soldier, sailor or laborer." Forbes knew that many wished for emancipation to be "done upon higher ground but the main thing is to have it *done strongly & to have it so backed* up by public opinion that it will strike the telling blow at the Rebellion and at slavery together." "In such a Proclamation," Forbes advised, "words become *things* and powerful things too—. . . a good strong Proclamation full of vigor, of Freedom and of *Democracy*—would almost compensate us for the dreadful repulse of Fredericksburgh." Privately, John DeFrees, who headed the Government Printing Office, wrote to Lincoln's secretary, John Nicolay: "Only a few events stand out prominently on the page of history of each century. The proposed proclamation of the President will be that *one* of this century. If the President can only put his whole mind to its composition, it will be done—but, I fear he will suffer himself to be so perplexed by 'outsiders' that he will not give it proper thought."[21]

Sumner updated Forbes on December 28. The senator had met with the president on the evening of the 27th. Sumner read aloud to him a memorial from clergymen calling on him to stand by the Proclamation. Lincoln then read aloud the address from the electors. More letters were handed over. Sumner "proceeded to dwell on the importance & grandeur of the act & how impatient we all are that it should be done in a way to enlist the most sympathy & to stifle opposition." Sumner had told Lincoln that it needed to be understood not only as an act of military necessity, but also as "an act of justice & humanity which must have the blessings of a benevolent Govt." Then, in his letter, he mentioned what Forbes must have been desperate to hear: "The Presdt. says that he could not stop the Proclamation if he would, & would not if he could."[22]

Also on December 28, Sumner wrote to Lincoln with a request. George Livermore—author of the *Historical Research* on slavery in the Revolutionary era and the uses of blacks as soldiers, a book that the senator had sent to the president—had written hoping "to get and to keep the pen" with which Lincoln would sign the Emancipation Proclamation. Sumner told the president of the request and said, "If nobody has yet spoken for it, let me."[23]

As if to buoy the president's resolve, the *Chicago Tribune* printed extracts from a letter it claimed to have received from an officer in an Illinois regiment: "Old Abe's proclamation is beginning to work. The negroes are counting the days and hours when the 1st of January shall come. They meet in little knots, and talk over the whole matter, and lay their plans for going. The day of Jubilee, they think, has surely come." And Sergeant Major Stephen Fleharty, of the 102nd Illinois, wrote to the *Rock Island Argus:* "Intelligence of 'Massa' Linkum's emancipation proclamation has doubtless reached every negro household from Mason and Dixon's line to the Gulf of Mexico."[24]

In New York, the *Tribune* reminded readers that "thus far we have been reaping all of the disadvantages and none of the advantages of such an Edict. We have had the exasperated South and the divided North, but no Liberty for the Slave. Having drawn the one weapon that can save us, we have been for one hundred days holding it by the blade instead of the hilt, and it has lacerated only our own hands." It was time for the president to "close his fingers firmly to hold the heart of Rebellion and Oppression in his grasp on New-Years Day, 1863."[25]

Frederick Douglass had never had any doubt that Lincoln would keep his word. In October he had expressed confidence that the president "is not the man to reconsider, retract or contradict words and purposes solemnly proclaimed over his official signature." In his address "The Day of Jubilee Comes," delivered on December 28, 1862, Douglass looked to the future, well beyond January 1. He told the congregation at the A.M.E. Zion Church in Rochester:

> Slavery has existed in this country too long and has stamped its character too deeply and indelibly, to be blotted out in a day or a year, or even in a generation.... Law and sword can and will, in the end abolish slavery. But law and the sword cannot abolish the malignant slaveholding sentiment which has kept the slave system alive in this country during two centuries. Pride of race, prejudice against color, will raise their hateful clamor for oppression of the negro as heretofore. The slave having ceased to be the abject slave of a single master, his enemies will endeavor to make him a slave of society at large.[26]

Douglass's comment would prove all too prescient, but first the problem of slavery had to be addressed. On Monday, December 29, the cabinet convened. According to Welles, "The President read the draft of his Emancipation Proclamation, invited criticism, and finally directed that copies should be furnished to each." The document that Lincoln read began by citing the preliminary decree of September 22, and, "in accordance with my purpose so to do publicly proclaimed for the full period of one hundred days, from the first day above mentioned," to designate those states and parts of states in rebellion.[27]

The final Proclamation differed in three significant ways from the preliminary Emancipation Proclamation. First, it made no mention of colonization. Perhaps the responses to his Annual Message of December 1 had finally made Lincoln see the impossibility of the scheme; in all likelihood, he had included colonization in the preliminary Emancipation Proclamation not only because he supported it, but also as an inducement to encourage slave states to adopt plans of abolition. With no states taking him up on his offer, or responding to his threat to issue a final Proclamation on January 1, there was no longer a need to include the incentive, certainly not as an official policy of an administration that was moving away from gradualist measures. And yet, personally, Lincoln had not abandoned the scheme altogether. It is perhaps revealing that when Caleb Smith resigned from his post as secretary of the interior, he appointed a rabid colonizationist, John Palmer Usher, to replace him. And on December 31, despite opposition by several cabinet members, he signed a contract with a shady businessman for the colonization of Ile à Vache, a tiny island off the coast of Haiti, and he did so despite being advised not to by Bates, Seward, and Smith. (Bates called the businessman "an errant humbug.") The experiment turned out to be a catastrophe, and several hundred surviving colonists, many still in the now tattered clothes they'd been wearing when they left in the spring of 1863, would be brought back to the United States in early 1864.[28]

Second, the final draft stated that blacks would be accepted into the armed services. Here, too, was reason to abandon colonization: it would be a cruel policy to allow blacks to serve the country and then expect them to leave. Perhaps Livermore's book had helped to convince the president. Enrolling blacks in the army also lent further credence to the argument that the Proclamation was justified as a military necessity—not only to keep the enslaved from supporting the rebellion, but also to enlist them to serve the Union. George E. Stephens, a black correspondent for the *Weekly Anglo-African*, predicted this development. Writing on December 31, he noted:

> If military necessity, three months earlier, required emancipation, the military necessity of the present time must require it still the more. The battle of Fredericksburg placed it beyond a doubt, and if it be withheld, it will be because slavery is preferred to honor, country, or right. When the proclamation comes it will be the signal for the commencement of

the war, and those men who are now spurned by the constituted authorities, must then be armed, and in the name of High Heaven the sorrows, tears, and anguish of millions shall be revenged. A proclamation will necessitate a general arming of the freedmen.[29]

Finally, Lincoln amended the sentence that had caused so much controversy. Instead of saying that the government "will do no act or acts to repress such persons, or any of them, in any efforts they may make for their actual freedom," he now wrote, in the final draft, that the government would do no acts to repress such persons in any "suitable efforts" they might make, and he added: "I hereby appeal to the people so declared to be free, to abstain from all disorder, tumult, and violence, unless in necessary self defence; and in all cases, when allowed, to labor faithfully for wages." He hoped this would put an end to the accusation that he sought to foment insurrection, and, at the same time, he provided a recommendation for what was to be done with the former slaves: allow them to work for wages.

While Lincoln did not believe, as his opponents argued, that the Emancipation Proclamation would lead to insurrection, he did come to believe the opposite: that withdrawing it would incite slave rebellion. The resourceful David Bartlett reported that when, on November 21, Lincoln met with a group of unconditional Unionists from Kentucky, Representative Samuel Lewis Casey was among them. According to Bartlett, Casey told the president that although he did not find the Proclamation suitable at first, he had come to accept it and would not "desire him to do so cowardly a thing as retrace your steps at the dictation of Democrats and slaveholders." The conversation turned to the issue of discontent on the part of the slaves. Bartlett reported that "the President . . . told Mr. Casey that the slaves of the South understood fully *now,* as they have never understood before, that the northern people are friendly to their freedom. Whether they are mistaken or not, the whole slave population of the South *expects its freedom at our hands.* These black millions are waiting patiently for their time to come, *and if the war ends without giving them their freedom,* THEY WILL TAKE IT!"[30]

Following the meeting on December 29, the president received memos from several cabinet members offering suggestions for revision. Bates thought the Proclamation should not state "what is proposed to be done in the future"; he was particularly aggravated by the final paragraph, which promised that the government would recognize and maintain freedom and planned to receive blacks into the military, terming it "wholly useless, and probably injurious—being a needless pledge of future action—which may be quite as well done without the pledge." Montgomery Blair suggested some paternalistic language about the behavior of the slaves, which "since the war began justifies confidence in their fidelity & humanity generally."

Seward thought Lincoln could improve upon the language in the draft that was intended to correct what was taken as an inflammatory sentence in the preliminary Proclamation. The secretary of state recommended elimination of the following language from the December 30 draft: "will do no act, or acts, to repress said persons, or any of them, in any suitable efforts they may make for their actual freedom." Lincoln accepted the advice. Seward also recommended that the start of the next sentence be changed from "I hereby appeal to the people so declared to be free" to "I hereby command and require." Lincoln declined this recommendation, but in the final version did substitute "I hereby enjoin the people so declared to be free to abstain from all violence, unless in necessary self-defence."

The group differed on whether fractional portions of states should be exempted. Welles and Chase thought not, whereas Bates thought the president had to declare, "as a simple matter of fact," which parts of states were in actual rebellion. Chase submitted fully revised paragraphs. Lincoln did not include a clause that read: "in accordance with my intention so to do publicly proclaimed for one hundred days as aforesaid." More striking, he also did not include Chase's phrase, "& hencefore forever shall be free." The preliminary Emancipation Proclamation had included the words "forever free"; his draft of December 30 also included the phrase "henceforward shall forever be free"; but Seward suggested that he omit the sentence containing the formulation. Why Lincoln dropped the phrase from the final draft is unknown; it does appear in the first of the two paragraphs he quotes from the Proclamation of September 22. Perhaps his anxiety, given the constitutional uncertainties of the decree, about actually being able to maintain freedom forever gave him pause. Perhaps now, with the deed done, the additional rhetoric seemed unnecessary. He did, however, adopt Chase's suggestion to add a final sentence, which bolstered the constitutional justification of the Proclamation and lent the necessarily dry legal document a measure of moral and emotional force. After Lincoln replaced one of Chase's phrases with a more incisive substitute, the sentence read: "And upon this act, sincerely believed to be an act of justice, warranted by the Constitution, *upon military necessity,* I invoke the considerate judgment of Mankind & the gracious favor of Almighty God."[31]

A reporter for the *New York Tribune* elaborated on the president's unwillingness to tie the decree to moral and humanitarian objectives:

> The President has been strongly pressed to place the Proclamation of Freedom upon high moral grounds, and to introduce into the instrument unequivocal language testifying to the negroes' right to freedom upon the precise principles expounded by the Emancipationists of both Old and New-England. This claim is resisted, for the reasons that policy requires that the Proclamation be issued as a war measure, and not a measure of morality; and that Law and Justice require that the slaves should be enabled to plead the Proclamation hereafter if necessary to establish judicially their title to freedom. They can do this, the President says, on a proclamation proceeding as a war measure from the Commander-in-Chief of the Army, but not on one issuing from the bosom of philanthropy.[32]

The *New York Times* picked up the *Tribune*'s report and argued that Lincoln should issue the Emancipation Proclamation in "the form of a military order, addressed to the Generals in command within the designated limits of the States in rebellion, and enjoining them to deprive the rebels of the military aid, rendered directly or indirectly, by their slaves. Against the justice and constitutional validity of such an order nothing could be said; while its practical results would be precisely the same as those of a Proclamation addressed to the world at large." In a letter to the president written on November 25, Henry J. Raymond, founding editor of the *Times* and a close White House advisor (according to one anecdote, Lincoln referred to Raymond as "my *Lieutenant-General* in politics"), recommended such a course, warning that "any attempt to make this war *subservient* to the sweeping abolition of Slavery, will revolt the Border States, divide the North and West, invigorate and make triumphant the opposition party, and thus defeat *itself* as well as destroy the Union." In reply, Lincoln wrote: "I shall consider and remember your suggestions."[33]

The logic was sound. Why antagonize the defenders of slavery for the sake of rhetorical flourish when an order from the commander-in-chief based on military necessity not only would accomplish the same result, but might also make emancipation more palatable to some opponents and more authoritative for the enslaved.

When Noah Brooks read the final document, he remarked on the "considerable improvement in tone and composition" from the preliminary Emancipation Proclamation, and observed that "even those who doubt the value and expediency of the measure cannot but admire the calm, judicious phraseology of . . . this extraordinary and important proclamation."[34]

At a meeting held at 10 A.M. on December 31, the cabinet discussed the Proclamation one last time. Welles thought that Chase had "proposed a felicitous closing sentence." The president considered the various suggestions, and spent part of the day finalizing the text. Nothing was left for anyone else to do but wait. Gather and wait—for a sign, for the word, for freedom. Wait for midnight to toll and for one hundred days of waiting to come to an end.

11. Lincoln signed forty-eight copies of this authorized edition of the Emancipation Proclamation—special souvenirs to be sold at the Philadelphia Great Central Sanitary Fair of June 1864. Approximately half of them have survived in public and private collections. Print of Emancipation Proclamation signed by Lincoln (1864; courtesy of Seth Kaller).

12. Francis Carpenter lived in the White House for six months and hoped to create a master-piece, a history painting that depicted the first reading of the Emancipation Proclamation. The painting did not succeed nearly as well as the book he published several years later: *Six Months at the White House with Abraham Lincoln*. Francis Carpenter, *First Reading of the Emancipation Proclamation of President Lincoln* (1864; United States Capitol).

13. Alexander Hay Ritchie's engraving of Carpenter's painting was far more popular than the original work. Lincoln himself was the first to sign up for a copy, which was delivered to his widow, Mary Todd, in 1866. Alexander Hay Ritchie, *First Reading of the Emancipation Proclamation before the Cabinet* (1866; courtesy of the American Antiquarian Society).

14. David Gilmour Blythe, a Pittsburgh artist, painted his political cartoons on canvas. None were more rich or complex than his depiction of Lincoln writing the Emancipation Proclamation. This print appeared in 1864. David Gilmour Blythe, *President Lincoln Writing the Proclamation of Freedom, January 1, 1863* (1864; Library of Congress).

ABRAHAM LINCOLN,

Abraham Lincoln

15. The eminent Philadelphia engraver John Sartain made this print of a spruced-up Lincoln from Edward Marchant's original, commissioned by the Union League of Philadelphia. Marchant resided at the White House prior to Carpenter's stay there. John Sartain after Edward Marchant, *Abraham Lincoln* (1864; Library of Congress).

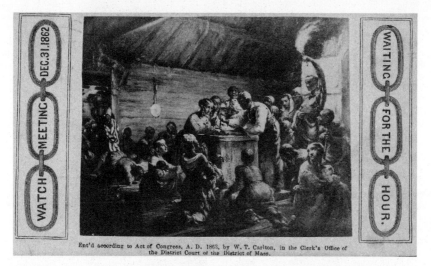

Ent'd according to Act of Congress, A. D. 1863, by W. T. Carlton, in the Clerk's Office of
the District Court of the District of Mass.

16. This rare carte de visite by William Tolman Carlton, based on his own painting that was presented to Lincoln as a gift, shows a gathering of slaves as they await the countdown to the midnight moment of emancipation. In the open doorway a man stands with the Union flag draped in his arms, and a white woman, likely the mistress of the household, views the event with tears in her eyes. *Watch Meeting, December 31, 1862: Waiting for the Hour* (1864; Library of Congress).

17. In this dramatic scene, a soldier stands inside a cabin and reads the Emancipation Proclamation to a group of attentive slaves. *Reading the Emancipation Proclamation* (1864; Library of Congress).

18. Many prints showed supplicating blacks kneeling before Lincoln, who has been transformed into the Great Emancipator. As he treads on the broken shackles, Lincoln points heavenward to the source of the slaves' freedom. *Emancipation of the Slaves, Proclamed* [*sic*] *on the 22nd September 1862, by Abraham Lincoln, President of the United States of North America* (circa 1862; Library of Congress).

UNCLE ABE — "*Sambo, you are not handsome, any more than myself, but as to sending you back to your old master, I'm not the man to do it—and what's more, I won't!*" (*Vide* President's Message.)

19. This cartoon offers a racial caricature of the black soldier, and a typical self-deprecating remark by the president, but also the reassurance that Lincoln will not under any circumstances repudiate the Emancipation Proclamation. "Uncle Abe," *Frank Leslie's Budget of Fun*, February 1, 1865.

PRESIDENT LINCOLN ENTERING RICHMOND, April 4, 1865.

20. Thomas Nast imagines the scene as it might have appeared when Lincoln and his twelve-year-old son, Tad, entered Richmond on April 4, 1865. A reporter observed, "The joy of the negro knew no bounds. It found expression in whoops, in contortions, in tears, and incessantly in powerful ejaculations and thanks." Thomas Nast, "Lincoln Entering Richmond," *Harper's Weekly*, February 24, 1866 (courtesy of the American Antiquarian Society).

The Proclamation
and Beyond

A man watches his pear-tree day after day, impatient for the ripening of the fruit. Let him attempt to *force* the process, and he may spoil both fruit and tree. But let him patiently *wait,* and the ripe pear at length falls into his lap!

—Abraham Lincoln, quoted in Francis B. Carpenter,
Six Months at the White House with Abraham Lincoln (1866)

10

Jubilee

On Thursday, January 1, 1863, Private John Boucher of the 10th Missouri sent a letter home: "Now Mother I am awaiting with great anxiety to here weather Old Abe stidcks up to his sept. proclamation if he shrinks back in the least from that the thing is done and my hope are gone. If they don't let us fight them in evry way that will tend to weaken them in evry way this war will go on and on the Lord knows when the end will come."[1]

The minister and historian Moses Coit Tyler also made special note of the date: "January 1, 1863. . . . I think the date at the top of this letter is the greatest one for America and perhaps for the human family since July 4, 1776. Today goes forth that glorious edict which strikes off the chains of those millions of slaves and liberates the nation from the viler slavery of a terrible iniquity."[2]

The "sticking up" and "going forth," however, were delayed. Lincoln had forwarded the final draft of the Emancipation Proclamation to secretary of state William Seward earlier in the morning. But when the formal document arrived at 10:45 from the printing office, Lincoln noticed an error. The formulaic superscription "In testimony whereof I have hereunto set my hand" had been omitted, and the president sent the Proclamation back to be corrected. This document, of all documents, would not go forth with any mistakes.

Lincoln's New Year's Day reception began at 11 A.M., and for the next three hours he greeted officers, diplomats, politicians, and members of the public, all eager to call on the president. Following the reception, Lincoln went to his study to sign the corrected copy. But as he reached down for his steel pen, with a gnawed wooden handle, his hand quivered. For a moment, superstition took hold of him. Perhaps this was an omen. And he certainly did not want anyone to think the signature appeared tremulous because he was uncertain about his action. Then he realized that he had been shaking hands nearly nonstop for three hours. He was quivering not from nerves but from exertion. "Three hours of hand-shaking is not calculated to improve a man's chirography," he said later that evening. Lincoln slowly signed his name. When he was done, he looked up and said, "That will do."[3]

In a letter to George Livermore, who did indeed receive the pen used by Lincoln, Charles Sumner reported: "The Proclamation was not signed till after three-hours of hand-shaking on New Year's Day, when the Presdt. found that his hand trembled, so that he held the pen with difficulty. The enemy would say—naturally enough, in signing such a doct. But it is done, & the act will be firm throughout time." Sumner could not help adding that he, and not Salmon Chase, had first proposed the final sentence: "And upon this act, sincerely believed to be an act of justice, warranted by the Constitution, upon military necessity, I invoke the considerate judgment of mankind, and the gracious favor of Almighty God."[4]

The assistant secretary of state, Frederick Seward, who was present with his father, William, at the signing, later wrote that Lincoln declared, "I never in my life felt more certain that I was doing right than I do in signing this paper. . . . If my name goes into history it will be for this act, and my whole soul is in it."[5]

It was late afternoon by the time the document was sent to the press, and by then the public's anxiety had begun to set in. "The morning papers. No proclamation! Has Lincoln played false to humanity?" shrieked the captious Adam Gurowski.[6]

For many, the wait had begun the previous evening. Hours before midnight, people massed in churches and halls, homes and slave quarters. They called it "watch night." Waiting and watching for news that the day of jubilee had arrived.

In New York City, starting at 9 P.M. on New Year's Eve, hundreds streamed into the Shiloh Presbyterian Church, where the Reverend Henry Highland Garnet served as pastor. Garnet, born a slave in Maryland, had escaped north as a child with his family and settled in New York. He had attended the African Free School, and in 1840 had graduated from the Oneida Institute in Troy. He had embraced radical abolitionism, forgoing the ideas of moral suasion and passive resistance that were advocated by men such as Garrison and Douglass; instead, he had embraced direct action—political and, if need be, violent—as the means to end slavery. In 1843, he had delivered a speech addressed to "the Slaves of the United States." "Brethren, arise, arise! Strike for your lives and liberties! Now is the day and the hour. Let every slave throughout the land do this, and the days of slavery are numbered. You cannot be more oppressed than you have been—you cannot suffer greater cruelties than you have already. *Rather die freemen than live to be slaves.* Remember that you are FOUR MILLIONS!"[7]

Nearly twenty years of prayer and activism had passed since that speech, and now the hour of freedom was drawing near. The pews were filled. A reporter described the audience as two-thirds black and one-third white. Starting with a prayer at 10 P.M., the program included speeches and songs. One speaker declared that "if the President's Emancipation Proclamation had been issued on the firing of the first gun at Fort Sumter the nation would have been saved the deluge of blood that had since flowed through the land." Another speaker was introduced as having been born in North Carolina; he said it "was a very good place to be born in, and a most excellent place to get out of." The congregation laughed heartily. A third speaker started to "grumble and find fault" because the Proclamation was being issued as a military necessity, not as an act of humanity and justice—but he was cut short. On this evening, complaining had no place.

At 11:45 an organist played a "solemn dirge." The audience then knelt for five minutes in silent prayer. As midnight arrived, the choir, joined by the congregation, sang "Blow, Ye Trumpets Blow, the Year of Jubilee Has Come." More songs, shouting, prayers, and rejoicing followed, "and the jubilee was kept up until a late hour in the evening."[8]

A similar scene took place in Washington, at a contraband camp. Three hundred people gathered at the schoolhouse at 8 P.M. on New Year's Eve.

Again, speeches and songs filled the air. A few minutes before midnight, the assembled knelt in prayer. And then, at two minutes past twelve, "an old colored man was called on to lead in prayer, and he eloquently prayed that the army might be successful, that the rebellion be speedily crushed, that the blessings of heaven would rest on President Lincoln, and that their friends left behind in Dixie might be saved. The whole number then united in singing a Hallelujah hymn." The singing, "including an extemporaneous song 'I'm a Free Man,'" continued until dawn. One contraband named Thornton wept all night. Asked what was the matter, he cried: "Tomorrow my child is to be sold neter more . . . No more dat, no more dat, no more dat. Can't sail your wife and children any more."[9]

In Boston, Moncure Conway and William Lloyd Garrison attended watch night at the African Church, and on New Year's Day two major events took place, one at the Music Hall in the afternoon and a second at Tremont Temple that ran all day. The Music Hall event, billed as the "Grand Jubilee Concert," was attended by New England's cultural elite: Henry Wadsworth Longfellow, John Greenleaf Whittier, Harriet Beecher Stowe, Charles Eliot Norton, Oliver Wendell Holmes, Ralph Waldo Emerson, and Francis Parkman. The assemblage heard selections from Beethoven and Mendelssohn. And then Emerson read his "Boston Hymn," composed for the occasion:

> To-day unbind the captive,
> So only are ye unbound;
> Lift up a people from the dust,
> Trump of their rescue, sound!
> Pay ransom to the owner
> And fill the bag to the brim.
> Who is the owner? The slave is owner,
> And ever was. Pay him.

At Tremont Temple, the all-day celebration overlapped in part with the Music Hall affair. The audience heard speech after speech, from distinguished abolitionists white and black: James Freeman Clarke, William C. Nell, William Wells Brown. Frederick Douglass spoke in the afternoon and again in the evening. Sumner sent a letter that offered his regrets at not being able to attend. Oddly, neither William Lloyd Garrison nor Wendell Phillips appeared. Anxiety mounted as the day wore on and the attendees awaited news of the Proclamation. Finally, during the evening session, a copy of the Proclamation, fresh off the telegraph wires, arrived and was read by Charles Slack, a local legislator who worked for "Equal School Rights." The "effect was electrical"—the audience rose to its feet. People threw their hats in the air, shouted at the top of their voices, and demonstrated "in every conceivable manner symptoms of gratification that the hour of deliverance had at length arrived."[10]

Thomas Wentworth Higginson couldn't be present at the Boston celebration—he was attending the festivities and services in South Carolina. Higginson had been one of the "secret six" who had supported John Brown's raid on Harpers Ferry in 1859, and he was now serving at Port Royal, South Carolina, as a colonel with the First South Carolina Volunteers, the first black regiment authorized by the federal government during the war. Port Royal—located in Beaufort County, fifty-five miles south of Charleston—had fallen into Union hands early in the war, and, since then, northern whites and local blacks had been participating in an experiment in free plantation labor. Edward S. Philbrick, one of many New Englanders who had rushed to Port Royal to supervise and educate, had welcomed the news of the preliminary Emancipation Proclamation: "I now feel more than ever the importance of our mission here, not so much for the sake of the few hundreds under my own eyes as for the sake of the success of the experiment we are now trying. It is, you know, a question even with our good President whether negroes can be made available as free laborers on this soil. I, for one, believe they can and I am more than ever in earnest to show it." Lincoln no doubt felt the same way: the Sea Islands, which were under Union military control, should have been made one of the exceptions included in the Emancipation Proclamation, but Lincoln had excluded Port Royal from the list of exemptions.[11]

At a plantation on Port Royal Island, the Proclamation was read and the colors presented. As Higginson saluted the flag, there was a spontaneous outpouring of emotion:

There suddenly arose, close beside the platform, a strong male voice, (but rather cracked and elderly), into which two women's voices instantly blended, singing, as if by an impulse that could be no more repressed than the morning note of the song-sparrow,—

> My Country 'tis of thee,
> Sweet land of liberty,
> Of thee I sing . . . !

I never saw anything so electric; it made all other words cheap; it seemed the choked voice of a race at last unloosed.[12]

Throughout the country, free blacks rejoiced. In Philadelphia, Benjamin Rush Plumly, an Ohio abolitionist who would go on to help recruit black troops and teach freedmen in Louisiana, wrote to Lincoln that he had spent January 1 in the "Crowded Churches of the Colored People," who "sang and shouted and wept and prayed. God knows, I cried, with them." All places of business were closed; in the churches "ministers and laymen, exhorted the people, to accept the Great Gift, with reverent joy; to make no public demonstration, no procession or parade; To indulge in no resentment for the past, and no impatience for the future, but to 'work and wait, trusting in God, for the final triumph of Justice,' Never [were] demonstrations so touching. Many wet eyes of the white people, testified to the profound pathos of the occasion." Plumly informed Lincoln that "the Black people all trust *you*. They *believe* that you desire to do them Justice. They do not believe that *You, wish* to expatriate them, or to enforce upon them any disability, but—that you *cannot* do *all*, that you would."[13]

The celebration of the "Year of Jubilee" continued through the weekend. On Friday, January 2, in Brooklyn, the African Methodist Church honored the Emancipation Proclamation. A banner was draped across the platform with various inscriptions: "Wilberforce," "Clarkson," "Our Country and the Day We Celebrate." At 8 P.M. the church was filled, "not a few of the audience being whites, among whom were numerous ladies." According to the *New York Times*, the pastor rejoiced over the Proclamation but regretted that "it did not extend to all who are held in Southern bondage." Yet providence was working for the benefit of the black man, and "the establishment of freedom throughout all our broad domain was only a work of time."[14]

Sunday brought more speeches and sermons across the Union, none more powerful than that delivered by Wendell Phillips at the Music Hall in Boston. The orchestra and balconies were filled and hundreds stood in the aisles to hear Phillips on the subject of the Proclamation. He did not disappoint. "For a hundred days your hearts have been full of this Proclamation. Every possible phase of thought must have been anticipated; every hope, every fear, canvassed. What can mortal lips add to the anxiety or to the joy of twenty million of people!" Phillips praised the Proclamation as the work of the people; it marked "the PEOPLE'S progress," because the government had been driven to take this action. The emphasis on the people was reminiscent of the phrase Lincoln had used in his address to Congress on July 4, 1861, when he had declared: "This is essentially a People's contest."[15]

Phillips marveled at the changes during the previous two years since Congress had resolved that the war had nothing to do with slavery. He marveled, as well, at the changes in the president during the previous one hundred days: "'Will you go away, if I venture to free you?' said the President on the 22d of September. 'May I colonize you among the sickly deserts or the vast jungles of South America!' On the first day of January, he says to the same four million, 'Let's colonize you in the forts of the Republic! Give us your hand to defend the perpetuity of the Union!' To that *colonization,*" added Phillips, "I have no criticism to suggest." Laughter and applause filled the hall.

Phillips went on to offer an answer to the question, heard on so many lips: What did the Proclamation mean? What would it "do for us now"? He answered: "It is not so much a step onward as it is launching into a new channel." It settled once and for all "the question of the right. . . . Battles are fought now for Justice." The president had made a mistake in exempting certain areas (portions of Virginia, the lower parishes of Louisiana, West Virginia, Tennessee), but this did not matter. "What care the counties of Louisiana whether they are excepted by the Proclamation or not?" Phillips asked. "With every surrounding locality free, how can they keep their slaves?" As for the border states, they too would follow, because "the moment you take out the bottom of the bucket, the contents fall to the ground [and] the Gulf States are the bottom." And so, in the end, "What is the President's Proclamation?" Phillips answered that, for the free, it was a "step in the progress of a people, rich, prosperous, independent." And for the enslaved, "it is sunlight, scattering the despair of centuries."[16]

Speaking at the North Church in Salem on Sunday, Edmund B. Willson, who later in the year would be commissioned chaplain of the 24th Massachusetts Volunteers, noted that the Proclamation had to be justified both on the grounds of military necessity and as an act of justice. Military necessity could not justify what is "grossly unjust," and justice could not govern the question without military necessity. The Proclamation, "like most human actions, is the product not of one but of many motives. . . . We have done two things in one in the emancipation. We have aimed a stroke of war policy at rebellion, and we have at the same time given back to millions of human beings rights which were *birth-rights* and inalienable, but of which they have been unjustly and cruelly robbed. It is this latter act of justice which is to live in history."[17]

And yet, for all the celebration and enthusiasm, at least one observer—the Reverend Nathaniel Hall—noted a certain reserve toward the decree. "Evidently," thought Hall, "we do not see . . . the moral magnitude and grandeur of this edict of Emancipation,—do not take in its vast proportions. There is, somehow, a striking want of correspondence between what has now been affirmed of it, and what seems to be the tone, or the degree, of the general feeling about it." He thought people had become so accustomed to accepting, however reluctantly, the presence of slavery in their midst, that they "fail to feel and see the Baseness." Also, he realized, "we are too near the event, perhaps, historically to be duly impressed by it." But even if the fact of freedom lagged behind the announcement of it, "the proclamation is the mighty fact. There it stands, irrevocable, sure,—the guaranty of their liberty, valid against the world."[18]

The culminating event during those days commemorating the Emancipation Proclamation took place on Monday night, January 5, at Cooper Union in New York. It was a fitting location for the celebration; nearly three years earlier, on February 27, 1860, Lincoln had come to this location and delivered a speech that, more than anything else, had made him a plausible contender for the presidency. Now, on January 5—as the *New York Times* reported—the auditorium was filled to capacity, three-fifths black and two-fifths white, with men and women equally represented. The proceedings began with an integrated band playing "The Star-Spangled Banner." The assembly then sang the "Emancipation Hymn" for 1863, which began:

> Hail to the brightness of Liberty's morning,
> Join all the earth in an anthem of praise
> Freedom's glad day in its glory is dawning,
> Light is dispensing its soul cheering rays.

Three cheers went up for Lincoln, three cheers for the Stars and Stripes, and three cheers as well for the abolitionists, "who for the last thirty years worked upon the mind of this nation." Henry Highland Garnet then spoke. He confessed the widespread fears that Lincoln, under severe pressure, would not redeem the promise of September 22; "but with eyes set on the God of Justice, and determined to disenthrall an injured race, and glorify God," the president had followed through. Garnet called Lincoln "an advancing and progressive man." He had kept his word, and now "no power could ever undo what he had done."[19]

Garnet then praised the black residents of New York, whose patriotism had led them from the start to offer their services to the war effort. But the offer had been spurned—"the white people were horror-stricken, and some of them turned up their noses till they almost met their foreheads." So black men had waited until called upon, and now the call had arrived. And they would go forth "to bequeath to future generations an heirloom in which their children and children's children would remember with pride that their fathers were not cowards when their country called them to its defense." The assembled then sang "John Brown's Body," a folk tune that had gained great popularity among Union troops during the war.[20]

Following Garnet, the Reverend George Barrell Cheever, pastor of the Church of the Puritans in Manhattan, spoke. The crowd stood and women waved their pocket handkerchiefs. Though in many ways a conservative Presbyterian minister, Cheever had long opposed slavery as a sin and a crime. Despite the high spirits and general mood, in his sermon on this occasion he gave little credit to Lincoln. Emancipation, he said, was a reluctant step on the part of an administration which, finally, was calling upon "the colored men . . . to come and help save the whites." "If the President had instead of waiting 100 days," declared Cheever, "issued an edict of unconditional Abolition three months ago, the Rebellion would have been crushed by this time." But now that it had been done, it was irrevocable, "never to be called back, never, never." And Cheever predicted that over time the policy of emancipation would become more popular, that "there will be a rivalry for the honor of the battle." Even such oppositional newspapers as the *Herald* and the *Journal of Commerce,* he averred, "would before long be claiming that they always claimed Emancipation as the policy that would lead to victory."[21]

Cheever had a point. The Emancipation Proclamation, now that it had been issued, compelled people to take sides and to be counted. In England, workingmen's meetings voted to support the president. On New Year's Eve, a group of London workingmen wrote to Lincoln: "We have watched with the warmest interest the steady advance of your policy along the path of emancipation; and on this eve of the day on which your proclamation of freedom takes effect, we pray God to strengthen your hands, to confirm your noble purpose, and to hasten the restoration of that lawful authority which engages, in peace or war, by compensation or by force of arms, to realize the glorious principle of which your constitution is founded—the brotherhood, freedom, and equality of all men." The president also heard from the workingmen of Manchester, who offered "high admiration of your firmness in upholding the proclamation of freedom."[22]

On January 19, Lincoln replied to the Manchester workingmen. He told them it had often been said that Europe would favor the Confederacy, and he realized the "severe trial" to which the workingmen of Europe had been subjected. "Under these circumstances," he concluded, "I cannot but regard your decisive utterance upon the question as an instance of sublime Christian heroism which has not been surpassed in any age or any country."[23]

From London, Henry Adams rejoiced: "The Emancipation Proclamation has done more for us here than all our former victories and all our diplomacy. It is creating an almost convulsive reaction in our favor all over this country." And John Murray Forbes heard from one correspondent that "so far from the Proclamation being a cause of embarrassment to the government, it has been and is, with regard to the feeling in Europe, the great source of their strength: and I did not hesitate to tell the President that had it not been for the anti-slavery policy of his government there would have been much greater difficulty in preventing a recognition of the Southern States."[24]

One writer, the abolitionist Maria Weston Chapman, could not find graceful expressions for her joy, so she resorted to exclamations: "Hurrah! Hosanna! Hallelujah! Laudamus! Nunc dimittis! Jubilate! Amen!"[25]

Perhaps the most eloquent celebration of the meaning of the Proclamation came in images, rather than in words. Thomas Nast, only twenty-three years old and at the beginning of a long and influential career as a cartoonist for *Harper's Weekly,* published an illustration titled "The Emancipation of the Negroes" on January 23. It offers a panorama of black history. At the center is a fanciful vision of middle-class domestic harmony, showing a free black family gathered by the hearth. The boy holds a book in his hand. According to the key published in the paper, "On the wall hangs a portrait of Abraham Lincoln, whom the family cannot sufficiently admire and revere." Also on the wall is a banjo, "a source of never-ending enjoyment and recreation."

At the top of the picture is the Goddess of Liberty. At the bottom, Father Time—holding a child, who represents the New Year—is "striking off the chains of the bondman and setting him at liberty forever." Prints of Nast's picture would include a significant change: instead of Father Time, a distinct portrait of Abraham Lincoln would occupy the pendant. The left side depicts scenes of slavery: fugitive slaves, a slave auction, a whipping, and a family group being separated. On the right side are images of the future, characterized by heroism, religion, education, and "negroes receiving pay for their faithful labor."

None of this is to suggest that criticism of the Emancipation Proclamation evaporated after January 1. As might be expected, Jefferson Davis, in his Message to the Confederate Congress on January 12, condemned the Proclamation as "the most execrable measure recorded in the history of guilty man." It was the "most startling political crime, the most stupid political blunder, yet known in American history," according to the *Richmond Enquirer.* The *Macon Weekly Telegraph* denounced the members of Lincoln's administration as "doubly-dyed scoundrels": "War or no war, they would have soon proclaimed emancipation, and thank God the proclamation finds our people with arms in their hands, and ready to fight in defence of law and social order." The *London Times* continued to hurl invective, and Democratic newspapers in the North recycled the arguments first rehearsed in September: the Proclamation was unconstitutional; it was a *brutum fulmen;* it would lead Europe to recognize the Confederacy; it would compel soldiers to desert; it would inaugurate servile insurrection. None of these concerns, though, had proven true in the fall. Why would they do so now?

Denunciations continued, but not with the vigor, energy, or focus that had greeted the preliminary Emancipation Proclamation. To be sure, speeches at the inaugurals of governors Horatio Seymour in New York and Joel Parker in New Jersey included denunciations of the Proclamation. More typical of the tone was the comment from a midwestern paper that called it "the most foolish joke ever got off by the six-foot-four Commander-in-Chief." According to the *New York Herald,* "this *pronunciamento* [was] unnecessary, unwise, and ill-timed, impracticable, outside of the constitution and full of mischief." But the paper also provided the numbers of slaves covered by the Proclamation (3,119,397) and of those exempted (830,000). Since the slaves freed were not under Union control, all the *Herald* could say was that "it is practically a dead letter, and for the present, at least, amounts to nothing as a measure of emancipation." That "present," however, included some occupied areas such as the Sea Islands of South Carolina and Georgia, and parts of North Carolina, Mississippi, Florida, and Arkansas. Slaves in those areas were indeed emancipated immediately, and, over time, millions more would be as well.[26]

The *Cincinnati Daily Commercial* expressed the feelings of most conservative Republicans: "The proclamation has been five days before the country in print and the sun, moon and stars seem to continue in their courses, unmindful of the decree—and the negroes, and white folks too, are pretty much where they were before Abraham Lincoln shed a drop of ink in writing his name at the bottom of probable sheet of foolscap on which the original draft of the proclamation was made."[27]

Now that the deed was done, some opponents may have relented in their criticism of the Emancipation Proclamation, but one Republican agitator did not. After suspecting that Lincoln had lost heart, Adam Gurowski initially praised the Proclamation as the "death-knell to slavery and to the slave-ocracy." He ridiculed "shallow and brainless diplomats [who] sneer at the proclamation. So did the Herodians sneer at the star of Bethlehem; and where now are the Herodians?" He even briefly praised the President: "In issuing the proclamation, Mr. Lincoln gives legal sanction, form, and record to what the storm of events and the loud cry of the best of the people have long demanded and now inexorably dictate."[28]

But then, as if catching himself, he resumed the vitriol: "History will piti-lessly tell the truth, the whole truth, and nothing but the truth; and small credit will history give to Lincoln beyond that of being the legal recorder of a righteous deed. . . . The proclamation is generated neither by Lincoln's brains, heart or soul, and what is born in such a way is always monstrous."[29]

Gurowski was not the only radical to feel aggrieved. While most abolition-ists muffled their disappointment, one black abolitionist, James H. Hudson, initially enthusiastic, ultimately turned bitter. "Our honest but incompetent President adopts a halfway measure, which purports to give freedom to the bulk of the slave population beyond the reach of our arms, while it ignores or defies justice, by clinching the rivets of the chain which binds those whom alone we have present power to redeem. The proclamation should have been made to include every bondsman on the soil of America; every chain should have been broken, and the oppressed bidden to go free."[30]

Norfolk was in one of the parts of Virginia excluded by the Emancipa-tion Proclamation. On January 14, the black abolitionist John Oliver wrote a wrenching letter to the Reverend Simeon S. Jocelyn, an abolitionist who, in 1829, had served as the first white minister of a black congregation, the United African Society in New Haven:

You must remember that Presedent Lincoln leves us as we were before his proclimation of freedom was issued. This will be another cause of delay, in many things I fear. Wither this place is a modern Sodom not to be saved under the blessing of Abraham I am Shore I do not know. . . . In contrary distinction to the proclamation however and not knowing what was coming the Slaves to the number of more than 5000 from miles around celebrated in Norfolk what they supposed was their free-dom on the first day of January, last. But since the proclimation has come to us the slaveholders have began again to maltreat their Slaves, at the same time tell them that no one on earth has the power to free them. The slaves here are feeling the most intence greaf from the effects of proclimation."[31]

Lincoln said in the Proclamation that the "excepted parts, are for the present, left precisely as if this proclamation was not issued." But nothing anywhere was left untouched. The word "emancipation" had been uttered, and the word had consequences, both intended and not. If in Norfolk, Virginia, which was explicitly exempted, the Proclamation could raise the hopes of slaves and then lead to a worsening of their condition, in Columbus, Kentucky, no party at all to the decree, the following could take place in a military chaplain's tent: "A colored woman brot his [the chaplain's] washing and he spoke to her as nicely as if she was a white woman. When she curtseyed and called him massa, he said, 'My poor woman, I am not your massa, you have no massa any more, President Lincoln has made all the colored people free just like the white folks.' The poor woman kept saying, 'bress de Lors, bress de Lord, dis am de yeah of jubilee.' When he handed her a fifty cent scrip to pay for the washing she looked at the picture of Lincoln in the corner of the bill, and putting it to her mouth, kissed it."[32]

11

"Men of Color, To Arms!"

The question that soon came to dominate discussion was not the Proclamation itself, but the statement in the Proclamation that blacks thus freed would "be received into the armed services of the United States." In a rousing speech at Cooper Union on February 6, 1863, Frederick Douglass addressed the Proclamation and the arming of black men.

> I stand here to-night not only as a colored man and an American, but, by the express decision of the Attorney-General of the United States, as a colored citizen, having, in common with all other citizens, a stake in the safety, prosperity, honor, and glory of a common country. [*Cheering.*] We are all liberated by this proclamation. Everybody is liberated. The white man is liberated, the black man is liberated, the brave men now fighting the battles of their country against rebels and traitors are now liberated, and may strike with all their might, even if they do by thus manfully striking hurt the Rebels, at their most sensitive point.— [*Applause.*] I congratulate you upon this amazing change—this amazing approximation toward the sacred truth of human liberty. . . . There are certain great national acts, which by their relation to universal principles, properly belong to the whole human family, and Abraham Lincoln's Proclamation of the 1st of January, 1863, is one of these acts.

Henceforth that day shall take rank with the Fourth of July. [*Applause.*] Henceforth it becomes the date of a new and glorious era in the history of American liberty."

Douglass's rhetoric continued to soar:

It is objected to the Proclamation of Freedom, that it only abolishes Slavery in the Rebel States. To me it seems a blunder that Slavery was not declared abolished everywhere in the Republic. Slavery anywhere endangers the National cause, and should perish everywhere. [*Loud applause.*] But even in this omission of the Proclamation the evil is more seeming than real. When Virginia is a free State, Maryland cannot be a slave State. When Missouri is a free State Kentucky cannot be a slave State. [*Cheers.*] Slavery must stand or fall together. Strike it at either extreme—either on the head or at the heel, and it dies. A brick knocked down at either end of the row brings every brick in it to the ground. [*Applause.*] . . . It is again objected to this Proclamation that it is only an ink and paper proclamation. I admit it. The objector might go it a step further, and assert that there was a time when this Proclamation was only a thought, a sentiment, an idea—a hope of some radical Abolitionist—for such it truly was. But what of it?—The world has never advanced a single inch in the right direction, when the movement could not be traced to some such small beginning. The bill abolishing Slavery, and giving freedom to eight hundred thousand people in the West Indies, was a paper bill.—The Reform bill, that broke up the rotten borough system in England, was a paper bill. The act of Catholic Emancipation was a paper act; and so was the bill repealing the Corn Laws. Greater than all, our own Declaration of Independence was at one time but ink and paper. [*Cheering.*]

If that paper proclamation was to be made into "iron, lead, and fire," blacks had to be enlisted in the army and used as soldiers. Objections to doing so were farcical and collapsed under the weight of contradiction. "In one breath," Douglass observed, "the Copperheads tell you that the slaves won't fight, and in the next they tell you that the only effect of the Proclamation is to make the slaves cut their masters' throats [*Laughter*] and stir up insurrections all over the South.—The same men tell you that the negroes are lazy and good for nothing, and in the next breath they tell you that they will all come North and take the labor away from the laboring white men here. [*Laughter and cheers.*] In one breath they tell you that the negro can never learn the military art, and in the next they tell you that there is danger that white men may be outranked by colored men. [*Continued laughter.*]" Douglass brought the lecture to a close by calling for whites to welcome blacks into the struggle.[1]

Following the Cooper Union address, Douglass devoted his energies to encouraging blacks to enlist. "Men of Color, To Arms!" became a motto of the recruitment campaign. "Liberty won by white men would lose half its luster," explained Douglass. "Can you ask for a more inviting, ennobling and soul enlarging work, than that of making one of the glorious Band who shall carry Liberty to your enslaved people?" Douglass also saw what military service would mean to the lives of blacks after the war: "Once let the black man get upon his person the brass letters U.S.; let him get an eagle on his button, and a musket on his shoulder, and bullets in his pocket, and there is no power on earth or under the earth which can deny that he has earned the right of citizenship in the United States."[2]

As Douglass recruited, Lincoln implemented. Some black military units were quietly allowed to form prior to the Emancipation Proclamation—for example, in South Carolina, Louisiana, and Kansas. Now, exercising the discretionary authority granted him by the Militia Act of 1862, the president used the Proclamation to approve, officially and publicly, the enrollment of black troops. On January 14, Lincoln wrote to Major General John Adams Dix and asked whether the army encampments at Fort Monroe and Yorktown, in Virginia, could be "garrisoned by colored troops," an expedient that would free up the white forces stationed there for action elsewhere. The Proclamation had been issued, he explained, and "now, that we have it, and bear all the disadvantages of it, (as we do bear some in certain quarters) we must also take some benefit from it, if practicable." In early March he received a letter from Thomas Richmond, a former member of the Illinois General Assembly. Richmond implored the president to "arm every Negro slave that can be animated with the hope of freedom and Justice and provide freedom to every Slave that will turn out and fight for it. No matter whether in loyal or rebelious States, press with all possible speed the securing of the muscle and Sinew of the Slave population." Richmond warned that if Lincoln did not do so, Jefferson Davis might. Of course, Richmond's was just one of many letters Lincoln had received during the previous year. For example, on September 26, 1862, he had received a letter from William Sprague, governor of Rhode Island: "You enlist into the Navy Colored men. Why not the Army? It will give strength to your proclamation." Since the Emancipation Proclamation already included a measure for enrolling blacks in the army, it is little wonder that Lincoln scrawled on the envelope: "Good advice." Later that month, writing to Andrew Johnson, he explained that "the colored population is the great *available* and yet *unavailed* of, force for restoring the Union. The bare sight of fifty thousand armed, and drilled black soldiers on the banks of the Mississippi, would end the rebellion at once." No longer did he worry, as he had in August, about losing the support of soldiers from the border states if blacks were armed.[3]

The Emancipation Proclamation led Representative Thaddeus Stevens of Pennsylvania, on January 12, to introduce a bill "to raise additional soldiers for the service of the Government." The bill authorized the president to "enroll, arm, equip, and receive" 150,000 persons of African descent for service of up to five years. There was a practical reason to do so: Union military leaders feared that with the impending expiration of two-year enlistments that had begun in the spring of 1861, and nine-month enlistments provided for by the Militia Act the previous July, there would be significant loss of manpower to fight the war. The Army of the Potomac had some fifty regiments that fit these categories. George Templeton Strong reported on January 26 that he had heard "we need not be uneasy about the regiments to be mustered out of service within a few months on expiration of their enlistments. There will be 300,000 enrolled Ethiops to fill the gap."[4]

But practical matters did not drive the caustic debate that occupied the House for more than a week. With the Emancipation Proclamation promulgated, opponents vented all their racial fears and hatreds on the bill, whereas supporters saw it as an essential step toward not only winning the war but also giving meaning to freedom. Charles Wickliffe of Kentucky expressed outrage that "this country cannot conquer and suppress this rebellion, unless he can employ the negro slave and put Sambo, or some other man meaner than Sambo, in command. Great God! Is that so?" He called blacks "poor, deluded, uninformed creatures [who] will not stand the firing of a gun. They will fall upon the ground or run away." "The negro is base, degraded, and cowardly, without aspiration, and incapable of discipline and military training," averred George Pendleton of Ohio. Henry May of Maryland insisted that "we who recognize the amiable disposition of the domesticated African, his inert nature, his slovenly habits, his clumsiness, his want of vigor, and his timidity, know that of all human beings he presents the least qualifications for a soldier." "The slave is not a soldier, and he cannot be a soldier. It is not in the nature of things," declared John J. Crittenden of Kentucky. "It is not in the nature of things that the black man is to save this union," thundered Hendrick Wright of Pennsylvania.[5]

Although most Democrats emphasized the docility of the slaves, others feared that the enlistment of runaway slaves in the army would lead to horrific scenes of bloodshed and slaughter. In either case, whether African Americans were submissive cowards or savage murderers, their presence, opponents believed, would demoralize the army and lead to desertions. William Wadsworth of Kentucky concluded, "We in the South could not live under this policy of arming the slaves. Let an army of one hundred and fifty thousand men, once slaves, be uniformed and armed, and commanded by the appointees of abolition, and it cannot be otherwise than that it would be the destruction of our homes, our families, our lives, our property, and our liberty."[6]

Democrats took special pleasure in chiding the Republican proponents of Thaddeus Stevens's bill, particularly Owen Lovejoy of Illinois, for their hypocrisy—a bold-faced accusation, in view of the fact that most Republicans opposed the Illinois ban on blacks settling within the state. Elijah Norton of Missouri reminded the gentleman from Illinois of the fall vote to prohibit any African American from moving into the state. "He is good enough for a soldier," admonished Norton, "but after the war is over and victory is won, if he goes to the gentleman's State he is driven out as one calculated to demoralize society and unfit to live in the same country with the free white man."[7]

Norton's point, viewed differently, suggested something so terrifying that opponents brought it up only as an indication of the absurdity of the measure: arming blacks could lead to equality. One congressman warned that "gentlemen cannot . . . lead the African through this war . . . without admitting the negro to an equality with themselves—at least a political equality." Another asserted that "the question is one of political and social equality with the negro everywhere. If you make him an instrument by which your battles are fought, the means by which victories are won, you must treat him as a victor is entitled to be treated, with all decent and becoming respect." And George Pendleton asked what would be done with them afterward: "Will you consign them again to political inferiority, to social isolation? Will you again deny to them those privileges which are guaranteed to every citizen by the Constitution, which they have helped you to maintain? Or will you take them to a political and social equality with yourselves? Will you give them the right to suffrage; the right to hold office? Will you put them side by side with the white citizens of the land?"[8]

For Thaddeus Stevens, the sponsor of the bill, the answer was a resounding yes. Stevens was a forceful presence. Age seventy, he wore a dark-brown wig and had deep-set, penetrating eyes. His club foot may have detracted from his appearance when he moved about; but standing at his desk, he always held his hands locked before him and "never makes a gesture, but calmly, slowly, and ponderously drops his sentences as though each one weighed a ton."[9]

Referring to Wickliffe, Stevens said: "The gentleman from Kentucky objects to their employment lest it should lead to the freedom of the blacks. He says that he fights *only* for the freedom of his own white race. That sentiment is unworthy . . . That patriotism that is wholly absorbed by one's own country is narrow and selfish. That philanthropy which embraces only one's own race, and leaves the other numerous races of mankind to bondage and to misery, is cruel and detestable." As to whether soldiers would object to arming blacks, Stevens thought "it would be a strange taste that would prefer, themselves, to face the death-bearing heights of Fredericksburg, and be buried in trenches at the foot of them, than to see it done by colored soldiers." Indeed, Stevens's argument had its own perversity. Why should whites alone bear the burden of fighting the war, he asked. "Why should our race be exposed to suffering and disease, when the African might endure his equal share of it?

Is it wise, is it humane, to send your kindred to battle and to death, when you might put the colored man in the ranks and let him bear a part of the conflict between the rebel and his enfranchised slaves?"[10]

Republicans tried to refute the arguments that claimed slaves could never make good soldiers. They offered testimony from generals Benjamin F. Butler and John C. Frémont; they pointed out the success of black sailors; they invoked historical precedents; and they quoted liberally from George Livermore's *Historical Research* on African Americans as soldiers—a book which, at the time, was also being excerpted in several newspapers. In response to the argument that black soldiers would be murdered if captured by the Confederates, the answer was simple, thought Thomas Edwards of New Hampshire: "I would hang or shoot one of their soldiers every time they hung or shot one of ours." William Dunn of Indiana responded to those who said blacks could not fight: "If they are ignorant of the use of arms, instruct them in that use. Teach their 'hands war, and their fingers to fight.' Are they so brutalized that they will not fight for their own liberty? Shall we receive them and educate them to arms for this purpose, or should we send our own sons there?" As for the argument that enlisting blacks would lead to savagery because they would seek revenge, Dunn turned the proslavery argument against itself and sarcastically asked, "Is it possible that these people, who for generations have been under the humanizing, civilizing, Christianizing influence of slavery, are still such barbarians that we cannot safely put arms into their hands without the commission by them of barbarous outrages upon their masters?" With respect to the question of equality, "I see no reason why we may not place the man who fights for the country, not only upon the same platform, and claim for him a position as the equal, but as the superior of the man who fights against my country."[11]

Finally, the enlistment of slaves was viewed as essential not only to advancing the cause of emancipation as enunciated by the Proclamation, but also to hastening the permanent abolition of slavery. "No man who has ever served under our flag," noted an opponent of the measure, "whether for a day or for an hour, can be made again a slave." Charles Sedgwick of New York understood that "the arming of the slave population is the end of the institution for all time, and no less the end of this rebellion."[12]

On February 3, a much-modified version of Stevens's bill passed the

House by a vote of 83 to 54. It included a provision that prohibited the placing of white soldiers under black command, forbade the enlistment of the slaves of loyal masters, and prohibited the establishment of recruitment offices in the border states. The Senate, however, referred the measure to the Military Affairs Committee, which recommended against its passage, because, under the Confiscation Act and Militia Act of July 17, 1862, the president already had the authority to enlist black soldiers. He would do so despite "great aversion to the Negro Soldier Bill" from numerous politicians who beseeched the president not to act. On February 6, Navy commander John Dahlgren noted in his diary, "I observe that the President never tells a joke now." But within a few weeks, Lincoln was himself again: "He was full of joke, and we had some hearty laughs."[13]

Through the late winter and spring, the recruitment of black troops accelerated. In January, secretary of war Edwin Stanton authorized Massachusetts governor John Andrew to form a black regiment, and the result was the 54th Massachusetts, the first black regiment created in the North. Two of Frederick Douglass's sons were members of the unit. In May, the War Department established the Bureau of Colored Troops; and several generals, most notably Adjutant General Lorenzo Thomas, set about recruiting freedmen for the military.[14]

By war's end, some 179,000 black soldiers had served—nearly 10 percent of the Union total—along with 19,000 sailors. Nearly 60 percent came from the states of the Confederacy, and 25 percent from the border states. Whether they originally came from the South or the North, all of the soldiers faced discrimination and hardship. All black regiments were led by white officers, only some of whom, such as Robert Gould Shaw of the Massachusetts 54th, accepted the commission because of their abolitionist principles. For others, commanding a black regiment was an avenue toward becoming an officer or moving up in rank and responsibility. Black soldiers received unequal pay—only $10 a month (which was $3 less than that of white soldiers), from which an additional $3 was deducted as a monthly clothing allowance. The inequity rankled, and a law for equal pay passed by Congress in June 1864 gave equal pay to men who were free at the start of the war from the date of their enlistment, and all others received equal pay retroactive to January 1, 1864. Black troops also suffered harsher discipline than their white counterparts.

And because they performed disproportionate amounts of fatigue duty involving arduous physical labor, and received worse medical care than their white counterparts, black soldiers were far more likely to die of disease than in battle. Blacks also suffered atrocities committed by Confederate soldiers, who executed them or returned captured soldiers to slavery. On May 1, 1863, the Confederate Congress passed a resolution that white officers who commanded or trained black men for military service were "guilty of inciting servile insurrection" and, if captured, would be tried under individual state laws against inciting slave rebellions. Lincoln responded with a General Order threatening reprisals for mistreatment of white officers or black troops, but anxiety over atrocities slowed the process by which blacks entered the field to fight.[15]

None of these deprivations, however, diminished the success of black soldiers, and early in 1863 reports began arriving of the competence and bravery of black troops in the field. One of the earliest came from Thomas Wentworth Higginson, whose First South Carolina Volunteers left Beaufort on January 23 on an expedition that "carried the regimental flag and the Emancipation Proclamation far into the interior of Georgia and Florida." The African Americans in his unit, he said, had been repeatedly under fire and "have, in every instance, come off not only with unblemished honor, but with undisputed triumph." The reports were much the same elsewhere—for example, at the battles of Port Hudson (May 27) and Milliken's Bend (June 7) along the Mississippi River, and in the assault on Fort Wagner (July 18) in Charleston Harbor. In a June editorial titled "The Negro Will Fight," the *Chicago Tribune* summed up the changed beliefs of many:

There is no longer any question about the fighting qualities of the [negro]. He has proved himself to be a good soldier on every occasion when his black metal [mettle] has been tried; and before the end of the war he will, if we are not vastly mistaken, have achieved a brilliant record. . . . Opposition to make a soldier of the negro has nearly ceased everywhere. . . . It is indeed a matter for great rejoicing that at last—although so late in the day—the government and the people have woke up to the importance of negro soldiers in the conduct of the war. . . . The thing, therefore, is now settled—the *negroes will fight.*"[16]

They fought, as well, for their rights. In some ways, becoming soldiers also offered a field for political action denied them in the civil arena. Soldiers of the Massachusetts 54th, for example, refused to accept their pay as long as it was unequal to the pay of white soldiers. In the fall, Corporal James Henry Gooding of the 54th wrote to President Lincoln. "We have done a Soldier's Duty," he declared. "Why Can't we have a Soldier's pay?" Whatever happened during the war, black soldiers knew that service would stand for something important afterward. Private Thomas Long, of the First South Carolina Volunteers, acting as a chaplain on Sunday, March 27, 1864, told his comrades in arms:

> If we hadn't become sojers, all might have gone back as it was before; our freedom might have slipped through de two houses of Congress & President Linkum's four years might have passed by & notin been done for we. But now tings can never go back, because we have showed our energy, our courage & our naturally [natural] manhood. Anoder ting is, suppose you had kept your freedom widout enlisting in dis army; your chilen might have grown up free, & been *well cultivated* so as to be equal to any business, but it would have always been flung in dere faces—"Your fader never fought for his own freedom"—and what could dey answer? *Neber can they say that to this African race any more.*[17]

Black military actions offered self-empowerment to black soldiers, and transformed the thinking of white soldiers. Emerson was right: the war was a teacher, and it taught through experience. But soldiers did not need a Concord philosopher to tell them that war educated. On September 22, 1863, one year to the day after the issuance of the preliminary Emancipation Proclamation, Silas Shearer, a private with the 23rd Iowa, wrote to his wife, whom he addressed as "Dear Companion": "My eyes don't see as they did when I left home. Since I have got down here and seen what Slavery was and where it had run to it changed me in a political since [sense] of view Slavery is what caused this War and the principle of it has changed me considerable." Months later, he returned to the topic. "My principles have changed since I last saw you," he reminded his wife. "When I was at home I was opposed to the medling of Slavery where it then Existed but since the Rebls got to such a pitch and it became us as a Military needsisity . . . to abolish Slavery and I say Amen to it and I believe the Best thing that has been done Since the War broke out is the Emancipation Proclimation."[18]

There were many soldiers, of course, who opposed the idea of fighting the war to free the slaves and said they would not fight alongside blacks. A lieutenant with the 35th Pennsylvania wrote to his stepfather: "I will never fight by the side of a Nigger & that is the feeling of the army where ever I have been & the sooner they drop the Nigger Question the better it will be for us all." Nearly as racist, but coming out on a different side of the question, was a private in the 9th Illinois who proclaimed, "I wouldn't lift my finger to free them if I had my say, but if we cant whip the rebels without taking the nigers I say take them and make them fite for us any way to bring this war to a close." Corporal Peter Welsh of the 28th Massachusetts, one of the regiments of the courageous Irish Brigade, averred that "the feeling against nigars is intensely strong in this army as is plainly to be seen wherever and whenever they meet them. They are looked upon as the principal cause of this war and this feeling is especially strong in the Irish regiments."[19]

But many others, some grudgingly and others generously, welcomed blacks into the struggle and over time came to respect their courage. Taylor Pierce, of the 22nd Iowa, informed his wife, "I think if old Abe will arm the Negroes and precipitate the whole mass of available bone and sinus [sinews] of the North they can either put down the rebellion or exterminate the accursed traitors. . . . I endorse the Proclimation to the fullest extent." Sergeant Lyman Ayer of the 2nd Minnesota reported in April that "the prejudice in the army against them is fast giving way. The majority of the troops in this Dept strongly endorse the policy of the administration including the proclamation." "There is not a Negro in the army," declared an officer in the 50th Ohio, "that is not a better man than a rebel, and for whom I have not a thousand times more respect than I have for a traitor." Captain Amos Hostetter of the 34th Illinois confessed, "We like the Negro no better now than we did then but we hate his master worse and I tell you when Old Abe carries out his Proclamation he kills this Rebellion and not before. I am thenceforth an *Abolitionist* and I intend to practice what I preach."[20]

Like many soldiers, Charles Wills changed his mind as the war progressed.

He enlisted as a private with the 8th Illinois and rose to be a lieutenant colonel with the 103rd Illinois. In August 1862 he wrote, "We are all rejoicing that 'Abe' refuses to accept the negroes as soldiers. Aside from the immense disaffection it would create in our army, the South would arm and put in the field three negroes to our one." Less than a year later, Wills confessed: "I never thought I would, but I am getting strongly in favor of arming them, and am becoming so blind that I can't see why they will not make soldiers. How queer. A year ago last January I didn't like to hear anything of emancipation. Last fall accepted confiscation of rebel's negroes quietly. In January took to emancipation readily, and now believe in arming the negroes."[21]

Stephen Pingree, a Dartmouth graduate and lawyer who served as a lieutenant colonel with the 3rd Vermont, also changed his opinion. In August 1863, Pingree admitted:

> I once doubted the policy of the negro soldier bill and, in fact, of the emancipation policy of the Gov't, but I was honest in both objections; the first on the ground that the negroes would be an unprofitable army, and the other on the ground that if we must emancipate, we could do so as we occupied the country, and not beforehand exasperate the South and cool the ardor of the border states by a course that must prove fruitless until military occupation could enforce it. Today, I believe not only in the justice but the policy of a war to restore the Union. I believe not only in Universal Emancipation, both in the border & rebel states . . . but I have faith in the effectiveness of Negro troops. . . . I have aided negroes to escape here and deliver themselves up to the military to be sent north, and I will always do it, because I hate Slavery and believe by destroying it we weaken this Rebellion.[22]

The views of Herman Lorenzo White, of the 22nd Massachusetts, also shifted over time, though not as dramatically. On January 25, 1863, he wrote his parents that he was "tired of this *nigger* war," opposed "Lincoln's proclamation," and "would do most anything to get out of this army." He detested blacks and thought whites and former slaves could never live side by side, "that the country would never enjoy peace and harmony if they were freed." But on August 4, 1864, near Petersburg, Virginia, he wrote his parents about the several regiments of black troops that were in camp: "It is astonishing to see the harmony that exists between them and the white troops. They fight, work & eat together without regard to color &c, set and chat together about the war and such like old chums, such is war, evry black soldier killed in battle is an equivalent for one white man."[23]

One soldier, Benjamin Stevens, even though he remained personally opposed to abolition as a war objective, joined the 10th Louisiana Infantry, which became the 48th United States Colored Infantry. After the fall of Vicksburg, he helped to recruit for the regiment. He explained to his mother, "I have talked with numbers of Parolled Prisoners in Vicksburg and they all admit it was the hardest stroke that there cause has received—the arming of the negroes. Not a few of them told me that they would rather fight two Regiments of White Soldiers than one of Niggers. Rebel citizens fear them more than they would fear Indians. . . . We are using their own strength against them."[24]

Benjamin Fordyce, an assistant surgeon with the 160th New York Volunteers, wrote with passion to his parents from LaFourche Crossing, Louisiana:

I saw this colored man who has been wounded at Port Hudson had two brothers killed in the same battle another and his last and only brother now in hospital with his wounds received in same battle A man who was born a slave and had been a slave till within a year past who had left a wife and family of children to fight for a government that had never guaranteed to him a single right above that of a hog or a horse till within one year past—when I heard him appeal to every strong bodied colored man he met; with an earnestness that secured seventy three in three days entirely alone and took them into quarters—hurrying from place to place, inviting, urging every man he met to come right along and join the army pointing to his own sacrifices that he had already made and the inestimable privilege of owning himself and family as a reward—I admit I felt ashamed of my own feeble efforts I had made to recruit the army—I felt satisfied that an element of strength has been developed and brought to the aid of our government of which we had no adequate idea.[25]

Perhaps the most far-reaching comment came from Daniel Sawtelle of the 8th Maine. Stationed at Port Royal, South Carolina, he wrote his sister in April: "I have thought that the negroes would not make good soldiers and so did most men in this regt, but in the several skirmishes they have had with the rebels they have won the praises of all and the rebels are as afraid of them as they would be of many tigers." This was a feeling expressed by many. It was what Sawtelle wrote next that distinguished him, and opened an avenue to the future: "There is one thing that I shall be glad I enlisted for. It is that I have had a chance to learn something about the institution of slavery. If I disliked it before, I utterly detest it now and I am not alone. Men that call themselves negro haters a while ago are compelled to say they are better than they thought they were. And why should not some of them (with the same advantage) be our equals."[26]

From the start of the war, wherever the Union army went, it traveled as a force of liberation. Brigadier General John White Geary, who headed the 2nd Division of the 12th Army Corps, made this clear when he wrote to Pennsylvania senator Edgar Cowan on August 4, 1863: "I also heartily approve of the President's Proclamation of January 1, 1863, and my own actions for a year previous, in liberating over 25,000 slaves is more than an endorsement upon it." To be sure, Geary was currying favor with Cowan in hopes of being recommended for a promotion to major general (which he did not receive), but the comment reveals much about the process of emancipation even before January 1.[27]

But with the Proclamation issued, one editor proclaimed, "wherever our armies go that proclamation goes with them and there slavery dies in consequence." The editor might have mentioned navies as well. On May 25, 1863, for example, Captain John J. Almy, commanding the USS *South Carolina*, spotted a group of blacks on Bull's Island Beach, north of Charleston, waving a white flag. He brought the runaway slaves aboard and explained to another captain, "In thus rescuing these persons from slavery and bringing them on board of a United States Federal vessel is, I consider, carrying out the spirit of the President's proclamation of January 1, 1863."[28]

Those armies and navies not only liberated slaves—they also enlisted tens of thousands, who fled bondage in ever greater numbers after the Emancipation Proclamation was issued. On January 13, James Freeman Clarke, Boston minister and author, visited a contraband camp near Washington: "I asked one colored woman, just from Virginia, if they had heard down there, among the slaves, of the President's Proclamation. She said, 'Oh yes, massa! We all knows about it; only we darsn't let on. We pretends not to know. I said to my ole massa, "what's this Massa, Lincoln is going to do what to the poor nigger? I hear he is going to cut 'em up awful bad. How is it, massa?" I just pretended foolish, sort of.' "[29]

In many cases the soldiers, white and black, literally carried the Emancipation Proclamation with them. John Murray Forbes reported that "with a view of placing the Proclamation of Emancipation in the hands of the negroes themselves, my father had 1,000,000 copies printed on small slips, one and a half inches square, put into packages of fifty each, and distributed among the Northern soldiers at the front, who scattered them about among the blacks, while on the march."[30]

Some soldiers wanted no part in spreading the word. They deeply resented the issuance of the Emancipation Proclamation, and considered resigning over it. One who eventually did was Henry Hubbell, a lieutenant colonel with the 3rd New York Volunteers. A Democrat, Hubbell volunteered at age thirty-three "to do my full duty to my country and myself." In a letter to his brother, Hubbell vented his racial hatred and his opposition to emancipation: "I did not come out to fight for the nigger or abolition of slavery, much less to make the nigger *better* than white men as they are every day becoming in the estimation and treatment of the powers at Washington." The "foolish and useless Emancipation Proclamation" showed Lincoln to be dishonest—"he releases the slaves where he has no power, & retains slavery where he has the power to free the slave." Fed up with Lincoln and the radicals, Hubbell resigned his commission in May 1863.[31]

Sergeant W. D. F. Landon of the 14th Indiana could not resign, but in a dispatch to a Vincennes newspaper, published under the pseudonym "Prock," he vented his racial hatred and gave voice to the cliché of not knowing whether to laugh or cry: "Old Abe's 'free papers' to all, including Africans and the rest of mankind, also the Apes, orangoutangs and monkies in

South America caused me an hour's hearty laugh, two hours tender cry, four hours big with mad, and I am swearing in all the languages known to American and Europeans."[32]

Major Henry Livermore Abbott, of the 20th Massachusetts, also opposed the Proclamation. "The president's proclamation is of course received with universal disgust, particularly the part which enjoins officers to see that it is carried out. You may be sure that we shan't see to any thing of the kind, having decidedly too much reverence for the constitution." Corporal John Ellis of the 111th Pennsylvania claimed, "There is a great deal of dissatisfaction in the army on account of the President's Proclamation." William Bluffton Miller of the 75th Indiana explained that soldiers condemned the Proclamation because "they are afraid of the effect in the north and fear it will cause a war there." "The spirits and patriotism of this army is dieing out every day," claimed Private John England of the 9th New York Volunteers. "This is occasioned by the general humbug that's carried on, the great want of a proper leader, and lastly the Presidents Emancipation Proclamation." John W. Chase, a private with the 1st Massachusetts Light Artillery, declared in a letter to his brother on January 11: "I am not willing to shed one drop of blood to fight Slavery up or down. Let the niggers go to *hell* for all [of] me and if a man wants to preach Abolition Emancipation or any other ism he must find somebody other than me to preach it." At the same time, he made it clear that "I am a strong union man" and "I hope to live long enough to see this thing through."[33]

In January, Valentine C. Randolph of the 39th Illinois recorded in his diary: "Some of the boys are strongly opposed to Lincoln's proclamation of freedom. They curse abolitionists and negroes and wish them all in Tophet [Hell] together." But Randolph also observed that "they are [by] no means martyrs to their doctrine. Many of them were today glad to get negroes to carry their knapsacks." The "bitter enmity towards the negroes," he believed, meant that "the white and the black races cannot live together without serious detriment to both."[34]

Soldiers may have accepted blacks when it was convenient for them to do so, but most had a long way to go before they could accept blacks as equals. Writing to his sister on January 2, Private John R. McClure of the 14th Indiana, exploded with racial hatred: "I think the Union is about played out. I use to think we were fighting for the union and constitution but we are not. We are fighting to free those colored gentlemen. If I had my way about things I would shoot every niggar I come across. I am thinking if old Abe makes his words true you folks will have an awful bad smell amonxt you by the time we get home, get all the niggars on an equality with you. But I don't think old Abe and all the rest of his niggar lovers can free the slaves because the south has a little to say about that. Old Abe has got to whip the south first and that is a thing he will not do very soon. Well that is enough about the war."[35]

McClure's vitriolic outburst came in the middle of an innocuous letter that began with a report of what he'd eaten for Christmas dinner (pork and crackers) and inquiries about friends. Despite his animosity to blacks and emancipation, McClure remained a soldier: he saw action at Gettysburg and was wounded in 1864 at the Battle of the Wilderness, in Virginia. It is odd that in his letter he does not see himself as part of the very force by which Lincoln hoped to "whip the south"; but after Fredericksburg, McClure feared "the north will never whip the south as long as there is a man left in the south. They fight like wild devles." Still, he continued in service and, but for this New Year's lapse, turned his thoughts away from political and military affairs.

Another Midwesterner, Charles Cort, a corporal with the 92nd Illinois, was unusual in that he seemed to backtrack on the issue of emancipation. On November 18, 1862, he wrote to his friends: "If the rebellion canot be put down with out emancepation I say emancepate and do not let slavery stand in the way in any shape." As the months passed, his racial attitudes stiffened. He referred to a group of contrabands as "fat, lazy and contented," and insisted that "most of the niggar loving individuals of Co. H [Company H] have cooled some what in their love and are the worst enemies the poor darky has and think he is better off in slavery than out of it. . . . Gradual emancipation is the only policy that will ever improve the condition of the slave." Cort concluded in March that "the Emancipation act has done a great deal of harm to the cause."[36]

Cort expressed his thoughts privately. Most soldiers did not take well to talk, particularly from civilians, opposing the policies of the administration. Private Charles Turner, an Ohio soldier in the Mississippi Marine Brigade, wrote that "nothing discourages soldiers so much as to hear men abusing president Lincoln or his proclamation. I would shoot a man as quick for that as I would if he called me a son of a bit[c]h." Another soldier, Corporal Newton Glazer of the 11th Vermont, believed that the Proclamation "separated the wheat from the chaff."

> It is an easy matter now to tell who is who. Those politicians who for a long time supported the President because he was so mild with the rebels, but when he came to make use of a means perfectly constitutional, to put down this rebellion, which touched their foster-child slavery, which would knock the very support on which the whole rebellion rested, O then where are they[:] cursing the government . . . cursing it because it was going to make slavery, not the Union, the Issue of the war. Their support is withdrawn from the government and they show just what they have been all the time, miserable traitors at heart.[37]

Jacob Behm of the 48th Illinois explained that "the necessity of Emancipation is forced upon us by the inevitable events of the war, and is made constitutional by the act of the Rebels themselves and the only road out of this war is by blows aimed at the heart of the Rebellion." George Greenville Benedict of the 12th Vermont, writing home to the Burlington *Free Press,* delighted that the army would no longer be "'playing at war.' . . . I for one—and I believe I am one of many thousand such—shall 'endure hardness' more cheerfully, and fight, when called to, more heartily, because Freedom has been proclaimed throughout the land for whose unity and welfare we struggle, though its full accomplishment may cost years of trial and trouble."[38]

"The men who are fighting our battles will welcome emancipation," predicted one writer. "It tells our soldiers that, while they give their lives to the cause of the Union, the lives of their enemies cannot be sheltered by four millions of another race. It makes their war a war for ideas." Of course, for some, it already *was* being fought on principles. In February, Thomas N. Stevens of the 28th Wisconsin declared: "I am not risking my life here merely for freedom for the Negro, though that may be one of the fruits of the war, but for the preservation of our constitutional liberties." In the rush to rechristen the war a fight for abolition, he was eager to provide a reminder of the original motivation of many soldiers.[39]

Union was a condition; liberty, an idea. The Emancipation Proclamation remade the war into a new cause. It gave meaning to lives lost, and it gave purpose to a conflict that seemed fatally directionless—a battle here, a battle there, but no vision beyond restoring the Union, which was no vision at all. This is not to say that Union was not an important ideal—only that it was a restorative rather than a transformative idea. Colonel Theodore Gates of the 20th New York Militia saw into the future: "President Lincolns emancipation proclamation will take its place among the most important papers of the age & will by & by stand side by side with our Declaration of Independence."[40]

It may have taken some time, but Private Lucius Wood of the 121st Ohio reported in March that "the Pres. Proclamation is gaining favor in the army every day. It certainly was the right move at the right time." And while there were no doubt some desertions as a result of the Emancipation Proclamation, the majority of the soldiers seemed to support it. "The proclamation has not diminished the ardor or the will of any but cowards and renegades," wrote Benjamin Stevenson, a surgeon with the 22nd Kentucky. "A few such have availed themselves of it as a pretext on which to abandon positions they were unworthy to fill. . . . In getting rid of such men we have had a happy riddance." Writing to his father in September 1863, Harvey Reid of the 22nd Wisconsin admitted that when the Emancipation Proclamation had first been introduced "I thought . . . it was unwise, but time and experience has, in my opinion, proved it most wise and one of the most powerful weapons yet employed against the rebellion." A private in the 18th Pennsylvania Cavalry declared, "I have always untill lately been opposed to abraham linkins proclamation but I have lately been convinced that it was just the right thing that was needed to weaken the strength of the rebls." Sergeant Cyrus Boyd of the 15th Iowa wrote about a regimental vote on a series of resolutions adopted by the officers of the brigade; among those resolutions was one that supported the Emancipation Proclamation. Boyd reported: "Near as I could tell about one half the men voted yes about one fourth nay and one fourth did not vote at all." But when the colonel asked those who had voted no to step to the side, only a few did so. Soldiers understood that whatever the act of voting meant, the army was not a democracy and it was their job to support the orders of the commander-in-chief.[41]

Some soldiers felt obliged to counteract rumors that were being spread by conservative northern Democrats, to the effect that entire companies were prepared to quit in opposition to the Proclamation and the arming of blacks. According to Sergeant James Dodds of the 114th Illinois, the rumor "stating that the soldiers were on the point of laying down their arms on account of the Proclamation that is all untrue. The army was never more united than now. They are all of one mind." Private Theodore Upson of the 100th Indiana provided a particularly candid and revealing account of the conflicting beliefs held by soldiers and the thought process by which they came, whatever their attitudes toward blacks and slavery, to support the policy of the administration: "The truth is none of our soldiers seem to like the idea of arming the Negros. Our boys say this [is] a white mans war and the Negro has no business in it, but a good many say they have stood [for] emancipation which came, of course, as fast as our armies occupied slave territory and no faster for we know they are holding slaves in the interior now. But we don't care to fight side by side with them. However, if Old Abe thinks it's the best thing to do, all right; we will stand by him. Lincoln is solid with the boys all right."[42]

12

"It Can Not Be Retracted"

Private Upson's word "solid" was an apt description of Lincoln, who refused to be swept away by the enthusiasm of the moment. He continued to monitor events in the border states, hoping that the Emancipation Proclamation and the enlistment of black soldiers, which certainly weakened the institution of slavery in those states, might hasten abolition. But he was to be disappointed. In Delaware and Kentucky, conservatives maintained political control and slavery would not be abolished until the ratification of the Thirteenth Amendment in 1865. In Maryland, a faction of Unionists committed to emancipation and the enlistment of black soldiers gained political control in the elections of November 1863; they called for a convention to rewrite the state's constitution so that it would abolish slavery. On March 7, 1864, Lincoln wrote a confidential letter to John Creswell, Republican representative from Maryland, and confessed, "I am very anxious for emancipation to be effected in Maryland in some substantial form." He said that his preference for gradual over immediate emancipation was misunderstood: "I had thought the *gradual* would produce less confusion, and destitution, and therefore would be more satisfactory; but if those who are better acquainted with the subject, and are more deeply interested in it, prefer the *immediate,* most certainly I have no objection to their judgment prevailing." On October 13, 1864, the electorate narrowly approved the new state constitution, which went into effect on November 1.[1]

On that day, blacks in Washington celebrated. After they held religious services, a spontaneous torchlight procession of several hundred people wound its way to the White House. The president appeared and inquired what the occasion was—to which someone shouted, "The emancipation of Maryland, suh!" The president then spoke: "it is not secret that I have wished, and still do wish, mankind everywhere to be free." He applauded the action of the state of Maryland and, before retiring, he urged those newly emancipated "to improve yourselves, both morally and intellectually."[2]

Of the border states, Missouri received the most attention, because a bill to provide compensation to loyal owners if the state abolished slavery occupied the members of the 37th U.S. Congress in its waning weeks. The House bill, introduced by Representative John Noell of Missouri on January 6, 1863, offered $10 million dollars in United States bonds, redeemable in thirty years, provided the state adopted a plan for immediate emancipation within one year. The measure, which also pledged congressional support for voluntary colonization of the freed people, passed later that day, 73 to 46. The Senate took up various substitutes and amendments; one offered up to $20 million in compensation if Missouri freed its slaves by 1865, or up to $10 million if emancipation was delayed to 1876. Massachusetts senator Henry Wilson said he was more than willing to "vote the money of Massachusetts with all my heart for emancipation in Missouri," but he wanted an assurance that emancipation would occur quickly. "I care less for money than for time. I am for making it a free State with free influences in my day and generation." Senator Samuel Pomeroy of Kansas predicted that "Missouri is destined to become a free State at any rate. You cannot keep slavery in Missouri thirteen years without a standing army." The Senate went back and forth, debating the amount of compensation and date of emancipations. An exasperated Charles Sumner of Massachusetts closed the debate:

> Procrastination is the thief, not only of time, but of virtue itself. . . . Every consideration of humanity, justice, religion, reason, common sense, and history, all demanded the instant cessation of an intolerable wrong, without procrastination or delay. But human nature would not yield;

and we have been driven to argue the question, whether an outrage, asserting property in man, denying the conjugal relation, annulling the parental relation, shutting out human improvement, and robbing the victim of all the fruits of his industry . . . should be stopped instantly or gradually.[3]

On February 12, 1863, the Senate approved a measure that was then sent to the Select Committee on Emancipation; there it died on March 3, when a motion to suspend the rules so the House could consider the matter failed to secure the required two-thirds majority. The next day, the 37th Congress adjourned. It had accomplished a great deal, and without its actions the process of emancipation would have evolved differently. Even the dyspeptic Adam Gurowski—"Count Growler," one reporter called him—concluded that the Congress had "inaugurated and directed a new evolution in the onward progress of mankind . . . and thoroughly vindicated the great social truth of genuine, democratic, self-government."[4]

Missouri would be left to act without congressional aid. In June 1863, a reconvened state convention adopted a gradual emancipation plan set to begin in 1870. The plan provided that all slaves alive on July 4, 1870, when abolition would take effect, would become "servants" for a specified period of time. Those over age forty on that date would remain "servants" for life; those ages twelve through forty would be freed from their temporary servitude on July 4, 1876; and those younger than twelve would remain "servants" until their twenty-third birthday. (Thus, a slave born on July 3, 1870, would not be freed until 1893.) The measure also specified that, effective July 4, 1870, no slave-become-servant could be sold or removed from the state.[5]

On June 22, 1863, Lincoln wrote to General John McAllister Schofield, who commanded Union forces in Missouri. The president reiterated his belief that "*gradual* can be made better than *immediate* for both black and white." He told Schofield that the government would protect slaveowners during the period of gradual emancipation, which, he believed, "should be comparatively short." He also expressed the belief that, as the measure provided, it "would be easier" to implement gradual emancipation if the act prevented persons from being sold "into more lasting slavery."[6]

The following month, Lincoln wrote to General Stephen Hurlbut. He wanted to clarify whether the Emancipation Proclamation applied to Arkansas. It did, he declared: "I think I shall not retract or repudiate it. Those who shall have tasted actual freedom I believe can never be slaves, or quasi slaves again." But for everyone still enslaved, "I believe some plan, substantially being gradual emancipation, would be better for both white and black." He had no objection to the proposed ending date of the Missouri proposal, "but I am sorry the beginning should have been postponed for seven years, leaving all that time to agitate for the repeal of the whole thing. It should begin at once, giving at least the new-born, a vested interest in freedom."[7]

Lincoln's comment may seem difficult to fathom. He delivered it six months after the Emancipation Proclamation, and well into the experience of black soldiers in the field. He praised the glory of freedom, yet was still willing to allow living persons to die as slaves. But as on so many other social questions, Lincoln's ideas were not stagnant. It was common for white Americans to think of emancipation as an experiment, one that had to be implemented gradually. Frederick Douglass called it "one of the strangest and most humiliating triumphs of human selfishness and prejudice over human reason, that it leads men to look upon emancipation as an experiment, instead of being, as it is, the natural order of human relations." Only the most radical abolitionists had consistently called for immediate emancipation. When the northern states abolished slavery after the Revolution, they did so with acts of gradual emancipation; it took New York, for example, nearly three decades to eliminate slavery after it first passed an act in 1799, and even then some children remained in apprenticeships. Lincoln's belief in gradualism was consistent with decades of social thought.[8]

And yet, between his letters to Schofield and Hurlbut in the summer of 1863, expressing a preference for gradual emancipation, and his letter to Creswell in March 1864, referring to his earlier preference in the past-perfect tense ("I had thought") and expressing support for immediate emancipation, Lincoln's position shifted. He was not alone, and a piece in the *New York Times,* titled "No Gradual Emancipation," marveled at the change. "It is extraordinary how completely the idea of gradual emancipation has been dissipated from the public mind everywhere by the progress of events," observed the writer. Even after it became clear during the war that slavery would end, "the idea still adhered that the emancipation must be gradual in order to be safe.... But all these gradual methods are now hardly more thought of than if they had been obsolete a century.... The change of opinion on this subject is a remarkable illustration of the practical aptitude of the American mind. With hardly an effort, theories and prejudices, that had apparently rooted themselves in it so deeply as to become a part of it, are discarded, and new ideas, in keeping with a new condition of affairs, are conceived, and con-formed to, almost by universal consent."[9]

In Missouri, a battle for control between conservatives and radicals raged for months, and the plan adopted in June 1863 was discarded with the elec-tion of a radical-controlled legislature in the fall of 1863. A new convention assembled, and would abolish slavery immediately in January 1865.

Lincoln continued to offer suggestions for new state constitutions that abol-ished slavery. On August 5, 1863, he wrote to General Nathaniel P. Banks, who headed the Department of the Gulf. He hoped Louisiana would "make a new Constitution recognizing the emancipation proclamation, and adopt-ing emancipation in those parts of the state to which the proclamation does not apply." Lincoln talked about formulating a plan by which "the two races could gradually live themselves out of their old relation to each other," and he emphasized the necessity of education for black children.[10]

Whether the question concerned Missouri or Louisiana or any other slave state, Lincoln was eager to see action taken soon. If the war ended quickly, what incentives would there be to abolish slavery, not only in border states but anywhere? Lincoln said time and again that he was "an anti-slavery man," that he was "naturally anti-slavery," and that "I certainly wish that all men could be free"; but he was always consistent in trying to keep his personal judgments separate from his constitutional obligations as president. "If slav-ery is not wrong, nothing is wrong. I can not remember when I did not so think and feel," Lincoln wrote in April 1864. "And yet," he added, "I have never understood that the Presidency conferred upon me an unrestricted right to act officially upon this judgment and feeling."[11]

These concerns troubled Lincoln, who believed the Emancipation Proc-lamation, justified as a measure of military necessity, might be inoperative once the military necessity had passed. While preparing the final Emancipa-tion Proclamation, he had consulted a book by the solicitor general, William

Whiting, entitled *The War Powers of the President*. Whiting confirmed that the president had the constitutional authority to impose the measures of confiscation and emancipation, but he also made clear that such proclamations "do not abolish slavery as a legal institution in the States; they act upon persons held as slaves; they alter no local laws in any of the States; they do not purport to render slavery unlawful; they merely seek to remove slaves from the control of rebel masters." Whiting's work had done much in the days leading up to January 1, 1863, to help persuade the president that he could lawfully exercise executive power to attack slavery as a "*means* of terminating the rebellion." At the same time, it made clear that, even with the Proclamation, slavery would continue to exist as a legal institution.[12]

Lincoln's scrupulous constitutionalism was evident in September 1863, when he responded to treasury secretary Salmon Chase, who had drafted an Executive Order that revoked the exemptions listed in the Emancipation Proclamation. Chase believed that the "existing rebellion will be more certainly, speedily & effectually suppressed if said exceptions" were revoked and annulled. In his reply, Lincoln reminded Chase:

> The original proclamation has no Constitutional or legal justification, except as a military measure. The exemptions were made because the military necessity did not apply to the exempted localities. Nor does the necessity apply to them now any more than it did then—If I take the step must I not do so, without the argument of military necessity, and so, without any argument, except the one that I think the measure politically expedient, and morally right? Would I not thus give up all footing upon Constitution and law? Would I not thus be in the boundless field of absolutism? Can this pass unnoticed, or unresisted? Could it fail to be perceived that without any further stretch, I might do the same in Delaware, Maryland, Kentucky, Tennessee, and Missouri; and even change any law in any state? Would not many of our own friends shrink away appalled? Would it not lose us the elections, and with them, the very cause we seek to advance?

The future chief justice chose not to respond.[13]

Quoting a line from Lincoln's Annual Message to Congress in December

1862, one soldier concluded: "As Uncle Abe has said, the whole subject is 'piled high with difficulties,' and it may be well for us to suspend judgement upon a question that cannot be decided by any opinion of ours. Time must work out the solution of the great problem that convulses our people —*What shall be the status of the negro in the future organization of our government?*"[14]

If Lincoln would not expand the Emancipation Proclamation, neither would he back away from it. In January 1863 he declared: "I have issued the emancipation proclamation, and I can not retract it. . . . To use a coarse, but an expressive figure, broken eggs can not be mended." On August 10, Lincoln met at the White House with Frederick Douglass, who had come to press for equal treatment of black soldiers. Several months later, Douglass recalled that the president had received him "just as you have seen one gentleman receive another!—with a hand and a voice well-balanced between a kind of cordiality and a respectful reserve." Lincoln mentioned a speech that Douglass had made in which the abolitionist labeled the president "tardy, hesitating, and vacillating." The president conceded that, at times, he may have been slow, eager to make certain that "preparatory work" had been done, but he claimed never to have vacillated. "I do not think that charge can be sustained," Lincoln admonished, "I think it cannot be shown that when I have once taken a position, I have ever retreated from it."[15]

Later that month, James Conkling, an Illinois attorney and politician, invited Lincoln to attend a rally of Unconditional Union men in Springfield. The president could not leave Washington, but he composed a lengthy letter, dated August 26, 1863, to be read aloud ("very slowly," he advised) on his behalf.

"You dislike the emancipation proclamation," he wrote, directing his remarks not to the enthusiastic Unionists who were assembled but to his critics, the Peace Democrats, "and, perhaps, would have it retracted. You say it is unconstitutional—I think differently. I think the constitution invests its commander-in-chief, with the law of war, in time of war. . . . But the proclamation, as law, either is valid, or it is not valid. If it is not valid, it needs no retraction. If it is valid, it can not be retracted, any more than the dead can be brought to life."[16]

He went on to discuss the enlistment of black soldiers, and claimed that "some of the commanders of our armies in the field who have given us our most important successes, believe the emancipation policy, and the use of colored troops, constitute the heaviest blow yet dealt to the rebellion." "You say you will not fight to free negroes. Some of them seem willing to fight for you," he noted. "But, no matter. Fight you, then exclusively to save the Union. I issued the proclamation on purpose to aid you in saving the Union." As for enlisting blacks, "I thought that whatever negroes can be got to do as soldiers, leaves just so much less for white soldiers to do, in saving the Union. Does it appear otherwise to you? But negroes, like other people, act upon motives. Why should they do anything for us, they must be prompted by the strongest motive—even the promise of freedom. And the promise being made, must be kept."

"Peace does not appear as distant as it did," he concluded. And when it comes, "there will be some black men who can remember that, with silent tongue, and clenched teeth, and steady eye, and well-poised bayonet, they have helped mankind on to this great consummation; while, I fear, there will be *some* white ones, unable to forget that, with malignant heart, and deceitful speech, they have strove to hinder it."[17]

Read before tens of thousands of people (the *Chicago Tribune* described the crowd as "like a hive in swarming time") and published widely in newspapers and separately as a pamphlet, the letter was a sensation. According to one report, listeners received it with "shouts, cheers, thanksgiving, and tears." George Templeton Strong called it "a straightforward, simple, honest, forcible exposition of [Lincoln's] views, and likely to be a conspicuous document in the history of our times." He also commented on the prose. The bookish Strong thought, "There are sentences that a critic would like to eliminate," and no doubt he had in mind a line such as "nor must Uncle Sam's Web-feet be forgotten," a reference to the Navy. But he also recognized the prose as "delightfully characteristic of the 'plain man' who wrote it and will appeal directly to the great mass of 'plain men' from Maine to Minnesota."[18]

The *Chicago Tribune* explained the significance of the message:

It has been feared that even as he looked upon his Proclamation as a temporary expedient, born of the necessities of the situation, to be adhered to or retracted as a short-sighted or time-serving policy dictated; and that when the moment for attempting compromise might come, he would put it aside . . . that he would grow faint-hearted at the moment when safety and patriotism required him to be brave and strong. . . . In a few plain sentences, than which none more important were ever uttered in this country, Mr. Lincoln exonerates himself from the crimes urged against him, shows the untenableness of the position that his enemies occupy, and gives the world assurance that that great measure of policy and justice, which, while it strikes a fatal blow at treason and rebellion, guarantees freedom to three millions of Slaves, is to remain the law of the Republic.

"One of those remarkably clear and forcible documents that come only from Mr. Lincoln's pen," the editorial concluded.[19]

More clear and forceful words were to come. On November 19, 1863, Lincoln spoke at Gettysburg and memorialized the dead who had given "the last full measure of devotion . . . that this nation, under God, shall have a new birth of freedom." The speech's rhetoric was historical and biblical: Lincoln grounded the meaning of the war in what had taken place in 1776 (four score and seven years earlier) and defined what had occurred as the creation of a nation devoted to liberty and equality. The cadences were musical: "We cannot consecrate, we cannot dedicate, we cannot hallow this ground"; "government of the people, by the people, for the people." Lincoln separated words from actions, knowing that in war the latter were the coin of victory, yet words gave meaning to deeds.

Lincoln's opponents were livid. Some saw what he had done: he had hijacked the meaning of the nation to make liberty and equality central to its identity, had taken the events of the year—from emancipation through the enlistment of black troops through the summer 1863 victories at Gettysburg and Vicksburg (on July 4 no less)—to define what this "great civil war" was about: not simply restoring the Union, but creating a nation dedicated to making palpable the principles of the Revolution. A Democratic newspaper called it "a perversion of history so flagrant that the most extended charity cannot regard it as otherwise than willful."[20]

On December 8, 1863, Lincoln addressed Congress. "The policy of emancipation, and of employing black soldiers, gave to the future a new aspect, about which hope, and fear, and doubt contended in uncertain conflict," he reported. Lincoln proceeded again to summarize the authority and logic behind his actions: "According to our political system, as a matter of civil administration, the general government had no lawful power to effect emancipation in any State, and for a long time it had been hoped that the rebellion could be suppressed without resorting to it as a military measure." The president continued using the passive voice: "It was all the while deemed possible that the necessity for it might come, and that if it should, the crisis of the contest would then be presented." "It came," said Lincoln, using a formulation he would return to again in his Second Inaugural (when he stated, "And the war came"). "It came, and as was anticipated, it was followed by dark and doubtful days. Eleven months having now passed, we are permitted to take another review."[21]

He liked what he saw. Union forces had opened the Mississippi Valley; Tennessee and Arkansas were clear of insurgent control; and the legislatures of states not included in the Emancipation Proclamation, which once would not have tolerated any discussion of putting restraints on slavery, now debated plans to remove it. Furthermore, "of those who were slaves at the beginning of the rebellion, full one hundred thousand are now in the United States military service, about one-half of which number actually bear arms in the ranks; this giving the double advantage of taking so much labor from the insurgent cause, and supplying the places which otherwise must be filled with so many white men. So far as tested, it is difficult to say they are not as good soldiers as any. No servile insurrection, or tendency to violence or cruelty, has marked the measures of emancipation and arming the blacks." It was a "new reckoning."[22]

The capstone of that new reckoning would be an amendment to the Constitution abolishing slavery. On December 14, 1863, the first of several proposals came forward, and the Senate Judiciary Committee resolved differences in language to present an amendment stating that "neither slavery nor involuntary servitude" was henceforth to exist in the United States. On April 8, 1864, the Senate passed the measure, by a vote of 38 to 6. The House voted twice, once in February on a measure drafted by Isaac Arnold, and once in

June on the amendment put forth by the Senate. Both amendments failed to muster the necessary two-thirds majority. One disappointed writer pointed out why it was so important to pass the amendment: "The Proclamation of Emancipation as a war measure is undoubtedly a proper proceeding; but, as a means of effecting organic changes, and as possible to operate beyond the period of actual war, it is open to many grave objections." The following June, at Lincoln's behest, the Republican Convention that renominated the president endorsed a constitutional amendment that "shall terminate and forever prohibit the existence of slavery within the limits of the jurisdiction of the United States."[23]

Disappointed that the House of Representatives had defeated the constitutional amendment banning slavery, Charles Sumner sought an alternate means by which to reinforce the Emancipation Proclamation: by writing emancipation into statutory law. Sumner had been thrilled in December 1863, when Lincoln, on the same day he delivered his Annual Message to Congress, issued a Proclamation of Amnesty and Reconstruction that specified conditions, including the elimination of slavery, under which states in rebellion could rejoin the Union. An overjoyed Sumner had written to John Bright: "The President's proclamation of reconstruction has *two* essential features,—1) the irrevocability of emancipation, making it a corner-stone of the new order of things, 2) the reconstruction or revival of the States by *preliminary process* before they take their place in the Union. I doubt if the detail will be remembered a fortnight from now. Any plan which features Emancipation beyond recall will suit me."[24]

The reaction of Lincoln's party to his December 1863 proclamation was largely favorable, but Republican lawmakers were eager to establish Congress's role in reconstruction. In April 1864, the House approved a bill sponsored by Representative Henry Winter Davis of Maryland that set more rigorous conditions than Lincoln had for rebel states to rejoin the Union and also required them to amend their respective constitutions to end slavery "forever." However, when the bill's cosponsor, Benjamin Wade of Ohio, brought it before the Senate on July 1, 1864, an amendment was adopted that struck out everything but its enacting clause, including the emancipation provision, and substituted language that, in effect, deferred a decision about reconstruction until the war was over. Sumner immediately proposed to add to the amended bill a statement "that the Proclamation of Emancipation is-sued by the President . . . so far as the same declares that the slaves in certain designated States and portions of States thenceforward should be free, is hereby adopted and enacted as a statute of the United States, and as a rule and article for the government of the naval and military forces thereof." Sum-ner explained that he sought "to recognize as a statute the proclamation of emancipation, to put it under the guarantee and the safeguard of an Act of Congress." He explained his fear: "We have been assured that that proclama-tion will not be changed, but who knows what may be hereafter the vicissi-tudes of elections. . . . I wish to make the present sure, and fix it forevermore and immortal in an act of Congress."[25]

Sumner's motion was defeated, 21 to 11. As it turned out, however, the next day the Senate reversed itself and approved the original Wade-Davis bill, in-cluding a requirement that before any rebel state could reenter the Union, it must amend its constitution so that "involuntary servitude is forever prohib-ited, and the freedom of all persons is guaranteed in said state." But Lincoln used a pocket veto to kill the bill, and on July 8 explained that he did so, among other reasons, because he was not willing to "declare a constitutional competency in Congress to abolish slavery in States." However much anxi-ety he shared with Sumner and others about the status of the stand-alone Emancipation Proclamation, its irrevocability would have to await passage of a constitutional amendment.[26]

Lincoln continued to explain his past actions, in effect becoming the first historian of the decision-making process that led to the Emancipation Proc-lamation. When Albert Hodges, editor of a newspaper in Frankfort, Ken-tucky, and Archibald Dixon, a former senator from the state, met with the president on March 26, 1864, to discuss border-state problems in general and, specifically, to complain about the enlistment of black soldiers, Lincoln justified his rationale using an analogy:

By general law life *and* limb must be protected; yet often a limb must be amputated to save a life; but a life is never wisely given to save a limb. I felt that measures, otherwise unconstitutional, might become lawful, by becoming indispensable to the preservation of the constitutions, through the preservation of the nation. Right or wrong, I assumed this ground, and now avow it. I could not feel that, to the best of my ability, I have even tried to preserve the constitution, if, to save slavery, or any minor matter, I should permit the wreck of government, country, and Constitution all together.

Lincoln had not exactly amputated the Constitution from the nation, but he had operated on it in such a way as to permit him to feel confident that, on the grounds of military necessity, he could go forward, emancipate the slaves, and save the gravely ill patient.[27]

A few weeks later, Lincoln turned from analogy to allegory. He was pondering the fact that both sides claimed to be fighting for liberty, but that only one side could be right, unless the meaning of words was seriously distorted. And so he told a tale:

The shepherd drives the wolf from the sheep's throat, for which the sheep thanks the shepherd as a *liberator*, while the wolf denounces him for the same act as a destroyer of liberty, especially as the sheep was a black one. Plainly, the sheep and the wolf are not agreed upon the definition of the word liberty; and precisely the same difference prevails to-day among us human creatures, even in the North, and all professing to love liberty. Hence we behold the process by which thousands are daily passing from under the yoke of bondage, hailed by some as the advance of liberty, and bewailed by others as the destruction of all liberty.

Lincoln's parable was clear: he was protecting the slaves from the avarice of the rebels, who sought to plunder the freedom of blacks in the name of their own liberty.[28]

But in midsummer 1864, the life of the nation was still very much in danger. The war had turned back again, and Lincoln had doubts as to whether he would be reelected. A year had passed since Gettysburg and Vicksburg, and still the Confederates—undermanned, undernourished, undersupplied —fought on, and not just defensively. In early July, Confederate infantry and cavalry under Jubal Early crossed the Potomac for a raid on Washington itself. On July 11, 1864, the raiders reached the outskirts of the capital, but were forced to withdraw the next day by the arrival of troops Grant had rushed to the city from the eastern Virginia front.

The wavering morale of the North gave sustenance to the peace movement, which called for an end to the war under conditions to be negotiated. Grant's Overland Campaign had incurred enormous casualties with seemingly little to show for it; Sherman's invasion of northern Georgia seemed bogged down; Lincoln had called for 500,000 volunteers, plus a draft if the goal wasn't reached. All of these events contributed to dissatisfaction and war weariness. "What a difference between now and last year!" wrote a visitor to Philadelphia. "No signs of any enthusiasm, no flags; most of the best men gloomy and despairing." Even Horace Greeley joined the chorus: "Our bleeding, bankrupt, almost dying country also longs for peace." Lincoln tried to maintain a public face of good cheer and abiding faith, but in July one visitor described him as "quite paralyzed and wilted down."[29]

During the summer of 1864, Greeley became involved in peace negotiations. He told the president a friend had informed him that Confederate representatives were waiting on the Canadian side of Niagara Falls to negotiate a settlement, and he urged Lincoln to "submit overtures for pacification to the southern insurgents." Lincoln sensed that the emissaries were interested less in peace than in enticing the administration into failed negotiations that would cost Lincoln politically. But there was also a risk to Lincoln, should word get out that he had declined an opportunity to end the war. Despite resistance from Greeley, Lincoln commissioned him to serve as emissary and provided him with a letter that said the president would consider "any proposition which embraces the restoration of peace, the integrity of the whole Union, and the abandonment of slavery."[30]

Negotiations collapsed, and Lincoln's letter was leaked to the press. George Templeton Strong regretted that the president "has given the disaffected and discontented a weapon that doubles their power of mischief"— and indeed northern Democrats howled that Lincoln had made the abolition of slavery a condition for ending hostilities. He heard from Charles Robinson, Democratic editor of the Green Bay *Advocate,* who said that as a War Democrat he had supported emancipation as "sound war policy," but wondered now how he could defend the war effort with the knowledge that Lincoln would not accept peace without abolition, which seemed to contradict the assurance he had provided in his response to Greeley's "Prayer of Twenty Millions" nearly two years earlier. Lincoln answered that he was sincere in his response to Greeley, and that when he "afterwards proclaimed emancipation, and employed colored soldiers," he was following what he had promised in that letter. Lincoln wrote to Robinson, "I am sure you would not desire me to say, or leave an inference, that I am ready to, whenever convenient, to join in re-enslaving those who shall have served us in consideration of our promise. As a matter of morals, could such treachery by any possibility, escape the curses of Heaven, or of any good man?"[31]

It was an animated retort, and Lincoln decided not to send the letter. On August 19, 1864, two days after drafting the response, he met with the assistant postmaster general, Alexander W. Randall of Wisconsin (who had personally delivered Robinson's letter to the president on the 16th), and the journalist Joseph T. Mills. According to Mills, Lincoln said:

> There have been men who have proposed to me to return to slavery the black warriors of Port Hudson & Olustee to their masters to conciliate the South. I should be damned in time & in eternity for so doing. The world shall know that I will keep my faith to friends & enemies, come what will. My enemies say I am now carrying on this war for the sole purpose of abolition. It is & will be carried on so long as I am President for the sole purpose of restoring the Union. But no human power can subdue this rebellion without using the Emancipation lever as I have done. . . . My enemies condemn my emancipation policy. Let them prove by the history of this war, that we can restore the Union without it.

Mills took note that "the President appeared to be not the pleasant joker I had expected to see, but a man of deep convictions & an unutterable yearning for the success of the Union cause." But as the meeting continued, Lincoln's spirits rose and he began to reminisce and engage in repartee. He told a humorous anecdote about a Democratic orator in Illinois who appealed to his audience by saying that if Republicans got into power, blacks would be allowed to vote. A white man came forward and, when asked whom he would vote for, said he would vote for Stephen A. Douglas. A black man then stepped forward and, when asked the same question, said he would vote for "Massa Lincoln." His point seemingly proven, the orator yelled out, "What do you think of that?" To which "some old farmer cried out, 'I think the darkey showed a damn sight more sense than the white man.'"[32]

Lincoln laughed heartily—but at the same time, he had come to believe that he would lose the election in November. On August 23, 1864, he prepared a memorandum that he asked his cabinet to sign without reading. It stated: "This morning, and for some days past, it seems exceedingly probable that this Administration will not be re-elected. Then it will be my duty to co-operate with the President elect, as to save the Union between the election and the inauguration; as he will have secured his election on such ground that he can not possibly save it afterwards."[33]

The next day he drafted a response to a suggestion made by Henry J. Raymond, chairman of Lincoln's national reelection campaign committee. Raymond had urged that Lincoln write to Jefferson Davis proposing an end to the war on the sole condition that the Confederacy recognize the supremacy of the national government. Arguing that "the tide is setting strongly against us," Raymond had warned that many members of the public were dissatisfied because they believed the administration would not make peace "until Slavery is abandoned," and rumors were widespread that "we *can* have peace with Union if we would." The suggestion was more political ploy than sincere proposal. Raymond was confidant that Davis would never accept such an offer, and that his rejection of a peace offer from the administration would strengthen Lincoln's position.

Lincoln responded by authorizing Raymond to arrange a conference with Davis and "propose, on behalf [of] this government, that upon restoration of the Union and the national authority, the war shall cease at once, all remaining questions to be left to adjustment by peaceful modes." But then the president had second thoughts. He never sent the letter; and after a meeting with Raymond and others on August 25, he decided against any peace overture.

The episode exposed tensions in Lincoln's thinking. Believing he would not be reelected, he was perhaps tempted to do what he could to end the war; in addition, he undoubtedly appreciated that if Davis rejected his proposal, it would improve Lincoln's own chances with some war-weary voters.

At the same time, however, he would alienate a broad constituency which had come to accept that the war for the Union and the war against slavery were now one and the same. Time and again since January 1, 1863, Lincoln had sustained emancipation. He and the Union cause had both come too far, since the beginning of the war, to turn back. In the end, both politics and justice dictated that he refrain from making any offers of peace.[34]

At month's end, the Democrats met in Chicago and nominated George Mc-Clellan for president. Since Lincoln had relieved him of his post in November 1862, the general had been living in New Jersey, writing reports defending his military service and cultivating Democratic leaders. His opposition to Lincoln on issues of emancipation and states' rights remained as vociferous as ever. In his letter of acceptance, McClellan declared that "the preservation of our union was the sole avowed object for which the war commenced. It should have been conducted for that object only. . . . The Union is the one condition of peace—we ask no more." The party platform, however, placed peace before union, proclaimed the war a failure, and suggested that after hostilities were halted a Convention of States would determine the basis of the Federal Union of the States. McClellan was a pro-war Democrat forced to run on a peace platform, a combination that could prove untenable.[35]

But McClellan's appeal to soldiers in the Army of the Potomac worried Lincoln. The Republicans knew how loyal the men were to the chivalrous McClellan ("no general could ask for greater love and more unbounded confidence than he receives from his men," wrote one officer) and feared the soldiers' vote in the field, since the soldiers might help to swing the election McClellan's way. (Eighteen states allowed the troops to vote while on active duty; eleven of those states counted the vote separately; Illinois, Indiana, New Jersey, Delaware, Rhode Island, Oregon, and Nevada had not authorized such voting.) Fall was approaching, and the Union needed something to help turn momentum its way.[36]

This arrived on September 3, 1864, in the form of a telegram from General William T. Sherman: "Atlanta is ours, and fairly won." In a campaign that had begun in May, Sherman's men had fought multiple battles around Atlanta, from July onward. They had tried to cut supply lines and had bombarded the city for weeks. Finally, in late August, Sherman had moved against General John Bell Hood's railroad supply lines. One Union soldier explained the general's tenacity this way: "Sherman dont know the word Cant."[37]

The news that Atlanta had fallen revived northern morale and Lincoln's chances for reelection. The *Chicago Tribune* declared, "The dark days are over. We see our way out." The *New York Times* said, "The skies begin to brighten. . . . The clouds that lowered over the Union cause a month ago are breaking away. . . . The public temper is buoyant and hopeful." George Templeton Strong, in his diary, effused, "Glorious news this morning—*Atlanta taken at last!!!*"[38]

In addition to news of Atlanta's capture, Lincoln had received word on August 5 that Admiral David G. Farragut had managed to overcome heavy fire from two forts, dodge a minefield, and sail into Mobile Bay, giving the Union control of the waterway and effectively closing Mobile as a port. Lincoln was so overjoyed by the double shot of Mobile and Atlanta that, on September 3, 1864, he issued a Proclamation of Prayer and Thanksgiving. He called for "devout acknowledgement to the Supreme Being in whose hands are the destinies of nations" and declared a special status for the following Sunday: thanksgiving was to be "offered to Him for His mercy in preserving our national existence against the insurgent rebels who so long have been waging a cruel war against the Government of the United States, for its overthrow."[39]

Those prayers were answered in September and October, with General Philip Sheridan's campaign through the Shenandoah Valley. Sheridan wreaked havoc on the rich farmland of the valley that sustained Robert E. Lee's army. He reported, "I have destroyed over 2,000 barns filled with wheat, hay, and farming implements; over seventy mills filled with flour and wheat; have driven in front of the army over 4,000 head of stock, and have killed and issued to the troops no less than 3,000 sheep." He promised he would leave the valley "with little in it for man or beast." Mary Chesnut, the wife of South Carolina's former senator James Chesnut and an inveterate diarist, spoke for many Southerners when, on hearing news of Sheridan's exploits, she wrote: "These stories of our defeats in the valley fall like blows upon a dead body. Since Atlanta I have felt as if all were dead within me."[40]

More good news arrived in the form of political initiatives. In September

1864, Louisiana, in response to Lincoln's plan for reconstruction, adopted a new state constitution and abolished slavery. Maryland's plan would soon go into effect. And three new states had been added to the Union: Kansas (in 1861), West Virginia (in 1863), and Nevada (in 1864)—states that would add to Lincoln's electoral total. Early returns from state elections also boded well: it seemed that Republicans were winning and that the earlier momentum of Democrats calling for peace had been reversed.

But Peace Democrats did not relent easily, and the election campaign through the fall of 1864 turned nasty. Opponents attacked Lincoln personally and suggested that, in the event he was reelected, blacks and whites would intermingle freely across the nation. A new word—"miscegenation"—was coined to describe the mixing of the races that, Democrats claimed, would necessarily follow a Republican victory. One political caricature, a print published in New York and titled "The Miscegenation Ball," showed interracial couples dancing and talking in a hall with a portrait of Lincoln and a banner reading, "Universal Freedom. One Constitution. One Destiny. Abraham Lincoln PRE[SIDENT]!!!"

The vituperative race-baiting did not succeed; Lincoln was reelected by an overwhelming margin. He won 55 percent of the popular vote. In the electoral college, he took 212 votes and carried twenty-three states. McClellan won twenty-one electoral votes and three states: New Jersey, Delaware, and Kentucky. The soldier vote also went overwhelmingly for Lincoln: he won at least 78 percent of the votes that were separately counted. Prior to the election, John Brobst of the 25th Wisconsin had written: "I want to see old Uncle Abe elected again. He is the only man that can settle this war up and do it as it should be settled. If McClellan gets the reins he will have peace sooner than Abe, but by letting them have their slaves. Then we can fight again in about ten years. But let Old Abe settle it, and it is always settled." One soldier from the 11th Iowa Infantry reported: "Our regiment is strong for Old Abraham—three hundred and fourteen votes for Lincoln and forty-two for McClellan." These men were not about to vote against the war's continuation and devalue the sacrifice of their fallen comrades. John Quincy Adams Campbell, of the 5th Iowa Volunteers, exulted: "A *glorious victory* for Loyalty, Liberty and Union. . . . The people with unanimity unparalleled, have declared that this war is *not* a failure, that Slavery must die, that treason must be punished and traitors hung, and that this war must continue till the old flag floats in proud supremacy over every foot of Uncle Sam's dominion."[41]

On November 10, 1864, Lincoln told a crowd that the election, even with all the strife, "has done good too. It has demonstrated that a people's government can sustain a national election, in the midst of a great civil war. Until now it has not been known to the world that this was a possibility. . . . We can not have free government without elections; and if the rebellion could force us to forego, or postpone a national election, it might fairly claim to have already conquered and ruined us."[42]

Charles Sumner celebrated the election as the beginning of "the new life of our country, born to-day into assured freedom, with all its attendant glory." A month later, in a letter to a public meeting in Philadelphia to celebrate the Emancipation Proclamation, he wrote, "That proclamation has done more than any military success to save the country. It has already saved the national character. The future historian will confess that it saved everything."[43]

Lincoln wasted no time pushing forward with an amendment abolishing slavery. In his Annual Message to Congress, he informed members that the results of the elections (Republicans had gained fifty House seats) made it clear that the next Congress would pass the amendment—so why wait? "May we not agree the sooner the better?" he asked. He also declared that if under any circumstances "the people should, by whatever mode or means, make it an Executive duty to re-enslave" those freed by the Emancipation Proclamation, "another, and not I, must be their instrument to perform it."[44]

Even as Lincoln denounced those who would reenslave the freedmen, a debate emerged in the Confederacy about enlisting and emancipating the slaves. Warren Akin, a member of the Confederate Congress from Georgia, offered a cogent assessment of the issues. "As for calling out the negro men and placing them in the army, with the promise they shall be free at the end of the war," he wrote in October 1864, "I can only say it is a question of fearful magnitude." He wondered whether the Confederate cause could triumph without such enlistment and emancipation; if it failed, "it is impossible for the evils resulting from placing our slaves in the army to be greater than those that will follow subjugation." At the same time, he asked: "Can we feed our soldiers and their families if the negro men are taken from the plantations?

Will our soldiers submit to having our negroes along side them in the ditches, or in line of battle? When the negro is taught the use of arms and the art of war, can we live in safety with them afterwards? . . . To call forth the negroes into the army, with the promise of freedom, will it not be giving up the great question involved by doing the very thing Lincoln is now doing?"[45]

Howell Cobb of Georgia, a Confederate major general who had served as Speaker of the U.S. House of Representatives and secretary of the treasury in the Buchanan administration, got to the crux of the issue: "You cannot make soldiers of slaves or slaves of soldiers. The day you make a soldier of them is the beginning of the end of the Revolution. And if slaves will make good soldiers, [then] our whole theory of slavery is wrong." Hearing the rumor that the rebels were considering arming the slaves, one Union colonel on General George Meade's staff observed that if the Confederates wound up doing so, "the slavery candle will burn at both ends." George Templeton Strong observed: "This sacrifice of the first principles of the Southern social system is a confession of utter exhaustion."[46]

Robert E. Lee had contemplated Confederate enlistment previously; but finally, on January 11, 1865, he wrote a letter that would have been unthinkable three years earlier. He began by asserting the slaveholders' common view that the relationship between master and slave was "controlled by humane laws and influenced by Christianity and an enlightened public sentiment." He did not want to disturb that relationship, but the course of the war required that the Confederate Congress consider recruiting slaves as soldiers. Lee pointed out that the Union army was already using slaves against southern troops—a practice that, in time, would lead to destruction of the institution anyhow. "We must decide," he concluded, "whether slavery will be extinguished by our enemies and the slaves be used against us, or use them ourselves at the risk of the effects which must be produced upon our social institutions. My opinion is that we should employ them without delay." He knew that a promise of freedom would have to accompany enlistment, and he was willing to make that promise in hopes of staving off defeat.[47]

On March 13, 1865, Jefferson Davis signed a bill authorizing the enlistment of up to 25 percent of male slaves of military age. That the Confederate Congress passed such an act (albeit by only one vote in the Senate and almost as narrow a margin in the House) reveals the strength of Confederate nationalism—a desire to establish an independent Confederacy even at the cost of slavery, the institution the rebel states had seceded from the Union to preserve in the first place. Thomas Goree, General James Longstreet's aide-de-camp, put the matter this way: "We had better free the negroes to gain our independence than be subjugated and lose slaves, liberty, and all that makes life dear."[48]

It was hard for anyone to imagine, however, that a promise of freedom from the Confederacy could be worth more than what Union forces were offering: actual freedom. One Georgia woman thought it "strangely inconsistent" to offer emancipation to an African American who had fought "to aid us in keeping in bondage a large portion of his brethren," whereas "by joining the Yankees he will instantly gain the very reward" of freedom. Henry Slade Tew, the mayor of Mount Pleasant, South Carolina, understood the arithmetic of freedom. In February 1865, he surrendered to military authorities who were occupying the city. He gave his assembled slaves $50 and told them to buy whatever they needed, as the Confederate script would soon be worthless. "I also told them," he informed his daughter, "that when the troops came they knew they were free to go or stay as they pleased. . . . No one answered a word, and I knew of course they would go."[49]

In April 1865, at war's end, Charles Page, a correspondent for the *New York Tribune,* came to Richmond, Virginia, determined "to ascertain the truth about negro troops in the rebel services." Rumors had spread that black men were volunteering and that the Confederates had even enlisted several regiments. Page gathered testimony; he discovered that only about fifty blacks had signed on, and that these were mere boys "who were ready to parade the streets, and live on Confederate rations, but who had no idea of fighting."

"Would you have fought against the Yankees?" Page asked.

"No, sir. Dey might have shot me through de body wid ninety thousand balls, before I would have fired a gun at my friends."

Another answered, "I'll tell you, massa, what I would have done. . . . I would have taken de gun and when I cotched a chance, I'd a shooted it at de Rebs and den run for de Yankees."[50]

By the time the Confederate government authorized the enlistment of slaves, Congress had approved the Thirteenth Amendment abolishing slavery and had forwarded it to the states for ratification. On January 31, 1865, the lame-duck House passed the amendment by a vote of 119 to 56, only two votes over the two-thirds needed. Lincoln personally involved himself in the legislative process: its passage "will bring the war, I have no doubt, rapidly to a close." Before the amendment was submitted to the states for ratification, Lincoln signed it, even though he was not obligated, constitutionally, to do so. The amendment would be ratified on December 6, 1865.

On February 1, a group came to serenade the president. According to the *New York Tribune,* Lincoln said he "had never shrunk from doing all that he could to eradicate Slavery by issuing an emancipation proclamation. But that proclamation falls far short of what the amendment will be when fully consummated. A question might be raised whether the proclamation was legally valid. It might be added that it only aided those who came into our lines and that it was inoperative as to those who did not give themselves up, or that it would have no effect on the children of the slaves born hereafter. In fact it would be urged that it did not meet the evil. But this amendment is a King's cure for all the evils. It winds the whole thing up."[51]

The Thirteenth Amendment wound up the status of slavery, but it did not address the status of the freedmen. Even before Lincoln issued the preliminary Emancipation Proclamation, some abolitionists were thinking ahead to the conditions of the former slaves. Samuel Gridley Howe had pushed for the creation of a bureau to address freedmen's needs. "We must be able," he wrote in September 1862, "to present as early as possible, a general and reliable coup d'oeil [glimpse] of the actual condition of those who are actually out of the house of bondage; their wants and their capacities. We must collect facts and use them as ammunition."[52]

Seizing on Howe's suggestion, in December 1862 the Emancipation League had sent out a questionnaire to its superintendents in various areas of the Confederacy. Included among the questions were inquiries about the freed people's work habits, attitudes toward learning, and general temperament. One of the questions read: "Have you found any disposition to revenge upon their masters,—to 'cut their masters' throats'?" From various locations, the committee heard that blacks "would readily become industrious and productive laborers under any liberal system which would offer a fair and reasonably certain compensation," that "they have an intense desire to learn . . . and their ability to learn to read is fully equal to that of whites," that they are "more pious than moral" and are "somewhat given to stealing and lying," and that few of them desired to go North. As for savagery, one superintendent reported: "I have very seldom seen any disposition to revenge upon their masters." Another respondent thought that African Americans were too dependent—a condition of slavery—and that the "spirit of *self-reliance* is hard to infuse into the soul." But it could be done if the old system were entirely eradicated.[53]

In March 1863, secretary of war Edwin Stanton appointed Samuel Gridley Howe, Robert Dale Owen, and James McKaye to the American Freedmen's Inquiry Commission. The commission was asked to investigate "the condition of the Colored population emancipated by acts of Congress and the proclamation of the president, and to consider and report what measures are necessary to give practical effect to those acts and proclamations, so as to place the Colored people of the United States in a condition of self-support and self-defense."[54]

On June 30, 1863, Stanton received a preliminary report. The commission concluded that "these refugees are, with rare exceptions, loyal men, putting faith in the Government, looking to it for guidance and protection, willing to work for moderate wages if promptly paid, docile and easily managed, not given to quarreling among themselves, of temperate habits, cheerful and uncomplaining under hard labor whenever they are treated with justice and common humanity, and (in the Southern climate) able and willing on the average, to work as long and as hard as white laborers, whether foreign or native born." As with the Emancipation League questionnaire, the commissioners found the freedmen eager to learn and devoted to religion. They expressed greater concern about slaves from South Carolina and Florida, where "humanity is the exception [and] the iron enters deep into the soul." Yet even there, "judicious management," particularly through the regular payment of wages and enlistment in the army, could rid the former slaves of bad habits born in bondage. The key was not to discourage the freedmen in their hopes of enjoying the fruits of their own labor. "The point on which they are peculiarly sensitive and chiefly need assurance," the report concluded, "is as to the absolute and irrevocable certainty of their freedom. . . .

They must have tangible proof of the reality and unchangeable character of their emancipation."[55]

That proof would come with the Thirteenth Amendment. And in time, additional amendments would be passed to address the issue not of reforming the ex-slaves, but of controlling the former masters. In 1864, James McKaye sent Stanton a supplemental report titled *The Emancipated Slave Face to Face with His Old Master*. McKaye observed, "The simple truth is, that the virus of slavery, the lust of ownership, in the hearts of these old masters, is as virulent and active today as it ever was. . . . They scoff at the idea of freedom for the negro. . . . They await with impatience the withdrawal of the military authorities, and the re-establishment of the civil power of the State to be controlled and used as hitherto for the maintenance of what, to them doubtless, appears the paramount object of all civil authority, of the State itself, some form of slave system."[56]

By 1865, Lincoln had begun to give thought to reconstruction and the condition of the freedmen, and he seemed to recognize that black men needed the vote, as well as work and education. On April 14, 1865, he expressed a desire to remake the country into a "Union of hearts and hands as well as of States." He would not be given that chance.

13

Emancipation Triumphant

How do you dramatize a decree? How do you turn emancipation into art? So wondered Francis Bicknell Carpenter, who desired, more than anything else, to embody the momentous event of the Emancipation Proclamation in a history painting that would win the applause of critics, draw crowds of admiring viewers, and, not incidentally, earn the artist a sizable fee.[1]

Born in 1830, Carpenter had studied at the Cortland Academy in Homer, New York, and in 1851 had established a studio in New York City. He had been elected an associate of the National Academy of Design, and had exhibited his work in group shows. Described as being of "middle height, rather slender, with delicate features, abundant straight hair, and dark gray eyes," Carpenter was primarily a portrait painter. But he was ambitious to execute something greater. As a student of art, he undoubtedly knew that the most distinguished critics ranked history painting as preeminent, above the lesser genres of domestic scenes, portraits, animal studies, and still lifes. For centuries, that had meant works focusing on classical or biblical topics, executed in a grand style. But the very idea of what constituted a suitable subject for history painting had itself undergone a revision around the time of the American Revolution. Benjamin West's *Death of General Wolfe* (1770) had shattered the paradigm. It was followed by such works as John Singleton Copley's *Watson and the Shark* (1778) and *The Death of Major Peirson* (1783), and

Théodore Géricault's *Raft of the Medusa* (1818–1819). John Trumbull, who drew upon West's earlier approach in his painting *The Death of General Warren at the Battle of Bunker Hill* (1786), went on to create several history paintings for the Capitol Rotunda, including one titled *The Declaration of Independence* (completed 1819), which showed the drafting of that foundational document.[2]

In seeking an audience with the president to discuss his idea, Carpenter enlisted the support of several politicians, including Owen Lovejoy. He explained to the Illinois congressman, "I wish to paint this picture *now*, while all the actors in the scene are living.... I wish to make it the standard authority for the portrait of ... Mr. Lincoln as it is the great act of his life by which he will be remembered and honored through all generations."[3]

Carpenter met the president on February 6, 1864. The following year, he recalled that first Saturday afternoon encounter: "Never shall I forget the thrill which went through my whole being as I first caught sight of that tall, gaunt form through a distant door, bowed down, it seemed to me, even then, with the weight of the nation he carried upon his heart, as a mother carries her suffering child." Lincoln spoke privately with the artist and said, "We will turn you loose here and try to give you a good chance to work out your ideas."[4]

Turn him loose, indeed. Shortly after their February interview, Carpenter moved into the White House, where he remained for six months. Lincoln and the cabinet posed for him again and again; Carpenter arranged for Lincoln and others to be photographed; he sketched each cabinet member; he borrowed books and maps, so as to better render them on the canvas; he took over the state dining room, much to the consternation of Mrs. Lincoln. Visitors would look at the artist engaged in his work, and Lincoln would explain, "Oh, you need not mind him; he is but a painter."[5]

Carpenter had already decided that the scene he would depict was the first reading of the Emancipation Proclamation to the cabinet, on July 22, 1862.

I conceived of that band of men, upon whom the eyes of the world centered as never before upon ministers of state, gathered in council, depressed, perhaps disheartened at the vain efforts of many months to restore the supremacy of the government. I saw, in thought, the head of the nation, bowed down with the weight of care and responsibility, solemnly announcing, as he unfolds the prepared draft of the Proclamation, that the time for the inauguration of this policy had arrived; I endeavored to imagine the conflicting emotions of satisfaction, doubt, and distrust with which such an announcement would be received by men of the varied characteristics of the assembled councilors.[6]

One newspaper learned that Carpenter was at work on the picture and used the information to poke fun at the cabinet:

What a field for color, for costume, for *pose,* for *chiaro-oscuro,* for drapery, for light, for rendition of passion and emotion! The President, with his feet on the round of the chair hugging his long knees. . . . Chase, with one hand on his breeches pocket and a pleasant smile wreathing one-half of his face—the other side of his countenance expressing disgust at the "two" term principle. Bates waking up, after three years of torpor, to the fact of increasing military power. Seward, with his brows knit, indicting a promise to end the rebellion in sixty days. Welles fast asleep, with an "intelligent contraband" brushing the flies off of him.[7]

Carpenter had indeed chosen a curious moment. Even Lincoln was unable to recollect the exact date of the first reading, telling the painter it "was the last of July, or the first part of the month of August." Lincoln thought the meeting had taken place on a Saturday, but it had actually been on a Tuesday. And he conflated a meeting from the previous day, when Blair had been absent, with the one on the following day, where he thought Blair had arrived late.[8]

Lincoln's failure to recall the specifics does not mean the first reading of the Emancipation Proclamation was unimportant or undramatic, or that it was an unworthy subject for a history painting. Trumbull, likewise, had declined to focus on an obvious moment—the signing of the Declaration of Independence—and had instead depicted the occasion when the drafting committee had presented the penultimate version of the document, on June 28, 1776.

But Carpenter might have picked any of a number of other occasions that could have proven more visually compelling and dramatic: September 22, 1862, for example, when a resolute Lincoln had read a story and spoken of God; or the signing, on January 1, 1863, when he had fretted about his quivering hand. And Carpenter might have considered a variety of scenes in which Lincoln would not have appeared: any of the celebrations on Jubilee Day, for example, or incidents in which soldiers had encountered contrabands and informed them of the Proclamation.

Carpenter, of course, was not the only artist attracted by the subject of the Emancipation Proclamation, though none sought to execute a work on the grand scale that he imagined. A variety of prints had already flooded the marketplace. The political satirist David Gilmour Blythe had painted *Abraham Lincoln Writing the Emancipation Proclamation* (1863), an engraving of which appeared the following year. Blythe's portrait depicts a weary Lincoln sitting in his nightshirt on a weathered chair. One foot has lost its slipper; the other steps on a paper written by the Peace Democrats. He is surrounded by dozens of books, letters, petitions, maps, and objects. The Bible and the Constitution rest on his lap. The presidential oath hangs behind him; the scales of justice are out of balance. Among the clutter are his maul (a large hammer used for splitting wood) lying on a map of the rebel states, George Washington's sword piercing a map of Europe (the first president had warned in his farewell address against entangling alliances), a bust of Andrew Jackson with his words "The union must and shall be preserved" written below, and a bust of James Buchanan (who preceded Lincoln) hanging by the neck. A trunk, stenciled "A. Lincoln, Springfield," lies open, and the president's coat hangs over the chair where he has thrown it. A paraphrase of Lincoln's sentiments adorns the cornice of the bookcase: "Without slavery the war would not exist, and without slavery it would not be continued." The painting, along with the subsequent print, had attracted little attention at the time; and given its less than heroic portrayal of a laboring president, one can easily understand why. But in its own way it captures an essential truth about the struggle to decide upon and compose the Emancipation Proclamation.[9]

By comparison, Edward Dalton Marchant, a well-known Philadelphia portrait painter, had accepted a commission for a commemorative portrait celebrating the signing of the Proclamation. In December 1862, Lincoln had received a letter from John Weiss Forney, founder of the pro-administration *Daily Morning Chronicle,* introducing the "eminent artist" Marchant and requesting that the president give him time to paint the picture, which would be hung in Independence Hall. Preceding Carpenter by a year, Marchant had maintained his studio in the White House. The artist later wrote that Lincoln "was seldom twice alike. Hence the endless variety observable in the photographs we have of him." He was "the most difficult subject who ever taxed" the skills of an artist. In his typical self-effacing manner, Lincoln had complimented the painter on making such a good picture out of such poor materials.[10]

Marchant's portrait, double the size of Blythe's, could not be more different. Classical in composition, it depicts a dapper Lincoln, with neatly combed hair and a white tie, seated at a table with the Proclamation beneath his arm and a quill at his side. Oversize columns lead to a pedestal that supports a towering statue of the goddess Liberty; broken manacles hang at her feet. "I have sought," Marchant said, "to symbolize, on canvas, the great, crowning act of our President." Marchant employed John Sartain, Philadelphia's preeminent printmaker, to engrave the portrait. The octavo-size mezzotint appeared in 1864, and thousands purchased the print, which portrays Lincoln as poised, thoughtful, refined, and at ease with the decree he has just signed.[11]

An alternative possibility was to focus not on Lincoln, but on the slaves— not on the writing of the Proclamation, but on the reaction to it. Such was Boston artist W. T. Carlton's approach in his painting *Watch Meeting: Waiting for the Hour* (1863), later engraved as a carte de visite. The scene is a barn, perhaps serving as a place of worship on a plantation, where slaves have gathered on December 31, 1862, to await Jubilee Day. In the open doorway a man stands with the Union flag draped in his arms. Mothers hold their children; other people, including the household's white mistress, pray. An altar is made from crates hammered together. An elderly man displays a gold timepiece in his hand; the fob is in the shape of an anchor. Under torchlight, all watch the minute hand move toward midnight. The Emancipation Proclamation is nailed up on the wall. William Lloyd Garrison personally made certain that the original of this painting was sent to Lincoln, who failed to acknowledge receipt. Several months later, after receiving a follow-up inquiry from Garrison, Lincoln replied that he had indeed received "the spirited and animated painting."[12]

Even more compelling than *Watch Meeting* was *Reading the Emancipation Proclamation,* printed in 1864. The scene is well composed, with a semicircle of three generations of slaves looking toward the Union soldier who is reading the decree. The women are variously depicted: the older ones have their heads covered, but the younger, lighter-skinned woman kneeling in prayer is without kerchief. At the top hangs a cotton plant, and on the floor is sugar cane—symbols of slave labor. A clean towel hangs on a clothesline. Lest there be any mistake as to who was responsible for the glorious moment, the bottom of the print includes a pendant of Lincoln.

Perhaps the most popular scenes consisted not of Lincoln *or* the slaves, but of the two interacting. These images nearly always showed submissive freedmen kneeling or bowing before the president. The effect was to minimize the role of blacks in their own liberation, while apotheosizing Lincoln as the Great Emancipator. When Thomas Ball's *Emancipation Memorial* was unveiled in 1876, Frederick Douglass murmured that the statue "showed the Negro on his knees when a more manly attitude would have been indicative of freedom." Earlier versions of the kneeling slave, which appeared in prints in 1865 and 1866, had presented a black man, his family behind him, kissing the president's hand as Lincoln stood on the broken manacles underfoot and pointed heavenward.[13]

Carpenter had in mind something greater than any of these works: a history painting that would capture the truth of a moment and give future generations an immediate grasp of its import and meaning. After all, Emanuel Leutze had succeeded famously with *Washington Crossing the Delaware* (1851). Carpenter, too, would make an epic painting, commemorating "an act unparalleled for moral grandeur in the history of mankind."[14]

The artist had Lincoln tell him the story of the Emancipation Proclamation, and Lincoln's account played into Carpenter's purpose of arranging the scene according to the different views of cabinet members:

There was a curious mingling of fact and allegory in my mind, as I assigned to each his place on the canvas. There were two elements in the Cabinet, the radical and the conservative. Mr. Lincoln was placed at the head of the official table, between two groups, nearest that representing the radical, but the uniting point of both. The chief powers of government are War and Finance: the ministers of these were at his right—the Secretary of War, symbolizing the great struggle, in the immediate foreground; the Secretary of Treasury, actively supporting the new policy, standing by the President's side. . . . The place for the Secretary of the Navy seemed . . . very naturally to be on Mr. Lincoln's left, at the rear of the table. To the Secretary of State, as the great expounder of the principles of the Republican party, the profound and sagacious statesman, would the attention of all at such a time be given. . . . The four chief officers of the government were thus brought, in accordance with their relations to the Administration, nearest the person of the President who, with the manuscript proclamation in hand, which he had just read, was represented leaning forward, listening to, and intently considering the views presented by the Secretary of State.[15]

Lincoln saw the design sketched on the stretched canvas and said, "It is as good as it can be made." He also reminded Carpenter that, following the cabinet meeting in July 1862, "I put the draft of the Proclamation aside, as you do your sketch for a picture, waiting for a victory."[16]

On July 22, 1864, two years after first announcing to his cabinet his intention to issue an Emancipation Proclamation, Lincoln and his councillors gathered in the state dining room to examine Francis Carpenter's huge canvas, nine feet by fourteen and a half feet. It was titled *First Reading of the Emancipation Proclamation of President Lincoln*. The men stood and stared.[17]

True to his word, Carpenter had created a tableau of the cabinet meeting on that 1862 day. In the painting, Lincoln sits just left of center, Proclamation and quill in hand. His is the only chair with arm rests. On the far left are Edwin Stanton and Salmon Chase. Gideon Welles is seated, with his back to the mantelpiece, and standing beside him are Caleb Smith and Montgomery Blair. On the far right of the canvas, arms crossed, sits Edward Bates. William

Seward, striking a statesman's pose, is in profile, and in the act of speaking. Eyes are on him. There are two portraits on the walls of the room: that of departed secretary of war Simon Cameron on the left, and that of Andrew Jackson above the mantel. Carpenter has included a selection of books, newspapers, and maps. The *New York Tribune* rests on the floor beside Stanton; on the table is a parchment copy of the Constitution and, before Bates, a map of the seat of war, in Virginia. Another map, showing the distribution of slave population is propped up on the right-hand side, and on the floor nearby are Whiting's *War Powers of the President* and Story's *Commentaries on the Constitution*. Beneath the table are volumes of the *Congressional Globe*. To remind all that the Proclamation was being signed as a military necessity, Carpenter had propped up a sword against an unoccupied chair.[18]

Lincoln's opinion of the painting, Carpenter wrote, "could not but have afforded the deepest gratification to any artist." A few days later, an insecure Carpenter pressed the topic again with the president, who said, "There is little to find fault with, the portraiture is the main thing, and that seems to me absolutely perfect. . . . It is as good as it can be made."[19]

In his dispatch to the Sacramento *Daily Union*, Noah Brooks was less diplomatic. He thought the painting raw, commonplace, and lacking in finish. The likeness of Lincoln was fair enough, "but too fresh-looking for the careworn hard-looking man that he is." The problem, Brooks thought, was that the scene just did not work as a history painting:

> A group of men, wearing the somber-hued garments of American gentlemen, assembled in a plainly furnished apartment, though earnestly discussing a matter which is now historic, does not furnish a tempting subject for the tricks and bewildering cheats of art, and no amount of accidental lights, warm coloring, and dramatic pose can invest Seward, Blair, and the "Marie Antoinette" of the Navy Department with the supernal glories which gleam on the canvas of painters who had for their subjects kings and emperors in gorgeous robes or renowned knights in "helm or hauberk's twisted mail."[20]

Brooks predicted, however, that the subsequent engraving, which would reduce the size of the painting and make its details more clear, "will be prized in every liberty-loving household." Lincoln was the first to subscribe for an artist's proof of the engraving, being made by Alexander Hay Ritchie. When it appeared in 1866, Lincoln's widow received the print. Advertisements for "Carpenter's Great National Picture, Engraved on Steel by A. H. Ritchie," included endorsements from Seward, Chase, Stanton, Welles, and Bates. All praised the portraits, and thought the execution more than satisfactory, but the comments lacked enthusiasm. Two years earlier, they had no doubt expressed greater criticism; but Lincoln was now gone, the war was over, and the painting inspired not rancor but, as Welles put it, "sadness . . . for the great and good man."

Salmon Chase was an exception. He publicly, and ambiguously, said, "I do not see that improvement is possible"; but privately, he wrote Carpenter a letter in which he criticized the print. That the image represented a meeting held in July 1862 jarred Chase, who exclaimed, "Now so little important did any Cabinet meeting in July relating to the Proclamation seem to me, that not the slightest trace of such a meeting remains on my memory." John Hay reported that Chase "objects to the whole picture being made subsidiary to Seward who is talking while every one else either listens or stares into vacancy. He thinks it would have been infinitely better to take the 22nd of September when the Proclamation was really read to the Cabinet."[21]

As for Seward, he didn't think the Emancipation Proclamation—whether on July 22, September 22, or January 1—had been "the central and crowning act of the administration." Seward even informed Carpenter he had told Lincoln "that you were painting your picture upon a false presumption. . . . You appear to think in common with many other foolish people, that the great business of this Administration is the destruction of slavery. Now allow me to say you are much mistaken." Instead, he suggested that the most momentous cabinet gathering might have been "the meeting at which it was resolved to relieve Fort Sumter." When Hay mentioned this to Chase, the secretary responded: "There was no such meeting."[22]

Another viewer was also unmoved and unimpressed. Lincoln's assistant secretary, William O. Stoddard, thought the image failed completely to capture the reality of what a cabinet meeting actually looked like: "When that half-dozen of overworked and anxious men did get together, it was not their habit, dignified as they were, and however important their business, to collect in studied stiffness around the table; but several times when I have been called in—to be sent for papers, &c.—I have seen one stretched on the sofa with a cigar [in] his mouth, another with his heels on the table, another nursing his knee abstractedly, the President with his leg over the arm of his chair, and not a man of them all in any wise sitting for his picture." Stoddard suggested that the title of the painting should have been *Table, Surrounded with Gentlemen Waiting To Have Their Picture Taken*.[23]

The painting, one critic wrote in the *New York Tribune*, "was far from being a masterly work." He cited any number of reasons for its failure: Carpenter's skills as an artist; the moment he chose to depict; the proximity to the event. Whereas Trumbull had completed his work on the Declaration thirty years after the Revolution, in 1864 Carpenter occupied a White House that still very much feared losing the war. It was too soon to represent emancipation as an accomplished deed, because, quite simply, it wasn't.[24]

The *New York Times* treated its native son more kindly:

> The picture will be viewed with satisfaction by succeeding generations for its special merits of portraiture. When slavery has become a surprise and a horror to everyone in the land; when the Proclamation of President Lincoln has passed into history as a splendid trophy of a sanguinary war; when the gratitude of a people that no longer knows a bondman reverts to the heroes that made them glorious, then will such a canvas be gazed upon with respectful admiration, and the features that are familiar to us to-day be regarded as typical of a stronger race of men than the world can always claim for its leaders.[25]

Whatever Carpenter's shortcomings as a painter, he succeeded as a writer. His book *Six Months at the White House with Abraham Lincoln* is subtitled *The Story of a Picture;* published in 1866, it was a sensation. So, too, was Ritchie's engraving, which sold thousands of copies, and which one newspaper predicted would "take its place among the pictures which the people hang upon their walls to commemorate one of the great acts in the nation's history."[26]

Compared with the book and the print, the painting has had a more limited public life. After it was viewed by the cabinet on July 22, 1864, and put on display in the East Room for a couple of days, Carpenter took the canvas to New York, Boston, Chicago, Milwaukee, and Pittsburgh. Special hinges in the frame allowed him to fold the enormous work, thus making it easy to transport. It also made an appearance on the occasion of Lincoln's inauguration for a second term. Carpenter then kept the painting in his studio, where he continued to tinker with the portraits. As early as 1866, one writer lamented that "it was not long ago made a national possession." In 1873, William Stoddard, despite his earlier disparagement of the painting, testified before the Joint Committee of the Library that Congress should purchase it for $25,000. The committee declined. In 1877, a philanthropist, Elizabeth Thompson, bought the canvas from Carpenter and donated it to Congress, where a ceremony to receive it was held on Lincoln's birthday in 1878. On that day, of the eight men depicted, only Montgomery Blair was still living.[27]

The picture now hangs near the west staircase in the Senate, far from the spotlight; whatever excitement it once generated has long since passed. But Carpenter is not entirely to blame for his failure to deliver a history painting that transcended the moment and lifted the viewer's spirits. No image of emancipation could ever equal the Proclamation itself, Lincoln's own plainly drawn canvas on which he boldly signed his name.

APRIL 4, 1865

Lincoln Visits Richmond

In October 1863, Lincoln decided to donate the manuscript of the Emancipation Proclamation. He had received a letter from Mrs. D. P. Livermore, one of the officials of the Chicago Sanitary Commission, a branch of the United States Sanitary Commission. Established by congressional legislation on June 18, 1861, the commission, among its many functions, helped to coordinate the volunteer work of women who devoted themselves to aiding sick and wounded soldiers. They sought donations, distributed supplies, and volunteered in hospitals. In the fall of 1863, the Northwestern Branch held the first Sanitary Fair; many more would follow in cities and towns across the Union. Organizers raised money in a variety of ways: by charging admission to exhibits, selling arts and crafts, offering baked goods, and soliciting the contribution of items for sale or auction.

It was for this last purpose that Mrs. Livermore wrote to the president: "It has been suggested to us from various quarters that the most acceptable donation you could possibly make, would be *the original manuscript of the Proclamation of emancipation*. . . . There would seem great appropriateness in this gift to Chicago, or Illinois, for the benefit of our Western soldiers, coming as it would from a Western President." In support of her appeal, Isaac Arnold and Owen Lovejoy sent notes to the president.

Lincoln could not resist the request. "I had some desire to retain the paper; but if it shall contribute to the relief or comfort of the soldiers that will be better," he wrote. Thanking him, Mrs. Livermore and Mrs. A. H. Hoge replied: "In the midst of so many varied and valuable donations, it has been reserved to you, Abraham Lincoln, the People's President, to bestow the most noble and valuable gift for the sick and suffering soldiers."[1]

Lincoln would do anything for the soldiers. His visits to the front invigorated him and he took strength from his contact with the men. As commander-in-chief, he despaired over having to sign execution warrants for deserters and sleeping sentries, and often responded to the personal pleas of parents to commute a sentence of death. Stories abounded of his generosity and warmth toward wounded soldiers, whom he saw on a daily basis in Washington. He took an interest in the construction of the Armory Square Hospital in 1862, and even helped to arrange the planting of flower beds between the wards. After he visited in June 1863, a nurse wrote: "It was a grand thing for him to come and cheer our soldier boys with his presence."[2]

At the time, Walt Whitman was in Washington, volunteering in the hospitals, sitting with soldiers, bringing them gifts of candy, fruit, or tobacco (an item forbidden by the Sanitary Commission, but Whitman did it on his own). In January 1863, he mourned at the sight of "America, already brought to Hospital in her fair youth." He often spotted Lincoln, usually as the president traveled on horseback between the White House and his summer cottage at the Soldiers' Home, three miles northeast of the White House.

In March 1863, Whitman had confessed: "I think well of the President. He has a face like a hoosier Michael Angelo, so awful ugly it becomes beautiful, with its strange mouth, its deep cut, criss-cross lines, and its doughnut complexion. My notion is, too, that underneath his outside smutched mannerism, and stories from third-class country bar-rooms, (it is his humor,) Mr. Lincoln keeps a fountain of first-class telling wisdom. . . . I more and more rely upon his idiomatic western genius, careless of court dress or court decorums." In June, Whitman had written to his mother: "I had a good view of the President last evening—he looks more careworn even than usual—his face with deep cut lines, seams, & his *complexion gray,* through very dark skin, a curious looking man, very sad—I said to a lady who was looking with me, 'Who can see that man without losing all wish to be sharp with him personally? Who can say he has not a good soul?'"[3]

And so, for the soldiers' benefit, Lincoln parted with the manuscript of the Emancipation Proclamation. It sold for $3,000, by far the highest amount of any donated item. In recognition, Lincoln received a gold watch from the organizers. The manuscript ended up in the Chicago Historical Society, where it perished in the fire of 1871. By then, slavery had been abolished, and the Constitution had been amended to guarantee equal protection, due process, and the right to vote without regard to race. Words had indeed become things, just as John Murray Forbes had predicted to Charles Sumner in December 1862.

Gratified by the money raised from the sale of the final Proclamation manuscript, Lincoln continued to empty his desk. In January 1864, he donated the manuscript of the preliminary Emancipation Proclamation for sale at the Albany Army Relief Bazaar. A special committee, formed to oversee how best to dispose of the document, decided to hold a lottery. A ticket sold for one dollar, and organizers printed only five thousand. On March 9, as a grand finale on closing day, the drawing was held. The winner turned out to be one of the members of the special committee, Gerrit Smith, a wealthy radical abolitionist, social activist, and former member of Congress. Smith allowed the document to remain with the Sanitary Commission, and in 1865, after Lincoln's funeral train stopped in Albany, the legislature purchased it for the New York State Library.[4]

Word of Lincoln's generosity quickly spread, and Sanitary Fair organizers bombarded him with requests for donations—a letter, an autograph, a photograph, and, on more than one occasion, a lock of his hair. So many people demanded so many things from him that once, after contracting a mild case of smallpox, with office seekers lined up in the hallway, he joked that at last he had something to give everyone. For a Sanitary Fair in Baltimore, he presented something more substantial than a trinket: he presented himself.

The president spoke at the opening of the event on April 18, 1864, and he reflected on the meaning of words: "We all declare for liberty; but in using the same *word* we do not all mean the same *thing*. With some the word liberty may mean for each man to do as he pleases with himself, and the product of his labor; while with others the same word may mean for some men to do as they please with other men, and the product of other men's labor. Here are two, not only different, but incompatible things, called by the same name —liberty." Lincoln went on to relate the parable of the shepherd who drives the wolf from the throat of the black sheep, and he praised the people of Maryland, who had called a convention to rewrite the state constitution and abolish slavery, thereby repudiating "the wolf's dictionary."[5]

Lincoln was not finished—he found additional ways to use the Emancipation Proclamation as an instrument to raise money for soldiers. For the Philadelphia Great Central Sanitary Fair, held in June 1864, he signed several dozen folio broadsheets that reprinted the Proclamation. The prints sold for $10 each.

Lincoln also attended the Philadelphia Sanitary Fair. One diarist, who met with the president at the Continental Hotel, recorded his impression: "The pictures of him do great injustice to his face. His features are irregular & would be coarse but for their expression, which is genial, animated & kind. He looked somewhat pale & languid & there is a soft shade of melancholy in his smile & in his eyes. Altogether an honest, intelligent, amiable countenance, calculated to inspire respect, confidence & regard." On June 16, 1864, Lincoln delivered an address. He declared, "War, at its best, is terrible, and this war of ours, in its magnitude and in its duration, is one of the most terrible. . . . We accepted this war for an object, a worthy object, and the war will end when that object is attained."[6]

It was the final speech Lincoln personally delivered outside Washington. Indeed, there were only two others during his entire tenure as president: the address at Gettysburg to dedicate the Soldiers' National Cemetery, and the address at the Baltimore Sanitary Fair. It is telling that on the three occasions he left Washington to speak officially, he did so on behalf of the Union soldiers, wounded and dead.

And it was on their behalf that time and again he made use of the Emancipation Proclamation as a treasure whose sale would aid the soldiers he cherished. That document played a central role in helping to obtain the objective he referred to in Philadelphia: restoring the Union. It also announced that a new objective—the emancipation of the slaves—was essential to the war effort. For Lincoln, the initial purpose of the war had been to save the Union; but he came to understand that preserving the nation required emancipation, and that the abolition of slavery was an act of justice in its own right.

It took time for Lincoln to accept and employ military necessity as the doctrine under which, as commander-in-chief, he could emancipate the slaves. It provided the only lever by which he could do so constitutionally. Saying, as some did, that the Constitution no longer applied to the Confederacy may have made for good radical politics, but it ignored his oath of office. Lincoln never recognized the legality of secession and, as a result, Confederates were still entitled to certain constitutional guaranties. Among these was the right to regulate their own internal institutions.

Lincoln dwelled on the problem of timing. Perhaps he agonized for too long about the border states; but after repeated entreaties, no one could say he had not given them every opportunity to act on their own terms to dismantle slavery. Perhaps he worried for too long about securing a plan of colonization to accompany emancipation; but he advanced the plan, and then relented to the reality that it was not feasible. Perhaps he fretted for too long about northern Democrats; but at last he realized that many of them would just as soon see the nation restored under terms that guaranteed and even extended slavery, and this he could never allow.

The moment mattered. Lincoln both led and responded to a transformation in public sentiment that made the Emancipation Proclamation sustainable when he issued it. That he did so in wartime, under the most intense pressure any American president has ever faced, makes his actions all the more remarkable. He was later quoted as saying, "It is my conviction that, had the proclamation been issued even six months earlier than it was, public sentiment would not have sustained it." The same was true with the enlistment of black men: "The step, taken sooner, could not, in my judgment, have been carried out."[7]

Even one of the president's most exasperated critics, William Lloyd Garrison, came to see the wisdom of Lincoln's way of proceeding. Garrison's impatience was understandable. He had once, decades earlier, supported colonization, but then converted to immediate emancipation. Since 1831, he had edited the *Liberator,* and in 1833 he had helped to found the American

Anti-Slavery Society. At times, it was Garrison who favored disunion, calling for separation from slaveholders and denouncing the Constitution as a pro-slavery covenant with Hell.

In the summer of 1864, Garrison confessed that he was mistaken to have expected the president to act on abolitionist principles: "The people do not elect a president to play the part of reformer or philanthropist, nor to enforce upon the nation his own peculiar ethical or humanitarian ideas, without regard to his oath or their will." It was the president's responsibility to maintain the Union and defend the Constitution to the best of his ability.[8]

Garrison also recanted his earlier accusation that Lincoln was "exceedingly slow." It was not for the restless activist to say. "It was for him to follow his own convictions, not mine. I may have been mistaken; he may have been more intelligent and accurate as to the possibilities. At the worst, it was wiser to be slow and sure, than premature and rash." As a result of Lincoln's patient yet persistent approach, "what long strides he has taken in the right direction, and never a backward step!"[9]

The Proclamation, Garrison declared, was "a virtual death-blow to the whole slave system." It was not a *brutum fulmen,* and it was not like the pope's bull against the comet. It made the abolition of slavery a means, and, in doing so, it became an end. It transformed the war. As one observer had written in November 1862, "The Proclamation has changed the conditions of the contest, and to be defeated now, driven out of the field for good and all, would be a far more mortifying termination of the war than it could have been if we had already failed utterly." It was one thing to be defeated and have to accept an independent Confederacy; it was another to be defeated after making emancipation part of the strategy and purpose of the war: "To fail now would be to place ourselves in the same position that is held by the commander of a ship of war who nails his colors to the mast, and yet has to get them down to prevent his conqueror from annihilating him."[10]

The Proclamation went beyond any previous measure in its assault upon slavery. Unlike the Second Confiscation Act, it applied to all slaves living in the designated areas, not just to those belonging to rebel owners. Furthermore, it acknowledged slaves as persons, not property. Even though the enslaved could be freed as enemy property, recognizing them as persons removed all discretion as to who claimed them as property, and made their liberation a legitimate objective of the war.[11]

Critics have perpetuated the myth that the Emancipation Proclamation did not free any slaves because it applied only to areas outside Union control; it exempted areas occupied by Union forces. But those areas had to be excluded in order to sustain the argument that military necessity demanded emancipation. How could there be a necessity where the Union ruled? Lincoln's response to Salmon Chase in September 1863 gave the treasury secretary a chance to make the case that the exemptions should be lifted; but Chase, unlike other correspondents over the years who had helped Lincoln to formulate counter-arguments (Orville Browning, Isaac Arnold, the Chicago clergymen), did not take the bait.

The exempted areas (the forty-eight counties in far western Virginia destined to become the new state of West Virginia, seven counties elsewhere in Virginia, thirteen parishes in southern Louisiana, and all of Tennessee) contained approximately 300,000 slaves. The Proclamation did not apply, of course, to the half million slaves in the border states. But Lincoln also refrained from adding to the list of exceptions some places he might have included—for example, eastern North Carolina, the Sea Islands of South Carolina, the northern area of the Shenandoah Valley, portions of northern Mississippi and northern Alabama, and parts of Georgia and Florida—which means tens of thousands of slaves did indeed immediately gain their freedom. Many northern newspapers included a chart that specified "on how large a number of human beings the President's benediction falls." The count came to 3.1 million slaves in the Confederacy outside Union military control. The Emancipation Proclamation declared these slaves free; in time, they would come to possess that freedom.[12]

Over the hundred days, Lincoln became bolder. Jurists, lawyers, and professors debated the Proclamation's constitutionality, and Lincoln felt reassured that he had the rightful power to act. Soldiers did not resign or desert in notable numbers; instead, they came to embrace the Proclamation. England blathered and blustered, but did not intervene—and that it would not was almost certain by January 1, 1863. Rather than feeling restrained by the fall 1862 election, Lincoln was energized by the results. He sacked McClellan, defended his own war policies, warded off pressure to remake his cabinet, and, despite his December message to Congress—which seemed to undercut his approach to emancipation, or to make it so gradual as to seem unrecognizable—he held fast to his intention to act on January 1.

The decision made during the hundred days to accept black men into the armed services was second in importance only to the proclamation of freedom itself. Those soldiers depleted the strength of the Confederate war effort and added to the fighting power of the Union forces. Those soldiers helped to win the war. And, by serving, they also helped to make the case that abolishing slavery and preserving the Union were inextricably tied: that slaves, too, were men.

As the war wound to its end, Lincoln needed to see for himself the fruits of victory. In late March 1865, he and his family sailed to City Point, Virginia, the location of General Ulysses Grant's headquarters and the supply base for the siege of Robert E. Lee's army at Petersburg. The president wanted to escape Washington. He was pallid and careworn. A trip to meet with the general and visit with the troops might provide just the lift he needed. He departed on March 20, and did not return until April 9. He enjoyed being away.

Richmond, the Confederate capital, fell while Lincoln was at City Point, and the president was eager to visit. On April 3, he wired Edwin Stanton, "It is certain now that Richmond is in our hands, and I think I will go there tomorrow." Mindful of Stanton's concern for his safety, he added, "I will take care of myself."[13]

On April 4, Lincoln entered Richmond. His journey up the James River had been risky, and he'd had to abandon a ship for a barge in order to avoid mines and obstructions. Buildings were on fire and there was confusion in the streets, but Lincoln strode forth from the waterfront with only a small guard of sailors behind and in front. He had brought along his youngest son, Thomas ("Tad"), a birthday adventure for the boy turned twelve that day. Walking hand in hand, they made their way into the city.

Word flashed that "the President" had been spotted. Hearing the news, a group of blacks thought it must be Jefferson Davis, captured and returned for trial, and yelled "Hang Him! Hang Him! Show Him No Quarter!" But then they saw the tall, ungainly man in black coat and stovepipe hat, striding along. "All could see him," reported an eyewitness. "He was so tall, so conspicuous."[14]

Blacks gathered in celebration and crowded around the presidential party.

Charles Carleton Coffin, a correspondent for the *Boston Journal,* was among the crowd. He turned to a black woman and said:

"There's the man who made you free."

"What, massa?"

"That is President Lincoln."

"Dat President Linkum?"

"Yes."

She gazed at him a moment, clapped her hands, and jumped up and down, shouting "Glory, glory, glory!" until "her voice was lost in the universal cheer."[15]

Another woman declared, "I know I am free for I have seen Father Abraham and felt him." "God bless you, Massa Linkum," screamed a woman who tossed her bonnet into the air. "The joy of the negro knew no bounds," reported Charles Page of the *New York Tribune.* "It found expression in whoops, in contortions, in tears, and incessantly in prayerful ejaculations of thanks."[16]

"President Lincoln walked in silence," Coffin wrote, "acknowledging the salutes of officers and soldiers and of the citizens, *black and white!* It was the man of the people among the people. It was the great deliverer meeting the delivered."[17]

A year later, Coffin added to the story: "The walk was long, and the President halted a moment to rest. 'May de good Lord bless you, President Linkum,' said an old negro, removing his hat and bowing with tears of joy rolling down his cheeks. The President removed his own hat and bowed in silence: it was a bow which upset the laws, forms, customs, and ceremonies of centuries of slavery."[18]

Twenty years later, Admiral David Dixon Porter, commander of the North Atlantic Squadron, recalled that some elderly black men and women had knelt before Lincoln. According to Porter, whose account must be treated as less reliable than those offered at the time of the event, the president said, "Don't kneel to me. . . . That is not right. You must kneel to God only, and thank him for the liberty you will hereafter enjoy."[19]

African Americans flooded into the city. A Confederate colonel in charge of the coal pits at Dover, Virginia, reported: "All the negroes are going or have gone, quick for Richmond. Never was change accomplished so silently

& so quietly." Garland White, a runaway slave who had traveled to Canada and then returned south to serve as chaplain of the 28th U.S. Colored Troops, was overcome with tears at the sight of thousands of slaves "shouting and praising God and father or master Abe, as they termed him."[20]

Lincoln reached Jefferson Davis's residence, the executive mansion of the Confederacy. "When he ascended the steps he faced the crowd," reported Thomas Morris Chester, a black correspondent to the *Philadelphia Press,* "and bowed his thanks for the prolonged exultation which was going up from the great concourse. The people seemed inspired by this acknowledgment, and with renewed vigor shouted louder and louder, until it seemed as if the echoes would reach the abode of those patriot spirits who had died without witnessing the sight."[21]

Lincoln entered the mansion and found his way to Davis's reception room and office. Tired from the excursion and commotion, the president sat down in Davis's easy chair. More than forty years later, John S. Barnes, the Navy captain responsible for transporting the presidential party from Washington to City Point, recalled that the group fell silent: "It was a supreme moment— the home of the fleeing President of the Confederacy invaded by his opponents after years of bloody contests for its possession, and now occupied by the President of the United States, Abraham Lincoln, seated in a chair almost warm from the pressure of the body of Jefferson Davis! What thoughts were coursing through the mind of this great man no one can tell."

"I wonder if I could get a drink of water," was all that Lincoln said.[22]

The president left Davis's residence and stepped into a carriage with Tad, Admiral Porter, and two generals for a ride through the city. A cavalry guard followed them. Chester reported, "There is no describing the scene along the route. The colored population was wild with enthusiasm. Old men thanked God in a very boisterous manner, and old women shouted upon the pavement as high as they had ever done at a religious revival."[23]

In a long, breathless sentence, Charles Carleton Coffin tried to narrate the scene, but he knew that "no written page or illuminated canvas can give the reality of the event."

The enthusiastic bearing of the people—the blacks and poor whites who have suffered untold horrors during the war, their demonstrations of pleasure—the shouting, dancing, the thanksgivings to God, the mention of the name of Jesus—as if President Lincoln was next to the son of God in their affections—the jubilant cries, the countenances beaming with unspeakable joy, the tossing up of caps, the swinging of arms of a motley crowd—some in rags, some barefoot, some wearing pants of Union blue, and coats of Confederate gray, ragamuffins in dress, through the hardships of war, but yet of stately bearing—men in heart and soul—free men henceforth and forever, their bonds cut asunder in an hour—men from whose limbs the chains fell yesterday morning, men who through many weary years have prayed for deliverance—who have asked sometimes if God were dead—who, when their children were taken from them and sent to the swamps of South Carolina and the cane breaks of Louisiana, cried to God for help and cried in vain— who told their sorrow to Jesus and asked for help but had no helper— men who have been whipped, scourged, robbed, imprisoned for no crime. All of these things must be kept in remembrance if we would have the picture complete.[24]

A few days later, back at City Point, Lincoln visited the army field hospital. Wilbur Fisk, a private with the 2nd Vermont who regularly wrote letters to the *Green Mountain Freeman,* recounted the event: "When the President came all the men that were able arranged themselves by common consent into line, on the edge of the walk that runs along by the door of the stockades, and Mr. Lincoln passed along in front, paying personal respect to each man. 'Are you well, sir?' 'How do you do to-day?' 'How are you sir?' looking each man in the face, and giving him a word and a shake of the hand as he passed. He went into each of the stockades and tents, to see those who were not able to be out. 'Is this Father Abraham?' says one very sick man to Mr. Lincoln. The President assured him, good naturedly, that it was."[25]

After the war, Septima Collis, wife of Colonel Charles H. T. Collis, published a memoir. She described City Point and the president's visit:

[The town was] one vast hospital for suffering humanity. As far as the eye could reach from the door-step of my humble home, the plain was dotted with tents which were rapidly filled with wounded men, Northern and Southern, white and black without distinction; army surgeons, and volunteer physicians just arrived, were kept sleeplessly at work; hospital nurses and the good Samaritans of the Sanitary Commission, laden with comforts for the sick and wounded, were passing to and fro, and amidst them all strode the tall gaunt figure of Abraham Lincoln, his moistened eyes even more eloquent than the lips, which had a kindly word of cheer for every sufferer. I had met Mr. Lincoln a few days before the crisis of which I am writing arrived, and was glad to know that he remembered me. My husband, who was present, asked him *en passant* how long he intended to remain with the army; "Well," said Mr. Lincoln, with as much caution as though he were being interviewed for publication, "I am like the western pioneer who built a log cabin. When he commenced he did n't know how much timber he would need, and when he had finished, he did n't care how much he had used up."[26]

And so it was with emancipation. Lincoln had utilized all his resources to restore the Union and prepare it for freedom. But when he was called away, there was still work to be done. As he prepared to depart, he smiled warmly and said, "I came down among you without any definite plans, and when I go home I sha'n't regret a moment I have spent with you."[27]

APPENDIX

NOTES

ACKNOWLEDGMENTS

INDEX

Texts of the Emancipation Proclamation

1. First Draft: July 22, 1862

In pursuance of the sixth section of the act of congress entitled "An act to suppress insurrection and to punish treason and rebellion, to seize and confiscate property of rebels, and for other purposes" Approved July 17, 1862, and which act, and the Joint Resolution explanatory thereof, are herewith published, I, Abraham Lincoln, President of the United States, do hereby proclaim to, and warn all persons within the contemplation of said sixth section to cease participating in, aiding, countenancing, or abetting the existing rebellion, or any rebellion against the government of the United States, and to return to their proper allegiance to the United States, on pain of the forfeitures and seizures, as within and by said sixth section provided.

And I hereby make known that it is my purpose, upon the next meeting of congress, to again recommend the adoption of a practical measure for tendering pecuniary aid to the free choice or rejection, of any and all States which may then be recognizing and practically sustaining the authority of the United States, and which may then have voluntarily adopted, or thereafter may voluntarily adopt, gradual abolishment of slavery within such State or States—that the object is to practically restore, thenceforward to be maintain[ed], the constitutional relation between the general government, and each, and all the states, wherein that relation is now suspended, or disturbed, and that, for this object, the war, as it has been, will be, prossecuted [*sic*]. And, as a fit and necessary military measure for effecting this object, I, as Commander-in-Chief of the Army and Navy of the United States, do order and declare that on the first day of January in the year of Our Lord one thousand, eight hundred and sixty three, all persons held as slaves within any state or states, wherein the constitutional authority of the United States shall not then be practically recognized, submitted to, and maintained, shall then, thenceforward, and forever, be free.

2. Preliminary Emancipation Proclamation: September 22, 1862

By the President of the
United States of America
A Proclamation

I, Abraham Lincoln, President of the United States of America, and Commander-in-chief of the Army and Navy thereof, do hereby proclaim and declare that hereafter, as heretofore, the war will be prosecuted for the object of practically restoring the constitutional relation between the United States, and each of the states, and the people thereof, in which states that relation is, or may be suspended, or disturbed.

That is my purpose, upon the next meeting of Congress to again recommend the adoption of a practical measure tendering pecuniary aid to the free acceptance or rejection of all slave-states, so called, the people whereof may not then be in rebellion against the United States, and which states, may then have voluntarily adopted, or thereafter may voluntarily adopt, immediate or gradual abolishment of slavery within their respective limits; and that the effort to colonize persons of African descent with their consent upon this continent, or elsewhere, with the previously obtained consent of the Governments existing there, will be continued.

That on the first day of January in the year of our Lord, one thousand eight hundred and sixty-three, all persons held as slaves within any state, or designated part of a state, the people whereof shall then be in rebellion against the United States shall be then, thenceforward, and forever free; and the executive government of the United States, will, including the military and naval authority thereof, recognize and maintain the freedom of such persons, and will do no act or acts to repress such persons, or any of them, in any efforts they may make for their actual freedom.

That the executive will, on the first day of January aforesaid, by proclamation, designate the States, and parts of states, if any, in which the people thereof respectively, shall then be in rebellion against the United States; and the fact that any state, or the people thereof shall, on that day be, in good faith represented in the Congress of the United States, by members chosen thereto, at elections wherein a majority of the qualified voters of such state shall have participated, shall, in the absence of strong countervailing testimony, be deemed conclusive evidence that such state and the people thereof, are not then in rebellion against the United States.

That attention is hereby called to an act of Congress entitled "An act to make an additional Article of War" approved March 13, 1862, and which act is in the words and figure following:

Be it enacted by the Senate and House of Representatives of the United States of America in Congress assembled, That hereafter the following shall be promulgated as an additional article of war for the government of the army of the United States, and shall be obeyed and observed as such:

Article—. All officers or persons in the military or naval service of the United States are prohibited from employing any of the forces under their respective commands for the purpose of returning fugitives from service or labor, who may have escaped from any persons to whom such service or labor is claimed to be due, and any officer who shall be found guilty by a court-martial of violating this article shall be dismissed from the service.

SEC. 2. *And be it further enacted,* That this act shall take effect from and after its passage.

Also to the ninth and tenth sections of an act entitled "An Act to suppress Insurrection, to punish Treason and Rebellion, to seize and confiscate property of rebels, and for other purposes" approved July 17, 1862, and which sections are in the words and figures following:

SEC. 9. *And be it further enacted,* That all slaves of persons who shall hereafter be engaged in rebellion against the government of the United States, or who shall in any way give aid or comfort thereto, escaping from such persons and taking refuge within the lines of the army; and all slaves captured from such persons or deserted by them and coming under the control of the government of the United States; and all slaves of such persons found on [or] being within any place occupied by rebel forces and afterwards occupied by the forces of the United States, shall be deemed captives of war, and shall be forever free of their servitude and not again held as slaves.

SEC. 10. *And be it further enacted,* That no slave escaping into any State, Territory, or the District of Columbia, from any other State, shall be delivered up, or in any way impeded or hindered of his liberty, except for crime, or some offense against the laws, unless the person claiming said fugitive shall first make oath that the person to whom the labor or service of such fugitive is alleged to be due is his lawful owner, and has not borne arms against the United states in the present rebellion, nor in any way given aid and comfort thereto; and no person engaged in the military or naval service of the United States shall, under any pretence whatever, assume to decide on the validity of the claim of any person to the service or labor of any other person, or surrender up any such person to the claimant, on pain of being dismissed from the service.

And I do hereby enjoin upon and order all persons engaged in the military and naval service of the United States to observe, obey and enforce, within their respective spheres of service, the act, and sections above recited.

And the executive will in due time recommend that all citizens of the United States who shall have remained loyal thereto throughout the rebellion, shall (upon restoration of the constitutional relation between the United States, and their respective states, and people, if that relation shall have been suspended or disturbed) be compensated for all losses by acts of the United States, including the loss of slaves.

In witness whereof, I have hereunto set my hand, and caused the seal of the United States to be affixed.

> Done at the City of Washington, this twenty second day of September, in the year of our Lord, one thousand eight hundred and sixty two, and of the Independence of the United States, the eighty seventh.

Abraham Lincoln

> By the President
> William H. Seward,
> Secretary of State

3. Draft: December 29–31, 1862

Whereas, on the twenty second day of September, in the year of our Lord one thousand, eight hundred and sixty-two, a proclamation was issued by the President of the United States, containing among other things the following, to wit: [*blank space for insertion*]

Now therefore I, Abraham Lincoln, President of the United States, by virtue of the power in me vested, as Commander-in-Chief, of the Army, and Navy of the United States in time of actual armed rebellion against the authority and government of the United States, and as a proper and necessary war measure for suppressing said rebellion, do, on this first day of January in the year of our Lord one thousand eight hundred and sixty three, and in accordance with my intention so to do, publicly proclaimed for one hundred days as aforesaid, order and designate as the States and parts of States in which the people thereof respectively are this day in rebellion against the United States, the following to wit: Arkansas, Texas, Louisiana, except the Parishes of [*blank space for insertion*], Mississippi, Alabama, Florida, Georgia, South Carolina, North Carolina, and Virginia, except the forty-eight counties designated as West Virginia, and also the counties of [*blank space for insertion*].

And by virtue of the power, and for the purpose aforesaid, I do order, and declare, that all persons held as slaves within said designated States, and parts of States, are, and henceforward forever shall be free; and that the Executive government of the United States, including the military and naval authorities thereof, will recognize and maintain the freedom of said persons and will do no act, or acts to repress said persons, or any of them, in any suitable efforts they may make for their actual freedom. And I hereby appeal to the people so declared to be free, to abstain from all disorder, tumult, and violence, unless in necessary self defence; and in all cases, when allowed, to labor faithfully, for wages.

And I further declare, and make known, that such persons of suitable condition, will be received into the armed service of the United States to garrison and defend forts, positions, stations, and other places, and to man vessels of all sorts in said service.

4. Emancipation Proclamation: January 1, 1863

By the President of the
United States of America:
A Proclamation.

Whereas, on the twenty second day of September, in the year of our Lord one thousand eight hundred and sixty two, a proclamation was issued by the President of the United States, containing, among other things, the following to wit:

That on the first day of January, in the year of our Lord one thousand eight hundred and sixty-three, all persons held as slaves within any State or designated part of a State, the people whereof shall then be in rebellion against the United States, shall be then, thenceforward, and forever free; and the Executive Government of the United States, including the military and naval authority thereof, will recognize and maintain the freedom of such persons, and will do no act or acts to repress such persons, or any of them, in any efforts they may make for their actual freedom.

That the Executive will, on the first day of January aforesaid, by proclamation, designate the States and parts of States, if any, in which the people thereof, respectively, shall then be in rebellion against the

United States; and the fact that any State, or the people thereof, shall on that day be, in good faith, represented in the Congress of the United States by members chosen thereto at elections wherein a majority of the qualified voters of such State shall have participated, shall, in the absence of strong countervailing testimony, be deemed conclusive evidence that such State, and the people thereof, are not then in rebellion against the United States.

Now therefore, I, Abraham Lincoln, President of the United States, by virtue of the power in me vested as Commander-in-Chief, of the Army and Navy of the United States in time of actual armed rebellion against [the] authority and government of the United States, and as a fit and necessary war measure for suppressing said rebellion, do, on this first day of January, in the year of our Lord one thousand eight hundred and sixty three, and in accordance with my purpose so to do publicly proclaimed for the full period of one hundred days, from the day first above mentioned, order and designate as the States and parts of States wherein the people thereof respectively; are this day in rebellion against the United States, the following to wit:

Arkansas, Texas, Louisiana, (except the Parishes of St. Bernard, Plaquemines, Jefferson, St. Johns, St. Charles, St. James[,] Ascension, Assumption, Terrebonne, Lafourche, St. Mary, St. Martin, and Orleans, including the City of New-Orleans), Mississippi, Alabama, Florida, Georgia, South-Carolina, North-Carolina, and Virginia, (except the forty-eight counties designated as West Virginia, and also the counties of Berkley, Accomac, Northampton, Elizabeth-City, York, Princess Ann, and Norfolk, including the cities of Norfolk & Portsmouth[)]; and which excepted parts are, for the present, left precisely as if this proclamation were not issued.

And by virtue of the power, and for the purpose aforesaid, I do order and declare that all persons held as slaves within said designated States, and parts of States, are, and henceforward shall be free; and that the Executive government of the United States, including the military and naval authorities thereof, will recognize and maintain the freedom of said persons.

And I hereby enjoin upon the people so declared to be free to abstain from all violence, unless in necessary self-defence; and I recommend to them that, in all cases when allowed, they labor faithfully for reasonable wages.

And I further declare and make known, that such persons of suitable condition, will be received into the armed service of the United States to garrison forts, positions, stations, and other places, and to man vessels of all sorts in said service.

And upon this act, sincerely believed to be an act of justice, warranted by the Constitution, upon military necessity, I invoke the considerate judgment of mankind, and the gracious favor of Almighty God.

In witness whereof, I have hereunto set my hand and caused the seal of the United States to be affixed.

> Done at the City of Washington, this first day of January, in the year of our Lord one thousand eight hundred and sixty three, and of the Independence of the United States of America the eighty-seventh.

Abraham Lincoln

By the President;
William H. Seward,
Secretary of State

Notes

Prologue

1. Charles Francis Adams, Jr., *Richard Henry Dana*, 2 vols. (Boston: Houghton Mifflin, 1890), 1:264. For an early collection that purports to gather some of Lincoln's humor, see *Old Abe's Jokes: Fresh from Abraham's Bosom* (New York: T. R. Dawley, 1864).

2. Artemus Ward, *His Book* (New York: Carleton, 1864), pp. 34–35.

3. Edward Dicey, *Six Months in the Federal States*, 2 vols. (London: MacMillan, 1863), 1:227; Davis quoted in Allan Nevins, *The War for the Union*, vol. 2: *War Becomes Revolution, 1862–1863* (New York: Scribner's, 1960), p. 235; William O. Stoddard, *Inside the White House in War Times: Memoirs and Reports of Lincoln's Secretary*, ed. Michael Burlingame (Lincoln: University of Nebraska Press, 2000), p. 93.

4. Thorndike Rice, *Reminiscences of Abraham Lincoln by Distinguished Men of His Time* (New York: Harper and Brothers, 1909), p. 156.

5. Salmon P. Chase, *The Salmon P. Chase Papers*, vol. 1: *Journals, 1829–1872*, ed. John Niven (Kent, OH: Kent State University Press, 1993), p. 393. Hawthorne originally included his description in his essay "Chiefly about War-Matters," *Atlantic Monthly* 10 (July 1862), pp. 43–62, but the editors cut it because they felt it "lacked reverence"; it was finally published in *Atlantic Monthly* 27 (April 1871), pp. 510–512. Theodore Lyman, *Meade's Headquarters, 1863–1865: Letters of Colonel Theodore Lyman from the Wilderness to Appomattox*, ed. George R. Agassiz (Boston: Atlantic Monthly Press, 1922), p. 325.

6. William Howard Russell, *My Diary North and South* (New York: Harper and Brothers, 1863), p. 20.

7. Dicey, *Six Months in the Federal States,* 1:234; John L. Motley, *The Correspondence of John Lothrop Motley,* ed. George William Curtis, 2 vols. (New York: Society of English and French Literature, 1889), 1:387.

8. Doris Kearns Goodwin, *Team of Rivals: The Political Genius of Abraham Lincoln* (New York: Simon and Schuster, 2005), p. 519.

9. Chase, *Journals,* 1:393–394.

10. Gideon Welles, *Diary of Gideon Welles,* ed. Howard K. Beale, 2 vols. (New York: W. W. Norton, 1960), 1:143.

11. This account is based on the diaries of Chase and Welles, as well as on Gideon Welles, "The History of Emancipation," *Galaxy* 14 (December 1872), pp. 838–851; and Welles, "An Interesting Leaf of History: How the Emancipation Proclamation Was Written," *Brooklyn Eagle,* June 21, 1865. On the Emancipation Proclamation, see John Hope Franklin, *The Emancipation Proclamation* (Garden City: Anchor Books, 1963); Allen C. Guelzo, *Lincoln's Emancipation Proclamation: The End of Slavery in America* (New York: Simon and Schuster, 2004); Michael Burlingame, *Abraham Lincoln: A Life,* 2 vols. (Baltimore: Johns Hopkins University Press, 2008), 2:407–418; William A. Blair and Karen Fisher Younger, eds., *Lincoln's Proclamation: Emancipation Reconsidered* (Chapel Hill: University of North Carolina Press, 2009); and Harold Holzer, *Emancipating Lincoln: The Proclamation in Text, Context, and Memory* (Cambridge, MA: Harvard University Press, 2012). Also see Eric Foner, *The Fiery Trial: Abraham Lincoln and American Slavery* (New York: W. W. Norton, 2010).

12. Maria Lydig Daly, *Diary of a Union Lady, 1861–1865,* ed. Harold Earl Hammond (New York: Funk and Wagnalls, 1962), p. 179.

13. Charles Sedgwick to John Murray Forbes, December 22, 1862, in John Murray Forbes, *Letters and Recollections of John Murray Forbes,* ed. Sarah Forbes Hughes, 2 vols. (Boston: Houghton Mifflin, 1899), 1:346.

14. Richard Hofstadter's pronouncement in 1948 that the Proclamation had "all the moral grandeur of a bill of lading" still clings to the document. See Hofstadter, *The American Political Tradition and the Men Who Made It* (New York: Knopf, 1973; orig. pub. 1948), p. 129. In the 1960s, some writers rejected Lincoln as the Great Emancipator and instead cast him as a racist and white supremacist who did not truly desire emancipation. See, for example, Lerone Bennett, Jr., "Was Lincoln a White Supremacist?" *Ebony,* February 1968, pp. 35–38; and Bennett, *Forced into Glory: Abraham Lincoln's White Dream* (Chicago: Johnson Publishing, 2000). In the 1990s, historians debated the question of who freed the slaves, as well as the relative roles of Lincoln and of the slaves themselves. For contrasting views, see James M. McPherson, "Who Freed the Slaves?" in McPherson, *Drawn with the Sword: Reflections on the American Civil War* (New York: Oxford University Press, 1996), pp. 192–207; and Ira Berlin, "Who Freed the Slaves? Emancipation and Its Meaning," in David W. Blight and Brooks D. Simpson, eds., *Union and Emancipation: Essays on Politics and Race in the Civil War Era* (Kent, OH: Kent State University Press, 1997), pp. 105–121. More recently, there has been a revival of Civil War

revisionism which seeks to debunk the importance of Lincoln, suggests that the war might have been avoided, and offers support for the Lost Cause of the Confederacy. For example, Thomas DiLorenzo (who is a libertarian economist, not a historian) has called the Emancipation Proclamation "little more than a political gimmick." See DiLorenzo, *The Real Lincoln: A New Look at Abraham Lincoln* (New York: Three Rivers Press, 2003), p. x.

15. *Douglass' Monthly*, March 1863; *Douglass' Monthly*, January 1863.

16. Taylor Peirce, *Dear Catherine, Dear Taylor: The Civil War Letters of a Union Soldier and His Wife*, ed. Richard L. Kiper (Lawrence: University Press of Kansas, 2002), p. 415.

1. Toward Emancipation

1. Salmon P. Chase, *The Salmon P. Chase Papers*, vol. 1: *Journals, 1829–72*, ed. John Niven (Kent, OH: Kent State University Press, 1993), p. 425.

2. Charles Sumner, *The Selected Letters of Charles Sumner*, ed. Beverly Wilson Palmer, 2 vols. (Boston: Northeastern University Press, 1990), 2:68; Hans L. Trefousse, *The Radical Republicans: Lincoln's Vanguard for Racial Justice* (Baton Rouge: Louisiana State University Press, 1975), p. 204; Orville Browning to AL, April 30, 1861, in Abraham Lincoln Papers, Library of Congress (hereafter ALP).

3. John Hay, *Inside Lincoln's White House: The Complete Civil War Diary of John Hay*, ed. Michael Burlingame and John R. Turner Ettlinger (Carbondale: Southern Illinois University Press, 1997), p. 22; William N. Slocum, *The War and How To End It* (San Francisco, 1861), p. 31.

4. Abraham Lincoln, *The Collected Works of Abraham Lincoln*, ed. Roy P. Basler, 9 vols. (New Brunswick: Rutgers University Press, 1953–1955), 5:160; 7:281–283 (hereafter cited as *CW*).

5. Henry Ward Beecher, *War and Emancipation* (Philadelphia: T. B. Peterson, 1861), p. 19. Beecher revised the sermon and titled it "Modes and Duties of Emancipation"; see Beecher, *Freedom and War: Discourses on Topics Suggested by the Times* (Boston: Ticknor and Fields, 1863), p. 188.

6. William Howard Russell, *My Diary North and South*, 2 vols. (London: Bradbury and Evans, 1863), 2:162; Benjamin F. Butler, *Private and Official Correspondence of Gen. Benjamin F. Butler*, 5 vols. (privately issued, 1917), 1:37.

7. Butler, *Private and Official Correspondence*, 1:40–41.

8. Ibid., p. 77.

9. The story is well told in Adam Goodheart, *1861: Civil War Awakening* (New York: Alfred A. Knopf, 2011), pp. 295–347.

10. Ibid., pp. 106, 119. On African Americans in the navy, see Barbara Brooks Tomblin, *Bluejackets and Contrabands: African Americans and the Union Navy* (Lexington: University Press of Kentucky, 2009).

11. *New York Times,* May 17, 1861.

12. *New York Herald,* May 30, 1861; *Boston Daily Advertiser,* May 29, 1861; Charles C. Nott, *The Coming Contraband* (New York: Putnam, 1862), pp. 2–3. For a full discussion of the term, see Kate Masur, "'A Rare Phenomenon of Philological Vegetation': The Word 'Contraband' and the Meanings of Emancipation in the United States," *Journal of American History* 93 (March 2007), pp. 1050–1084.

13. Doris Kearns Goodwin, *Team of Rivals: The Political Genius of Abraham Lincoln* (New York: Simon and Schuster, 2005), p. 369; Chase to Butler, June 24, 1862, in Butler, *Private and Official Correspondence,* 1:633.

14. *New York Herald,* May 30, 1861; *Douglass's Monthly,* July 1861; *Liberator,* June 28, 1861; *New York Times,* July 20, 1861; Henry Ward Beecher, "Modes and Duties of Emancipation," pp. 192–193.

15. *New York Times,* June 9, 1861.

16. Frederick Law Olmsted, *The Papers of Frederick Law Olmsted,* vol. 4: *Defending the Union: The Civil War and the U.S. Sanitary Commission,* ed. Jane Turner Censer (Baltimore: Johns Hopkins University Press, 1986), pp. 118, 236.

17. Charles Harvey Brewster, *When This Cruel War Is Over: The Civil War Letters of Charles Harvey Brewster,* ed. David W. Blight (Amherst: University of Massachusetts Press, 1992), pp. 57, 61, 78.

18. Ibid., 90, 92, 96.

19. On the reactions of slaves to the war, see Stephanie McCurry, *Confederate Reckoning: Power and Politics in the Civil War South* (Cambridge, MA: Harvard University Press, 2010), pp. 216–309.

20. Worthington Chauncey Ford, ed., *A Cycle of Adams Letters, 1861–1865,* 2 vols. (Boston: Houghton Mifflin, 1920), 1:26; Sumner, *Selected Letters,* 2:74.

21. Henry Wilson, *History of the Antislavery Measures of the 37th and 38th United States Congresses, 1861–65* (Boston: Walker, Fuller, 1865), pp. 1–16.

22. John Murray Forbes, *Letters and Recollections of John Murray Forbes,* ed. Sarah Forbes Hughes, 2 vols. (Boston: Houghton Mifflin, 1899), 1:241.

23. *Chicago Tribune,* September 5, 1861; *Liberator,* September 13, 1861; *Chicago Tribune,* September 18, 1861.

24. *CW,* 4:506; Joshua Speed to Abraham Lincoln, September 1 and September 3, 1861, in ALP.

25. *CW,* 4:518; Orville Browning to Abraham Lincoln, September 17, 1861, in ALP.

26. *CW,* 4:531–532. Browning responded to the president on September 30, 1861. He argued that the rebel states had dissolved the state of society that had existed and, therefore, "all their property, both real and personal, is subject, by the law of nations, to be taken, and confiscated." Browning cited Jean Jacques Burlamaqui, *The Principles of Natural and Politic Law* (1748), as an authority.

27. William R. Prince to AL, September 20, 1861; Erastus Wright to AL, Septem-

ber 20, 1861; W. McCaully to AL, September 20, 1861; John L. Scripps to AL, September 23, 1861; Thomas O'Reilly to AL, October 24, 1861; Samuel Camp to AL, September 17, 1861; all in ALP.

28. *Liberator,* July 5, 1861.

29. Charles L. Brace, "The Key to Victory," *The Independent,* August 22, 1861, p. 1.

30. *The War and Slavery: or, Victory Only through Emancipation* (Boston: R. F. Wallcut, 1861), p. 6; *New York Times,* August 9, 1861; Sidney George Fisher, *A Philadelphia Perspective: The Civil War Diary of Sidney George Fisher,* ed. Jonathan W. White (New York: Fordham University Press, 2007), p. 107.

31. Orestes Brownson, "Slavery and the War," in *The Works of Orestes Brownson,* ed. Henry Brownson, 20 vols. (New York: Arno Press, 1966), 17:144–178. Also see *Liberator,* October 11, 1861.

32. Brownson, "Slavery and the War," pp. 144–178.

33. Edward Dicey, *Six Months in the Federal States,* 2 vols. (London: MacMillan, 1863), 1:236–237.

34. Charles Sumner, "Emancipation Our Best Weapon," in *The Works of Charles Sumner,* 15 vols. (Boston: Lee and Shepard, 1874), 6:12, 19, 20–21, 28; Edward L. Pierce, *Memoir and Letters of Charles Sumner,* 4 vols. (Boston: Roberts Brothers, 1893), 4:49. For an acute discussion of military necessity and the law of war, see Burrus M. Carnahan, *Act of Justice: Lincoln's Emancipation Proclamation and the Law of War* (Lexington: University Press of Kentucky, 2007).

35. Criticisms from Boston papers quoted in "Appendix," *Works of Charles Sumner,* 6:38–42; *Weekly Caucasian,* October 12, 1861; Ford, ed., *A Cycle of Adams Letters, 1861–1865,* 1:54, 58.

36. Yates told the story in a speech delivered some two years later, on October 20, 1863, and several newspapers reported it, including the *Washington Chronicle* and the *New York Herald.* Noah Brooks, Washington correspondent for the *Sacramento Daily Union,* also reported the story; see Brooks, *Lincoln Observed: Civil War Dispatches of Noah Brooks,* ed. Michael Burlingame (Baltimore: Johns Hopkins University Press, 1998), p. 72; George B. McClellan, *The Civil War Papers of George B. McClellan: Civil War Correspondence, 1860–1865,* ed. Stephen W. Sears (Cambridge, MA: Da Capo Press, 1992), p. 128; Ulysses S. Grant, *The Papers of Ulysses S. Grant,* ed. John Y. Simon, 31 vols. (Carbondale: Southern Illinois University Press, 1970), 3:227.

37. Wilson, *History of the Antislavery Measures,* pp. 179–180.

38. Amanda Foreman, *A World on Fire: An Epic History of Two Nations Divided* (London: Allen Lane, 2010), pp. 234–238; A. Taylor Milne, "The Lyons-Seward Treaty of 1862," *American Historical Review* 38 (April 1933), pp. 511–525.

39. *CW,* 5:35–53. See Gary W. Gallagher, *The Union War* (Cambridge, MA: Harvard University Press, 2011).

40. *Liberator,* December 20, 1861; William Lloyd Garrison, *Let the Oppressed Go*

Free, 1861–1867: The Letters of William Lloyd Garrison, ed. Walter M. Merrill, 6 vols. (Cambridge, MA: Harvard University Press, 1979), 5:37, 47; Charles Eliot Norton, *Letters of Charles Eliot Norton,* 2 vols. (Boston: Houghton Mifflin, 1913), 1:246.

41. *Congressional Globe,* 37th Congress, 2nd Session, Appendix, p. 38 (hereafter *CG*).

42. James M. McPherson, *For Cause and Comrades: Why Men Fought in the Civil War* (New York: Oxford University Press, 1997), pp. 120–121.

43. Oliver Willcox Norton, *Army Letters* (Privately printed, 1903), pp. 29, 42.

44. Chandra Manning, *What This Cruel War Was Over* (New York: Vintage, 2007), pp. 45, 49; James K. Newton, *A Wisconsin Boy in Dixie: The Selected Letters of James K. Newton,* ed. Stephen E. Ambrose (Madison: University of Wisconsin Press, 1961), p. 28; William Thompson Lusk, *War Letters of William Thompson Lusk* (New York: privately printed, 1911), p. 101.

45. *CG,* 37th Congress, 2nd Session, p. 83.

46. Wendell Phillips, "The War for the Union," in Phillips, *Speeches, Lectures, and Letters* (New York: Negro University Press, 1968), p. 431.

47. George S. Boutwell, *Emancipation: Its Justice, Expediency and Necessity as the Means of Securing a Speedy and Permanent Peace* (Boston: Wright and Potter, 1861), p. 11; *Liberator,* March 14, 1862.

48. Sumner, *Selected Letters,* 2:76, 85; Sumner, *Works,* 6:152.

49. Gideon Welles, *Diary of Gideon Welles,* ed. Howard K. Beale, 2 vols. (New York: W. W. Norton, 1960), 1:187; Hay, *Inside Lincoln's White House,* p. 192.

50. *New York Herald,* quoted in LeRoy H. Fischer, *Lincoln's Gadfly, Adam Gurowski* (Norman: University of Oklahoma Press, 1964), p. 166; *North American Review* 98 (April 1864), p. 619.

51. Adam Gurowski, *Diary from March 4, 1861, to November 12, 1862* (Boston: Lee and Shepard, 1862), pp. 98, 54, 85, 129–130, 143, 157–158, 144.

2. Messages and Measures

1. George Templeton Strong, *Diary of the Civil War: George Templeton Strong,* ed. Allen Nevins (New York: MacMillan, 1962), p. 279. In Greek mythology dealing with the Trojan War, Thersites was a common soldier who alone says what others may be thinking.

2. Ibid, pp. 204–205.

3. Charles Sumner, *The Selected Letters of Charles Sumner,* ed. Beverly Wilson Palmer, 2 vols. (Boston: Northeastern University Press, 1990), 2:93; N. H. Eggleston, "Emancipation," *New Englander and Yale Review* 21 (October 1862), p. 783.

4. David Herbert Donald, *Charles Sumner and the Rights of Man* (New York: Random House, 1970), p. 52.

5. Abraham Lincoln, *The Collected Works of Abraham Lincoln,* ed. Roy P. Basler, 9 vols. (New Brunswick: Rutgers University Press, 1953–1955), 5:144–146 (hereafter *CW*).

6. James M. McPherson, *The Struggle for Equality* (Princeton: Princeton University Press, 1964), p. 97; Adam Gurowski, *Diary from March 4, 1861, to November 12, 1862* (Boston: Lee and Shepard, 1862), p. 167; Charles Eliot Norton, *Letters of Charles Eliot Norton,* ed. Sara Norton and Mark DeWolfe Howe (Boston: Houghton Mifflin, 1913), pp. 252–253.

7. Frederick Douglass, "The War and How To End It: An Address Delivered in Rochester, New York, on March 25, 1862," in *The Frederick Douglass Papers, Series One: Speeches, Debates and Interviews,* ed. John W. Blassingame, 5 vols. (New Haven: Yale University Press, 1985), 3:518.

8. Samuel Gridley Howe, *Letters and Journals of Samuel Gridley Howe,* ed. Laura E. Richards (Boston: Dana Estes, 1909), pp. 500–501; Henry Ward Beecher, *Freedom and War: Discourses on Topics Suggested by the War* (Boston: Ticknor and Fields, 1863), p. 224.

9. William Aikman, *The Future of the Colored Race in America* (New York: Anson Randolph, 1862), p. 8.

10. *Independent,* March 13, 1862; *Tribune,* quoted in David Herbert Donald, *Lincoln* (New York: Simon and Schuster, 1995), p. 347; *New York Herald,* April 1, 1862; *New York Times,* March 8, 1862; *CW,* 5:152–153. Persuaded by Lincoln's argument, Raymond wired his editors to support the proposal without qualification.

11. Statement to Frank Blair quoted in Charles M. Segal, ed., *Conversations with Lincoln* (New York: G. P. Putnam's Sons, 1961), p. 164.

12. John G. Nicolay, *With Lincoln in the White House: Letters, Memoranda, and Other Writings of John G. Nicolay, 1860–1865,* ed. Michael Burlingame (Carbondale: Southern Illinois University Press, 2000), pp. 73–74. On Lincoln's Delaware plan, see Michael Burlingame, *Abraham Lincoln: A Life,* 2 vols. (Baltimore: Johns Hopkins University Press, 2008), 2:229–231.

13. Don E. Fehrenbacher and Virginia Fehrenbacher, comps. and eds., *Recollected Words of Abraham Lincoln* (Stanford: Stanford University Press, 1996), p. 122.

14. On this subject, see William C. Harris, *Lincoln and the Border States: Preserving the Union* (Lawrence: University Press of Kansa, 2011).

15. Segal, *Conversations with Lincoln,* pp. 166–168.

16. *Congressional Globe,* 37th Congress, 2nd Session, pp. 1174, 1154 (hereafter *CG*).

17. Henry Wilson, *History of the Antislavery Measures of the 37th and 38th United States Congresses, 1861–65* (Boston: Walker, Fuller, 1865), pp. 17–37.

18. On the abolition of slavery in Washington, D.C., see Kate Masur, *An Example for All the Land: Emancipation and the Struggle for Equality in Washington, D.C.* (Chapel Hill: University of North Carolina Press, 2010).

19. *CG,* 37th Congress, 2nd Session, p. 1632, Appendix, pp. 83–84, 1191, 1300–1301, 1338.

20. Ibid., pp. 1351–1352, 1357.

21. Nearly a year later, on January 27, 1863, Saulsbury would turn violent on the floor of the Senate. He denounced Lincoln as "weak and imbecile"—language that was a violation of Senate rules of conduct. Called to order, the senator, who by all accounts was drunk, persisted. The vice president called the sergeant-at-arms, Isaac Bassett, to remove him, at which point Saulsbury "drew a revolver and kept it pointed . . . saying 'D—n you Bassett, if you touch me I'll shoot you dead.'" He left, returned, and then was forcibly removed. See *CG,* 37th Congress, 3rd Session, pp. 649–650; and the account in Noah Brooks, *Mr. Lincoln's Washington: Selections from the Writing of Noah Brooks, Civil War Correspondent,* ed. P. J. Staudenraus (South Brunswick, NJ: A. S. Barnes, 1967), pp. 87–89.

22. *CG,* 37th Congress, 2nd Session, pp. 1472, 1520.

23. *Report of the Select Committee on Emancipation and Colonization* (Washington, DC: Government Printing Office, 1862), pp. 14–15.

24. Charles Sumner, *The Works of Charles Sumner,* 15 vols. (Boston: Lee and Shepard, 1875), 9:466.

25. Sumner, *Works,* 6:28; *CG,* 37th Congress, 2nd Session, pp. 1449, 1451.

26. Sumner, *Selected Letters,* 2:109.

27. Orville H. Browning, *The Diary of Orville Hickman Browning,* vol. 1, ed. Theodore Calvin Pease and James G. Randall (Springfield: Illinois State Historical Library, 1925), p. 541.

28. Frederick Douglass to Charles Sumner, April 8, 1862, in Frederick Douglass, *Life and Writings of Frederick Douglass,* ed. Philip S. Foner, 5 vols. (New York: International Publishers, 1950–1975), 3:233.

29. *Douglass' Monthly* (Rochester, NY), January 1862; *CG,* 37th Congress, 3rd Session, p. 1172.

30. Beecher, *Freedom and War,* p. 236.

31. *CG,* 37th Congress, 2nd Session, Appendix, p. 85; B. S. Hedrick to AL, September 23, 182 in Abraham Lincoln Papers, Library of Congress (hereafter ALP).

32. Lydia Maria Child, *The Right Way the Safe Way* (New York, 1860), p. 80.

33. Elizur Wright, *The Lesson of St. Domingo: How To Make the War Short and the Peace Righteous* (Boston: A. Williams, 1861), p. 18.

34. Orestes Brownson, *The Works of Orestes Brownson,* ed. Henry Brownson, 20 vols. (New York: Arno Press, 1966), 17:206; Eggleston, "Emancipation," pp. 791–792. For a discussion of transatlantic comparisons, see Edward Bartlett Rugemer, *The Problem of Emancipation: The Caribbean Roots of the American Civil War* (Baton Rouge: Louisiana State University Press, 2008).

35. Sumner, *Works,* 6:383–384; Sumner, *Selected Letters,* 2:105; Brownson, *Works,* 17:236.

36. *CG*, 37th Congress, 2nd Session, p. 786.

37. Worthington Chauncey Ford, ed., *A Cycle of Adams Letters, 1861–1865*, 2 vols. (Boston: Houghton Mifflin, 1920), 1:139–140.

38. Peter Sturtevant to AL, May 16, 1862, and Reverdy Johnson to AL, May 16, 1862, in ALP; *Philadelphia Inquirer*, May 17, 1862; *North American*, May 17, 1862.

39. Strong, *Diary of the Civil War*, p. 226; Salmon P. Chase, *The Salmon P. Chase Papers*, vol. 1: *Journals, 1829–1872*, ed. John Niven (Kent, OH: Kent State University Press, 1993), p. 344; *Portland Daily Advertiser*, May 19, 1862.

40. Carl Schurz to AL, May 16, 1862, ALP.

41. *CW*, 5:222–223.

42. *The Salmon P. Chase Papers*, vol. 3: *Correspondence, 1858–March 1863*, ed., John Niven (Kent: Kent State University Press, 1996), p. 219; *CG*, 37th Congress, 2nd Session, Appendix, p. 185; William Lloyd Garrison, *Let the Oppressed Go Free, 1861–1867: The Letters of William Lloyd Garrison*, ed. Walter M. Merrill, 6 vols. (Cambridge, MA: Harvard University Press, 1979), vol. 5, pp. 60, 93; *Liberator*, May 30, 1862.

43. *Harper's Weekly*, May 31, 1862; *Weekly Patriot and Union*, May 1862; Gurowski, *Diary*, pp. 210–211.

44. George Gordon Meade, *The Life and Letters of George Gordon Meade*, 2 vols. (New York: Scribner's, 1913), 1:267.

45. *CG*, 37th Congress, 2nd Session, 1628, 1779, 1627, 1991, 1790. Leonard P. Curry, *Blueprint for Modern America* (Nashville: Vanderbilt University Press, 1968), pp. 75–100, is indispensable for sorting through the legislative history.

46. *CG*, 37th Congress, 2nd Session, 2233, 1719, 2302, 2191.

47. Ibid., 1880.

48. Ibid., 1138, 1880, Appendix 107, 1923, Appendix 108, 1604, 1158.

49. Ibid., 1904.

50. Ibid., 945, Appendix 212, 944, Appendix 67, 1904, Appendix 172.

51. Ibid., Appendix, 244–246, 249.

52. Ibid., 1655, Appendix 166–167.

53. Ibid., 2358, 2304, 1797, 1881, 1783.

54. Ibid., 1903, 1896.

55. *CW*, 5:330.

3. A New Departure

1. *Congressional Globe*, 37th Congress, 2nd Session, 1918 (hereafter *CG*).

2. Ibid., 1181, 1897–1898, Appendix 114, 1237, 1875.

3. Leonard P. Curry, *Blueprint for Modern America* (Nashville: Vanderbilt University Press, 1968), pp. 68–70, 88–89.

4. John Murray Forbes, *Letters and Recollections of John Murray Forbes*, ed. Sarah Forbes Hughes, 2 vols. (Boston: Houghton Mifflin, 1899), 1: 315, 318.

5. *CG,* 37th Congress, 2nd Session, 2274.

6. Abraham Lincoln, *The Collected Works of Abraham Lincoln,* ed. Roy P. Basler, 9 vols. (New Brunswick: Rutgers University Press, 1953–1955), 5:278 (hereafter cited as *CW*).

7. *Liberator,* July 4, 1862; July 25, 1862.

8. Orville H. Browning, *The Diary of Orville Hickman Browning,* vol. 1, ed. Theodore Calvin Pease and James G. Randall (Springfield: Illinois State Historical Library, 1925), p. 355.

9. Charles Sumner, *The Selected Letters of Charles Sumner,* ed. Beverly Wilson Palmer, 2 vols. (Boston: Northeastern University Press, 1990), 2:122, 115; David Herbert Donald, *Charles Sumner and the Rights of Man* (New York: Random House, 1970), p. 60.

10. *CW,* 5:184–185.

11. Daniel H. Hill, quoted in Grady McWhiney and Perry Jamieson, *Attack and Die: Civil War Military Tactics and the Southern Heritage* (Tuscaloosa: University of Alabama Press, 1984), p. 4.

12. Browning, *Diary,* p. 556; Jeffrey D. Wert, *Army of the Potomac* (New York: Simon and Schuster, 2005), pp. 126–127.

13. McClellan to AL, July 7, 1862, in Abraham Lincoln Papers, Library of Congress (hereafter ALP).

14. David Herbert Donald, *Lincoln* (New York: Simon and Schuster, 1995), p. 359.

15. Gideon Welles, *Diary of Gideon Welles,* ed. Howard K. Beale, 2 vols. (New York: W. W. Norton, 1960), 1:71.

16. George Templeton Strong, *Diary of the Civil War: George Templeton Strong,* ed. Allen Nevins (New York: MacMillan, 1962), p. 239; Salmon P. Chase, *The Salmon P. Chase Papers,* vol. 3: *Correspondence,* ed. John Niven (Kent, OH: Kent State University Press, 1993), p. 229.

17. Adam Gurowski, *Diary from March 4, 1861, to November 12, 1862* (Boston: Lee and Shepard, 1862), 106, 148, 180, 191, 211.

18. Strong, *Diary of the Civil War,* pp. 244, 246, 256.

19. *CW,* 5:317–319.

20. Border-State Congressmen to AL, July 14, 1862; and Border-State Congressmen to AL, July 15, 1862. Both in ALP.

21. Welles, *Diary,* pp. 70–77; and Gideon Welles, "The History of Emancipation," *Galaxy* 14 (December 1872), pp. 838–851. For an account of the various recollections of when Lincoln may have decided on emancipation, see Matthew Pinsker, "Lincoln's Summer of Emancipation," in Harold Holzer and Sara Vaughn Gabbard, eds., *Lincoln and Freedom: Slavery, Emancipation and the Fifteenth Amendment* (Carbondale: Southern Illinois University Press, 2007), pp. 79–99.

22. Welles, *Diary,* 1:70–77.

23. *New York Times,* July 17, 1862.

24. Browning, *Diary,* 1:558.

25. Ibid., 1:558–559.

26. See Michael Burlingame, *Abraham Lincoln: A Life,* 2 vols. (Baltimore: Johns Hopkins University Press, 2008), 1:359.

27. *CW,* 5:328–331.

28. *CG,* 37th Congress, 2nd Session, 2972, Appendix 122.

29. Ibid., 3198, 3204, 3206, 3235, 3251. For a history of the confiscation acts, see Silvana R. Siddali, *From Property to Person: Slavery and the Confiscation Acts, 1861–62* (Baton Rouge: Louisiana State University Press, 2005).

30. Horace Binney, *The Life of Horace Binney,* ed. Charles Chauncey Binney (Philadelphia: J. B. Lippincott, 1903), p. 358.

4. Movement

1. Salmon P. Chase, *The Salmon P. Chase Papers,* vol. 3: *Correspondence,* ed. John Niven (Kent, OH: Kent State University Press, 1993), 3:231; John Hay, *At Lincoln's Side: John Hay's Civil War Correspondence and Selected Writings,* ed. Michael Burlingame (Carbondale: Southern Illinois University Press, 2000), p. 23; Charles Eliot Norton, *Letters of Charles Eliot Norton* (Boston: Houghton Mifflin, 1913), p. 255.

2. Chase, *Papers,* vol. 1: *Journals,* pp. 348–352.

3. *Liberator,* August 8, 1862.

4. Chase, *Journals,* 1:351.

5. F. B. Carpenter, *Six Months at the White House with Abraham Lincoln: The Story of a Picture* (New York: Hurd and Houghton, 1866), pp. 20–21.

6. Gideon Welles, "The History of Emancipation," *Galaxy* 14 (December 1872), pp. 838–851.

7. Abraham Lincoln, *The Collected Works of Abraham Lincoln,* ed. Roy P. Basler, 9 vols. (New Brunswick: Rutgers University Press, 1953–1955), 5:336–337 (hereafter *CW*).

8. Chase, *Journals,* 1:351; "An Interesting Leaf of History—How the Emancipation Proclamation Was Written," *Brooklyn Eagle,* June 21, 1865; Welles, "History of Emancipation," p. 845. Welles's comment that Bates's views were also Lincoln's must be taken with some skepticism. Lincoln clearly was opposed to compulsory colonization, and Welles was writing more than ten years after the meeting.

9. Welles, "History of Emancipation," pp. 838–851.

10. Francis Cutting to Edwin Stanton, February 20, 1869, in Stanton Papers, Library of Congress.

11. Ibid.

12. James Speed to AL, July 28, 1862, in Abraham Lincoln Papers, Library of Congress (hereafter ALP).

13. *CW,* 5:342–346, 350–351; Asa Gray, *Letters of Asa Gray,* ed. Jane Loring Gray, 2 vols. (Boston: Houghton Mifflin, 1894), 2:487.

14. Leonard Swett to Laura Swett, August 10, 1862, quoted in David Herbert Donald, *Lincoln* (New York: Simon and Schuster, 1995), p. 366.

15. Benjamin Bannen to AL, July 24, 1862, in ALP.

16. Adam Gurowski, *Diary from March 4, 1861, to November 12, 1862* (Boston: Lee and Shepard, 1862), p. 245.

17. Thurlow Weed, *Memoir of Thurlow Weed,* ed. Thurlow Weed Barnes (Boston: Houghton Mifflin, 1884), p. 230; Donn Piatt, *Memories of the Men Who Saved the Union* (New York: Belford, Clarke, 1887), pp. 150–151; Donald, *Lincoln,* p. 91.

18. Francis Cutting to Edwin Stanton, February 20, 1869, in Stanton Papers, Library of Congress; Charles Sumner, *The Selected Letters of Charles Sumner,* ed. Beverly Wilson Palmer, 2 vols. (Boston: Northeastern University Press, 1990), 2:131.

19. Donald, *Lincoln,* p. 239; *New York Times,* January 4, 1862; *CW,* 5:169; Gideon Welles, *Diary of Gideon Welles,* ed. Howard K. Beale, 2 vols. (New York: W. W. Norton), 2:112.

20. *CW,* 5:388–389.

21. Thurlow Weed to AL, August 24, 1862, and Sydney Gay to AL, August 1862, in ALP; Allen C. Guelzo, *Lincoln's Emancipation Proclamation: The End of Slavery in America* (New York: Simon and Schuster, 2004), p. 151; Gurowski, *Diary,* p. 252; *Liberator,* September 12, 1862.

22. *CW,* 5:534. See Eric Foner, "Lincoln and Colonization," in *Our Lincoln: New Perspectives on Lincoln and His World,* ed. Eric Foner (New York: W. W. Norton, 2008), pp. 135–166; and Phillip W. Magness and Sebastian N. Page, *Colonization after Emancipation: Lincoln and the Movement for Black Resettlement* (Columbia: University of Missouri Press, 2011).

23. *CW,* 5:370–375. See Kate Masur, "The African American Delegation to Abraham Lincoln: A Reappraisal," *Civil War History* 56 (June 2010), 117–144.

24. *Liberator,* August 29, 1862; N. H. Eggleston, "Emancipation," *New Englander and Yale Review* 21 (October 1862), 811; Gurowski, *Diary,* p. 251; Chase, *Journals,* 1:362.

25. *Liberator,* August 29, 1862.

26. *Douglass' Monthly,* September 1862.

27. *Forney's War Press,* August 23, 1862.

28. Frederick Douglass, "Fighting the Rebels with One Hand: An Address Delivered in Philadelphia, Pennsylvania, on January 14, 1862," *The Frederick Douglass Papers, Series One: Speeches, Debates and Interviews,* ed. John W. Blassingame, 5 vols. (New Haven: Yale University Press, 1985), 3:482–483.

29. Simon Cameron, quoted in James M. McPherson, *Battle Cry of Freedom* (New York: Oxford University Press, 1988), p. 357; Stanton to Saxton, August 25, 1862, in *War of the Rebellion: A Compilation of the Official Records of the Union and Confeder-*

ate Armies (Washington, DC: Government Printing Office, 1880–1901), Series 1, vol. 14, pp. 377–378.

30. Chase, *Journals,* 1:351; *CW,* 5:357; Whitelaw Reid, *A Radical View: The "Agate" Dispatches of Whitelaw Reid, 1861–1865,* ed. James G. Smart, 2 vols. (Memphis: Memphis State University Press, 1976), 2:75.

31. *Army Life of an Illinois Soldier* (Washington: Globe Printing, 1906), p. 125; Edward L. Pierce, *Memoir and Letters of Charles Sumner,* 4 vols. (Boston: Roberts Brothers, 1894), 4:84.

32. James M. McPherson, *Crossroads of Freedom: Antietam* (New York: Oxford University Press, 2002), pp. 85, 86; Donald, *Lincoln,* p. 372; Welles, *Diary,* 1:131.

33. *CW,* 5:403–404.

34. Ibid., 419–425.

35. Hay, *At Lincoln's Side,* p. 127.

36. John McClure, *Hoosier Farm Boy in Lincoln's Army: The Civil War Letters of Pvt. John R. McClure,* ed. Nancy Niblack Baxter (privately printed, 1971), p. 40; William Child to his wife, n.d., in Andrew Carroll, ed., *War Letters* (New York: Washington Square Press, 2001), p. 76.

37. McPherson, *Crossroads of Freedom,* p. 135; Gurowski, *Diary,* p. 252.

38. Robert Dale Owen, *The Policy of Emancipation in Three Letters* (Philadelphia: Lippincott, 1863), p. 28. In the original letter to Lincoln, dated September 17, Owen miscalculated and wrote that the "25th of September approaches." He meant the 23rd, and the date was corrected for publication. Also see his letter to Chase of August 20, when he first brought up the expiration date of the president's Proclamation as to the Sixth Section of the Confiscation Act. Chase, *Correspondence,* 3:254–255. Horace Greeley also implored the president to act on the same date Owen originally specified. See "The 25th of September," in *Independent,* September 18, 1862.

39. Chase, *Correspondence,* 3:277.

40. John Hay, *Lincoln's Journalist: John Hay's Anonymous Writings for the Press, 1860–1864,* ed. Michael Burlingame (Carbondale: Southern Illinois University Press, 1998), p. 308.

41. Ibid., pp. 307–310.

5. Judgments

1. Gideon Welles, *Diary of Gideon Welles,* ed. Howard K. Beale, 2 vols. (New York: W. W. Norton, 1960), 1:147; Abraham Lincoln, *The Collected Works of Abraham Lincoln,* ed. Roy P. Basler, 9 vols. (New Brunswick: Rutgers University Press, 1953–1955), 5:438–439 (hereafter *CW*).

2. Whitelaw Reid, *A Radical View: The "Agate" Dispatches of Whitelaw Reid, 1861–1865,* ed. J. G. Smart, 2 vols. (Memphis: Memphis State University Press, 1976), 1:235–236.

3. John Hay, *Inside Lincoln's White House: The Complete Civil War Diary of John Hay,* ed. Michael Burlingame and John R. Turner Ettlinger (Carbondale: Southern Illinois University Press, 1997), p. 41; *CW,* 2:320–323. On the hundred days, see Roland C. McConnell, "From Preliminary to Final Emancipation Proclamation: The First Hundred Days," *Journal of Negro History* 48 (October 1963), pp. 260–276; John Hope Franklin, *The Emancipation Proclamation* (Garden City: Anchor Books, 1963), pp. 55–88; and Michael Burlingame, *Abraham Lincoln: A Life,* 2 vols. (Baltimore: Johns Hopkins University Press, 2008), 2:419–473.

4. "Occasional," in *Forney's War Press,* October 4, 1862.

5. *Daily Evening Bulletin,* October 15, 1862; *New York Tribune,* September 23, 1862; *Lowell Daily Citizen,* September 23, 1862; *Albany Evening Journal* and *New York Evening Post,* quoted in *Portland Daily Advertiser,* September 26, 1862; *New York Times,* September 23, 1862; *Philadelphia Press,* September 24, 1862.

6. *Peninsular News and Advertiser,* September 29, 1862; *Harper's Weekly,* October 11, 1862.

7. Abiel A. Livermore to AL, September 24, 1862; James W. Stone to AL, September 23, 1862; Benjamin Gratz Brown to AL, September 27, 1862; W. B. Lowry, H. Catlin, and J. F. Downing to AL, September 23, 1862; George Cassara to AL, September 25, 1862. All in Abraham Lincoln Papers, Library of Congress (hereafter ALP).

8. AL to Hannibal Hamlin, September 28, 1862, in *CW,* 5:444.

9. *Letters of a Family during the War for the Union, 1861–1865* (privately printed, 1899), p. 484.

10. Charles Eliot Norton, *Letters of Charles Eliot Norton,* 2 vols. (Boston: Houghton Mifflin, 1913), 1:256–257.

11. William Furness, *A Word of Consolation for the Kindred of Those Who Have Fallen in Battle* (Philadelphia: Crissy and Markley, 1862), pp. 8–9.

12. *North American,* September 24, 1862.

13. *New York World* and *Journal of Commerce,* quoted in *Baltimore Sun,* September 24, 1862; *Boston Post,* quoted in *Portland Daily Advertiser,* September 25, 1862.

14. *Boston Journal,* quoted in *Liberator,* November 14, 1862.

15. *New York World,* September 24, 1862; *New York Herald,* quoted in *Baltimore Sun,* September 24, 1862; *Harrisburg Weekly Patriot,* September 25, 1862; *Louisville Journal,* quoted in Cleveland *Plain Dealer,* September 29, 1862; *Springfield Register,* quoted in *San Francisco Bulletin,* October 22, 1862.

16. *Liberator,* November 14, 1862.

17. *Daily Evening Bulletin,* October 20, 1862; also see Charles Sumner to John Bright, October 28, 1862, in Charles Sumner, *The Selected Letters of Charles Sumner,* ed. Beverly Wilson Palmer, 2 vols. (Boston: Northeastern University Press, 1990), 2:127–128; Welles, *Diary,* 1:158.

18. C. C. Hazewell, "The Hour and the Man," *Atlantic* 10 (November 1862), p. 632.

19. *New York Times,* October 5, 1862; *Boston Journal,* September 25, 1862; *New York Times,* October 7, 1862.

20. *Boston Herald,* quoted in *Liberator,* October 3, 1862; *Richmond Enquirer,* October 17, 1862.

21. Quoted in Gary Gallagher, *Lee and His Army in Confederate History* (Chapel Hill: University of North Carolina Press, 2001), pp. 13, 19–20.

22. *New York Times,* September 27, 1862. Also see William B. Hesseltine and Hazel C. Wolf, "The Altoona Conference and the 'Emancipation Proclamation,'" *Pennsylvania Magazine of History and Biography* 71 (July 1947), pp. 195–205.

23. James M. McKim to AL, September 27, 1862, ALP; *The Independent,* December 25, 1862; Madeleine Vinton Dahlgren, *Memoir of the Life of John A. Dahlgren* (Boston: James R. Osgood, 1882), p. 380; Albert G. Browne, *Sketch of the Official Life of John A. Andrew* (New York: Hurd and Houghton, 1868) p. 74; *Independent,* September 25, 1862.

24. Harriet Beecher Stowe, *Life and Letters of Harriet Beecher Stowe,* ed. Annie Fields (Boston: Houghton Mifflin, 1897), pp. 262, 269. See Wendy F. Hamand, "'No Voice from England': Mrs. Stowe, Mr. Lincoln, and the British in the Civil War," *New England Quarterly* 61 (March 1988), pp. 3–24.

25. Harriet Beecher Stowe, *A Reply* (London: Sampson, Low, 1863), pp. 45–47.

26. William Lloyd Garrison to Fanny Garrison, September 25, 1862, in *The Letters of William Lloyd Garrison,* ed. Walter M. Merrill, 6 vols. (Cambridge, MA: Harvard University Press, 1979), 5:114–115.

27. Orestes Brownson, "The President's Policy," in *The Works of Orestes Brownson,* ed. Henry Brownson, 20 vols. (New York: Arno Press, 1966), 17:389; N. H. Eddleston, "Emancipation," *New Englander and Yale Review* 21 (October 1862), p. 818.

28. Horace Greeley, "Aurora," *Continental Monthly* 2 (November 1862), pp. 623–624.

29. "Emancipation Proclaimed," *Douglass' Monthly,* October 1862.

30. Charles Francis Adams, Jr., *Richard Henry Dana,* 2 vols. (New York: Chelsea House, 1983), 2:263.

31. Lydia Maria Child to Mrs. S. B. Shaw, 1863, in *Letters of Lydia Maria Child* (Boston: Houghton Mifflin, 1883), p. 171.

32. Adam Gurowski, *Diary from March 4, 1861, to November 12, 1862* (Boston: Lee and Shepard, 1862), pp. 277–278.

33. Karl Marx to Friedrich Engels, October 29, 1862, trans. anonymous, www.marxists.org/archive/marx/works/1862/letters/62_10_29.htm; *Die Presse* (Vienna), October 12, 1862, trans. anonymous, at www.marxists.org/archive/marx/works/1862/10/12.htm.

34. *Weekly Patriot and Union* (Harrisburg, Pennsylvania), quoted in *Liberator,* October 3, 1863 (General John W. Phelps had issued a proclamation condemning slavery); *Chicago Times* characterized in *Milwaukee Daily Sentinel,* September 25, 1862.

35. *New York Express,* quoted in *Portland Daily Advertiser,* September 26, 1862.

36. *Quincy Whig Republican* (Quincy, Illinois), October 4, 1862.

37. *Springfield Republican,* September 24, 1862.

38. Henry C. Knowlton to [Harlow Higginbotham], September 26, 1862, GLC05244, Gilder Lehrman Collection of American History, New-York Historical Society. "Hunky" meant fine or satisfactory.

6. The Reactions of Scholars and Soldiers

1. Isaac N. Morris to Abraham Lincoln, November 20, 1862, in Abraham Lincoln Papers, Library of Congress (hereafter ALP).

2. Gideon Welles, *Diary of Gideon Welles,* ed. Howard K. Beale, 2 vols. (New York: W. W. Norton, 1960), 1:150.

3. James Brooks, *The Two Proclamations: Speech of Hon. James Brooks, before the Democratic Union Association,* September 29, 1862, p. 6; *New York Weekly Caucasian,* October 4, 1862.

4. *Albany Atlas & Argus,* December 27, 1862.

5. Benjamin R. Curtis, *Executive Power* (Boston: Little, Brown, 1862), pp. 14, 28. Also see Joel Parker, *Constitutional Law and Unconstitutional Divinity* (Cambridge: H. O. Houghton, 1863); and the response by Leonard Bacon, "Reply to Professor Parker," *New Englander and Yale Review* 22 (April 1863), pp. 191–259. Joel Parker further developed his argument on the unconstitutionality of the Emancipation Proclamation in his book *The War Powers of Congress, and of the President* (Cambridge: H. O. Houghton, 1863).

6. Curtis, *Executive Power,* pp. 18, 21.

7. Theophilus Parsons, letter to *Boston Daily Advertiser,* reprinted in *Christian Inquirer,* December 27, 1862; *New York Times,* September 30, 1862.

8. Libertas [Charles Mayo Ellis], *The Power of the Commander-in-Chief to Declare Martial Law and Decree Emancipation, as Shown by B. R. Curtis* (Boston: A. Williams, 1862), pp. 5–6, 10, 13.

9. Grosvenor P. Lowrey, *The Commander-in-Chief: A Defence upon Legal Grounds of the Proclamation of Emancipation, and an Answer to Ex-Judge Curtis' Pamphlet, Entitled "Executive Power"* (New York: G. P. Putnam, 1862), pp. 9, 13, 16, 20.

10. Charles P. Kirkland, *A Letter to Benjamin R. Curtis* (New York: Latimer Bros. and Seymour, 1862), pp. 3, 9.

11. Ibid., pp. 13, 15–16.

12. John C. Gray and John C. Ropes, *War Letters, 1862–1865, of John Chipman Gray and John Codman Ropes,* ed. Worthington Chauncey Ford (Boston: Houghton Mifflin, 1927), pp. 72–73; N. H. Eggleston, "Emancipation," *New Englander and Yale Review* 21 (October 1862), p. 787.

13. Curtis, *Executive Power,* p. 16.

14. Kirkland, *Letter to Curtis,* pp. 15–16; Lowrey, *Commander-in-Chief,* pp. 25–26.

15. Charles A. Dana to William H. Seward, September 23, 1862, ALP.

16. *Harrisburg Weekly Patriot and Union,* quoted in *Liberator,* October 3, 1862; *Richmond Whig,* quoted in *Saturday Evening Post,* October 11, 1862; *Charleston Daily Courier,* October 3, 1862; *Southern Illustrated News,* November 8, 1862.

17. *Richmond Whig,* September 30, 1862.

18. *Christian Recorder,* October 25, 1862; Charles Sumner, *Emancipation! Its Policy and Necessity as a War Measure for the Suppression of the Rebellion* (Boston: n.p., 1862), p. 17.

19. *Speech of Richard Busteed, Delivered at Faneuil Hall, Boston, October 31, 1862* (New York: Westcott, 1862), p. 21.

20. Adam Gurowski, *Diary from March 4, 1861, to November 12, 1862* (Boston: Lee and Shepard, 1862), p. 299.

21. Sumner, *Emancipation!* p. 14; *Wisconsin Patriot,* December 6, 1862.

22. Salmon P. Chase, *The Salmon P. Chase Papers,* vol. 1: *Journals, 1829–1872,* ed. John Niven (Kent, OH: Kent State University Press, 1993), p. 399; Gideon Welles, "The History of Emancipation," *Galaxy* 14 (December 1872), pp. 844–855; *Liberator,* November 19, 1862.

23. On the Chiriqui plan, see Paul T. Scheips, "Lincoln and the Chiriqui Colonization Project," *Journal of Negro History* 37 (October 1952), pp. 418–453. Also see Eric Foner, "Lincoln and Colonization," in Eric Foner, ed., *Our Lincoln: New Perspectives on Lincoln and His World* (New York: W. W. Norton, 2008), pp. 135–166.

24. *New York Times,* October 3, 1862.

25. Sumner, *Emancipation!* pp. 2, 3, 16.

26. Thomas T. Ellis, *Leaves from the Diary of an Army Surgeon* (New York: John Bradburn, 1863), pp. 306–307; James M. McPherson, *Tried by War: Abraham Lincoln as Commander in Chief* (New York: Penguin, 2008), p. 133. William C. Davis, *Lincoln's Men: How President Lincoln Became Father to an Army and a Nation* (New York: Free Press, 1999), pp. 88–108.

27. *New York Herald,* October 7, 1862.

28. *Charleston Mercury,* October 14, 1862.

29. McPherson, *Tried by War,* p. 134; Gurowski, *Diary,* p. 295.

30. Allen C. Guelzo, *Lincoln's Emancipation Proclamation: The End of Slavery in America* (New York: Simon and Schuster, 2004), p. 185; Oliver Willcox Norton, *Army Letters* (privately printed, 1903), p. 101; Charles Fessenden Morse, *Letters Written during the Civil War, 1861–1865* (privately printed, 1898), p. 96.

31. Morse, *Letters,* p. 98.

32. *New York Tribune,* September 30, 1862; *Boston Journal,* quoted in *Tribune,* September 30, 1862.

33. *New York Times,* September 29, 1862; Civil War Diary of Sergeant Henry Tisdale, www.civilwardiary.net/.

34. *Chicago Tribune,* October 16, 1862; John Quincy Adams Campbell, *The Union Must Stand: The Civil War Diary of John Quincy Adams Campbell, Fifth Iowa Volunteer Infantry,* ed. Mark Grimsley and Todd D. Miller (Knoxville: University of Tennessee Press, 2000), p. 63; John P. Jones to his wife, October 3, 1863, GLC05981.09, Gilder-Lehrman Collection, New-York Historical Society; Frederick Wilkinson to his wife, October 4, 1862, GLC3523.13.059, Gilder-Lehrman Collection; Levi Hines to parents, September 26, 1862, Levi Hines Papers, Schoff Civil War Collection, Clements Library, University of Michigan.

The majority of manuscript letters cited in this section come from the research compiled by Chandra Manning for her exhaustive study *What This Cruel War Was Over: Soldiers, Slavery, and the Civil War* (New York: Vintage, 2007). Professor Manning shared with me her unpublished research on soldiers and the Emancipation Proclamation. I am deeply indebted to her for her generosity.

See also David Wallace Adams, "Illinois Soldiers and the Emancipation Proclamation," *Journal of the Illinois State Historical Society* 67 (September 1974), p. 413; James M. McPherson, *For Cause and Comrades: Why Men Fought in the Civil War* (New York: Oxford University Press, 1997), pp. 117–130; and William C. Davis, *Lincoln's Men: How President Lincoln Became Father to an Army and a Nation* (New York: Free Press, 1999), pp. 88–108.

35. *Liberator,* December 5, 1862; Manning, *What This Cruel War Was Over,* p. 89; Campbell, *The Union Must Stand,* p. 61; Roland E. Bowen, *From Ball's Bluff to Gettysburg: The Civil War Letters of Private Roland E. Bowen,* ed. Gregory A. Coco (Gettysburg: Thomas, 1994), p. 136; Allan Nevins, *The War for the Union,* vol. 2: *War Becomes Revolution, 1862–1863* (New York: Scribner's, 1960), p. 239.

36. Charles W. Wills, *Army Life of an Illinois Soldier* (Washington: Globe Printing, 1906), p. 150; Jasper Barney to John Dinsmore, October 24, 1862, John C. Dinsmore Letters, Illinois State Historical Society; Michael Gapen, December 7, 1862, Michael Gapen Letters, Chicago Historical Society.

37. Simon P. Newman, "A Democrat in Lincoln's Army: The Civil War Letters of Henry P. Hubbell," *Princeton University Library Chronicle* 50 (Winter 1989), p. 161; McPherson, *For Cause and Comrades,* pp. 120–121; Adams, "Illinois Soldiers," p. 420.

38. Norman C. Delaney, ed., "Letters of a Maine Soldier Boy," *Civil War History* 5 (March 1959), pp. 54–55.

39. William Ross to father, November 2, 1862, William H. Ross letters, Chicago Historical Society; Robert Stoddart Robertson, quoted in Jeffry Wert, *The Sword of Lincoln: The Army of the Potomac* (New York: Simon and Schuster, 2005), p. 176; John W. Chase, *Yours for the Union: The Civil War Letters of John W. Chase, First Massachusetts Light*

Artillery, ed. John S. Collier and Bonnie B. Collier (New York: Fordham University Press, 2004), pp. 156–157; Norton, *Army Letters,* p. 125.

40. Norton, *Army Letters,* pp. 43, 88, 102.

41. Charles B. Haydon, *For Country, Cause and Leader: The Civil War Journals of Charles B. Haydon,* ed. Stephen Sears (New York: Houghton Mifflin, 1993), p. 291; Wilder Dwight, *Life and Letters of Wilder Dwight* (Boston: Ticknor and Fields, 1868), p. 55; Adams, "Illinois Soldiers," p. 416.

42. Norton, *Army Letters,* p. 79; Dwight, *Life and Letters,* pp. 205, 240.

43. S. F. Fleharty, *Jottings from Dixie: The Civil War Dispatches of Sergeant Major Stephen Fleharty, USA,* ed. Philip J. Reyburn and Terry L. Wilson (Baton Rouge: Louisiana State University Press, 1999), 90–91; Joseph Richardson Ward, *An Enlisted Soldier's View of the Civil War: The Wartime Papers of Joseph Richardson Ward, Jr.,* ed. D. Duane Cummins and Daryl Hohweiler (West Lafayette: Belle Publications, 1981), p. 40; Moncure Conway's views in Oliver Wendell Holmes, Sr., to John Lothrop Motley, February 3, 1862, in *The Correspondence of John L. Motley,* ed. George William Curtis, 2 vols. (London: John Murray, 1889), 2:57–58; Louis Hughes, *Thirty Years a Slave: From Bondage to Freedom: The Institution of Slavery as Seen on the Plantation and in the Home of the Planter* (Milwaukee: South Side Printing Company, 1897), p. 117; *Douglass' Monthly,* November 1862.

44. Hughes, *Thirty Years a Slave,* p. 155.

45. Manning, *What This Cruel War Was Over,* p. 106; McPherson, *For Cause and Comrades,* pp. 107–108.

46. George Tillotson's letter is included in Robert E. Bonner, *The Soldier's Pen: Firsthand Impressions of the Civil War* (New York: Hill and Wang, 2006), p. 116; Robert Gould Shaw, *Blue-Eyed Child of Fortune: The Civil War Letters of Colonel Robert Gould Shaw,* ed. Russell Duncan (Athens: University of Georgia Press, 1992), pp. 245, 252.

47. Edward Edes to his mother, September 25, 1862, Edward Edes Correspondence, Massachusetts Historical Society; Jacob Behm to his sister and brother-in-law, October 1, 1862, Jacob Behm Correspondence, U.S. Army Military History Institute, Carlisle, PA; Adams, "Illinois Soldiers," p. 418.

7. Intervention and Election Fever

1. Adam Gurowski, *Diary from March 4, 1861, to November 12, 1862* (Boston: Lee and Shepard, 1862), p. 233.

2. Charles Sumner to Sydney Howard Gay, [July 26, 1862], in Charles Sumner, *The Selected Letters of Charles Sumner,* ed. Beverly Wilson Palmer, 2 vols. (Boston: Northeastern University Press, 1990), 2:120–121.

3. Howard Jones, *Union in Peril: The Crisis over British Intervention in the Civil War* (Chapel Hill: University of North Carolina Press, 1992), p. 84.

4. John L. Motley, *The Correspondence of John L. Motley,* ed. George William Curtis, 2 vols. (London: John Murray, 1889), 2:67, 1:373.

5. Ibid., 1:382, 394, 387, 390, 383.

6. Ibid., 1:35, 46, 54, 64–65.

7. Kinley J. Brauer, "The Slavery Problem in the Diplomacy of the American Civil War," *Pacific Historical Review* 46 (August 1977), p. 448; Worthington Chauncey Ford, ed., *A Cycle of Adams Letters, 1861–1865,* 2 vols. (Boston: Houghton Mifflin, 1920), 1:150.

8. Motley, *Correspondence,* 2:78, 80.

9. Ford, *Cycle of Adams Letters,* 1:190.

10. Motley, *Correspondence,* 2:81, 91.

11. Brauer, "Slavery Problem," p. 452.

12. Abraham Lincoln, *The Collected Works of Abraham Lincoln,* ed. Roy P. Basler, 9 vols. (New Brunswick: Rutgers University Press, 1953–1955), 5:422 (hereafter cited as *CW*).

13. *New York Tribune,* October 28, 1862.

14. James M. McPherson, *For Cause and Comrades: Why Men Fought in the Civil War* (New York: Oxford University Press, 1997), p. 122; *Lowell Daily Citizen,* September 24, 1862; *Douglass' Monthly,* October 1862.

15. Howard Jones, *Abraham Lincoln and a New Birth of Freedom* (Lincoln: University of Nebraska Press, 1999), p. 94; *New York Times,* October 22, 1862.

16. *Guardian,* October 7, 1862.

17. John Hope Franklin, *The Emancipation Proclamation* (Garden City: Anchor Books, 1963), p. 67; Brauer, "Slavery Problem," p. 463; Jones, *Abraham Lincoln,* p. 119.

18. For a thorough account of internal British politics and the question of intervention, see Amanda Foreman, *A World on Fire: The Epic History of Two Nations Divided* (London: Allen Lane, 2010); quote from Gladstone, p. 319.

19. *London Times,* October 7, 1862.

20. Keith Wilson, "'The Beginning of the End': An Analysis of British Newspaper Coverage of Lincoln's Emancipation Proclamation," *Journalism History* 34 (Winter 2009), p. 234; Franklin, *Emancipation Proclamation,* p. 71.

21. Wilson, "'Beginning of the End,'" p. 233; Howard Jones, *Blue and Gray Diplomacy: A History of Union and Confederate Foreign Relations* (Chapel Hill: University of North Carolina Press, 2010), p. 232; *Raleigh Register,* October 1, 1862.

22. Gurowski, *Diary,* p. 292.

23. Motley, *Correspondence,* 2:101–102.

24. Ford, *Cycle of Adams Letters,* 1:192; Joseph M. Hernon, Jr., "British Sympathies in the American Civil War: A Reconsideration," *Journal of Southern History* 33 (1967), p. 359.

25. Henry Adams, *The Education of Henry Adams* (New York: Library of America, 1983), p. 867.

26. *Brooklyn Eagle,* June 21, 1865; John Sherman to Salmon P. Chase, September 28, 1862, in Salmon P. Chase, *The Salmon P. Chase Papers,* vol. 3: *Correspondence,* ed. John Niven (Kent, OH: Kent State University Press, 1993), p. 287.

27. *Saturday Evening Post,* November 15, 1862; Francis P. Blair to Abraham Lincoln, November 14, 1862, Abraham Lincoln Papers, Library of Congress (hereafter ALP); Chase, *Correspondence,* 3:316.

28. John G. Nicolay, *With Lincoln in the White House: Letters, Memoranda, and Other Writings of John G. Nicolay, 1860–1865,* ed. Michael Burlingame (Carbondale: Southern Illinois University Press, 2000), p. 89.

29. See Allan Nevins, *The War for the Union,* vol. 2: *The War Becomes Revolution, 1862–1863* (New York: Scribner's, 1960), p. 319; and James M. McPherson, *Battle Cry of Freedom* (New York: Oxford University Press, 1988), pp. 561–562.

30. Motley, *Correspondence,* 2:101; Gurowski, *Diary,* p. 312.

31. Gurowski, *Diary,* p. 300.

32. Hezekiah S. Bundy to Salmon P. Chase, October 3, 1862, in Salmon P. Chase Papers, microfilm edition, reel 23, series 1. I am indebted to Professor Michael Vorenberg for bringing this letter to my attention.

33. Bruce Tap, "Race, Rhetoric, and Emancipation: The Election of 1862 in Illinois," *Civil War History* 39 (1993), pp. 102–125; McPherson, *Battle Cry of Freedom,* p. 560. Also see V. Jacques Voegeli, *Free but Not Equal: The Midwest and the Negro during the Civil War* (Chicago: University of Chicago Press, 1967). On Northern Democrats generally, see Jennifer L. Weber, *Copperheads: The Rise and Fall of Lincoln's Opponents in the North* (New York: Oxford University Press, 2006); Joel H. Sibley, *A Respectable Minority: The Democratic Party in the Civil War Era, 1860–1868* (New York: Norton, 1977); Jean H. Baker, *Affairs of Party: The Political Culture of Northern Democrats in the Mid-Nineteenth Century* (Ithaca: Cornell University Press, 1983).

34. "The Constitution as It Is—the Union as It Was," *Continental Monthly* 2 (October 1862), 377–383.

35. Adelaide E. Case to Charles N. Tenney, November 9, 1862, Electronic Text Center, University of Virginia Library.

36. Tap, "Race, Rhetoric, and Emancipation," pp. 111, 114; David Herbert Donald, *Lincoln* (New York: Simon and Schuster, 1995), p. 382.

37. *CW,* 5:474; James K. Moorhead to AL, October 24, 1862, ALP; James M. McPherson, *Crossroads of Freedom: Antietam* (New York: Oxford University Press, 2002), p. 150; *North American,* November 5, 1862.

38. Horace White to Abraham Lincoln, October 22, 1862, ALP; *Independent,* October 23, 1862.

39. *New York Tribune,* November 1, 1862.

40. Sidney David Brummer, *Political History of New York State during the Period of the Civil War* (New York, 1911), pp. 231–232; Gideon Welles, *Diary of Gideon Welles,* ed. Howard K. Beale, 2 vols. (New York: W. W. Norton, 1960), 1:154.

41. Brummer, *Political History,* pp. 239–240, 252; *Chicago Evening Journal,* November 15, 1862.

42. Chase to Richard C. Parson, October 31, 1862, Chase, *Correspondence,* 3:311; Chase to Charles Sumner, November 9, 1862, Chase, *Correspondence,* 3:314.

43. J. B. Jones, *A Rebel War Clerk's Diary* (Philadelphia: J. B. Lippincott, 1866), 1:185; *Charleston Mercury,* November 5, 1862.

44. *Charleston Mercury,* November 8 and November 10, 1862.

45. *Congressional Globe,* 37th Congress, 3rd Session, pp. 94–100 (hereafter *CG*); *CG,* 37th Congress, 3rd Session, Appendix, p. 39.

46. *New York Herald,* October 19, 1862; *New York Evening Post,* November 7, 1862; *Illinois Daily State Journal,* November 29, 1862; Owner, quoted in Allen C. Guelzo, *Lincoln's Emancipation Proclamation: The End of Slavery in America* (New York: Simon and Schuster, 2004), p. 190. Mark Neely, Jr., argues that Northern Democrats misread the results as signs of war weariness whereas they were actually a sign of being "defeat-weary." See Mark E. Neely, Jr., "The Constitution and Civil Liberties under Lincoln," in *Our Lincoln: New Perspectives on Lincoln and His World,* ed. Eric Foner (New York: W. W. Norton, 2008), pp. 48–49.

47. *New York Times,* November 7, 1862; Isaac N. Morris to AL, November 20, 1862, ALP.

48. Isaac N. Morris to AL, November 20, 1862, ALP.

49. Orville Hickman Browning, *The Diary of Orville Hickman Browning,* vol. 1, ed. Theodore Calvin Pease and James G. Randall (Springfield: Illinois State Historical Library, 1925), pp. 588–589.

50. Mark Krug, "Lincoln: The Republican Party and the Emancipation Proclamation," *History Teacher* 7 (November 1973), p. 60.

51. Francis Springer to Hawkins Taylor, October 19, 1862, ALP.

52. David D. Field to AL, November 8, 1862, ALP.

53. John Cochrane to AL, November 5, 1862, ALP; John C. Gray and John C. Ropes, *War Letters, 1862–1865, of John Chipman Gray and John Codman Ropes,* ed. Worthington Chauncey Ford (Boston: Houghton Mifflin, 1927), p. 19; George Templeton Strong, *Diary of the Civil War: George Templeton Strong,* ed. Allan Nevins (New York: MacMillan, 1962), pp. 268, 272.

54. *CG,* 37th Congress, 3rd Session, p. 78; *Boston Evening Transcript,* October 20, 1862.

55. William T. Sherman, *The Sherman Letters,* ed. Rachel Sherman Thorndike (New York: Charles Scribner's Sons, 1894), pp. 167–168.

56. Carl Schurz to AL, November 8, 1862, ALP.

57. *CW,* 5:493–496.

58. Carl Schurz to AL, November 20, 1862, ALP; *CW,* 5:509–511.

59. Benjamin F. Butler, *Private and Official Correspondence of Gen. Benjamin F. Butler,* 5 vols. (privately issued, 1917), 2:534; Charles Sumner to John Bright, October 28, 1862, in Sumner, *Selected Letters,* 2:127; *North American,* October 25, 1862.

60. Karl Marx, [The Election Results in the Northern States], *Die Presse,* November 23, 1862, www.marxists.org/archive/marx/works/1862/11/23.htm.

61. Fessenden to J. M. Forbes, November 13, 1862, in John Murray Forbes, *Letters and Recollections of John Murray Forbes,* ed. Sarah Forbes Hughes, 2 vols. (Boston: Houghton Mifflin, 1899), 1:365; Sumner to John Bright, November 18, 1862, in Sumner, *Selected Letters,* 2:131.

62. Sumner to John Bright, October 28, 1862, in Sumner, *Selected Letters,* 2:127.

63. William G. Christie to James C. Christie, February 16, 1863, Minnesota Historical Society, www.mnhs.org/library/Christie/letters/0216631.html.

64. Noah Brooks, *Lincoln Observed: Civil War Dispatches of Noah Brooks,* ed. Michael Burlingame (Baltimore: Johns Hopkins University Press, 1998), p. 14.

65. Nicolay, *With Lincoln in the White House,* pp. 89–91; Gurowski, *Diary,* p. 313.

66. *Illinois Daily State Journal,* November 29, 1862; January 6, 1863.

67. *Independent,* November 13, 1862.

8. "We Cannot Escape History"

1. Charles Sumner to AL, November 8, 1862, in Charles Sumner, *The Selected Letters of Charles Sumner,* ed. Beverly Wilson Palmer, 2 vols. (Boston: Northeastern University Press, 1990), 2:130.

2. George Livermore, *An Historical Research Respecting the Opinions of the Founders of the Republic on Negroes as Slaves, as Citizens, and as Soldiers* (Boston: John Wiley and Son, 1862), pp. 21, 28, 53.

3. Ibid., pp. 114, 150, 170, 195.

4. *Opinion of Attorney General Bates on Citizenship* (Washington: Government Printing Office, 1863), pp. 7, 12.

5. Doris Kearns Goodwin, *Team of Rivals: The Political Genius of Abraham Lincoln* (New York: Simon and Schuster, 2005), p. 675; Eric Foner, *The Fiery Trial: Abraham Lincoln and American Slavery* (New York: W. W. Norton, 2010), p. 236.

6. Frederick Starr, Jr., *What Shall Be Done with the People of Color in the United States* (Albany: Weed, Parsons, 1862), pp. 17–18.

7. Samuel T. Spear, *The Nation's Blessing in Trial* (Brooklyn: W. W. Rose, 1862), pp. 26, 39.

8. Albert Barnes, *The Conditions of Peace* (Philadelphia: William B. Evans, 1863), pp. 19–20, 28.

9. See David Leverenz, *Manhood and the American Renaissance* (Ithaca: Cornell University Press, 1989); *Independent,* January 8, 1863. Also see "The Manhood of the Negro," *Liberator,* December 26, 1862.

10. Ralph Waldo Emerson, *The Journals and Miscellaneous Notebooks of Ralph Waldo Emerson,* vol. 15, *1860–1866,* ed. Linda Allardt and David W. Hill (Cambridge, MA: Harvard University Press, 1982), p. 299.

11. Emerson, *Journals,* pp. 187, 291; R. W. Emerson, "The President's Proclamation," *Atlantic Monthly* 10 (November 1862), pp. 638–642.

12. Abraham Lincoln, *The Collected Works of Abraham Lincoln,* ed. Roy P. Basler, 9 vols. (New Brunswick: Rutgers University Press, 1953–55), 5:503 (hereafter *CW*).

13. "Annual Message to Congress," December 1, 1862, in *CW,* 5:518–537.

14. Allen Thorndike Rice, *Reminiscences of Abraham Lincoln by Distinguished Men of His Time* (New York: North American Review, 1888), p. 62.

15. Charles Sumner to Wendell Phillips, December 4, 1862, in Sumner, *Selected Letters,* 2:133; Chase to AL, November 28, 1862, in Salmon P. Chase, *The Salmon P. Chase Papers,* vol. 3: *Correspondence,* ed. John Niven (Kent, OH: Kent State University Press, 1993), p. 320.

16. Adam Gurowski, *Diary from November 18, 1862, to October 18, 1863* (New York: Carleton, 1864), 2:22; *San Francisco Bulletin,* December 3, 1862; "The President's Message," *Douglass' Monthly,* January 1863.

17. Dawes to his wife, December 2, 1862, quoted in Michael Burlingame, *Abraham Lincoln: A Life,* 2 vols. (Baltimore: Johns Hopkins University Press, 2008), 2:441.

18. *New York Weekly Caucasian,* December 6, 1862.

19. *New York Times,* December 2, 1862; *New York Herald,* December 2, 1862; Oliver Willcox Norton, *Army Letters* (privately printed, 1903), p. 128; Daniel S. Dickinson, *Speeches, Correspondence, etc. of the Late Daniel S. Dickinson,* ed. John R. Dickinson, 2 vols. (New York: G. P. Putnam, 1867), 2:593.

20. *Boston Journal,* December 2 and December 4, 1862.

21. *Harper's Weekly,* December 13, 1862; Orestes Brownson, "The President's Policy," in *The Works of Orestes Brownson,* ed. Henry Brownson, 20 vols. (New York: Arno Press, 1966), 17:409; *Congressional Globe,* 37th Congress, 3rd Session, Appendix, p. 39 (hereafter *CG*).

22. Orville H. Browning, *The Diary of Orville Hickman Browning,* vol. 1, ed. Theodore Calvin Pease and James G. Randall (Springfield: Illinois State Historical Library, 1925), p. 591; *Liberator,* December 12, 1862; *CG,* 37th Congress, 3rd Session, Appendix, p. 79; *Vanity Fair,* February 1863.

23. Brownson, "President's Policy," pp. 392, 403.

24. *Independent,* December 4, 1862; Cleveland *Plain Dealer,* December 4, 1862.

25. *Liberator,* December 12, 1862.

26. *Chicago Tribune,* December 3, 1862.

27. *Charleston Mercury,* December 11, 1862; *Girard Union,* quoted in *Liberator,* December 19, 1862.

28. *Boston Daily Advertiser,* December 9, 1862; Sumner to Phillips, December 4, 1862, in Sumner, *Selected Letters,* 2:133.

29. *Independent,* December 4, 1862.

30. *Liberator,* December 12, 1862.

9. Standing Firm

1. *Speech of Hon. Geo. H. Yeaman of Kentucky on the President's Proclamation* (Baltimore: John Murphy, 1863), pp. 21, 30.

2. *Congressional Globe,* 37th Congress, 3rd Session, p. 148 (hereafter *CG*).

3. *CG,* 37th Congress, 3rd Session, pp. 77, 152; *Pacific Appeal,* December 20, 1862.

4. George Templeton Strong, *Diary of the Civil War: George Templeton Strong,* ed. Allen Nevins (New York: MacMillan, 1962), pp. 281–282; James M. McPherson, *Tried by War: Abraham Lincoln as Commander in Chief* (New York: Penguin Press, 2008), p. 145.

5. Parker's letter appeared in the *Boston Post* and is reprinted in Joel Parker, *Constitutional Law and Unconstitutional Divinity* (Cambridge, MA: H. O. Houghton, 1863), pp. 43–44; John C. Gray and John C. Ropes, *War Letters, 1862–1865, of John Chipman Gray and John Codman Ropes,* ed. Worthington Chauncey Ford (Boston: Houghton Mifflin, 1927), p. 50.

6. *The Independent,* December 25, 1862.

7. Gideon Welles, *Diary of Gideon Welles,* ed. Howard K. Beale, 2 vols. (New York: W. W. Norton, 1960), 1:198–199; Abraham Lincoln, *The Collected Works of Abraham Lincoln,* ed. Roy P. Basler, 9 vols. (New Brunswick, NJ: Rutgers University Press, 1953–1955), 5:600 (hereafter cited as *CW*); Orville H. Browning, *The Diary of Orville Hickman Browning,* vol. 1, ed. Theodore Calvin Pease and James G. Randall (Springfield: Illinois State Historical Library, 1925), p. 600.

8. Noah Brooks, *Mr. Lincoln's Washington: Selections from the Writing of Noah Brooks, Civil War Correspondent,* ed. P. J. Staudenraus (South Brunswick, NJ: A. S. Barnes, 1967), p. 29; *CW,* 6:16–17.

9. Leonard Curry, *Blueprint for Modern America* (Nashville: Vanderbilt University Press, 1968), pp. 48–52.

10. Edward Bates to AL, December 27, 1862, Abraham Lincoln Papers, Library of Congress (hereafter ALP); Welles, *Diary,* pp. 208–209; William Seward to AL, Decem-

ber 26, 1862, ALP; Salmon Chase to AL, December 29, 1862, ALP; Salmon P. Chase, *The Salmon P. Chase Papers,* vol. 3: *Correspondence,* ed. John Niven (Kent, OH: Kent State University Press, 1993), p. 346.

11. *CW,* 6:26–28. In *Virginia v. West Virginia* (1871), the Supreme Court implicitly ruled in favor of the constitutionality of the creation of the new state.

12. Harriet Beecher Stowe to Charles Sumner, December 12, 1862, Harriet Beecher Stowe Center Library, Hartford, CT; Strong, *Diary of the Civil War,* pp. 282–284; *Liberator,* December 26, 1862.

13. Samuel Du Pont, *Samuel Francis Du Pont: A Selection from His Civil War Letters,* ed. John D. Hayes, 2 vols. (Ithaca: Cornell University Press, 1969), 2:282, 318; *Independent,* December 25, 1862.

14. William L. Utley to AL, November 17, 1862, ALP.

15. George Robertson to AL, November 19, 1862, ALP; AL to Robertson, August 15, 1855, *CW,* 2:317–319.

16. AL to Robertson, November 20 and November 26, 1862, ALP.

17. Taylor Peirce, *Dear Catherine, Dear Taylor: The Civil War Letters of a Union Soldier and His Wife,* ed. Richard L. Kiper (Lawrence: University Press of Kansas, 2002), p. 62; Thomas Hawley to parents and siblings, December 10, 1862, Thomas S. Hawley Papers, Missouri Historical Society.

18. John Murray Forbes, *Letters and Recollections of John Murray Forbes,* ed. Sarah Forbes Hughes, 2 vols. (Boston: Houghton Mifflin, 1899), 1:344, 349; Browning, *Diary,* pp. 606–607.

19. *Commercial Advertiser,* December 26, 1862; *North American,* November 25, 1862.

20. *Chicago Tribune,* December 29, 1862.

21. John Forbes to Charles Sumner, December 27, 1862, ALP. An edited version of the letter appears in Forbes, *Letters and Recollections,* 1:349–350; John D. DeFrees to John G. Nicolay, December 17, 1862, in ALP.

22. Sumner to Forbes, December 28, 1862, in Charles Sumner, *The Selected Letters of Charles Sumner,* ed. Beverly Wilson Palmer, 2 vols. (Boston: Northeastern University Press, 1990), 2:135–136.

23. Sumner to AL, December 28, 1862, in ALP.

24. *Chicago Tribune,* December 20, 1862; S. F. Fleharty, *Jottings from Dixie: The Civil War Dispatches of Sergeant Major Stephen Fleharty, USA,* ed. Philip J. Reyburn and Terry L. Wilson (Baton Rouge: Louisiana State University Press, 1999), p. 91.

25. *New York Tribune,* December 31, 1862.

26. Frederick Douglass, "The Day of Jubilee Comes: An Address Delivered in Rochester, New York, December 28, 1862," in *The Frederick Douglass Papers, Series One: Speeches, Debates and Interviews,* ed. John W. Blassingame, 5 vols. (New Haven: Yale University Press, 1985), 3:544–545.

27. Welles, *Diary,* 1:209.

28. For Lincoln's continued, tacit support of colonization, see Phillip W. Magness and Sebastian N. Page, *Colonization after Emancipation: Lincoln and the Movement for Black Resettlement* (Columbia: University of Missouri, 2011).

29. Donald Yacavone, ed., *A Voice of Thunder: A Black Soldier's Civil War* (Urbana: University of Illinois Press, 1998), pp. 218–219.

30. *Independent,* November 27, 1862. A year later, Lincoln made the same point to John Hay: "Now, the slaves are quiet, choosing to wait for the deliverance they hope from us, rather than endanger their lives by a frantic struggle for freedom." John Hay, *Inside Lincoln's White House: The Complete Civil War Diary of John Hay,* ed. Michael Burlingame and John R. Turner Ettlinger (Carbondale: Southern Illinois University Press, 1997), p. 117.

31. Edward Bates, December 31, 1862; Montgomery Blair, December 31, 1862; Salmon P. Chase [December 30–31, 1862]; all in ALP. Seward's revisions are contained in Abraham Lincoln, December 30, 1862 (Final Emancipation Proclamation—Preliminary Draft, with suggested changes by William Henry Seward).

32. *New York Tribune,* December 30, 1862.

33. *New York Times,* December 31, 1862; Frank B. Carpenter, "Anecdotes and Personal Reminiscences of President Lincoln," in Henry J. Raymond, *The Life and Public Services of Abraham Lincoln* (New York: Derby and Miller, 1865), p. 758; *CW,* 5:544–545.

34. Brooks, *Mr. Lincoln's Washington,* p. 57.

10. Jubilee

1. John Boucher to wife Polly, January 1, 1863, Boucher Family Papers, Civil War Misc. Coll., 2nd ser., U.S. Army Military History Institute, Carlisle, PA.

2. Moses Coit Tyler, *Moses Coit Tyler: Selections from His Letters and Diaries,* ed. Jessica Tyler Austin (Garden City: Doubleday, 1911), p. 19.

3. Francis Carpenter, *Six Months at the White House with Abraham Lincoln: The Story of a Picture* (New York: Hurd and Houghton, 1866), pp. 87, 270.

4. Charles Sumner to George Livermore, January 9, 1863, in Charles Sumner, *The Selected Letters of Charles Sumner,* ed. Beverly Wilson Palmer, 2 vols. (Boston: Northeastern University Press, 1990), 1:139–140.

5. Frederick W. Seward, *Seward at Washington, as Senator and Secretary of State: A Memoir of His Life, with Selections from His Letters, 1861–1872* (New York: Derby and Miller, 1891), p. 151.

6. Adam Gurowski, *Diary from November 18, 1862, to October 18, 1863* (New York: Carleton, 1864), 2:61.

7. Henry Highland Garnet, "An Address to the Slaves of the United States," in *A Memorial Discourse* (Philadelphia: Joseph Wilson, 1865), p. 49.

8. *New York Times,* January 1, 1863.

9. *New York Evening Post,* January 2, 1863.

10. *Liberator,* January 2, 1863; *Christian Inquirer,* January 17, 1863.

11. Elizabeth Ware Pearson, ed., *Letters from Port Royal* (Boston: W. B. Clarke, 1906), p. 92. For a thorough account, see Willie Lee Rose, *Rehearsal for Reconstruction: The Port Royal Experiment* (New York: Oxford University Press, 1964).

12. Thomas Wentworth Higginson, *The Complete Civil War Journals and Collected Letters of Thomas Wentworth Higginson,* ed. Christopher Looby (Chicago: University of Chicago Press, 2000), pp. 74–78.

13. Benjamin Rush Plumly to AL, January 1, 1863, in Abraham Lincoln Papers, Library of Congress (hereafter ALP). Edward Bates called Plumly "a scatter-brained zealot." See Edward Bates, *The Diary of Edward Bates, 1859–1866,* ed. Howard K. Beale (Washington, DC: Government Printing Office, 1933), p. 392.

14. *New York Times,* January 4, 1863. William Wilberforce was an English politician and abolitionist who led the movement against the British slave trade. Thomas Clarkson was a leading English abolitionist who worked alongside Wilberforce to effect passage of the Slave Trade Act in 1807 and the Slavery Abolition Act of 1833.

15. Both Phillips and Lincoln, no doubt, would have appreciated William T. Sherman's gloss on the phrase: "'The People' is a vague expression," he wrote, and "people may be wrong as well as right." William T. Sherman, *The Sherman Letters,* ed. Rachel Sherman Thorndike (New York: Charles Scribner's Sons, 1894), p. 161.

16. *Liberator,* January 9, 1863.

17. Edmund Burke Willson, *The Proclamation of Freedom* (Salem, MA: T. J. Hutchinson, 1863), pp. 8, 11.

18. Nathaniel Hall, *The Proclamation of Freedom* (Boston: Crosby and Nichols, 1863), pp. 4–6.

19. *New York Times,* January 6, 1863.

20. Ibid.

21. Ibid.

22. London England Workingmen to AL, December 31, 1862, ALP.

23. Abraham Lincoln, *The Collected Works of Abraham Lincoln,* ed. Roy P. Basler, 9 vols. (New Brunswick: Rutgers University Press, 1953–1955), 6:63–65.

24. Worthington Chauncey Ford, ed., *A Cycle of Adams Letters, 1861–1865,* 2 vols. (Boston: Houghton Mifflin, 1920), 2:243; John Murray Forbes, *Letters and Recollections of John Murray Forbes,* ed. Sarah Forbes Hughes, 2 vols. (Boston: Houghton Mifflin, 1899), 1:78.

25. Abby Hopper Gibbons, *The Life of Abby Hopper Gibbons, Told Chiefly through Her Correspondence,* ed. Sarah Hopper Emerson (New York: Putnam's, 1897), p. 384.

26. Jefferson Davis to Confederate Congress, January 12, *War of the Rebellion: A Com-*

pilation of the Official Records of the Union and Confederate Armies (Washington, DC: Government Printing Office, 1880–1901), Series 4, vol. 2, p. 345; *Richmond Enquirer,* January 7, 1863; *Macon Weekly Telegraph,* January 12, 1863; *Chatfield Democrat,* quoted in Frank L. Klement, "Midwestern Opposition to Lincoln's Emancipation Policy," *Journal of Negro History* 49 (July 1964), p. 181; *New York Herald,* January 3, 1863.

27. *Cincinnati Daily Commercial,* January 7, 1863.

28. Gurowski, *Diary,* pp. 62–63.

29. Ibid., 70.

30. *Pacific Appeal,* March 7, 1863.

31. John Oliver to Simeon Jocelyn, January 14, 1863, in C. Peter Ripley, ed., *The Black Abolitionist Papers, The United States, 1859–1865* (Chapel Hill: University of North Carolina Press, 1992), p. 173.

32. Chauncey Herbert Cooke, *Soldier Boy's Letters to His Father and Mother, 1861–85* (Independence, WI: News-Office, 1915), p. 27.

11. "Men of Color, To Arms!"

1. "Frederick Douglass at the Cooper Institute," *Douglass' Monthly* 5 (March 1863), 804–808.

2. Frederick Douglass, "Negroes and the National War Effort: An Address Delivered in Philadelphia, Pennsylvania, July 6, 1863," *The Frederick Douglass Papers, Series One: Speeches, Debates and Interviews,* ed. John W. Blassingame, 5 vols. (New Haven: Yale University Press, 1985), 3:596.

3. Abraham Lincoln, *The Collected Works of Abraham Lincoln,* ed. Roy P. Basler, 9 vols. (New Brunswick: Rutgers University Press, 1953–1955), 6:56 (hereafter cited as *CW*); Thomas Richmond to AL, March 2, 1863, Abraham Lincoln Papers, Library of Congress (hereafter ALP); William Sprague to AL, September 26, 1862, ALP; *CW,* 6:149–150.

4. George Templeton Strong, *Diary of the Civil War: George Templeton Strong,* ed. Allan Nevins (New York: MacMillan, 1962), p. 291.

5. *Congressional Globe,* 37th Congress, 3rd Session, pp. 601, 685 (hereafter *CG*).

6. Ibid., p. 629.

7. Ibid., p. 684.

8. Ibid., pp. 628, Appendix, 93, 653.

9. Noah Brooks, *Mr. Lincoln's Washington: Selections from the Writing of Noah Brooks, Civil War Correspondent,* ed. P. J. Staudenraus (South Brunswick, NJ: A. S. Barnes, 1967), pp. 103–104.

10. *CG,* 37th Congress, 3rd Session, Appendix, p. 79.

11. Ibid., p. 604.

12. Ibid., p. 630.

13. Madeleine Vinton Dahlgren, *Memoir of the Life of John A. Dahlgren* (Boston: James R. Osgood, 1882), pp. 387, 391.

14. See Leonard P. Curry, *Blueprint for Modern America* (Nashville: Vanderbilt University Press, 1968), pp. 64–67.

15. On black soldiers, see Dudley T. Cornish, *The Sable Arm: Negro Troops in the Union Army, 1861–65* (New York: Longmans, Green, 1956); James M. McPherson, *The Negro's Civil War* (New York: Vintage, 1965); Joseph T. Glatthaar, *Forged in Battle: The Civil War Alliance of Black Soldiers and White Officers* (New York: Penguin, 1990); and Ira Berlin, Joseph P. Reidy, and Leslie S. Rowland, eds., *Freedom's Soldiers: The Black Military in the Civil War* (New York: Cambridge University Press, 1998).

16. *Harper's Weekly,* March 14, 1863; *Chicago Tribune,* June 16, 1863.

17. Virginia M. Adams, ed., *On the Altar of Freedom* (New York: Warner Books, 1991), p. 119; Thomas Wentworth Higginson, *The Complete Civil War Journals and Collected Letters of Thomas Wentworth Higginson,* ed. Christopher Looby (Chicago: University of Chicago Press, 2000), pp. 209–210.

18. Harold D. Brinkman, ed., *Dear Companion: The Civil War Letters of Silas I. Shearer* (Ames: Sigler, 1995), pp. 56, 68.

19. Benjamin Ashenfelter to stepfather, March 1, 1863, Benjamin Ashenfelter Letters, Harrisburg Civil War Round Table Collection, U.S. Army Military History Institute (hereafter cited as USAMHI), Carlisle, PA; James McPherson, *For Cause and Comrades* (New York: Oxford University Press, 1997), p. 129; Peter Welsh, *Irish Green and Union Blue: The Civil War Letters of Peter Welsh,* ed. Lawrence Frederick Kohl, with Margaret Cosse Richard (New York: Fordham University Press, 1986), p. 62.

20. Taylor Peirce, *Dear Catherine, Dear Taylor: The Civil War Letters of a Union Soldier and His Wife,* ed. Richard L. Kiper (Lawrence: University Press of Kansas, 2002), pp. 64, 66; Lyman Ayer to Sela Wright, April 25, 1863, Lyman Ayer Letters, Civil War Collection, Federal Collection, Reel 17, Box F25, Folder 6, Tennessee State Library and Archives; Amos Hostetter to sister and brother-in-law, January 29, 1863, Illinois State Historical Society.

21. Charles W. Wills, *Army Life of an Illinois Soldier* (Washington: Globe Printing, 1906), pp. 125, 183–184.

22. Kelly A. Nolin, ed., "The Civil War Letters of S. M. and S. E. Pingree, 1862–64," *Vermont History* 63 (Spring 1995), pp. 80–94.

23. Kathleen Kroll and Charles Moran, eds., "The White Papers," *Massachusetts Review* 18 (Summer 1977), pp. 257, 263.

24. Richard N. Ellis, ed., "The Civil War Letters of an Iowa Family," *Annals of Iowa* 39 (Spring 1969), p. 582.

25. Benjamin A. Fordyce, *Echoes: From the Letters of a Civil War Surgeon,* ed. Lydia P. Hecht (n.p.: Bayou Publishing, 1996), pp. 67–68.

26. Daniel W. Sawtelle, *All's for the Best: The Civil War Reminiscences and Letters of Daniel W. Sawtelle,* ed. Peter H. Buckingham (Knoxville: University of Tennessee Press, 2001), p. 226.

27. John White Geary to Edgar Cowan, August 4, 1863, GLC00673, Gilder-Lehrman Collection of American History, New-York Historical Society.

28. *North American,* January 1, 1863; Barbara Brooks Tomblin, *Bluejackets and Contrabands: African Americans and the Union Navy* (Lexington: University Press of Kentucky, 2009), pp. 42–43.

29. James Freeman Clarke, *James Freeman Clarke: Autobiography, Diary and Correspondence,* ed. Edward Everett Hale (Boston: Houghton Mifflin, 1892), p. 286.

30. John Murray Forbes, *Letters and Recollections of John Murray Forbes,* ed. Sarah Forbes Hughes, 2 vols. (Boston: Houghton Mifflin, 1899), 1: 348.

31. Simon P. Newman, "A Democrat in Lincoln's Army: The Civil War Letters of Henry P. Hubbell," *Princeton University Library Chronicle* 50 (Winter 1989), pp. 158, 163–164.

32. Nancy Niblack Baxter, *Gallant Fourteenth: The Story of an Indiana Civil War Regiment* (Carmel: Guild Press, 1980), p. 126.

33. Henry Livermore Abbott, *Fallen Leaves: The Civil War Letters of Major Henry Livermore Abbott,* ed. Robert Garth Scott (Kent, OH: Kent State University Press, 1991), p. 161; John Ellis to nephew, February 1863, Ellis-Marshall Family Papers, Harrisburg Civil War Round Table Collection, USAMHI, Carlisle, PA; William Bluffton Miller, *Fighting for Liberty and Right: The Civil War Diary of William Bluffton Miller,* ed. Jeffrey L. Patrick and Robert J. Willey (Knoxville: University of Tennessee, 2005), p. 69; John England to fiancée, Ellen, January 25, 1863, John England Letters, U.S. Army Boxes, New York Public Library; John W. Chase, *Yours for the Union: The Civil War Letters of John W. Chase, First Massachusetts Light Artillery,* ed. John S. Collier and Bonnie B. Collier (New York: Fordham University Press, 2004), pp. 189, 175.

34. Valentine C. Randolph, *A Civil War Soldier's Diary: Valentine C. Randolph, 39th Illinois Regiment,* ed. David D. Roe (De Kalb: Southern Illinois University Press, 2006), pp. 131, 141.

35. John R. McClure, *Hoosier Farm Boy in Lincoln's Army: The Civil War Letters of Pvt. John R. McClure,* ed. Nancy Niblack Baxter (privately printed, 1971), p. 44.

36. Charles E. Cort, *"Dear Friends": The Civil War Letters and Diary of Charles Edwin Cort,* ed. Helyn Tomlinson (n.p., 1962), pp. 29, 52, 77, 61.

37. Charles Turner, February 19, 1863, Charles Albert Turner Letters, Folder 2, Western Reserve Historical Society; Newton Glazier, February 8, 1863, Nelson Newton Glazier Letters, Vermont Historical Society.

38. Jacob Behm, "Emancipation: A Soldier's View," *Civil War Times Illustrated* 21 (February 1983), pp. 46–47; George Granville Benedict, *Army Life in Virginia* (Burlington: Free Press Association, 1895), pp. 111–112.

39. *Philadelphia Press,* January 1, 1863; Thomas N. Stevens, *"Dear Carrie . . .": The Civil War Letters of Thomas N. Stevens,* ed. George M. Blackburn (Mount Pleasant, MI: Clarke Historical Library, 1984), p. 62.

40. Theodore B. Gates, *The Civil War Diaries of Col. Theodore B. Gates, 20th New York State Militia,* ed. Seward R. Osborne (Hightstown, NJ: Longstreet House, 1991), p. 60. On ideas of Union and nationalism, see Gary W. Gallagher, *The Union War* (Cambridge, MA: Harvard University Press, 2011); and Melinda Lawson, *Patriot Fires: Forging a New American Nationalism in the Civil War North* (Lawrence: University Press of Kansas, 2002).

41. Lucius Wood to parents, March 5, 1863, E. G. Wood Family Papers, Folder 3, Western Reserve Historical Society; B. F. Stevenson, *Letters from the Army 1862–1864* (Cincinnati: Robert Clarke, 1886), pp. 208–209; Harvey Reid, *The View from Headquarters: Civil War Letters of Harvey Reid,* ed. Frank L. Byrne (Madison: State Historical Society of Wisconsin, 1965), p. 92; James M. McPherson, *For Cause and Comrades,* p. 125; Cyrus F. Boyd, Diary, March 6, 1863, 2:19–20, Cyrus F. Boyd Collection, Kansas City Public Library, Special Collections.

42. James Dodds, March 18, 1863, John L. Harris Papers, Illinois State Historical Library; Theodore Frelinghuysen Upson, *With Sherman to the Sea: The Civil War Letters, Diaries and Reminiscences of Theodore F. Upson,* ed. Oscar Osburn Winther (Baton Rouge: Louisiana State University Press, 1943), pp. 55–56.

12. "It Can Not Be Retracted"

1. Abraham Lincoln, *The Collected Works of Abraham Lincoln,* ed. Roy P. Basler, 9 vols. (New Brunswick, NJ: Rutgers University Press, 1953–55), 7:226 (hereafter *CW*).

2. Noah Brooks, *Mr. Lincoln's Washington: Selections from the Writing of Noah Brooks, Civil War Correspondent,* ed. P. J. Staudenraus (South Brunswick, NJ: A. S. Barnes, 1967), pp. 381–383.

3. Leonard P. Curry, *Blueprint for Modern America* (Nashville: Vanderbilt University Press, 1968), pp. 52–54; Henry Wilson, *History of the Antislavery Measures of the 37th and 38th United States Congresses, 1861–65* (Boston: Walker, Fuller, 1865), pp. 231, 246.

4. Adam Gurowski, *Diary from March 4, 1861, to November 12, 1862* (Boston: Lee and Shepard, 1862), p. 163; Whitelaw Reid, *A Radical View: The "Agate" Dispatches of Whitelaw Reid, 1861–1865,* ed. James G. Smart, 2 vols. (Memphis: Memphis State University Press, 1976), 2:183.

5. See Dennis K. Boman, "All Politics Are Local: Emancipation in Missouri," in Brian Dirck and Allen Guelzo, eds., *Lincoln Emancipated: The President and the Politics of Race* (De Kalb: Northern Illinois University Press, 2007).

6. *CW*, 6:291.

7. Ibid., 6:358–359.

8. Frederick Douglass, "The Black Man's Future in the Southern States: An Address Delivered in Boston, Massachusetts, on 5 February 1862," in *The Frederick Douglass Papers, Series One: Speeches, Debates, and Interviews,* vol. 3, *1855–63,* ed. John W. Blassingame, 5 vols. (New Haven: Yale University Press, 1985), p. 505.

9. *New York Times,* February 25, 1864.

10. *CW,* 6:364–365.

11. Ibid., 6:365, 281.

12. William Whiting, *The War Powers of the President* (Boston: John L. Shorey, 1862), pp. ii, vi. Francis Carpenter recalled telling the president, "I learned that you frequently consulted, during the period you were preparing the Proclamation, Solicitor Whiting's work on the 'War Powers of the President.'" See Henry J. Raymond, *The Life and Public Services of Abraham Lincoln* (New York: Derby and Miller, 1865), p. 763. In 1865, after Whiting submitted his resignation, Lincoln wrote to Stanton, "I like Mr. Whiting very much" (*CW,* 8:373).

13. *CW,* 6:428–429.

14. S. F. Fleharty, *Jottings from Dixie: The Civil War Dispatches of Sergeant Major Stephen Fleharty, USA,* ed. Philip Reyburn and Terry Wilson (Baton Rouge: Louisiana State University Press, 1999), p. 99. Lincoln wrote, "The occasion is piled high with difficulty, and we must rise with the occasion" (*CW,* 5:537).

15. Frederick Douglass, "Emancipation, Racism, and the Work before Us: An Address Delivered in Philadelphia, Pennsylvania, December 4, 1863," in *Frederick Douglass Papers,* 3:606–607. Also see James Oakes, *The Radical and the Republican* (New York: W. W. Norton, 2007); and John Stauffer, *Giants: The Parallel Lives of Frederick Douglass and Abraham Lincoln* (New York: Twelve, 2008).

16. *CW,* 6:48, 406–410.

17. Ibid.

18. *Chicago Tribune,* September 4, 1863; George Templeton Strong, *Diary of the Civil War: George Templeton Strong,* ed. Allen Nevins (New York: MacMillan, 1962), p. 355.

19. *Chicago Tribune,* September 3, 1863; David Donald, *Lincoln* (New York: Simon and Schuster, 1995), p. 457. Also see Allen Guelzo, "Defending Emancipation: Abraham Lincoln and the Conkling Letter, 1863," *Civil War History* 48 (2002), pp. 313–337.

20. Donald, *Lincoln,* p. 466.

21. *CW,* 7:50.

22. Ibid.

23. "The Constitutional Amendment," *Continental Monthly* 6 (September 1864), p. 323. Also see Alex Twining, "President Lincoln's Proclamation of Freedom to the Slaves," *New Englander* 24 (January 1865), pp. 178–186.

24. *CW,* 7:53–56; Charles Sumner to John Bright, December 15, 1863, in Charles Sumner, *The Selected Letters of Charles Sumner,* ed. Beverly Wilson Palmer, 2 vols. (Boston: Northeastern University Press, 1990), 2:214.

25. *CG*, 38th Congress, 1st Session, pp. 346–361.

26. *CW*, 7:433.

27. Ibid., 7:281. Francis Carpenter quotes Lincoln using a similar analogy in his conversation with the British abolitionist George Thompson on April 7, 1864: "I have sometimes used the illustration in this connection of a man with a diseased limb, and his surgeon. So long as there is a chance of the patient's restoration, the surgeon is solemnly bound to try and save both life and limb; but when the crisis comes, and the limb must be sacrificed as the only chance of saving the life, no honest man will hesitate." Francis B. Carpenter, *Six Months at the White House with Abraham Lincoln: The Story of a Picture* (New York: Hurd and Houghton, 1866), p. 77.

28. *CW*, 7:301–302. For further discussion of this theme, see James M. McPherson, "Lincoln and Liberty," in *Abraham Lincoln and the Second American Revolution* (New York: Oxford University Press, 1991), pp. 43–64; and Ronald C. White, Jr., "Lincoln and the Rhetoric of Freedom," in Harold Holzer and Sarah Vaughn Gabbard, eds., *Lincoln and Freedom: Slavery, Emancipation, and the Thirteenth Amendment* (Carbondale: Southern Illinois University Press, 2007), pp. 130–142.

29. James M. McPherson, *This Mighty Scourge* (New York: Oxford University Press, 2007), p. 171; James M. McPherson, *Battle Cry of Freedom* (New York: Oxford University Press, 1988), p. 762.

30. Horace Greeley to AL, July 7, 1864 in ALP; *CW*, 7:451.

31. Strong, *Diary of the Civil War*, p. 474; *CW*, 7:499–502.

32. *CW*, 7:506–508.

33. Ibid., 7:514.

34. Ibid., 7:517–518.

35. George B. McClellan, *The Civil War Papers of George B. McClellan*, ed. Stephen Sears (Cambridge, MA: Da Capo Press, 1992), p. 595.

36. Oliver Willcox Norton, *Army Letters, 1861–1865* (privately printed, 1903), p. 101. On the soldier vote, see Davis E. Long, *Jewel of Liberty: Abraham Lincoln's Re-election and the End of Slavery* (Mechanicsburg: Stackpole Books, 1994).

37. Henry Orendorff, *We Are Sherman's Men: The Letters of Henry Orendorff*, ed. William M. Anderson (Macomb: Western Illinois University, 1986), p. 115.

38. Charles Bracelen Flood, *1864: Lincoln at the Gates of History* (New York: Simon and Schuster, 2009) p. 280; Strong, *Diary of the Civil War*, p. 480.

39. *CW*, 7:533–534.

40. James M. McPherson, *Tried by War: Abraham Lincoln as Commander in Chief* (New York: Penguin, 2008), pp. 245–246; Mary Boykin Miller Chesnut, *Mary Chesnut's Civil War*, ed. C. Vann Woodward (New Haven: Yale University Press, 1982), p. 648.

41. John F. Brobst, *Well Mary: Civil War Letters of a Wisconsin Volunteer*, ed. Margaret Brobst Roth (Madison: University of Wisconsin Press, 1960), p. 92; Alexander G. Downing, *Downing's Civil War Diary*, ed. Olynthus B. Clark (Des Moines: Historical

Department of Iowa, 1916), p. 227; Mark Grimsley and Todd D. Miller, eds., *The Union Must Stand* (Knoxville: University of Tennessee Press, 2000), p. 193.

42. *CW,* 8:101.

43. Charles Sumner, *The Works of Charles Sumner,* 15 vols. (Boston: Lee and Shepherd, 1874), 9:136, 192.

44. *CW,* 8:149–152.

45. Warren Akin, *Letters of Warren Akin, Confederate Congressman,* ed. Bell Irvin Wiley (Athens: University of Georgia Press, 2010), pp. 32–33. The most complete treatment of the issue can be found in Bruce Levine, *Confederate Emancipation: Southern Plans to Free and Arm Slaves during the Civil War* (New York: Oxford University Press, 2006).

46. Howell Cobb, quoted in James M. McPherson, *Ordeal by Fire: The Civil War and Reconstruction* (New York: Alfred A. Knopf, 1982), p. 77; Theodore Lyman, *Meade's Headquarters, 1863–1865: Letters of Colonel Theodore Lyman from the Wilderness to Appomattox,* ed. George R. Agassiz (Boston: Atlantic Monthly Press, 1922), p. 245; Strong, *Diary of the Civil War,* p. 564.

47. Robert E. Lee to Andrew Hunter, January 11, 1865, www.sonofthesouth.net/lee-foundation/LettersAndrewHunter.htm.

48. Thomas Jewett Goree, *Longstreet's Aide: The Civil War Letters of Major Thomas J. Goree,* ed. Thomas W. Cutrer (Charlottesville: University Press of Virginia, 1995), p. 137. The Confederate Congress refused to include an emancipation clause, but the enabling legislation, Jefferson Davis's General Order No. 14, did so. See Levine, *Confederate Emancipation,* pp. 118–119; and Stephanie McCurry, *Confederate Reckoning: Power and Politics in the Civil War South* (Cambridge, MA: Harvard University Press, 2011), pp. 350–351.

49. Ella G. C. Thomas, *The Secret Eye: The Journal of Ella Gertrude Clanton Thomas, 1848–1889,* ed. Virginia Ingraham Burr (Chapel Hill: University of North Carolina Press, 1990), p. 243; Henry Slade Tew, "An Eye Witness Account of the Occupation of Mt. Pleasant," *South Carolina Historical Magazine* 66 (January 1965), pp. 8–14.

50. Charles A. Page, *Letters of a War Correspondent,* ed. J. R. Gilmore (Boston: L. C. Page, 1899), pp. 337–338.

51. *CW,* 8:254.

52. James M. McPherson, *The Struggle for Equality* (Princeton: Princeton University Press, 1964), p. 180.

53. Emancipation League, *Facts Concerning the Freedmen* (Boston: Commercial Printing, 1863).

54. "American Freedmen's Inquiry Commission Preliminary Report," in *War of the Rebellion: A Compilation of the Official Records of the Union and Confederate Armies* (Washington, DC: Government Printing Office, 1880–1901), Series 3, vol. 3, pp. 430–454.

55. Ibid.

56. James McKaye, *The Emancipated Slave Face to Face with His Old Master* (New York: W. C. Bryant, 1864), p. 22.

13. Emancipation Triumphant

1. These questions are inspired by Julian Barnes, who, in his brilliant story "Shipwreck," which explores Théodore Géricault's painting *The Raft of the Medusa,* asks, "How do you turn catastrophe into art?" *New Yorker,* June 12, 1989, pp. 40–50.

2. Frederic B. Perkins, *The Picture and the Men* (New York: A. J. Johnson, 1867), p. 18. For an introduction to history painting, see William Ayres, ed., *Picturing History: American Painting, 1770–1930* (New York: Rizzoli, 1993).

3. Harold Holzer, Gabor S. Boritt, and Mark E. Neely, Jr., "Francis Bicknell Carpenter (1830–1900): Painter of Abraham Lincoln and His Circle," *American Art Journal* 16 (Spring 1984), p. 69.

4. Francis Carpenter, "Anecdotes and Reminiscences," in Henry J. Raymond, *The Life and Public Services of Abraham Lincoln* (New York: Derby and Miller, 1865), p. 759. In Francis B. Carpenter, *Six Months at the White House with Abraham Lincoln: The Story of a Picture* (New York: Hurd and Houghton, 1866), Carpenter would revise and embellish some of the anecdotes first told in Raymond's volume.

5. Carpenter, *Six Months,* p. 30.

6. Ibid., pp. 12–13.

7. *The Daily Age,* March 7, 1864.

8. Carpenter, *Six Months,* p. 21.

9. For a survey of images of the Emancipation Proclamation, see Harold Holzer, "Picturing Freedom: The Emancipation Proclamation in Art, Iconography, and Memory," in Harold Holzer, Edna Greene Medford, Frank J. Williams, *The Emancipation Proclamation: Three Views* (Baton Rouge: Louisiana State University Press, 2006), pp. 83–136; and Harold Holzer, *Emancipating Lincoln: The Proclamation in Text, Context, and Memory* (Cambridge, MA: Harvard University Press, 2012). Also see Barry Schwartz, "Picturing Lincoln," in Ayres, *Picturing History,* pp. 135–155; and Harold Holzer, Gabor S. Boritt, and Mark E. Neely, Jr., *The Lincoln Image: Abraham Lincoln and the Popular Print* (New York: Charles Scribner's Sons, 1984). On Blythe, see Bruce W. Chambers, *The World of David Gilmour Blythe* (Washington, DC: Smithsonian Institution Press, 1980).

10. J. W. Forney to AL, December 30, 1862, Abraham Lincoln Papers, Library of Congress; Holzer, Boritt, and Neely, *The Lincoln Image,* pp. 109–110.

11. Andrew L. Thomas, "Edward Dalton Marchant's *Abraham Lincoln,*" in Katherine Martinez and Page Talbott, eds., *Philadelphia's Cultural Landscape: The Sartain Family Legacy* (Philadelphia: Temple University Press, 2000), p. 64.

12. Abraham Lincoln, *The Collected Works of Abraham Lincoln,* ed. Roy P. Basler, 9 vols. (New Brunswick, NJ: Rutgers University Press, 1953–1955), 8:265–266.

13. Frederick Douglass, *The Frederick Douglass Papers, Series One: Speeches, Debates, Interviews,* ed. John W. Blassingame and John R. McKivigan, 5 vols. (New Haven: Yale University Press, 1991), 4:428. See Kirk Savage, *Standing Soldiers, Kneeling Slaves: Race, War, and Monument in Nineteenth-Century America* (Princeton: Princeton University Press, 1997).

14. Carpenter, *Six Months,* pp. 10–11.

15. Ibid., pp. 27–28.

16. Ibid., pp. 28, 22.

17. Salmon Chase had resigned in June 1864 and was not present.

18. For an illuminating discussion of the maps contained in the painting, see Susan Schulten, "The Cartography of Slavery and the Authority of Statistics," *Civil War History* 56 (March 2010), pp. 5–32.

19. Carpenter, *Six Months,* p. 350.

20. Noah Brooks, *Mr. Lincoln's Washington: Selections from the Writing of Noah Brooks, Civil War Correspondent,* ed. P. J. Staudenraus (South Brunswick, NJ: A. S. Barnes, 1967), pp. 361–363. Twisted mail is a type of mesh-like armor made from small metal rings. Brooks is quoting (and slightly altering) a line from Thomas Gray's poem "The Bard: A Pindaric Ode" (1768).

21. Salmon Chase, *The Salmon P. Chase Papers,* vol. 5: *Correspondence, 1865–1873,* ed. John Niven (Kent, OH: Kent State University Press, 1998), pp. 92–93; John Hay, *Lincoln and the Civil War in the Diaries and Letters of John Hay,* ed. Tyler Dennett (New York: Dodd and Mead, 1939), p. 272.

22. John Hay, *Inside Lincoln's White House: The Complete Civil War Diary of John Hay,* ed. Michael Burlingame and John R. Turner Ettlinger (Carbondale: Southern Illinois University Press, 1997), pp. 211–212; Carpenter, *Six Months,* pp. 72–73; Hay, *Lincoln and the Civil War,* p. 272. Welles also recounts that, in March 1864, Seward directly told Carpenter he thought the Emancipation Proclamation was "an incident following and wholly subordinate to other and much greater events." Gideon Welles, *Diary of Gideon Welles,* ed. Howard K. Beale, 2 vols. (New York: W. W. Norton, 1960), 1:549.

23. William Osborn Stoddard, *Inside the White House in War Times: Memoirs and Reports of Lincoln's Secretary,* ed. Michael Burlingame (Lincoln: University of Nebraska Press, 2000), p. 182.

24. *New York Tribune,* June 2, 1866.

25. *New York Times,* October 21, 1864.

26. Holzer, Boritt, and Neely, "Francis Bicknell Carpenter," p. 77.

27. *New York Tribune,* June 2, 1866.

Epilogue

1. Abraham Lincoln, *The Collected Works of Abraham Lincoln,* ed. Roy P. Basler, 9 vols. (New Brunswick: Rutgers University Press, 1953–1955), 6:539–540 (hereaf-

ter *CW*); Mrs. A. H. Hoge and Mrs. D. P. Livermore to AL, November 11, 1863, in Abraham Lincoln Papers, Library of Congress.

2. Amanda Akin Stearns, *The Lady Nurse of Ward E* (New York: Baker and Taylor, 1909), p. 42. Also see Ida Tarbell, "Lincoln's Love for the Private Soldier," *New York Times,* December 6, 1908.

3. Walt Whitman to Ralph Waldo Emerson, [January 17, 1863]; WW to Nathaniel Bloom and John F. S. Gray, March 19, 1863; WW to Louisa Van Velsor Whitman, June 30, 1863; in Walt Whitman, *The Correspondence of Walt Whitman,* vol. 1: *1842–1867,* ed. Edwin Haviland Miller (New York: New York University Press, 1961), pp. 69, 83, 113.

4. On the Albany Army Relief Bazaar and the preliminary Emancipation Proclamation, see www.nysl.nysed.gov/library/features/ep/acquisition.htm.

5. *CW,* 7:301–303.

6. Sidney George Fisher, *A Philadelphia Perspective: The Civil War Diary of Sidney George Fisher,* ed. Jonathan W. White (New York: Fordham University Press, 2007), pp. 226–227; *CW,* 7:394–396.

7. Francis B. Carpenter, *Six Months at the White House with Abraham Lincoln: The Story of a Picture* (New York: Hurd and Houghton, 1866), p. 77.

8. William Lloyd Garrison to Francis W. Newman, [July 15, 1864], in Garrison, *Let the Oppressed Go Free: The Letters of William Lloyd Garrison, 1861–1867,* ed. Walter M. Merrill, 6 vols. (Cambridge, MA: Harvard University Press, 1979), 5:220–226. The letter appeared in the *Liberator* and the *National Anti-Slavery Standard.*

9. Ibid.

10. C. C. Hazewell, "The Hour and the Man," *Atlantic* 10 (November 1862), p. 633.

11. This interpretation draws on the insights of Burrus M. Carnahan, *Act of Justice: Lincoln's Emancipation Proclamation and the Law of War* (Lexington: University of Kentucky Press, 2007), esp. pp. 93–115.

12. *Independent,* January 8, 1863. See William C. Harris, "After the Emancipation Proclamation: Lincoln's Role in the Ending of Slavery," *North and South* 5 (December 2001), pp. 42–53, as well as the discussion in Eric Foner, *The Fiery Trial: Abraham Lincoln and American Slavery* (New York: W. W. Norton, 2010), pp. 240–247.

13. *CW,* 8:384–385. For an acute reading of Lincoln's entry into Richmond, see Richard Wightman Fox, "Lincoln's Practice of Republicanism: Striding through Richmond, April 4, 1865," in Thomas A. Horrocks, Harold Holzer, and Frank J. Williams, eds., *The Living Lincoln* (Carbondale: Southern Illinois University Press, 2011), pp. 131–151.

14. Thomas Morris Chester, *Thomas Morris Chester, Black Civil War Correspondent: His Dispatches from the Virginia Front,* ed. R. J. M. Blackett (Baton Rouge: Louisiana State University Press, 1989), p. 294; [Charles Carleton Coffin], "The President's Entry into Richmond," *Littell's Living Age* 85 (April 22, 1865), p. 138. Coffin revised the account and published another version as "Late Scenes in Richmond," *Atlantic Monthly* 15 (June 1865), pp. 753–756.

15. [Coffin], "The President's Entry into Richmond," pp. 137–138.

16. Chester, *Thomas Morris Chester,* p. 297; Charles A. Page, *Letters of a War Correspondent,* ed. J. R. Gilmore (Boston: L. C. Page, 1899), p. 325.

17. [Coffin], "The President's Entry into Richmond," pp. 137–138.

18. Charles Carleton Coffin, *Four Years of Fighting: A Volume of Personal Observation with the Army and the Navy* (Boston: Ticknor and Fields, 1866), pp. 511–512.

19. David Dixon Porter, *Incidents and Anecdotes of the Civil War* (New York: Appleton, 1885), p. 295.

20. William M. E. Rachal, ed., "The Occupation of Richmond, April 1865: The Memorandum of Events of Colonel Christopher Q. Tompkins," *Virginia Magazine of History and Biography* 73 (April 1965), pp. 192–193; Garland White, "Letter from Richmond," *Christian Recorder,* April 22, 1865.

21. Chester, *Thomas Morris Chester,* pp. 294–295.

22. John S. Barnes, "With Lincoln from Washington to Richmond in 1865," *Appleton's Magazine* 9 (January–June 1907), pp. 748–749.

23. Chester, *Thomas Morris Chester,* p. 295.

24. [Coffin], "The President's Entry into Richmond," p. 138.

25. Wilbur Fisk, *Hard Marching Every Day: The Civil War Letters of Private Wilbur Fisk, 1861–1865,* ed. Emil Rosenblatt and Ruth Rosenblatt (Lawrence: University Press of Kansas, 1992), p. 322.

26. Septima M. Collis, *A Woman's War Record, 1861–65* (New York: G. P. Putnam's Sons, 1889), p. 60.

27. Ibid.

Acknowledgments

I became interested in Lincoln in my first graduate research seminar in 1979. That it took me some thirty years to write about him highlights the unexpected paths my work has taken. I can only hope that my experiences as a teacher and historian have enriched this narrative.

Thankfully, I have not had to labor alone. I was thrilled when Joyce Seltzer offered to publish my manuscript. Her superb editorial skills, legendary in the profession, have made this a better book. I am grateful as well to Brian Distelberg and Maria Ascher of Harvard University Press for seeing the manuscript through the publication process.

This is my third book with my agent, Zoe Pagnamenta. She has many distinguished clients on her list, and I am honored that she treats me as if I am one of them. I am grateful as well to Sara Levitt.

It is likely that without James McPherson this book would never have come to fruition. It was Jim who taught that first seminar of mine. I was lucky to serve as a research assistant on his book *Ordeal by Fire,* to precept for his undergraduate Civil War course, and to walk Gettysburg with him and some two dozen Princeton students one drizzly fall day in the early 1980s. When the idea for this book first emerged, I did what any historian would do: I asked Jim for his opinion. He thought there might be something to it, and that was enough. For the past three years we've met often to discuss the topic, and he was kind enough to read an early draft of the manuscript. I would not be the historian I am without his example, and I thank him for all he has done, not only for me personally but also for the study of Lincoln and the Civil War era.

I am also deeply indebted to my colleague Ron Spencer. Ron played a key role in hiring me at Trinity College in 2004, and he quickly became a dear friend and advisor. Until his recent retirement, Ron taught courses on the Civil War and Reconstruction. His knowledge of the era is vast and his skills as an editor are unparalleled. I benefited from both as Ron saved me from numerous factual errors and various assaults upon the English language. There is not a paragraph in this book (except for this one) that has not been improved by Ron's insistence on clarity and economy of expression. I will forever be grateful to him for all that he has done for me.

I delivered a part of this work as a lecture at Rutgers University in spring 2011. I am indebted to the members of the American Studies and History Departments for their good response and warm embrace. I would like especially to thank the chairpersons of each department, Ben Sifuentes and James Masschaele. I am also grateful to my colleagues at Trinity who encouraged me to pursue my writing and teaching wherever it might lead: Zayde Antrim, Davarian Baldwin, Jeff Bayliss, Jack Chatfield, Sean Cocco, Scott Gac, Cheryl Greenberg, Christopher Hager, Joan Hedrick, Paul Lauter, Eugene Leach, Michael Lestz, Kevin McMahon, Diana Paulin, and Scott Tang. My administrative assistant, Nancy Rossi, not only keeps the American Studies program running—she also keeps the coffee coming.

Several Trinity College students helped with the research for this book: Grace Green, Sara Ickow, Kathryn Murdock, and Catherine Shortliffe. Sara deserves special mention for the outstanding work she did at the Library of Congress. I owe a special debt to Gigi Barnhill and Lauren Hewes, curators of the graphic arts department at the American Antiquarian Society.

I offer my thanks to Bob Allison, Scott Gac, Christopher Hager, Peter Mancall, James Oakes, and Aaron Sachs for having read all or part of this manuscript. Their insights proved indispensable. Jim Goodman, Doug Greenberg, and Tom Slaughter also read the manuscript, but that is the least of their contribution. We've shared a journey filled with laughs and tears, joys and sorrows, good times and hard. I am blessed by their presence in my life. I am also blessed by my ongoing friendship with my childhood companions Mark Richman and Bruce Rossky.

This book is dedicated to my brother, who is four years my senior and displays a bit too much pleasure when people ask if I'm the older one. Dave has done everything for me, and is a steadfast publicist for my books. He has also picked up more checks than any younger brother has a right to expect. More important, he set an example and encouraged me to pursue my path. I would not have succeeded without him.

While writing this book, my late-teen children, Ben and Sophie, somehow became young adults. It adds special delight that together we share a passion for American culture. In 1999, when they were thirteen and eight, I took them to see Bruce Springsteen and the E Street Band at Madison Square Garden. Since then we've been to many shows, and I look forward to many more. "My Love Will Not Let You Down," Bruce sings. Never has, never will.

I took Jani to her first Springsteen concert in 1978, fifth row at the Academy of Music. She married me three years later, though I am uncertain of the cause and effect. There are no words that can encompass our life together, except once again these: Thank you for guarding my dreams and visions and for showing me that "love is wild, love is real."

Index

by, 36; and exclusions under Emancipation Proclamation, 218; as forfeiting slaves, 76; fugitive slaves of loyal, 6; of Kentucky, 26; legal rights of, 102; loyal, 65, 77, 226, 240; McKaye on former, 263; and Militia Act debate, 76; Missouri, 240; and Motley, 144; nonslaveholding states as taxed to pay, 45; and racial amalgamation, 172; in rebellion, 55; slaves as children of, 135; Spear on, 173; and Starr, 172; and Charles Sumner, 29; Wade on, 65

Slavery: and Henry Adams, 30; and John Quincy Adams, 29; and Aikman, 42; and AL, 4–5, 33, 87–88, 90, 97, 178, 192; AL's official vs. personal feelings about, 87, 88; AL's opposition to, 14, 44, 243; AL's willingness to accept, 40; amendment of February 11, 1861, prohibiting interference with, 33; assault of Emancipation Proclamation on, 280; and Barnes, 173–174; Beecher on, 15; black soldiers returned to, 227; and border states, 40, 45; and Brownson, 27; John W. Chase on, 234; and Salmon Chase, 18, 141–142; Cheever on, 213; Child on, 53; common charge for costs of, 178; in Confederacy vs. border states, 45; Congressional authority over, 54; and Constitution, 14, 15, 28, 248–249; constitutional amendment to abolish, 121; continued existence as legal institution, 244; as creation of state or local laws, 14; and Crittenden resolution, 34; and Cutting, 82; and Delaware, 43; in District of Columbia, 46–51, 174; Douglass on, 90, 174, 196, 220; and elections of 1862, 154; and Thomas Eliot, 33; and Emancipation Proclamation, 220; and Emancipation Proclamation first draft, 81; and Emerson, 175, 176; and European nations, 146–150; eventual destruction of, 8; evil effects on whites, 88; evolution of opinions about, 65; financial aid for abolition of, 40; and foreign nations, 146; and Fort Sumter, 13; Grant on, 30; and Great Britain, 141, 142–143, 149; and Greeley, 86, 111; Nathaniel Hall on, 212; and Harding, 33–34; and Hunter, 55–57; as intact after war, 40; and Livermore, 169–170; Lowrey on, 121; in loyal states, 111, 112; and McClellan, 30; and meeting of September 22, 1862, 4–5; in Missouri, 44, 240; Motley on, 142; national effects of, 178; and noninterference within states, 14, 34, 40, 54, 72, 112, 185; and Oliver Willcox Norton, 35; Wendell Phillips on, 211; and preliminary Emancipation Proclamation, 111, 112, 116; and preservation of Union, 87–88, 109; and presidential proclamations, 244; in rebel states, 106, 111, 112; and Robertson, 191, 192; Ropes on, 122–123; and Seward, 30,

272; Spear on, 173; James Speed on, 83; and Starr, 172; state control of, 54–55; and Stowe, 15; and Sumner, 28–30, 128; in territories, 97; and Thirteenth Amendment, 7; Union soldiers' firsthand encounters with, 134–136; Union soldiers' opinions of, 34–35, 133–134; as unlawful, 244; and U.S.-European relations, 140; Wade on, 65; war's effect on attitudes toward, 15; and Weed, 85, 87; in West Virginia, 189, 190; Yeaman on, 185

Slaves: ability as soldiers, 259; AL depicted interacting with, 269; AL on liberation of, 25; arming of, 76, 80, 81, 91–92, 118, 221–222, 259; in Ball's *Emancipation Memorial,* 269; beyond reach of Union military, 217; and Butler, 15–18; Carlton's depiction of, 268; as children of slaveholders, 135; as citizens, 118; and citizenship, 171; and Confederacy, 63, 248; Confederate debate over enlistment and emancipation of, 258–261; and Confederate livelihood, 258–259; Confederate use of, 73; and Confiscation Act of 1862, 6, 75; confiscation without emancipation of, 61; as contraband of war, 17–21; depicted in *Reading the Emancipation Proclamation,* 269; and desire for freedom, 242; Douglass on freed, 51–52; and Emancipation Proclamation, 216; Emancipation Proclamation as raising hopes of, 218; and Emancipation Proclamation exclusions, 218; and Emancipation Proclamation first draft, 81; as expecting freedom, 198, 323n30; freed as soldiers, 248; freed by war as free forever, 178; freed under Emancipation Proclamation, 199, 209, 216, 217–218, 220, 281; future of freed, 45, 47, 49, 51–52; inhumane treatment of, 134; insurrections by, 7, 15–16, 34, 52, 76, 94, 116, 123–125, 141, 145, 148, 185, 186, 198, 220–221, 248; Kirkland on, 122; knowledge of Emancipation Proclamation, 233; labor of, 16–17, 22, 48, 63, 94, 248; labor of freed, 126; light-skinned, 135; of loyal masters as ineligible for enlistment, 226; as men, 282; and Militia Act debate, 76–77; in Missouri, 24; as persons vs. property, 280; and preliminary Emancipation Proclamation, 7; as property, 16–17; provision for freed, 29, 93, 178; reenslavement of freed, 121, 253, 258; and Santo Domingo, 16; self-defense by freed, 198; Spear on, 173; in Union army, 118; Union army liberation of, 232; under Union control, 216; wages for freed, 198. *See also* Blacks; Contrabands

Slaves, fugitive, 48; and AL, 46, 68, 97; and Beecher, 19; and Butler, 16–17; and Confiscation Act of 1862, 75; and Congress, 46; and